J.K. LASSER

1001 DEDUCTIONS AND TAX BREAKS 2018

J.K. LASSER'S™

1001 DEDUCTIONS AND TAX BREAKS 2018

Your Complete Guide to Everything Deductible

Barbara Weltman

WILEY

978-1-119-38048-1 (paper)
978-1-119-38047-4 (ePDF)
978-1-119-38039-9 (ePub)

Printed in the United States of America

10 9 8 7 6 5 4 3 2 1

Contents

Introduction

Discussions about tax reform has got people talking about taxes. But say the word "taxes" and most people groan. There are good reasons for this response: First of all, the cost of paying your taxes annually can be a financial burden. You may feel taken to the cleaners every time you view your paycheck *after* withholding for federal income taxes (not to mention state income taxes as well as Social Security and Medicare taxes). And taxes are time consuming—costing individuals 8.9 billion hours annually to file their returns.

Second, you may not even have to deal personally with taxes, other than paying them. The IRS says that nearly 60% of taxpayers use paid preparers for their returns.

Third, the tax law is very complicated and changing all the time. According to the Tax Foundation, the Internal Revenue Code (Tax Code) has about 2.4 million words. There were only 11,400 words in the Tax Code in 1914, one year after the constitutional amendment authorizing the levy of an income tax. Between 2001 and 2012, there were 4,600 changes (which works out to more than one a day). Today the Tax Code is twice as long as it was in 1985. There have been major changes in the tax law nearly every year over the past 50 years—and this year is no exception! In addition, new court decisions and IRS rulings appear each day, providing guidance on how to interpret the law. The Tax Foundation says taxpayers spend more than $409 billion each year complying with federal tax rules.

Fourth, you have to know what the tax rules are and can't claim ignorance to avoid taxes and penalties. Even if you use a tax professional or tax preparation software to prepare your return, you remain responsible for your taxes. The Tax Court has noted that using software is not an automatic excuse to avoid underpayment penalties.

How can you combat the feeling of dread when it comes to taxes? It helps to know that the tax law is peppered with many, many tax breaks to which you may be entitled. These breaks allow you to *not* report certain economic benefits you enjoy or to subtract certain expenses from your income or even directly from your tax bill. As the famous jurist Judge Learned Hand once stated (in the 1934 case of *Helvering v. Gregory* in the Court of Appeals for the Second Circuit):

Anyone may arrange his affairs so that his taxes shall be as low as possible; he is not bound to choose that pattern which best pays the treasury. There is not even a patriotic duty to increase one's taxes. Over and over again the Courts have said that there is nothing sinister in so arranging affairs as to keep taxes as low as possible. Everyone does it, rich and poor alike, and all do right, for nobody owes any public duty to pay more than the law demands.

So get your tax affairs in order and reduce what you pay each year to Uncle Sam!

In getting a handle on how to do this by taking advantage of every tax break you may be entitled to without running afoul of the Internal Revenue Service (IRS), there are some simple rules to keep in mind. They include:

- You must report all of your income unless a specific law allows you to exclude or exempt it (so that it is never taxed) or defer it (so that it is taxed at a later time).

- You can claim deductions only when and to the extent the law allows. Deductions are referred to as a "matter of legislative grace"; Congress doesn't have to create them and does so only for some purpose (for example, to encourage economic activity or to balance some perceived inequity in the tax law).

- Tax credits are worth more than tax deductions. A credit reduces your tax payment on a dollar-for-dollar basis; a $1,000 credit saves you $1,000 in taxes. A deduction is worth only as much as the top tax bracket you are in. Suppose you are in the 28% tax bracket, which means this is the highest rate you pay on at least some of your income. If you have a $1,000 deduction, it is worth $280 (28% of $1,000) because it saves you $280 in taxes you would otherwise have to pay.

- Even if your income is modest, you may have to file Form 1040 (the so-called long form), rather than a simplified return (Form 1040A or 1040EZ), in order to claim certain tax benefits.

- In a number of cases, different deduction rules apply to the alternative minimum tax (AMT), a shadow tax system that ensures you pay at least some tax if your regular income tax is lower than it would have been without certain deductions.

Whether you prepare your return by hand (as 6% of filers do), use computer software or an online solution (39%), or rely on a professional (55%), this book is designed to tell you how to get every tax edge you're entitled to. Knowing what to look out for will help you plan ahead and organize your activities in such a way that you'll share less of your hard-earned money with Uncle Sam.

Tax-Favored Items

There are 5 types of tax-advantaged items receiving preferential or favorable treatment under the tax law:

1. *Tax-free income*—income you can receive without any current or future tax concerns. Tax-free income may be in the form of exclusions or exemptions from tax. In many cases, tax-free items do not even have to be reported in any way on your return.

2. *Capital gains*—profits on the sale or exchange of property held for more than one year (long-term). Long-term capital gains are subject to lower tax rates than the rates on other income, such as salary and interest income, and may even be tax free in some cases. Ordinary dividends on stocks and capital gain distributions from stock mutual funds are taxed at the same low rates as long-term capital gains.

3. *Tax-deferred income*—income that isn't currently taxed. Since the income builds up without any reduction for current tax, you may accumulate more over time. However, at some point the income becomes taxable.

4. *Deductions*—items you can subtract from your income to reduce the amount of income subject to tax. There are 2 classes of deductions: those "above the line," which are subtracted directly from gross income, and those "below the line," which can be claimed only if you itemize deductions instead of claiming the standard deduction (explained later).

5. *Credits*—items you can use to offset your tax on a dollar-for-dollar basis. There are 2 types of tax credits: one that can be used only to offset tax liability (called a "nonrefundable" credit) and one that can be claimed even if it exceeds tax liability and you receive a refund (called a "refundable" credit). Usually you must complete a special tax form for each credit you claim.

This book focuses on different types of tax-favored items: exclusions (tax-free income), above-the-line deductions that don't require itemizing, itemized deductions, tax credits, and other benefits, such as subtractions that reduce income. At the end of this Introduction you'll see symbols used to easily identify the type of benefit being explained.

Limits on Qualifying for Tax-Favored Items

In many cases, eligibility for a tax benefit, or the extent to which it can be claimed, depends on adjusted gross income (AGI) or modified adjusted gross income (MAGI).

Adjusted gross income is gross income (all the income you are required to report) minus certain deductions (called "adjustments to gross income"). Adjustments or subtractions you can make to your gross income to arrive at your adjusted gross income are limited to the following items:

Alimony payments

Archer Medical Savings Accounts (MSAs) (for accounts set up prior to 2008)

Business expenses

Capital loss deductions of up to $3,000

Domestic production activities deduction

Educator expenses up to $250

Employer-equivalent portion of self-employment tax

Forfeiture-of-interest penalties because of early withdrawals from certificates of deposit (CDs)

Health Savings Account (HSA) contributions

Individual Retirement Account (IRA) deductions

Jury duty pay turned over to your employer

Legal fees for unlawful discrimination claims

Moving expenses

Net operating losses (NOLs)

Performing artist's qualifying expenses

Qualified retirement plan contributions for self-employed individuals

Rent and royalty expenses

Repayment of supplemental unemployment benefits required because of the receipt of trade readjustment allowances

Self-employed health insurance deduction

Simplified employee pension (SEP) or savings incentive match plan for employees (SIMPLE) contributions for self-employed individuals

Student loan interest deduction up to $2,500

Travel expenses to attend National Guard or military reserve meetings more than 100 miles from home

Tuition and fees deduction up to $4,000 (if this deduction is extended for 2017; it expired at the end of 2016)

Figuring AGI may sound complicated, but in reality it's merely a number taken from a line on your tax return. For example, AGI is the figure you enter on line 37 of the 2017 Form 1040, line 21 of the 2017 Form 1040A, or line 4 of 2017 Form 1040EZ.

Modified adjusted gross income is merely AGI increased by certain items that are excludable from income and/or certain adjustments to gross income. *Which* items are added back varies for different tax breaks. For example, the MAGI limit on eligibility to claim the student loan interest deduction is AGI (disregarding the student loan interest deduction) increased by the tuition and fees deduction as well as the exclusion for foreign earned income and certain other foreign income or expenses. All of these items are explained in this book.

Household income is a term in tax law used to determine eligibility for the premium tax credit under the Affordable Care Act, as well as whether a penalty applies to individuals who don't have minimum essential health coverage for 2017 and are not exempt from this requirement. Household income is explained further in this book in connection with these tax rules.

Standard Deduction versus Itemized Deductions

Every taxpayer, other than someone who can be claimed as a dependent on another taxpayer's return, is entitled to a standard deduction. This is a subtraction from your income, and the amount you claim is based on your filing status. Table I.1 shows the standard deduction amounts for 2017. In 2015, 70.5% of all filers used the standard deduction.

In addition to the basic standard deduction, certain taxpayers can increase these amounts. An additional standard deduction amount applies to those age 65 and older and for blindness. For 2017, the additional amount is $1,550 for

TABLE I.1 Standard Deduction Amounts for 2017

Filing Status	Standard Deduction
Married filing jointly	$12,700
Head of household	9,350
Single (unmarried)	6,350
Qualifying widow(er) (surviving spouse)	12,700
Married filing separately	6,350

individuals who are not married and are not a surviving spouse and $1,250 for those who are married or a surviving spouse.

Example

In 2017, you are single, age 68, and *not* blind (and do not own a house and did not buy a car this year). Your standard deduction is $7,900 ($6,350 + $1,550).

Instead of claiming the standard deduction, you can opt to list certain deductions separately (i.e., *itemize* them). Itemized deductions include:

Medical expenses

Taxes

Interest payments

Gifts to charity

Casualty and theft losses

Unreimbursed employee business expenses

Investment expenses

Legal fees to earn income

Gambling losses

Estate tax payments on income in respect of decedents

You cannot claim any additional standard deduction that applies to those 65 or older and/or blind if you choose to itemize deductions in lieu of claiming the basic standard deduction amount.

Generally, claim the standard deduction when it is greater than the total of your itemized deductions. However, it may save overall taxes to itemize, even when total deductions are less than the standard deduction, if you are subject to the alternative minimum tax (AMT). **The reason:** The standard deduction cannot be used to reduce income subject to the AMT, but certain itemized deductions can.

If a married couple files separate returns and one spouse itemizes deduction, the other must also itemize and cannot claim a standard deduction.

Overall Limit on Itemized Deductions

High-income taxpayers have an overall limit on the total amount of itemized deductions they can claim. Itemized deductions are reduced by the lesser of 3% of the amount that adjusted gross income (AGI) exceeds the applicable threshold amount (see Table I.2) or 80% of itemized deductions subject to the

TABLE I.2 2017 Thresholds for the Itemized Deduction Phaseout

Filing Status	MAGI Start of Phaseout
Married filing jointly	$313,800
Head of household	287,650
Single (unmarried)	261,500
Qualifying widow(er) (surviving spouse)	313,800
Married filing separately	156,900

phaseout. Thus you cannot lose more than 80% of itemized deductions subject to the phaseout.

Itemized deductions subject to the phaseout include taxes, interest (other than investment interest), charitable contributions, and miscellaneous itemized deductions not subject to the 2%-of-adjusted-gross-income limit (other than gambling losses). Itemized deductions *not* subject to the phaseout are medical expenses, investment interest, casualty and theft losses, and gambling losses. These itemized deductions are already subject to special limitations.

Impact of Deductions on Your Chances of Being Audited

Did you know that the IRS collects statistics from taxpayers to create profiles of average deductions? If you claim more than the average for your income range, the computer *may* select your return for further examination.

Table I.3 shows the average itemized deductions for taxpayers in various adjusted gross income ranges.

Tax experts agree that you should claim every deduction you are entitled to, even if your write-offs exceed these statistical ranges. Just make sure to have

TABLE I.3 Average Itemized Deductions for 2015*

AGI	Medical	Taxes	Interest	Donations
Under $15,000	$ 8,210	$ 3,667	$ 6,397	$ 1,533
$ 15,000 ≤ 30,000	8,646	5,497	6,572	2,483
$ 30,000 ≤ 50,000	8,761	4,027	6,357	2,812
$ 50,000 ≤ 100,000	9,426	6,323	7,382	3,244
$100,000 ≤ 200,000	11,305	11,052	8,905	4,155
$200,000 ≤ 250,000	17,625	17,711	11,370	5,779
$250,000 and over	37,032	51,906	16,580	21,769

*The latest year for which statistics are available.

the necessary proof of your eligibility and other records you are required to keep in case your return is examined.

How to Use This Book

The chapters in this book are organized by subject matter so you can browse through them to find the subjects that apply to you or those in which you have an interest.

Each tax benefit is denoted by an icon to help you spot the type of benefit involved:

 Exclusion

 Above-the-line deduction

 Itemized deduction (a deduction taken *after* figuring adjusted gross income)

 Credit

 Other benefit (e.g., a subtraction other than an above-the-line or itemized deduction that reduces income)

For each tax benefit you will find an explanation of what it is, starting with the maximum benefit or benefits you can claim if you meet all eligibility requirements. You'll learn the conditions or eligibility requirements for claiming or qualifying for the benefit. You'll find both planning tips to help you make the most of the benefit opportunity as well as pitfalls to help you avoid problems that can prevent your eligibility. You'll see where to claim the benefit (if reporting is required) on your tax return and what records you must retain to support your tax position.

You'll find hundreds of examples to show you how other taxpayers have successfully taken advantage of the benefit. Over the years, taxpayers have been able to write off literally thousands of items; not every one is listed here because space does not allow it. And you'll learn what *isn't* allowed even though you might otherwise think so. There are references to free IRS publications on a variety of tax topics that you can download from the IRS website (www.irs.gov) or obtain free of charge by calling 800-829-1040.

In the appendices, you'll find a listing of items that can be adjusted each year to reflect cost-of-living changes so you can plan ahead, as well as a checklist of items that are tax free, and a checklist of items that are not deductible.

Throughout the book you will find alerts to possible changes to come. For a *free* update on tax developments, look for the Supplement to this book in February 2018, by going to www.jklasser.com, as well as to my website, www.barbaraweltman.com.

You and Your Family

Alert

At the time this book was completed, Congress was considering important tax changes that could affect 2017 tax returns and planning for 2018. Check the online Supplement in February 2018 at www.jklasser.com or www.barbaraweltman.com to see what changes have been enacted and when they are effective.

Do the old clichés still ring true? Can two still live as cheaply as one? Are things really cheaper by the dozen? For tax purposes, there may be a penalty or bonus for being married versus single, but there are certain tax breaks for building a family.

This chapter explains family-related tax benefits, such as exemptions and tax credits related to your children and the consequences of marital dissolutions.

For more information on these topics, see IRS Publication 501, *Exemptions, Standard Deduction, and Filing Information*; IRS Publication 503, *Child and Dependent Care Expenses*; IRS Publication 504, *Divorced or Separated Individuals*; IRS Publication 596, *Earned Income Credit*; and IRS Publication 972, *Child Tax Credit*.

Marital Status

Whether you are married or single has a significant impact on your taxes. In some cases, being married results in a "marriage bonus," such as effectively averaging taxes when one spouse works and the other does not. In other cases, being married results in a "marriage penalty," which means that two working spouses earning about the same likely will pay higher total tax than if they were single. For some tax rules, a married couple has the identical tax break as a single individual, such as the $3,000 capital loss deduction against ordinary income, which is a distinct disadvantage for those who are married. For some tax rules, a married couple has double the tax break for singles, such as the ordinary loss deduction for so-called Section 1244 stock, so marital status makes no difference here.

Technically, there are a number of filing statuses that determine eligibility for various tax breaks:

- Married filing jointly
- Married filing separately
- Head of household
- Unmarried (single)
- Qualifying widow(er) with a dependent child

You need to know which term applies to you. The terms are not further defined here and often cause confusion, so check IRS Publication 501 if you are unsure. Note that under federal tax law, the terms "husband," "wife," and "spouse" are gender neutral. The term "husband and wife" means two individuals lawfully married to each other. However, those in a civil union or domestic partnership are not married for federal income tax purposes.

Personal Exemption

Each taxpayer (other than someone who is another taxpayer's dependent) automatically is entitled to a deduction just for being a taxpayer. The amount of the deduction, called the exemption amount, is a fixed dollar amount ($4,050 in 2017).

TABLE 1.1 Value of Your Personal Exemption in 2017

Your Top Tax Bracket	Value of Your Exemption
10%	$ 405
15%	608
25%	1,013
28%	1,134
33%	1,337
35%	1,418
39.6%	1,604

Benefit

You can claim a deduction for yourself, called a personal exemption. In 2017, the exemption amount is $4,050 (each year it is indexed for inflation). Table 1.1 shows you the value of your personal exemption for your tax bracket in 2017 (the amount of taxes you save by claiming it).

Conditions

There are no conditions to claiming this deduction; it's yours because you are a taxpayer and the law says you are entitled to it.

Each spouse is entitled to his or her own personal exemption. On a joint return, 2 personal exemptions are claimed. If you are married but file a separate return, you can claim both deductions (an exemption for you and an exemption for your spouse) if your spouse has no income and is not the dependent of another taxpayer.

However, you *cannot* claim the personal exemption if you can be claimed as a dependent on another taxpayer's return. For example, a child who is the parent's dependent cannot claim a personal exemption on the child's own return.

Planning Tip

You cannot claim any personal or dependency exemption for alternative minimum tax (AMT) purposes, a shadow tax system designed to ensure that all taxpayers pay at least some tax. A large number of exemptions can substantially reduce or even eliminate any regular tax. So if you have a large number of exemptions, you may trigger or increase AMT liability. You may wish to engage in some tax planning to minimize or eliminate your AMT liability.

Pitfalls

The deduction for personal exemptions can be reduced or even eliminated entirely if your income is high enough. Personal exemptions are subject to a

TABLE 1.2 2017 Phaseout for Personal Exemptions

Filing Status	AGI—Beginning of Phaseout	AGI—Completed Phaseout
Married filing jointly and surviving spouses	$313,800	$436,300
Heads of households	$287,650	$410,150
Singles	$261,500	$384,000
Married filing separately	$156,900	$218,150

phaseout when adjusted gross income (AGI) exceeds a set amount based on filing status. Table 1.2 shows the AGI threshold for the start of the phaseout; it also shows the point at which the deduction for personal exemptions is completely eliminated. The phaseout is 2% of each $2,500 (or fraction of $2,500) of AGI over your threshold amount.

Example

You are single (with no dependents) and your adjusted gross income for 2017 is $263,000. You are subject to the phaseout of your $4,050 personal exemption. Your exemption is reduced by 2% because your income exceeds your $261,500 threshold by $1,500, which is a fraction of $2,500. Your exemption amount is $3,969 ($4,050 − [$4,050 × 2% = $81]). If your AGI is more than $384,000, you cannot claim any exemption amount.

If a parent waives the exemption for a child to enable the child to claim an education credit (see Chapter 3), the child cannot claim his or her own exemption.

Where to Claim the Personal Exemption

You claim the exemption directly on your tax return in the "Tax and Credits" section of Form 1040 or the "Tax, Credits, and Payments" section of Form 1040A; no special form or schedule is required. If you are filing Form 1040EZ, the exemption amount is built into the tax table (you can file this return only if you are single or married filing jointly with no dependents); you don't have to subtract it anywhere on the return.

If your AGI exceeds the beginning of the phaseout range, use a worksheet in the instructions for the return to figure the phaseout of your exemption.

Dependency Exemption

A fixed deduction ($4,050 in 2017) is allowed to every taxpayer who supports another person and meets other tests described later. This deduction is called a dependency exemption.

Benefit ⬤

You may be entitled to a dependency exemption for each person you support if certain conditions are met. Like the personal exemption, each dependency exemption in 2017 is a deduction of $4,050.

Conditions

There are 2 classes of dependents: qualifying children and all other qualifying individuals. Different conditions apply to each class of dependents.

For a qualifying child, there are 5 conditions:

1. Being your child
2. Modified support test
3. Citizenship test (see end of "Conditions" section)
4. Joint return test (see end of "Conditions" section)
5. Social Security number test (see end of "Conditions" section)

BEING YOUR CHILD

For purposes of a qualifying child, your children include your natural children, stepchildren, adopted children (including those placed for adoption), and eligible foster children (those placed with you by an authorized adoption agency or court). A qualifying child also includes grandchildren, brothers and sisters (including stepsiblings), and children of siblings (nieces and nephews who are younger than you). The child must be under age 19, under age 24 and a full-time student, or permanently disabled (any age).

Your child must live in your household for more than half the year. A child kidnapped by someone other than a family member continues to be treated as a member of your household until the year in which he or she would have attained age 18.

The child must be younger than you or your spouse, unless the child is permanently or totally disabled. Thus, you cannot take a dependency exemption for your older sibling, unless he or she is disabled.

MODIFIED SUPPORT TEST

A qualifying child must not have provided more than half of his or her own support (you do not have to show you paid more than half the child's support).

Amounts received as scholarships are *not* counted as support. There is no gross income test for a qualifying child as there is for a qualifying relative explained later.

Special rule for divorced or separated parents: The exemption belongs to the noncustodial parent if these conditions are met:

- The child receives more than half of his/her support from the parents.
- A decree of divorce or separation agreement between the parents states that the noncustodial parent is entitled to claim the dependency exemption or the custodial parent signs a written declaration (IRS Form 8332) that he/she will not claim the exemption.

If there is no divorce decree or separation agreement with a statement on the dependency exemption for the noncustodial parent or the custodial parent fails to sign a written declaration waiving the exemption, then a so-called tie-breaker rule applies. Under this rule, the exemption belongs to the parent with whom the child resided for the greater amount of time, or if equal time, then to the parent with the higher adjusted gross income. Thus, the custodial parent will usually prevail because the child is a member of the custodial parent's household for more time during the year than the child is a member of the noncustodial parent's household.

There are 5 tests for claiming a dependency exemption for someone who is not a qualifying child. You must satisfy *all* of them:

1. Relationship or member of the household test
2. Gross income test
3. Support test
4. Citizenship or residency test
5. Joint return test

RELATIONSHIP OR MEMBER OF THE HOUSEHOLD TEST

The person you claim as a dependent must either be a relative (whether or not they live with you) or a member of your household. Relatives who do not have to live with you in order to qualify as your dependent include:

- Child, adopted child, or stepchild (other than a qualifying child)
- Grandchild (other than a qualifying child)
- Great-grandchild (other than a qualifying child)
- In-law (son, daughter, father, mother, brother, or sister)
- Parent or stepparent
- Sibling, stepbrother or stepsister, half-brother or half-sister
- Uncle, aunt, nephew, or niece if related by blood

Any other individual, including, for example, a cousin, must be a member of your household for the entire year (not counting temporary absences).

GROSS INCOME TEST

The person you claim as a dependent must have gross income of less than the exemption amount—$4,050 in 2017.

Gross income means income that is subject to tax. It does not include tax-free or excluded items, such as municipal bond interest, employee fringe benefits, or gifts. Social Security benefits are gross income only to the extent they are taxable (which may be 50% or 85%, depending on the recipient's income and Social Security benefits).

SUPPORT TEST

You must provide more than half of the person's support for the year (or meet the multiple support rules discussed later). Generally, this test does not present a problem; you may be the person's only means of support.

But where the person pays some of his or her own support while receiving help from you and other sources, you need to look closely at whether you pay more than half of the person's support. "Support" is different from "income." You need to look at what is *spent* on personal living needs and not what the person *receives* in the way of income. Government benefits payable to the person, including Social Security benefits, are treated as the person's own payment of support (whether or not actually spent on personal living needs).

EXAMPLES OF SUPPORT ITEMS

Clothing

Education expenses (If your child takes out a student loan that he or she is primarily obligated to repay, the loan proceeds count as the child's own payment of support.)

Entertainment

Food

Lodging (If the person shares your home, support is based on the fair rental value of the room or apartment in your home, including a reasonable allowance for heat and other utilities.)

Medical expenses (for details see Chapter 2)

Recreation, including the cost of a television, summer camp, dance lessons, vacations, and a wedding

CITIZENSHIP OR RESIDENCY TEST

The person you claim as a dependent must be a U.S. citizen or national, or a resident of the United States, Canada, or Mexico.

JOINT RETURN TEST

If you are claiming an exemption for someone who is married, the person may not file a joint return with his or her spouse. However, this joint return test is not failed if a joint return is filed merely to claim a refund and both spouses have income under the exemption limit.

> **Example**
>
> You are supporting your married daughter. Both she and her husband are graduate students who each earned $3,000 as teaching assistants and file a joint return to claim a refund of taxes paid on these earnings. Even though your daughter files a joint return, you can still claim her as a dependent (assuming other tests are met).

Planning Tips

Even if you do not provide more than half the support of another person, you may still qualify for the deduction if you contribute more than 10% of the person's support and, together with others, contribute more than half the person's support. Then each of the other supporters who contribute more than 10% must agree among themselves who claims the exemption (it cannot be prorated among the supporters).

> **Example**
>
> You and your 2 sisters support your elderly mother. You contribute 40%, Ann contributes 35%, and Betty contributes 5% (your mother pays 20% of her own support). Since you and your sisters contribute more than half of your mother's support, a multiple support agreement is warranted.
>
> However, only you and Ann qualify since you each contribute more than 10% of the support. You and Ann can decide who claims the exemption—it does not matter that you paid more than Ann.

In deciding which person should claim the exemption when more than one person qualifies, the decision should be based on who would benefit more. Factors to consider include:

- Which person is in the higher tax bracket and whether such person is subject to the phaseout of exemptions for high-income taxpayers
- Who examined the exemption in the prior year and who will claim it next year

If all things are equal, then rotate from year to year who claims the exemption (for example, one year you claim the exemption for a parent and the following year your sibling claims it).

Even if you do not qualify to claim a dependency exemption for your child who is over 23 and no longer a full-time student, you may still cover your child under your health care plan up to age 26. The child does not have to be your dependent, or even live with you, in order to be covered by your medical policy.

For couples with a child and who are getting divorced, deciding which one should claim the exemption can be contentious. As said earlier, the exemption belongs to the spouse who has physical custody of the child for the greater part of the year. The custodial spouse can waive the exemption in favor of the non-custodial spouse by signing Form 8332; the waiver can be made on an annual or permanent basis. The fact that the divorce decree awards the exemption to the noncustodial spouse does not alleviate the need to obtain the written waiver from the custodial spouse on the IRS form.

Social Security Number Test

The dependent must have a Social Security number. If a dependent is ineligible for one, make sure that he or she has an up-to-date Individual Taxpayer Identification Number (ITIN). File Form W-7, *Application for IRS Individual Taxpayer Identification Number (ITIN)*. In the case of a foreign adoption, obtain an Adoption Taxpayer Identification Number (ATIN), which is a temporary number. File Form W-7A, *Application for Taxpayer Identification Number Pending Adoptions*.

Pitfalls

The same phaseout for personal exemptions applies equally to dependency exemptions. Check Table 1.2 earlier in this chapter to see whether you are subject to any phaseout of the deduction for dependency exemptions.

Because of the phaseout for personal exemptions, parents who are splitting up should decide which of them could benefit more from the exemption. For instance, a high-income father who is the custodial parent may wish to negotiate for some consideration by foregoing the dependency exemption for the child. This allows the mother to claim the exemption and increase the overall after-tax income for the family.

When parents do not decide between themselves, then a "tie-breaker rule" applies:

- If only one of the persons who want to claim the exemption is the child's parent, the child is treated as the qualifying child of the parent.

- If the parents of the child are married to each other, file jointly, and can claim the child as a qualifying child, the child is treated as the qualifying child of the parents and no one else.
- If the parents don't file a joint return together (e.g., they are unmarried) but both parents claim the child as a qualifying child, the IRS will treat the child as the qualifying child of the parent with whom the child lived for the longer period of time during the year. If the child lived with each parent for the same amount of time, the IRS will treat the child as the qualifying child of the parent who had the higher adjusted gross income (AGI) for the year.
- If no parent can claim the child as a qualifying child, the child is treated as the qualifying child of the person (e.g., a grandparent) who had the highest AGI for the year.
- If a parent can claim the child as a qualifying child but no parent does so, the child is treated as the qualifying child of the person who had the highest AGI for the year, but only if that person's AGI is higher than the highest AGI of any of the child's parents who can claim the child.

If you support a domestic partner or lover and meet all of the tests, you can claim a dependency exemption as long as the relationship does not violate local law. For example, in North Carolina, a man was prohibited from claiming the exemption for his live-in girlfriend because under North Carolina law this cohabitation was a misdemeanor. (Technically, it remains illegal in Michigan and Mississippi—the law was repealed in Florida in 2016—but these laws against cohabitation may not withstand a challenge today.) In contrast, a man in Missouri was permitted to claim the exemption for his live-in girlfriend because the relationship there was not in violation of state law.

If you can claim an exemption for a partner, you may or may not be able to claim one for the partner's qualifying child. Usually, you do not qualify for an exemption for your partner's child because the child is not your qualifying relative (he or she is the qualifying child of your partner). Under an exception, however, the exemption for the child can be claimed if your partner (for whom the child is a qualifying child) is not required to file a tax return because of low income and does not file a return or files one only to get a refund of withheld income taxes (see the tie-breaker rule discussed earlier). If, for example, your partner files a return to claim the earned income credit in addition to claiming a refund of withheld income taxes, then this exception to the general rule does not apply and you cannot claim a dependency exemption for your partner's child.

Where to Claim the Dependency Exemption

You claim the exemption directly on your tax return in the "Tax and Credits" section of Form 1040 or the "Tax, Credits, and Payments" section of Form 1040A; no special form or schedule is required. You cannot claim a dependency exemption if you file Form 1040EZ.

If your AGI exceeds the beginning of the phaseout range, use a worksheet in the instructions for the return to figure the phaseout of your exemption.

In the case of divorced or separated parents, the noncustodial parent should attach to his or her return Form 8332, *Release of Claim to Exemption for Child of Divorced or Separated Parents*, signed by the custodial parent.

Child Tax Credit

The U.S. Department of Agriculture estimates that it costs a middle-class family over $233,610 to raise a child born in 2015 (the most recent year for statistics) to age 18 (without adjustment for inflation). In recognition of this cost, you can claim a tax credit each year until your child reaches the age of 17. The credit is currently up to $1,000 per child. This credit is in addition to the dependency exemption for the child.

Benefit ✚

You may claim a tax credit of up to $1,000 for each child under the age of 17. If the credit you are entitled to claim is more than your tax liability, you may be entitled to a refund under certain conditions.

Generally, the credit is refundable to the extent of 15% of earned income over $3,000.

If you have 3 or more children for whom you are claiming the credit, you are entitled to an additional child tax credit. In reality, the additional child tax credit is merely a larger refund of the credit you are ordinarily entitled to. There are 2 ways to figure your refundable amount (the additional child tax credit) and you can opt for the method that results in the larger refund:

1. Fifteen percent of earned income over $3,000
2. Excess of your Social Security taxes (plus the so-called employer share of self-employment taxes, if any) over your earned income credit for the year (the earned income credit is explained in the next main section)

Conditions

To claim the credit, you must meet 2 conditions:

1. You must have a qualifying child.
2. Your income must be below a set amount.

QUALIFYING CHILD

You can claim the credit only for a "qualifying child." This is a child who is under age 17 at the end of the year and meets the definition of a qualifying child

TABLE 1.3 Phaseout of Child Tax Credit over MAGI Limits in 2017

Filing Status	MAGI Limit
Married filing jointly	$110,000
Head of household	75,000
Unmarried (single)	75,000
Qualifying widow(er)	75,000
Married filing separately	55,000

explained earlier in this chapter. This age limit applies even if the child is permanently and totally disabled.

MAGI LIMIT

You must have modified adjusted gross income (MAGI) below a set amount. The credit you are otherwise entitled to claim is reduced or eliminated if your MAGI exceeds a set amount. MAGI for purposes of the child tax credit means AGI increased by the foreign earned income exclusion, the foreign housing exclusion or deduction, or the possession exclusion for American Samoa residents.

The credit amount is reduced by $50 for each $1,000 of MAGI or a fraction thereof over the MAGI limit for your filing status. The phaseout begins if MAGI exceeds the limits found in Table 1.3.

Example

In 2017, you are a head of household with 2 qualifying children. Your MAGI is $80,000. Your credit amount of $2,000 ($1,000 × 2) is reduced by $250 ($80,000 − $75,000 = $5,000 MAGI ÷ [$1,000 × $50]). Your credit is $1,750 ($2,000 − $250).

REFUNDABLE CREDIT

If the credit you are entitled to claim is more than your tax liability, you can receive the excess amount as a "refund." The refund is limited to 15% of your taxable earned income (such as wages, salary, tips, commissions, bonuses, and net earnings from self-employment) over $3,000. If your earned income is not over $3,000, you may still qualify for the additional credit if you have 3 or more children.

If you have 3 or more children for whom you are claiming the credit, you may qualify for a larger refund, called the additional child tax credit. You can figure your refund in the usual manner as explained earlier, or, if more favorable, you can treat your refundable amount as the excess of the Social Security taxes you paid for the year (plus the employer equivalent portion of self-employment taxes, if any) over your earned income credit (explained later in this chapter).

Planning Tip

If you know you will become entitled to claim the credit (e.g., you expected the birth of a child in 2017), you may wish to adjust your withholding so that you don't have too much income tax withheld from your paycheck. Increase your withholding allowances so that less income tax is withheld from your pay by filing a new Form W-4, *Employee's Withholding Allowance Certificate*, with your employer.

Pitfalls

If you claim the foreign earned income exclusion to exclude income earned abroad up to the annual dollar limit ($102,100 in 2017), you cannot receive a refundable child tax credit.

For 2017 returns filed in 2018, the IRS is not permitted to issue tax refunds for the refundable child tax credit before February 15, 2018.

Where to Claim the Credit

You figure the credit on a worksheet included in the instructions for your return. You claim the credit in the "Tax and Credits" section of Form 1040 or the "Tax, Credits, and Payments" section of Form 1040A. You cannot claim the credit if you file Form 1040EZ.

If you are eligible for the additional child tax credit, you figure this on Form 8812, *Additional Child Tax Credit*.

Earned Income Credit

Low-income taxpayers are encouraged to work and are rewarded for doing so by means of a special tax credit, called the earned income credit. The earned income credit is the second-largest program, after Medicaid, that provides assistance to low-income people. The amount of the credit varies with income, filing status, and the number of dependents, if any. The credit may be viewed as a "negative income tax" because it can be paid to taxpayers even if it exceeds their tax liability. On 2015 returns, more than 28.4 million taxpayers claimed the earned income credit, totaling $69.8 billion.

Benefit ⊕

If you are a working taxpayer with low or moderate income, you may qualify for a special tax credit of up to $6,318 in 2017. The amount of the credit depends

TABLE 1.4 Maximum Earned Income Credit for 2017

Number of Qualifying Children	Maximum Earned Income Credit
No qualifying child	$ 510
1 qualifying child	3,400
2 qualifying children	5,616
3 or more qualifying children	6,318

on several factors, including your adjusted gross income, earned income, and the number of qualifying children that you claim as dependents on your return. Table 1.4 shows the maximum credit you may claim based on the number of your qualifying children, if any.

The credit is "refundable" because it can be received in excess of the tax owed.

Conditions

To be eligible for the credit, you must have earned income from being an employee or a self-employed individual. The amount of the credit you are entitled to claim depends on several factors.

QUALIFYING CHILDREN

You may claim the credit even if you have no qualifying child. But you are entitled to a larger credit if you have one qualifying child and a still larger credit for 2 or more qualifying children.

To be a qualifying child, the child must:

- Be a qualifying child as defined earlier in the chapter under the dependency exemption
- Be under age 19 or under age 24 and a full-time student or permanently and totally disabled
- Live in your U.S. household for more than half the year
- Qualify as your dependent if the child is married at the end of the year
- Be a U.S. citizen or resident (or a nonresident who is married to a U.S. citizen and elects to have all worldwide income subject to U.S. tax)

EARNED INCOME

Earned income includes wages, salary, tips, commissions, jury duty pay, union strike benefits, certain disability pensions, U.S. military basic quarters and subsistence allowances, and net earnings from self-employment (profit from your

TABLE 1.5 Earned Income Needed for Top Credit in 2017

Number of Qualifying Children	Earned Income Needed for Top Credit
No qualifying child	$ 6,670
1 qualifying child	10,000
2 or more qualifying children	14,040

self-employment activities). Military personnel can elect to treat tax-free combat pay as earned income for purposes of the earned income credit.

Nontaxable employee compensation, such as tax-free fringe benefits or salary deferrals—for example, contributions to company 401(k) plans—is not treated as earned income.

Earned income does not include pensions and retirement plan distributions, long-term disability and military disability pensions, welfare, and Social Security benefits (for retirement or disability).

To qualify for the maximum credit, you must have earned income at or above a set amount. Table 1.5 shows the earned income you need to obtain the top credit (depending on the number of your qualifying children, if any).

ADJUSTED GROSS INCOME

If your adjusted gross income is too high, the credit is reduced or eliminated. Table 1.6 shows the AGI phaseout range for the earned income credit. This depends not only on the number of qualifying children, if any, but also on your filing status, as shown in the table.

JOINT RETURN

If you are married, you usually must file a joint return with your spouse in order to claim an earned income credit. However, this requirement is waived if your spouse did not live in your household for the last 6 months of the year. In this case, assuming you paid the household expenses in which a qualifying child lived, you qualify as head of household and can claim the earned income credit (using "other taxpayers" limits on AGI).

TABLE 1.6 AGI Phaseout Range for the Earned Income Credit in 2017

Number of Qualifying Children	Married Filing Jointly	Other Taxpayers
No qualifying child	$13,930–20,600	$ 8,340–15,010
1 qualifying child	$23,930–45,207	$18,340–39,617
2 qualifying children	$23,930–50,597	$18,340–45,007
3 or more qualifying children	$23,930–53,930	$18,340–48,340

Example

You are married and file a joint return. You and your spouse have 1 qualifying child. In 2017, if your AGI is less than $23,930, your earned income credit is *not* subject to any phaseout. If your AGI is $45,207 or higher, you cannot claim *any* earned income credit; it is completely phased out. If your AGI is between these amounts (within the phaseout range), you may claim a reduced credit.

Planning Tips

The credit is based on a set percentage of earned income. However, you don't have to compute the credit. You merely look at an IRS Earned Income Credit Table, which accompanies the instructions for your return.

You can have the IRS figure your credit for you (you don't even have to look it up in the table). To do this, just complete your return up to the earned income credit line and put "EIC" on the dotted line next to it. If you have a qualifying child, complete and attach Schedule EIC to the return. Also attach Form 8862, *Information to Claim Earned Income Credit after Disallowance*, if you are required to do so as explained next.

If you are barred from claiming a dependency exemption for a child because of the tie-breaker rule (discussed earlier in this chapter), you may claim the earned income credit with no qualifying child. For example, a grandmother has a home in which her daughter and the baby (granddaughter) live. Under the tie-breaker rule, while the baby could be a qualifying child of the grandmother and mother, she is the daughter's qualifying child. The grandmother can claim the earned income tax credit with no qualifying child, assuming all other requirements for the credit are met. Alternatively, if the daughter foregoes the dependency exemption, the grandmother can claim it and the earned income tax credit, assuming that her AGI exceeds the daughter's AGI. In this instance, the daughter could claim the earned income tax credit with no qualifying child, assuming all other requirements for the credit are met.

Pitfalls

You lose eligibility for the credit if you have unearned income over $3,450 in 2017 from dividends, interest (both taxable and tax-free), net rent or royalty income, net capital gains, or net passive income that is not self-employment income.

You lose out on the opportunity to claim the credit in future years if you negligently or fraudulently claim it on your return. You are banned for 2 years from claiming the earned income credit if your claim was reckless or in disregard of the tax rules. You lose out for 10 years if your claim was fraudulent. If you become ineligible because of negligence or fraud, the IRS issues a deficiency notice. You may counter the IRS's charge by filing Form 8862, *Information to Claim Earned Income Credit after Disallowance*, to show you are eligible.

If the IRS accepts your position and recertifies eligibility, you don't have to file this form again (unless you again become ineligible). For 2017 returns filed in 2018, the IRS is not permitted to issue tax refunds for the refundable earned income tax credit before February 15, 2018.

Where to Claim the Earned Income Credit

You can claim the earned income credit on *any* income tax return (Form 1040, 1040A, or 1040EZ) as follows: in the "Payments" section of Form 1040; the "Tax, Credits, and Payments" section of Form 1040A; or the "Payments and Tax" section of Form 1040EZ.

You can check your eligibility to claim the credit on Schedule EIC, Earned Income Credit, which must be attached to your return.

Dependent Care Expenses

Many taxpayers must pay for the care of a child in order to work. According to a 2016 report from the National Association of Child Care Resource and Referral Agencies, the annual cost of child care for an infant currently ranges from $3,675 to $17,062 per year. The tax law provides a limited tax credit for such costs, called the dependent care credit. The amount of the credit you can claim depends on your income. Or, if your employees help with child care costs, you may exclude the payments from your income. (At the time this book was prepared there were several important tax-related child care proposals under consideration; see the Supplement for any developments.)

Benefit

If you hire someone to care for your children or other dependents to enable you to work or incur other dependent care expenses, you may be eligible for a tax credit of up to $2,100. More specifically, this credit is a percentage of eligible dependent care expenses (explained later). The credit percentage ranges from a low of 20% to a high of 35%. The maximum amount of expenses that can be taken into account in figuring the credit is $3,000 for one qualifying dependent and $6,000 for 2 or more qualifying dependents.

If your employer pays for your dependent care expenses, you may be able to exclude this benefit from income up to $5,000.

Conditions for the Tax Credit

There are a number of conditions for claiming the dependent care credit; you must satisfy all 6 of them to claim the credit:

1. Incur the expenses to earn income.
2. Pay expenses on behalf of a qualifying dependent.

3. Pay over half the household expenses.

4. File a joint return if you are married.

5. Have qualifying expenses in excess of employer reimbursements.

6. Report information about the child care provider.

INCUR THE EXPENSES TO EARN INCOME

The purpose of the dependent care credit is to enable you to work. This generally means that if you are married, you both must work, either full time or part time.

However, a spouse who is incapacitated or a full-time student need not work; he or she is treated as having earned income of $250 per month if there is one qualifying dependent or $500 per month if there are 2 or more qualifying dependents.

Example

You are a single mother and a full-time student with 1 child. You are treated as having earned income of $3,000 for the year ($250 × 12). You can use this income in figuring your credit, even though you didn't actually receive this income.

PAY EXPENSES ON BEHALF OF A QUALIFYING DEPENDENT

This is for your child under the age of 13, your incapacitated dependent of any age, or your spouse who is incapacitated.

If your child has his or her 13th birthday during the year, you can take into account expenses incurred up to this birthday.

PAY OVER HALF THE HOUSEHOLD EXPENSES

You (and your spouse) must pay more than half of the maintenance expenses of the household.

FILE A JOINT RETURN IF MARRIED

Generally, to claim the credit you *must* file a joint return if eligible to do so. However, you can claim the credit even though you are still married if you live apart from your spouse for over half the year, you pay over half the household expenses for the full year, and your spouse is not a member of your household for the last 6 months of the year. In this case, you qualify to file as unmarried (single).

HAVE QUALIFYING EXPENSES IN EXCESS OF EMPLOYER REIMBURSEMENTS

Only certain types of child care expenses can be taken into account in figuring the credit. Qualifying expenses can be incurred in your home or outside the home (using a day care center). You cannot include amounts paid to you, your child who is under age 19 at the end of the year, your spouse, or any other person you can claim as a dependent.

EXAMPLES OF QUALIFYING EXPENSES

Babysitter

Day camp, including a specialty camp such as soccer or computers (but only the day cost of a sleep-away camp)

Day care center

Housekeeper (the portion of compensation allocated to dependent care)

Nursery school

Private school (The costs for first grade and higher do not qualify unless the child is handicapped, provided the child spends at least 8 hours per day in your home.)

Transportation, if supervised (so that it is part of care), such as to a day camp or after-school program not on school premises, but not the cost of personally driving a dependent to and from a dependent care center

You do not have to find the least expensive means of providing dependent care. For example, just because your child's grandparent lives in your home doesn't mean you must rely on the grandparent for child care; you can pay an unrelated person to babysit in your home or take your child to day care.

The expenses you incur for dependent care must be greater than any amount you exclude as employer-provided dependent care.

REPORT INFORMATION ABOUT THE DEPENDENT CARE PROVIDER

You must list the name, address, and employer identification number (or Social Security number) of the person you pay for dependent care. No employer identification number is required if payment is made to a tax-exempt charity providing the care.

If the person has not completed Form W-4, *Employee's Withholding Allowance Certificate*, as your household employee, you can obtain the necessary information by asking the provider to complete Form W-10, *Dependent Care Provider's Identification and Certification*, or by looking at a driver's license or other government-issued photo ID, business letterhead, or invoice. This may seem like a lot of bother and formality for a baby-sitter, but if you want to claim the credit, you must comply with this information-reporting requirement.

HOW TO FIGURE YOUR CREDIT PERCENTAGE BASED ON AGI

The amount of the credit you claim depends on your AGI. However, no matter how large your AGI, you are entitled to a minimum credit of 20% of eligible

TABLE 1.7 Dependent Care Credit Limits

AGI	Credit Percentage	1 Dependent	2 or More Dependents
$15,000 or less	35%	$1,050	$2,100
$15,001–17,000	34	1,020	2,040
$17,001–19,000	33	990	1,980
$19,001–21,000	32	960	1,920
$21,001–23,000	31	930	1,860
$23,001–25,000	30	900	1,800
$25,001–27,000	29	870	1,740
$27,001–29,000	28	840	1,680
$29,001–31,000	27	810	1,620
$31,001–33,000	26	780	1,560
$33,001–35,000	25	750	1,500
$35,001–37,000	24	720	1,420
$37,001–39,000	23	690	1,380
$39,001–41,000	22	660	1,320
$41,001–43,000	21	630	1,260
$43,001 and over	20	600	1,200

expenses. Table 1.7 shows you the maximum credit you may claim based on your AGI and number of dependents.

Example

You have 1 qualifying child and adjusted gross income of $40,000. Your credit is 22% of your dependent care expenses up to $3,000, for a top credit of $660.

Conditions for the Exclusion

Benefits must be provided by your employer under a written plan that does not discriminate in favor of owners or highly compensated employees (for example, top executives cannot obtain greater benefits than you). The dollar limit on this benefit is $5,000 (or $2,500 if you are married and file separately).

The same limits apply to a flexible spending arrangement (FSA), which is an employer plan to which you contribute a portion of your pay to be used for dependent care expenses. This salary reduction amount is *not* currently taxable to you; it becomes tax-free income that you withdraw from the FSA to cover eligible expenses.

Planning Tip

If you have the option of making salary reduction contributions to your company's flexible spending arrangement (FSA) for dependent care expenses, decide carefully on how much to contribute each month. You can use the funds in the FSA only for dependent care expenses; you cannot, for example, use any of the funds for your medical expenses or other costs. Any funds not used up by the end of the year (or within the first two and a half months of the next year if your employer has a grace period) are forfeited; they do not carry over.

Pitfall

If you qualify to receive an exclusion, you must reduce the amount of eligible expenses used in figuring the credit by the amount of the exclusion.

Example

You have 1 child and receive reimbursement from your employer's plan for the year of $2,500. In figuring your tax credit, you can use only $500 of eligible expenses ($3,000 − $2,500). In essence, once your exclusion is $3,000 for 1 child or $6,000 if you have 2 or more children, you cannot claim any tax credit.

If you participate in a dependent care FSA, distributions from the plan are treated as employer reimbursements. Like excludable benefits, distributions from FSAs reduce the amount of expenses you can use to figure the credit.

There is no option to carry over any unused contributions to a dependent care FSA as there is in the case of a medical FSA. However, if you don't use up your contributions to a dependent care FSA, your plan may have a run-out period during which you can continue to submit claims for child care expenses in the contribution year.

If you pay someone to care for your dependent in your home, you are the worker's employer. You are responsible for employment taxes. For more information about these employment taxes, see IRS Publication 926, *Household Employer's Tax Guide*, at www.irs.gov.

Where to Claim the Tax Credit or Exclusion

You figure the credit and the exclusion on Form 2441, *Dependent Care Expenses*. If you file Form 1040, the credit is then entered in the "Tax and Credit" section of your return. If you file Form 1040A, the credit is figured on Schedule 2 of the return. You may not claim the credit if you file Form 1040EZ.

If you owe employment taxes for a dependent care worker, you must file Form 1040 and complete Schedule H, *Household Employment Taxes*, which is attached to the return. You include employment taxes you owe in the "Other Taxes" section of your return.

Adoption Costs

Each year, more than 125,000 children are adopted in the United States (more than 30,000 of whom were from foreign countries in 2009, the most recent year for statistics), with costs as much as $40,000 or more. Taxpayers who adopt a child may qualify for a tax credit. The amount of the credit may or may not fully offset actual costs for the adoption. If an employer pays for adoption costs, a worker may be able to exclude this fringe benefit from income.

Benefit

If you adopt a child, you may be eligible to claim a tax credit for the expenses you incur. The maximum credit is $13,570 per child in 2017. The credit is 100% of eligible adoption expenses up to this dollar limit. If you adopt a child that the state has determined as having special needs (e.g., a medical condition), the credit is $13,570 without regard to your actual adoption expenses. The credit, including one for a special needs child, is subject to income limits.

Example

In 2017, your income is $100,000; you pay $9,000 in attorney's and adoption agency fees to adopt a child who is not a special needs child (the adoption becomes final in 2017). You can claim a tax credit of $9,000 (100% of your eligible costs that do not exceed $13,570).

If your employer pays or reimburses you for adoption expenses, you may exclude this benefit from your income; it is tax free to you if you meet eligibility conditions. The exclusion has the same dollar limit and income limits as the credit.

If a tax-exempt organization makes a payment to help pay adoption costs, the payment is not taxable. The payment is viewed as a gift to the recipient.

Conditions

To claim the adoption credit or exclusion, 2 key conditions apply:

1. You must pay qualified adoption expenses.

2. Your modified adjusted gross income cannot exceed a set amount.

There is an additional condition for married persons; they must file jointly unless they are legally separated or live apart for the last 6 months of the year. This requirement applies even if only one spouse is adopting a child.

The determination of whether a child is a special needs child must be made by the state; a taxpayer cannot make this call on his or her own.

QUALIFIED ADOPTION EXPENSES

Qualified expenses include any reasonable and necessary expenses related to the adoption.

EXAMPLES OF QUALIFIED ADOPTION EXPENSES

Adoption agency fees

Attorney's fees

Court costs

Travel expenses while away from home (including meals and lodging)

Nonqualifying expenses include those related to your adoption of your spouse's child, expenses related to a surrogate parenting arrangement, expenses paid for adopting your spouse's child, expenses paid using funds received from a government program, and expenses that violate the law.

MODIFIED ADJUSTED GROSS INCOME LIMIT

To be eligible for the full credit or the exclusion, your modified adjusted gross income in 2017 cannot exceed $203,540. If your MAGI is over $243,540, the credit is completely phased out.

Example

You adopt a child in 2017 and your MAGI is $223,540. You can only claim a credit of up to $6,785; half of the credit limit is phased out because of your MAGI.

Modified adjusted gross income for this purpose is AGI increased by the foreign earned income exclusion; the foreign housing exclusion or deduction; and the exclusion for income from Guam, American Samoa, Northern Mariana Islands, or Puerto Rico.

Planning Tips

The amount of the adoption credit cannot be more than your tax liability for the year. Tax liability for this purpose means your regular tax, plus your tentative alternative minimum tax (without regard to the foreign tax credit), dependent care credit, credit for the elderly or disabled, education credit, child tax credit, or mortgage interest credit if any.

However, if the credit exceeds your tax liability, you can carry the excess credit forward for up to 5 years.

If your employer has an adoption assistance program but you aren't entitled to some or all of the exclusion (e.g., your MAGI is too high or your expenses

TABLE 1.8 Year to Claim the Credit for Adoption of a U.S. Citizen or Resident Child

When You Pay Expenses	When You Claim Credit
Any year before year the adoption becomes final (or falls through)	Year after year of payment
Year adoption becomes final (or falls through)	Year adoption becomes final (or falls through)
Any year after year adoption becomes final (or falls through)	Year of payment

exceeded the dollar limit), plan to pay tax on the amount your employer pays or reimburses you. The employer is *not* required to withhold income tax on these payments. Employer-paid expenses are reported on your Form W-2.

Obtain a taxpayer identification number for the child if he/she does not have one. Use Form W-7A, *Application for Taxpayer Identification Number For Pending Adoption*, to obtain a temporary tax ID for a child in a domestic adoption who does not have or is unable to obtain his or her own Social Security number.

Pitfall

The year for which you are entitled to claim the credit depends on the type of child you are adopting.

CHILD WHO IS A U.S. CITIZEN OR RESIDENT

If you adopt or are adopting a child who is a U.S. citizen or resident, use Table 1.8 to see the year for which to claim the credit for payments you make.

FOREIGN CHILD

You can take the credit only if the adoption becomes final. Use Table 1.9 to see the year in which to claim the credit.

Where to Claim the Adoption Credit or Exclusion

You figure the adoption credit on Form 8839, *Qualified Adoption Expenses*, which is attached to your return. You can claim the credit only if you file Form 1040 or Form 1040A; you cannot claim the credit if you file Form 1040EZ.

TABLE 1.9 Year to Claim the Credit for Adoption of a Foreign Child

When You Pay Expenses	When You Claim Credit
Any year before year adoption becomes final	Year adoption becomes final
Year adoption becomes final	Year adoption becomes final
Any year after year adoption becomes final	Year of payment

To claim the credit, you must retain certain documents; they do not have to be attached to the return.

- For U.S. adoptions, attach a copy of the adoption order or decree.
- For adoptions finalized abroad, include the child's Hague Adoption Certificate, an IH-3 visa, or a foreign adoption decree translated into English. If the child's country of origin is not a party to the Hague Convention, then attach a copy of the translated decree or an IR-2 or IR-3 visa.
- If you adopt a special needs child, also attach the state determination of the child's special needs status certificate so you can claim the full $13,570, regardless of the adoption costs you paid.

Example

In 2016, you start the adoption process, hiring a lawyer and paying a retainer of $3,000. In 2016, the lawyer helps you work with an authorized adoption agency to which you pay a fee of $10,000 to adopt your daughter, a U.S. resident. The child is placed with you at that time. In 2017, you pay the lawyer an additional $4,000 and the adoption becomes final in this year. You may *not* claim any credit in 2016. In 2017, you may claim a credit up to $13,570, comprised of $13,000 [retainer and adoption fee] paid in 2016 and $570 of the $4,000 additional attorney's fee paid in 2017. The excess expenses of $3,460 [$4,000 − $380]) are not carried over and cannot be used in the future.

If your employer paid or reimbursed you for qualified expenses, you must also complete this form to figure excludable benefits.

Foster Care

Taxpayers who care for children in foster care and receive funds for expenses may not be taxed on those funds. Instead, they may be able to exclude the payments they receive from income.

Benefit

Exclusion for foster care payments. If you receive foster care payments to care for a child placed with you by a state or local agency or a tax-exempt foster care placement agency, you are not taxed on those payments. They are fully excludable; there is no dollar limit.

Qualified payments include payments for the provision of foster care. They also include difficulty-of-care payments to account for the additional care required for a child with physical, mental, or emotional handicaps. Payments under a state Medicaid Home and Community-Based Services Waiver (Medicaid waiver) program are treated as difficulty-of-care payments.

However, the exclusion for foster care payments is limited to payments received for 5 qualifying individuals who are over age 18. The exclusion for difficulty-of-care payments is limited to payments received for 10 qualifying individuals who are over age 18. There are no limits on the number of children age 18 or under for whom the exclusion may be claimed.

Deduction for out-of-pocket costs. See Chapter 6.

Condition

Foster care payments include only those made by a state or local government or qualified foster care placement agency for the care of a qualified foster child or a difficulty-of-care payment. Also, you and the foster child must live in the same home.

Planning Tip

If you are a foster care parent dealing with a private agency, make sure the placement entitles you to exclude payments received for the care of the child.

Pitfalls

Payments received from private agencies that are not tax-exempt entities, even though licensed by the state, are not excludable from income.

Payments made to a child's biological parent cannot be excluded, even if labeled "foster care payment" because such parent is never a foster parent.

Where to Claim the Exclusion

Foster care payments are not reported on the return if they are excludable. If you care for more than the allowable number of children over age 18, you must include the payments in income. Report this as "other income" on your return.

Child Support

Divorced or separated parents may be ordered by a court to make support payments for a child of the marriage. Even an unwed parent may be instructed to support his or her child. The recipient of child support payments, typically the parent with whom the child resides, is not taxed on these payments. (The parent making the payments cannot deduct them, but paying child support may entitle the parent to other tax write-offs discussed throughout this chapter, such as the dependency exemption.)

Benefit

Child support payments are not taxable to the child, nor to the parent who receives them on behalf of the child. There is no dollar limit to this benefit.

Conditions

Payments for child support should be fixed. If they are set by a decree of divorce or separate maintenance or a separation agreement, they are considered to be fixed.

In addition, if payments made to a parent will be reduced or terminated upon a contingency related to the child, then those payments are treated as being fixed for child support. Contingencies for this purpose include:

- Reaching the age of majority (generally age 18 or 21, depending on the law in your state)
- Leaving school
- Marrying
- Entering military service
- Moving out of the custodial parent's home
- Starting to work and/or attaining a set income level

Planning Tip

If a parent is required to pay both alimony and child support but makes a single payment that is less than the total amount due, the first dollars are considered tax-free child support.

Example

Ed owes his former spouse $1,000 each month to cover alimony of $600 and child support of $400. In March 2017, Ed pays only $500. Of this amount, $400 is treated as child support; $100 is treated as alimony.

Pitfalls

The parent who makes child support payments cannot deduct them. They are not considered to be part of deductible alimony payments (explained in the next section).

If a reduction in child support payments to a parent is not specifically tied to the child's age of majority but is scheduled to occur within 6 months before or after such date, the reduction is treated as if it was tied to the child. This means that the amount subject to reduction is viewed as child support and not as deductible alimony. The same rule applies if you are making payments on behalf of more than one child and there are at least 2 reductions, each of which is within a year of a child's reaching the age of majority.

If you are due a refund of federal income tax because you overpaid it through withholding or estimated taxes, you won't receive it if you are delinquent on your child support payments. The IRS is authorized to divert your refund to the parent owed the child support payments as long as the state provides notice to you and a procedure you can follow to contest this action.

Where to Claim the Exclusion

Child support payments received need not be reported on the return.

Alimony

Taxpayers who are required by a court to make payments to a spouse or former spouse can deduct such payments. The payments may be called alimony, support, or spousal maintenance, depending on state law (called "alimony" here for convenience). The tax law, in most cases, imposes symmetry on the treatment of alimony so that the government effectively comes out even; the spouse receiving the payments reports them as income while the spouse making the payments gets to deduct them.

Benefit

If you make payments to a spouse or former spouse for alimony, support, or spousal maintenance, you can deduct the payments if certain conditions are met. There is no dollar limit on this deduction. The deduction is claimed as an adjustment to gross income; you do not have to itemize your other deductions to write off alimony payments you make.

Conditions

There are 4 conditions that must be met for payments made to a spouse or former spouse to be considered alimony:

1. Amounts must be paid pursuant to a legal requirement, such as a court decree.
2. Payments must be made in cash.
3. You must live apart from your spouse or former spouse.
4. Your responsibility to make payments must terminate on the death of your spouse or former spouse.

Typically, alimony that is deductible by the payer is taxable to the recipient—the government effectively nets no additional tax revenue from the arrangement. But this symmetry is not required. If you meet all of the conditions, you can deduct your alimony payments even if your former spouse is not required to pay tax on them (for example, your former spouse lives abroad where alimony is exempt income).

PAYABLE UNDER A COURT DECREE

You can't deduct alimony if you voluntarily make payments. You must either be ordered to do so under a decree of divorce, legal separation, or support or agree to make payments under a written separation agreement.

If the marriage is annulled and you are ordered to make payments, they can be treated as alimony if the other conditions are satisfied.

CASH PAYMENTS

You can deduct only payments made in cash. But you don't necessarily have to make these payments directly *to* your spouse or former spouse. Payments made *on behalf of* your spouse or former spouse qualify for the deduction if required by the divorce decree or separation agreement. For example, if you are ordered to pay your former spouse's rent with a check directly to the landlord, you can treat the payment as alimony if the other conditions are met.

If you continue to own the home in which your former spouse resides (i.e., own it by yourself or jointly with your former spouse) and you pay the mortgage and other expenses, only some of these expenses qualify as deductible alimony—even if you are required to make the payments under the terms of a divorce decree or separation agreement. If you own the home, you benefit from the payment of the mortgage, real estate taxes, and other maintenance on the property and cannot deduct these payments. If you own the home jointly, only one-half of your payments can be treated as alimony because only one-half benefits your spouse or former spouse. (Of course, you can deduct mortgage interest and real estate taxes as itemized deductions as explained in Chapter 4.)

LIVING APART

You and your spouse or former spouse must not live in the same household. This means separate residences; merely having separate bedrooms in the same home is not good enough for payments to be treated as alimony.

However, payments made while you are preparing to leave can be deducted. There is a one-month limit so that only payments made within one month prior to your departure can be treated as alimony. If it takes you longer to move out, your earlier payments are not deductible.

PAYMENT RESPONSIBILITY ENDS ON DEATH

Your responsibility to make payments to your spouse or former spouse must end if that person dies. If your obligation to make payments continues beyond the recipient's death (for example, you must continue to pay until total payments reach a set amount), you cannot treat *any* of the payments as alimony (even those made before death).

Generally, the divorce decree should state that your obligation to make payments ends on the recipient's death. But this isn't necessary as long as this condition is part of the law in your state.

The fact that your estate continues to be liable for payments after your death does not prevent you from treating your payments as alimony.

Planning Tip

Don't make voluntary payments if you want to deduct them. For example, don't make payments prior to a court order or separation agreement and don't voluntarily increase your payments. If you want to ensure that increased payments qualify as deductible alimony, you need to amend the court order or separation agreement to incorporate the change.

Pitfalls

Payments made to someone who was never legally your spouse cannot be treated as alimony. For example, if you make payments to a domestic partner, you cannot deduct them even though they otherwise have all the earmarks of alimony.

Property settlements are not deductible. If you make payments that decline by more than $15,000 in the second or third year, in the third year, you may lose some of the deductions you've already claimed. This reduction is viewed as front-loading—trying to make a property settlement appear to be alimony so that you can deduct it (a property settlement isn't deductible).

In effect, deductible payments in year 1 and year 2 are recaptured in the 3rd year if payments decline by too much. The recipient removes them from income and you lose your deductions, and this is reported on the return for the third year (you don't go back and amend the returns in years 1 and 2).

Where to Claim the Deduction

The deduction for alimony payments is claimed on Form 1040 in the section labeled "Adjusted Gross Income." You cannot deduct alimony if you file Form 1040A or Form 1040EZ.

There is no separate form or schedule to complete when deducting alimony. However, you *must* include the recipient's Social Security number on your return (to allow the IRS to cross-check whether the recipient reported the alimony as income).

ABLE Accounts

If you have a disabled child or are under age 26 and meet certain eligibility conditions, you can have a special savings account that generally does not adversely impact eligibility for means-tested government programs (e.g., Medicaid). The account can be used on a tax-free basis for various disability-related expenses (including funeral and burial costs). See details in Chapter 2.

Medical Expenses

Alert

At the time this book was completed, Congress was considering important tax changes that could affect 2017 tax returns and planning for 2018. Check the online Supplement in February 2018 at www.jklasser.com or www.barbaraweltman.com to see what changes have been enacted and when they are effective.

Rising premiums and government mandates are headline news. Certain medical-related tax rules were uncertain when this book was prepared, so check the Supplement for any updates. As things stand now, the tax law provides you with some relief for the high cost of coverage by allowing you to treat your medical expenses in special tax-advantaged ways, as explained in this chapter. These tax benefits apply whether coverage is paid for you by your employer or you pay health costs yourself.

To learn more about medical and dental expenses, see IRS Publication 502, *Medical and Dental Expenses*, IRS Publication 969, *Health Savings Accounts and Other Tax-Favored Health Plans*, IRS Publication 974, *Premium Tax Credit*, and IRS Publication 5187, *Affordable Care Act: What You and Your Family Need to Know*.

Employer-Provided Health Insurance

Employers with 50 or more employees are required to offer affordable health coverage for their staff and dependents. Many employers not required to provide coverage do so anyway. Of these, many employees enjoy coverage through their employers at no cost to them; others pay a portion of coverage and the employers pay the rest. The value of employer-paid coverage is tax free, regardless of amount.

Benefit ✖

The value or amount that an employer pays for premiums to cover you, your spouse, your dependent, and a child under the age of 27 is not taxable. There is no dollar limit on the amount of coverage you can receive on a tax-free basis.

Conditions

There are none; as long as you are an employee, your company-paid coverage is tax free to you. This is so even though the amount of this employee benefit is reported on your Form W-2.

Planning Tips

If both you and your spouse work and each is entitled to health coverage, compare the medical plans and choose the one that offers the better coverage. If you must contribute toward your coverage, but your spouse does not and can include you, it may be preferable to decline your employer's coverage so you can use your spouse's plan.

If you do not have a group health plan at work but your employer reimburses you for the premiums of individual coverage, the reimbursement may be tax free; see the discussion on Health Reimbursement Arrangements later in this chapter.

Pitfalls

While employer-paid coverage for spouses of the same or opposite sex is tax free, this treatment does not apply to domestic partners. Employees are taxed on employer-paid coverage for their domestic partners.

If you are 65 and older and covered by an employer plan of a company with fewer than 20 employees, Medicare is your primary payer. Be sure to apply for Medicare within 3 months before and 3 months after you turn age 65 (7-month enrollment period).

Where to Report the Benefit

You do not have to report this tax-free fringe benefit. Even if your employer reports the value of the coverage on your W-2 form, this does not change the tax-free treatment of the benefit to you.

Premium Tax Credit

Every individual (other than those who are exempt under the law) must have minimum essential coverage. This is health coverage that meets certain standards, which is provided through:

- CHIP
- Employer plans (including COBRA)
- Health care exchanges (marketplaces such as HealthCare.gov)
- Medicaid
- Medicare
- Private insurance
- Refugee medical assistance
- Student health plans (most qualify as minimum essential coverage but check with the school)
- TRICARE

Lower-income taxpayers who cannot qualify for Medicaid may be eligible for a tax credit to help pay for coverage if they purchase it through a government health care exchange. The credit is refundable (it can exceed the amount of taxes owed) and can even be applied toward premiums throughout the year.

Benefit

If you have low or moderate income, you may qualify for the premium tax credit. It is an advanceable, refundable tax credit for eligible people who purchase coverage through a government health care exchange. The credit amount varies with household income for eligible taxpayers.

You can choose to have the credit paid in advance to your insurance company you've chosen from the exchange, or you can claim all of the credit when you file your tax return for the year. If you choose to have the credit paid in advance, you will have to reconcile on your tax return the amount paid in advance with the actual credit to which you are entitled.

Conditions

To qualify for the credit, all of the following conditions apply:

- You must obtain coverage through a government health care exchange (also called the Marketplace), such as HealthCare.gov.
- You must apply for the credit at the time you purchase your coverage by estimating household income, unless you are waiting until you file your return to claim the credit.
- Your household income must fall within federal poverty guidelines.
- If your employer offers coverage, it is not *affordable* to you.
- You are not eligible for a government program (e.g., Medicare, Medicaid, CHIP, or TRICARE).
- If you are married, you must file jointly, unless you are a domestic abuse victim and file separately.
- You cannot be claimed as a dependent on another taxpayer's return.

COVERAGE THROUGH AN EXCHANGE

Only coverage purchased through an exchange can entitle you to the credit. However, it is not necessary that you obtained the coverage online; you may have submitted paper returns or obtained coverage by telephone.

APPLY FOR THE CREDIT

The federal government does not automatically give you the credit. You must prove eligibility for the credit, either at the time you purchase your health coverage from an exchange or when you file your return.

HOUSEHOLD INCOME LIMITS

Only individuals and families whose household income is between 100% and 400% of the federal poverty line for their family size are eligible for the premium tax credit. Household income has a special meaning for purposes of the premium assistance credit. It is modified adjusted gross income (MAGI) of everyone in your household (you, your spouse, and anyone claimed as

TABLE 2.1 Poverty Amounts in the Contiguous States and D.C.*

Household Size	Household Income
One individual	$11,880 (100%) up to $47,520 (400%)
Family of 2	$16,020 (100%) up to $64,080 (400%)
Family of 3	$20,160 (100%) up to $80,640 (400%)
Family of 4	$24,300 (100%) up to $97,200 (400%)
Family of 5	$28,440 (100%) up to $113,760 (400%)
Family of 6	$32,580 (100%) up to $130,320 (400%)
Family of 7	$36,730 (100%) up to $146,920 (400%)
More than 8*	$40,890 (100%) up to $163,560 (400%)

*Add $4,160 for each additional person. Note that Hawaii and Alaska use different guidelines.

a dependent). MAGI for this purpose is adjusted gross income plus any excluded foreign income, nontaxable Social Security benefits (including tier 1 Railroad Retirement benefits), and tax-exempt interest. It does *not* include Supplemental Security Income (SSI).

The credit amount depends on your household income relative to the federal poverty level. The 2017 credit is based on 2016 poverty amounts listed in Table 2.1.

UNAFFORDABLE EMPLOYER COVERAGE

Even if your employer offers coverage, you may still be eligible for the premium tax credit. Coverage in 2017 is deemed "unaffordable" if premiums for self-only coverage (even if you have family coverage) exceed 9.69% of your household income (see the definition of household income under *household income limits* earlier). If your employer offers multiple health coverage options, the affordability test applies to the lowest-cost option available to you that also satisfies the minimum value requirement (i.e., the plan covers at least 60% of the expected total allowed costs for covered services). If your employer offers any wellness programs, the affordability test is based on the premium you would pay if you received the maximum discount for any tobacco cessation programs, and did not receive any other discounts based on wellness programs.

However, you cannot claim the credit if you enroll in an employer plan or receive reimbursement from your employer for individually-obtained coverage under a QSEHRA (discussed later in this chapter), even if it is unaffordable.

INFORMATION RETURNS

There are 3 information returns that contain information about your health coverage.

1. Form 1095-A, *Health Insurance Marketplace Statement*. This is issued by the government Marketplace to anyone who obtained coverage through it (whether through the federal or state exchange).

2. Form 1095-B, *Health Coverage*. This is issued by an insurance company for private coverage. If you work for a small business (fewer than 50 employees), the form is issued by your employer if it has a self-insured plan, such as a Health Reimbursement Arrangement. As a practical matter, most small businesses do not have self-insured plans, so if you buy coverage individually (not through an exchange) or have employer coverage from a small business, you'll receive the Form 1095-B.

3. Form 1065-C, *Empower-Provided Health Insurance Offer and Coverage*. This is issued by a large employer (50 or more employees); it describes the coverage you have (or don't have).

There is confusion about what to do with the form(s) you receive. The form(s) you receive are not attached to your return; retain the form(s) with your tax papers for the year. Only Form 1095-A is relevant to the premium tax credit because the credit applies only to coverage obtained through the Marketplace. You use information on Form 1095-A, second-lowest-cost Silver Plan (SLCSP), to compute the credit on Form 8962, *Premium Tax Credit*.

Forms 1095-B and C are used to determine whether you have coverage in order to escape the shared responsibility payment (Form 8965, *Health Coverage Exemptions*).

Planning Tips

If you are 26 or younger, you may obtain coverage through an employer plan of your parent. Such coverage satisfies the minimum essential coverage requirement.

Looking ahead to health coverage for 2018 and eligibility for the premium tax credit (assuming rules are not changed), use your 2017 income, increases in the poverty amounts, and an increase in the percentage used to determine whether coverage is unaffordable to 9.56% to make projections.

Pitfalls

You are not required to have health coverage if you can't afford it. The law says this is so if the minimum amount you're required to pay is more than 8.16% of your household income.

If you do not have minimum essential coverage and are not exempt from this requirement, you are subject to a penalty tax which is politely called the shared responsibility payment. For 2017, the penalty is the *greater of* $695 per person ($347.50 per dependent under age 18) up to a maximum of $2,085, or 2.5% of household income in excess of your filing threshold ($10,400 for singles; $20,800 for married couples filing jointly). The penalty is capped at the national average premium for a bronze level plan from the exchange (Marketplace). For 2017, the national average monthly premium for a bronze plan is $272 per individual, which is $3,264 for the year (no more than $16,320 for a family of 5 or more).

Your actual premium tax credit may differ from the initial credit granted when you applied for health coverage. Changes during the year in your marital status, number of dependents, or household income may work to increase or decrease the initial credit amount. Again, this will be reconciled when you complete Form 8962, *Premium Tax Credit*, at the time you file your tax return for 2017.

Where to Claim the Credit

Figure the credit on Form 8962, *Premium Tax Credit*. If you claimed the credit on an advanced basis when you signed up for coverage through the Marketplace and now determine that the allowable credit is *more* than the amounts advanced during the year, claim the additional credit on Form 8962 and on line 46 of Form 1040 or line 29 of Form 1040A. If the allowable credit is *less* than the amount advanced to you during the year, the shortfall is reported as an additional tax you owe to the federal government on line 69 of Form 1040 or line 45 of Form 1040A (you must file either of these returns if you owe any excess credit amount and cannot file Form 1040EZ).

Health Coverage Tax Credit

If you qualify for Trade Adjustment Assistance (TAA), you may be able to claim a refundable tax credit for a portion of your health insurance premiums for you and your family.

Benefit ⊕

If you qualify, the government pays a percentage of your health insurance premiums for coverage under any of the following:

- COBRA (Consolidated Omnibus Budget Reconciliation Act of 1986)
- A health insurance program offered to state employees or a comparable program
- A group health plan that is available through the employment of an eligible individual's spouse

The portion of health insurance premiums paid by the federal government is 72.5%. There is no dollar limit on the credit you can claim or any restrictions on claiming the credit because of your income level.

> **Example**
>
> You lose your job in June 2017 because of foreign competition and, as an eligible recipient, begin to pay health coverage starting July 1, 2017, and through the end of the year. The cost of the premiums is $4,000. You pay $1,100 (27.5% of $4,000); the government pays $2,900 (72.5% of $4,000).

Conditions

To claim the credit, you must meet 2 conditions:

1. You are an eligible recipient ("eligible individual")
2. You pay for certain health coverage ("qualifying health coverage")

ELIGIBLE INDIVIDUAL

To be an eligible individual, you must fall within either of 2 categories:

1. You are a worker who lost your job due to foreign trade competition. You must be treated as someone eligible to receive a trade adjustment allowance (TAA) or an alternative TAA.
2. You are a retiree age 55 or older receiving benefits from the Pension Benefit Guaranty Corporation (you are called a PBGC pension recipient). This means that to claim the credit in 2017, you must have been born before 1961.

You claim the credit if you spouse or dependent is an eligible individual. If you file a joint return, only one spouse has to meet the eligibility conditions. You cannot claim the credit if you can be claimed as another taxpayer's dependent.

Eligibility is determined on a month-by-month basis. You are eligible in a month if, as of the first day of the month, you meet the eligibility requirements. You may, for example, only be entitled to a credit for a portion of the year (the months in which you are an eligible individual).

You do not qualify if you are imprisoned under federal, state, or local authority.

As a practical matter, you don't have to determine whether you're an eligible individual; the government does this for you. It will send you Form 8887, *Health Insurance Credit Eligibility Certificate,* stating that you are an eligible TAA, alternative TAA, or PBGC pension recipient.

QUALIFYING HEALTH INSURANCE

Even if you are an eligible individual, you do not qualify for the credit if you have health coverage under Medicare Part A, Medicare Part B, Medicaid, State

Children's Health Insurance Program (S-CHIP), Federal Employees Health Benefit Plan (FEHBP), Tricare (for certain military personnel and their families), or any coverage if at least 50% is paid by your (or your spouse's) employer.

EXAMPLES OF QUALIFYING HEALTH INSURANCE

Certain state-sponsored health insurance if your state elects to have it apply.

COBRA (see later in this chapter).

Coverage under a group plan available through employment of your spouse.

Coverage under individual health insurance, provided you were covered during the entire 30-day period that ends on the date you separated from the employment that makes you an eligible individual.

Planning Tips

You can include as part of the credit any distributions taken from a Health Savings Account or Archer Medical Savings Account (discussed later in this chapter to pay qualified health coverage).

You can claim the credit in advance of filing your tax return and are entitled to it even if you don't owe any taxes. As long as you obtain the proper certification, you pay only your required percentage of health insurance premiums, and the federal government pays the balance.

Of course, you cannot claim a tax credit on your tax return if the credit has been obtained on an advanced basis by means of government payment of your health insurance. The amount of the credit you claim on your tax return is reduced by the amount of the credit you receive in advance.

Pitfalls

Even if you are an eligible individual, not all health insurance qualifies for the credit. Examples of nonqualifying health insurance (in addition to those listed earlier) include:

- Accident and/or disability insurance
- Automobile medical insurance
- Coverage for on-site medical clinics
- Coverage for only a specified disease or illness
- Coverage under a flexible spending arrangement (FSA)
- Credit-only insurance
- Hospital indemnity or other fixed indemnity coverage
- Liability insurance or a supplement to liability insurance
- Medicare supplemental insurance ("Medigap")

- Tricare supplemental insurance (for military personnel and their families)
- Workers' compensation or similar insurance

Check for enrollment requirements. State programs can require eligible individuals to enroll within a reasonable period after becoming qualified and deny enrollment for failure to make timely payments (and can restrict eligibility to state residents).

If you claim the credit, you cannot include the same premiums in determining your itemized medical deduction on Schedule A, your self-employed health insurance deduction, or tax-free distributions from any medical or health savings account. What's more, if you claim the premium tax credit for coverage obtained through a government Marketplace, you cannot use the health coverage tax credit; no double benefit is allowed.

Where to Claim the Credit

There are 2 ways to obtain the credit: by registering in advance so that a portion of the credit is applied toward your premiums (register by calling toll free 866-628-4282) or by claiming it on your tax return.

You figure the credit on Form 8885, *Health Insurance Credit for Eligible Recipients.* You claim the credit as "Other Credits" on Form 1040.

You cannot claim the credit on Form 1040A or Form 1040EZ.

Itemized Medical Expenses

Medical care for most Americans today is very costly. Even those with insurance still pay out-of-pocket for many things, including copayments, noncovered procedures, and, often, the insurance premiums themselves. The tax law recognizes that medical costs, even though they are personal expenses, should be deductible if they exceed a set percentage of your income.

Benefit

If you itemize deductions (instead of claiming the standard deduction), you can write off medical expenses that are not covered by insurance, employer payments, or government programs to the extent they exceed 10% of adjusted gross income.

Example

Your adjusted gross income is $100,000. You have $12,000 of medical costs that are not covered by insurance. You can deduct $2,000—the first 10% ($10,000) is nondeductible.

There is no dollar limit on what you can deduct for medical expenses (once you pass the AGI threshold).

Conditions

To be treated as qualified medical expenses, payments must be for the diagnosis, cure, mitigation, treatment, or prevention of disease, or any treatment that affects a part or function of your body.

Deductible expenses include those paid not only for yourself but also for a spouse and dependents. A dependent, for this purpose, includes not only someone for whom you claim a dependency exemption but also someone you could have claimed the exemption for except for the fact that the person has gross income in excess of the exemption amount ($4,050 in 2017).

Example

In 2017, you provide more than half of your mother's support, including the payment of all her medical expenses. Her gross income is $12,000 so you cannot claim her as a dependent. You can, however, include your payment of her medical expenses with yours when figuring your medical expense deduction.

Examples of Deductible Medical Expenses

PROFESSIONAL SERVICES

Annual physical

Chiropodist

Chiropractor

Christian Science practitioner

Dermatologist

Dentist

Full body electronic scans

Gynecologist

Neurologist

Nurse, including board, wages, and employment taxes on wages

Nurse's aide for an elderly person in need of supervision and assistance

Obstetrician

Ophthalmologist

Optician

Optometrist

Osteopath

Pediatrician

Physician

Physiotherapist

Plastic surgeon for medically necessary surgery

Podiatrist

Practical nurse

Psychiatrist

Psychoanalyst

Psychologist

Registered nurse

Surgeon

DENTAL SERVICES

Artificial teeth

Cleaning teeth

Dental x-rays

Extracting teeth

Filling teeth

Gum treatment

Oral surgery

Orthodontia

EQUIPMENT AND SUPPLIES

Abdominal supports

Arches

Artificial eyes and limbs

Autoette

Back supports

Blood sugar test kit

Braces

Braille books and magazines

Contact lenses

Crutches, canes, and walkers

Elastic hosiery

Eyeglasses

Hearing aids and their batteries

Heating devices

Home exercise equipment for doctor-prescribed weight loss

Home pregnancy test

Invalid chair

Iron lung

Lactation equipment and supplies

Mattress to alleviate arthritic condition

Orthotics and orthopedic shoes (but only the excess over the cost of regular shoes)

Oxygen or oxygen equipment to relieve breathing problems caused by a medical condition

Protheses

Reclining chair if prescribed by a doctor

Repair of special telephone equipment for someone who is hearing impaired

Sacroiliac belt

Seeing-eye dog and its maintenance

Splints

Telephone-teletype costs and television adapter for closed-caption service for someone who is hearing impaired

Television adapter to display the audio part of programs as subtitles for the hearing impaired

Truss

Wheelchair

Whirlpool baths prescribed by a doctor

Wig advised by a doctor as essential to the mental health of a person who lost all hair from disease

HOME IMPROVEMENTS

Air conditioner where necessary for relief from an allergy or for relieving difficulty in breathing

Cost of installing stair-seat elevator for a person with a heart condition

Fluoridation unit

Lead-based paint removal to prevent a child with lead poisoning from eating the paint (but not the cost of repainting the scraped area)

Ramps for wheelchair access

Swimming pool (the portion of the cost that does not increase the home's value)

INSURANCE

Blue Cross and Blue Shield

Contact lens replacement insurance

Health insurance premiums you pay to cover hospital, surgical, and other medical expenses (Health insurance paid by your employer is not deductible by you, but you aren't taxed on this benefit.)

Long-term care insurance to the extent permitted for your age (explained later in this chapter)

Medicare Part B (and Medicare Part A for those not covered by Medicare)

Medicare Part D

Medigap (supplemental Medicare insurance)

Membership in a medical service cooperative

Student health fee

MEDICINE AND DRUGS

Birth control pills

Insulin

Prescription drugs

Viagra if medically prescribed

TESTS

Blood tests

Cardiograms

Full body electronic scans

Metabolism tests

Spinal fluid tests

Sputum tests

Stool examinations

Urine analyses

X-ray examinations

TREATMENTS AND PROGRAMS

Abortion

Alcoholism inpatient treatment at a therapeutic center

Acupuncture

Blood transfusion

Breast reconstructive surgery following a mastectomy

Childbirth classes for expectant mothers

Childbirth delivery

Clarinet lessons advised by a dentist for the treatment of tooth defects

Convalescent home—for medical treatment only

Diathermy

Drug treatment center—inpatient care costs

Egg donor fees (including legal fees for preparation of a contract between the taxpayer and the donor)

Electroshock therapy

Fertility treatments, including in vitro fertilization and surgery to reverse prior sterilization

Health institute fees for exercises, rubdowns, and so on that are prescribed by a doctor as treatments necessary to alleviate a physical or mental defect or illness

Hearing services

Hospitalization

Hydrotherapy

Kidney donor's or possible donor's expenses

Laser eye surgery or keratotomy

Lifetime care (see "Continuing Care Facilities and Nursing Homes" section later in this chapter)

Long-term care costs for someone who is chronically or terminally ill

Navajo healing ceremony ("sings")

Organ transplant (including the costs of a donor or prospective donor)

Prenatal and postnatal visits

Psychotherapy

Radium therapy

Remedial reading for someone with dyslexia

Sex reassignment surgery for someone with gender identity disorder (GID)

Special school for a mentally or physically impaired person if the main reason for attendance is to use its resources for relieving the disability

Sterilization

Stop-smoking programs

Surgery to remove loose skin following 100-pound weight loss

Tutoring for severe learning disabilities

Umbilical cord blood banking services if needed to treat an existing or imminently probable disease

Vaccines

Vasectomy

Weight-loss program to treat obesity, high blood pressure, or other condition

TRAVEL

Ambulance hire

Autoette (auto device for handicapped person)

Bus fare to see doctors, obtain treatment (including attendance at AA meetings), or pick up prescriptions

Cab fare to see doctors, obtain treatment (including attendance at AA meetings), or pick up prescriptions

Car use to see doctors, obtain treatment (including attendance at AA meetings), or pick up prescriptions at 17¢ per mile for travel in 2017

Conference expenses (travel costs and admission fees) for medical conferences on an illness or condition suffered by you, your spouse, or dependent

Lodging to receive outpatient care at a licensed hospital, clinic, or hospital-equivalent facility, up to $50 per night ($100 per night if you accompany a sick child)

Train fare to see doctors, obtain treatment (including attendance at AA meetings), or pick up prescriptions

Planning Tips

Payments by credit card are deductible in the year of the charge (not in the year of paying the credit card bill), so year-end charges for unreimbursed expenses (such as prescription sunglasses) are deductible in the year of the purchase.

If you don't expect your medical expenses to be sufficient to exceed the AGI floor this year, hold off on elective procedures until next year. Then you can effectively bunch expenses (this year's and next year's) into one year to exceed the AGI floor.

Pitfalls

Not every expense of a medical nature is deductible. Here is a listing of instances where no deduction was allowed by the IRS:

- Antiseptic diaper services
- Bottled water purchased to avoid the city's fluoridated water
- Breast augmentation surgery for a male who undergoes sex reassignment surgery
- Burial, cremation, and funeral costs
- Child care so a parent can see a doctor
- Cosmetic surgery *unless* it is medically necessary (For example, a nose job to improve appearance is not a qualified medical expense, but one done following a car accident to repair a nose broken in the accident is a qualified expense.)
- Dancing lessons
- Ear/body piercing
- Hair transplant
- Health club and gym memberships for maintaining general good health or appearance
- Illegal drugs and controlled substances (e.g., laetrile) in violation of federal law
- In vitro fertilization costs incurred to enable a healthy man to have a woman carry his child
- Marijuana, even if prescribed by a doctor in a state permitting the prescription (it is contraband under federal law)
- Marriage counseling fees
- Massages recommended by a doctor to relieve stress
- Maternity clothes
- Nicotine patches and gums
- Nutritional supplements, including vitamins, and herbal supplements
- Organ donations (e.g., a kidney)
- Over-the-counter medicines
- Premiums on policies guaranteeing a specified income each week in the event of hospitalization
- Prescription drugs purchased abroad, such as from Canada
- Scientology fees (but see Chapter 6)
- Sex change operation

- Special foods or beverage substitutes (in lieu of what is normally consumed)
- Swimming lessons
- Tattooing
- Teeth-whitening treatment
- Toothpaste
- Umbilical cord blood banking services to treat a disease that might possibly develop in the future
- Veterinary fees (other than for service animals)
- Weight-loss program to improve general good health or appearance

When figuring the deductible portion of home improvements made for medical reasons, such as a swimming pool used to alleviate a medical condition, only the portion of the cost that does not increase the home's value is deductible. However, the cost of making improvements to accommodate a disability, such as installing ramps or widening doors, usually doesn't add any value to the home and is fully deductible.

Medical expenses are deductible for purposes of the alternative minimum tax (AMT) *only* to the extent they exceed 10% of AGI.

Where to Claim the Deduction

Itemized medical expenses are reported in the first part of Schedule A of Form 1040. You cannot deduct medical expenses if you file Form 1040A or Form 1040EZ.

RECORDKEEPING

Retain all canceled checks, doctors' statements, receipts, and other evidence of medical expenses you paid. If you are deducting car mileage for medical-related travel, keep a detailed record of the date and distance of each trip in a diary, logbook, or other record keeper.

Self-Employed Health Insurance Deduction

Self-employed individuals (owning more than 2% S corporation shareholders) cannot deduct their health insurance costs from their business income. This means that health insurance costs do not reduce net earnings from self-employment. But these individuals are permitted to deduct premiums as an adjustment to gross income (an "above-the-line deduction") even if they do not itemize other deductions.

Benefit

Self-employed individuals and shareholders owning more than 2% of S corporations can deduct all of their health insurance directly from gross income. Thus, the write-off can be taken even if other deductions are not itemized.

This deduction includes not only payments for normal medical care but also long-term care insurance. There is no dollar limit on this deduction.

Conditions

To qualify for this write-off, you and your spouse may not have any employer-subsidized coverage. This condition applies on a month-by-month basis.

Example

If you (or your spouse) are eligible for employer-subsidized coverage in January but opt to pay your own coverage that month, you do not qualify for the deduction. But if, in February, you are no longer qualified under the employer plan, you can deduct your premium for this month.

Also, the deduction cannot exceed the net earnings from the business in which the medical insurance plan is established. These earnings may not be aggregated with earnings from other businesses. For S corporation shareholders, the deduction cannot be more than wages from the corporation (if this was the business in which the insurance plan was established).

Planning Tips

You can claim the deduction whether you buy the insurance through the business or individually, as long as you meet the conditions explained earlier.

Premiums for Medicare Part B coverage for a self-employed individual can qualify for the above-the-line deduction. The IRS has yet to rule on whether COBRA coverage also qualifies as eligible coverage for purposes of this above-the-line deduction.

If you are paying for your medical insurance, you may wish to combine this with a Health Savings Account (explained later in this chapter).

Pitfall

The deduction does not offset business expenses. In the case of S corporation shareholders owning more than 2% of the corporation, the shareholder can deduct his or her premiums from gross income only if the corporation pays the premiums or reimburses the shareholder for the premiums *and* includes the premiums as wages on the shareholder's Form W-2. In the past, the IRS had required that the corporation take out the policy, but this is no longer required.

Where to Claim the Deduction

The deduction is claimed in the "Adjusted Gross Income" section on Form 1040 (whether or not you itemize other medical expenses).

You cannot claim the self-employed health insurance deduction if you file Form 1040A or Form 1040EZ.

Long-Term Care Coverage

Individuals who are suffering from chronic conditions such as Alzheimer's disease or are merely elderly and incapable of self-care (such as feeding and bathing themselves) require long-term care, either in their own homes or in nursing homes. According to a Genworth survey in 2016 (the most recent year for statistics), the average annual cost of a nursing home stay in a private room is now $92,345 ($82,125 for a semiprivate room); it is $297,840 for a private room in Alaska. This cost generally is *not* covered by Medicare or supplemental Medicare insurance. Only special insurance, called long-term care insurance, pays for this type of care. The tax law allows a portion of this special medical insurance to be deductible.

Benefit

You can deduct a portion of long-term care insurance premiums as a qualified medical expense (based on your age).

Benefits received under a long-term care policy generally are treated as tax-free income (the benefits are an exclusion from income).

Conditions

Since there are 2 benefits—a deduction for the payment of long-term care insurance premiums and an exclusion from income for benefits received under the policy—different conditions apply for each.

CONDITIONS FOR THE DEDUCTION

You can deduct only a portion of premiums based on your age. For 2017, the federal deduction is limited to the amounts shown in Table 2.2.

The premium limit is on a per-person basis.

TABLE 2.2 Deductible Long-Term Care Premiums for 2017

Age by Year-End	Deduction Limit
Age 40 or younger	$ 410
Age 41–50	770
Age 51–60	1,530
Age 61–70	4,090
Age 71 or older	5,110

Example

Both you and your spouse carry long-term care insurance. You are age 65 and your spouse is age 60. Your annual premium is $4,200 and your spouse's premium is $1,800. You can treat $5,620 ($4,090 for you and $1,530 for your spouse) of your total $7,000 premiums as a deductible medical expense if the sum of your medical expenses exceeds 10% of your AGI.

CONDITIONS FOR THE EXCLUSION

The exclusion applies only to qualified long-term care services provided to a person who is chronically ill and that are necessary for medical or personal care and are provided under a plan of care prescribed by a licensed health care practitioner. You are chronically ill if a licensed health care practitioner certifies that within the past 12 months you meet *either* of these conditions:

- You are unable for at least 90 days to perform at least 2 activities of daily living without substantial assistance, due to loss of functional capacity. Activities of daily living include eating, toileting, transferring, bathing, dressing, and continence.
- You require substantial supervision for your safety due to severe cognitive impairment.

If the policy pays your long-term care expenses, you can exclude these payments.

Benefits paid under an indemnity-type contract are fully excludable to the extent they cover long-term care expenses. If you receive benefits under a per diem contract, there is a per-day dollar limit on what you can exclude. For 2017, the exclusion is $360 per day, even if your actual expenses are less.

Planning Tips

Since the average annual cost of a nursing home now is $92,345 for a private room ($82,125 for a semiprivate room), you might want to carry long-term care coverage to pay some or all of this cost if it arises. The younger you are when you purchase the policy, the smaller your annual premiums will be (they are fixed at the time of purchase and generally do not increase thereafter).

Long-term care insurance may be available as an employee fringe benefit under your company's cafeteria plan. If you opt for this coverage, you are not taxed on this benefit.

If you add a long-term care rider to a life insurance or annuity contract, the portion of the premium related to long-term care may qualify as a deductible medical expense (within the limits discussed in this section).

Many states allow more generous deductions or credits, even if you receive no benefit at the federal level. In New York, for example, there is a 20% tax credit, with no age or dollar limitation.

Commercial annuities can offer a long-term care rider. Such annuities usually cost from 35% to 50% more than stand-alone annuities. Similarly, life insurance policies may offer a long-term care rider.

Pitfall

Since long-term care insurance usually pays a fixed dollar amount and, hopefully, you won't need long-term care for many years to come, it can be difficult to know how much insurance to carry. Consider including a cost-of-living rider to adjust your dollar coverage for inflation.

Where to Claim the Deduction and/or Exclusion

The deduction for long-term care insurance premiums is treated like other deductible medical expenses. Generally, they are included with your other itemized medical expenses (up to your allowable dollar limit). However, if you are self-employed, you can include this amount with your other medical insurance claimed as part of the self-employed health insurance deduction, which is an adjustment to gross income.

If you receive benefits under a long-term care policy that are fully excludable, you do not have to report anything on your return. But if you are limited in what you can exclude (as explained earlier), excess benefits are reported as "Other Income" on Form 1040.

Flexible Spending Accounts for Health Care

Companies are increasingly forced to make employees pay for some or all of their medical expenses. But they can assist them by creating special arrangements, called flexible spending accounts (health FSAs), that enable employees to pay for medical expenses on a pretax basis. This means employees can dedicate some of their wages to special accounts used for medical expenses. Amounts put into these accounts are not currently taxed. The maximum amount you can contribute to an FSA in 2017 is $2,600. The limit for 2018 will be adjusted for inflation; check the Supplement for an update.

Benefit ⊗

Businesses can set up flexible spending accounts (FSAs) to allow employees to pay for expenses not covered by insurance on a pretax basis. At the start of the year employees agree to a salary reduction amount as their contribution to the FSA. These amounts are not treated as taxable compensation and are not subject to Social Security and Medicare (FICA) taxes. Employees then use these amounts any time during the year to pay for medical costs, including health insurance premiums or other expenses not covered by insurance, such as orthodontia and prescription eyeglasses.

For purposes of health FSAs, reimbursable medical expenses include prescription medications and insulin, as well as doctor-prescribed over-the-counter medications.

Conditions

The plan can set the limits on how much you can commit to the FSA each year up to the dollar limit allowed for the year (e.g., $2,600 for 2017). It may be fixed as a percentage of your compensation (e.g., up to 6%). Ask your plan administrator for details on your contribution limits and the deadline for signing up each year (just because you were in the FSA this year does not automatically cover you for next year; you may be required to complete the same paperwork all over again).

Planning Tips

You can tap into your annual contribution at any time during the year (even before you have fully paid into the FSA).

Example

In January you agree to contribute $1,800 for the year, which is $150 each month, to your company's FSA. In February, when you have contributed only $300, you pay a dental bill of $1,500 that is not covered by insurance. You submit the paid bill to your plan administrator and receive the full reimbursement of $1,500.

Your employer can adopt an IRS-approved grace period of up to 2½ months. If so, you have up to March 15, 2018, to incur medical expenses that can be reimbursed out of your 2017 FSA amounts.

Example

In 2017, you contribute $200 per month to your FSA. At the end of December you have used up only $2,000 of this amount. Assuming your employer adopted the IRS grace period, you have until March 15, 2018, to incur additional medical expenses of $400 so you can use up your account. If you incur $600 of medical expenses between January 1, 2018, and March 15, 2018, the first $400 is applied against your 2017 FSA contributions; the balance is applied against your 2018 FSA contributions (assuming you have agreed to these contributions).

Instead of a grace period, the plan can allow for a limited carryover of unused amounts to the following year. Currently the carryover is capped at $500. The carryover is not cumulative, so you can carry over only $500 each year (you cannot "bank" your carryovers). Assuming the plan allows for a carryover, it does not impact your annual contribution.

Example

In 2016, you failed to use $600 of your $2,500 contribution to your employer's medical FSA. The plan allows for a $500 carryover. In 2017, you contribute $2,600 to the plan. Your available reimbursements in 2017 are $3,100 ($2,600 annual contribution + $500 carryover). But $100 of your unused 2016 contribution is lost forever.

An employer can transfer funds in an FSA to an employee's Health Savings Account (HSA). The limit on the transfer is the lesser of the account balance on the date of transfer or on September 21, 2006. This is a one-time opportunity.

Reservists called to active duty can take penalty-free withdrawals from their FSAs for any purpose (not just medical).

Pitfalls

FSAs operate on a use-it-or-lose-it basis subject to the grace period or limited carryover discussed earlier. If you contribute more than your covered medical expenses for the year and cannot use it up in the contribution year or grace period (if applicable) and cannot take advantage of the limited carryover, you can't get the money back. Don't agree to a salary reduction amount in excess of what you reasonably expect to use for medical expenses.

FSAs cannot pay for any expenses that would not qualify as a deductible medical expense. For example, FSAs cannot be used to pay for cosmetic surgery (unless it is medically necessary—for example, to correct a birth defect) or for a breast pump (which is helpful to a working mother but does not treat or mitigate a medical condition).

If you leave the job before using up your FSA contributions for the year, you usually have to spend the unused amount within a time fixed by the plan (usually by the end of the month in which the employment ends). However, if you opt for COBRA (see later in this chapter), then FSA funds can continue to be used through the end of the year (and through the grace period if applicable); no additional contributions can be made to the FSA after termination of employment.

Where to Claim the Benefit

Since this benefit is an exclusion from income, you do not have to report anything on your return. Compensation reported on your Form W-2 is reduced to the extent of your FSA contributions.

However, you are required to account to the FSA administrator in order to receive payments from the plan. For example, you may be asked to submit a paid bill for prescription sunglasses in order to receive reimbursement from the FSA, and the bill must be submitted within a certain period after incurring the expense. Talk to your plan administrator for rules on how to obtain reimbursements from the plan.

Health Reimbursement Arrangements

Companies are continually looking for ways to reduce their health care costs for employees. Within the past few years, a new type of a company can set up a plan, called a health reimbursement arrangement, to reimburse employees up to the dollar limit fixed by the plan for out-of-pocket expenses (amounts not covered by insurance or other reimbursement arrangements). An employee can use funds in his or her account within the plan to pay for medical costs without being taxed when funds are contributed or when they are withdrawn for approved medical expenses. A special type of health reimbursement arrangement called a Qualified Small Employer Health Reimbursement Arrangement (QSEHRA) covers premiums only. This is discussed later in this chapter.

Benefit ⊗

Employers may set up health reimbursement arrangements (HRAs) to allow employees to pay for unreimbursed medical expenses without any cost to them. Here's how they work. The company sets up accounts for each employee and contributes a flat dollar amount (typically about half of the deductible under the employer-paid health insurance policy). You are not taxed on employer contributions. Similarly, when you use funds in your account to cover qualified medical costs (prescription medications and insulin, as well as doctor-prescribed over-the-counter medications), you are not taxed on withdrawals. There is no dollar limit on employer contributions on your behalf, nor on amounts you can withdraw tax free to pay for medical expenses.

Condition

Your company (not the IRS) sets any and all participation requirements, so talk with the HRA administrator about anything you must do to participate in and receive reimbursements from the HRA.

Planning Tips

You can use the funds in your account whenever you need to within the year. Any amounts remaining in the account at year-end automatically carry over to the next year and can be used to cover your future medical expenses.

Funds in an HRA can be transferred by an employer to an employee's Health Savings Account (HSA). The limit on the transfer is the lesser of the account balance on the date of transfer or on September 21, 2006. This is a one-time opportunity.

Pitfalls

There are no pitfalls for participating in your company's HRA. You are receiving a tax-free fringe benefit to the extent you use the coverage under the HRA.

Where to Claim the Benefit

Since this benefit is an exclusion from income, you do not have to report anything on your return.

However, you are required to account to the HRA administrator in order to receive payments from the plan. For example, you may be asked to submit a paid bill for prescription sunglasses in order to receive reimbursement from the HRA. Talk to the plan administrator for rules on how to obtain reimbursement.

QSEHRAs

The 21st Century Cures Act of 2016 created a new type of health benefit plan exclusively for employees in small businesses called Qualified Small Employer Health Reimbursement Arrangements (QSEHRAs). These plans enable employers to reimburse employees for their individually obtained health coverage on a tax-free basis. This benefit is paid entirely by employers; no employee salary reduction contributions are made.

Benefit

The value of the reimbursement received from your employer is not includible in gross income. This is so even though it may be reported on your Form W-2.

Conditions

There are several conditions for the exclusion to apply:

- Your employer must be a "small employer" (fewer than 50 full time/full-time equivalent employees) and not have any other group health plan.
- You must submit proof to your employer that you obtained health coverage.
- The amount of the annual reimbursement is capped at $4,950 for self-only coverage or $10,000 for family coverage.

Planning Tips

While the Tax Code does not specify that reimbursement can cover an employee's cost under a spouse's plan through the spouse's employer, the IRS suggested in informal advice in 2015 that this could be possible. More IRS guidance is needed on this point.

Pitfalls

You cannot claim a premium tax credit for your coverage, even though your income is low enough that you'd otherwise qualify for it. If you claim the credit, the QSEHRA benefit is reduced dollar for dollar.

If you don't have coverage for the full year, the dollar limit for reimbursement is prorated. For example, if you have family coverage from July through December, your exclusion is limited to $5,000 (half of the $10,000 annual limit).

Benefits under a QSEHRA do not have to be given to an employee who has not completed 90 days of service, is under age 25, or is a part-time or seasonal employee. If you are in any of these categories, check with your employer about reimbursements for your premiums.

Health Savings Accounts

Individuals who are covered by health insurance policies with high deductibles may be eligible to contribute money to a special savings account, called a Health Savings Account (HSA). HSAs have become a way to obtain needed health coverage now on an affordable basis. There are an estimated 20–22 million people who now have HSAs. HSAs can be obtained individually or through an employer if such a benefit is offered. Many employers are offering these accounts along

TABLE 2.3 Health Savings Account Contribution Limits for 2017

Your Age	Self-Only Plan	Family Plan
Under age 55	$3,400	$6,750
55 or older	$4,400	$7,750

with high-deductible health insurance (defined later), either as an employee's health care choice or the only option available.

Contributions to the account are tax deductible. Earnings on the account are not subject to immediate tax. If withdrawals are made to pay for medical expenses, they are fully tax free. Otherwise, withdrawals are taxable and subject to a 20% penalty unless taken when age 65 or older or disabled. Spouses who inherit an account can roll over the funds tax free.

Benefit

If you have a "high-deductible" health insurance policy (defined in the "Conditions" section), you can contribute to a special savings account. Benefits to HSAs include:

- Contributions within set limits are deductible as an adjustment to gross income (you do not have to itemize deductions to claim this benefit). See Table 2.3 for 2017 limits. The limits for those under age 55 can be indexed for inflation and may increase slightly for 2018; the additional contribution limit for those age 55 and older remains at $1,000.
- Interest or other earnings in the account are tax deferred.
- Withdrawals used to pay medical costs are tax free.

Conditions

To contribute to an HSA, you must meet 2 conditions:

1. You are not covered by Medicare.
2. You are covered by a high-deductible health plan (HDHP). In the past this had been a "bronze" plan on a government Marketplace, but with changes in the policy offering, a Marketplace option you select may or may not be an HDHP.

MEDICARE

HSAs are designed to cover individuals who do not qualify for Medicare. Therefore, you are ineligible for an HSA once you are covered by Medicare. Since

TABLE 2.4 2017 High-Deductible Policy Limits

	Self-Only Coverage	Family Coverage
Annual deductible at least	$1,300	$ 2,600
Limit on expenses	$6,550	$13,100

determination of eligibility is made month by month, you may be qualified for a deduction for the portion of the year before you are covered by Medicare.

QUALIFYING HIGH-DEDUCTIBLE HEALTH INSURANCE

You must have a high-deductible health insurance policy for at least all of December in 2017. This can be a policy that you have obtained personally or coverage provided by your employer. The determination of whether you have such coverage is made on the first day of the month.

A high-deductible policy is one that falls within certain limits. (See Table 2.4.)

You cannot have any other health coverage, other than accident insurance, dental care, disability coverage, disease-specific coverage (such as cancer insurance), long-term care, vision care, and workers' compensation.

Like individual retirement accounts (IRAs), contributions to HSAs can be made up to the due date for the return (without extensions). For example, contributions for 2017 can be made up to April 17, 2018.

Tax-Free Withdrawals

Only account distributions used to pay qualified medical expenses are tax free. Qualified medical expenses include:

- Any expense that could be claimed as an itemized medical deduction (see the section earlier in this chapter)
- COBRA premiums
- Over-the-counter medications if prescribed by a doctor
- Premiums for long-term care insurance
- Periodic health evaluations, such as annual physicals
- Routine prenatal and well-child care
- Child and adult immunizations
- Tobacco cessation programs
- Obesity weight-loss programs
- Screening services, such as those listed

Examples of Screening Services Treated as Medical Expenses for HSAs

CANCER SCREENING

Breast cancer (e.g., mammogram)

Cervical cancer (e.g., Pap smear)

Colorectal cancer

Oral cancer

Ovarian cancer

Prostate cancer (e.g., prostate-specific antigen [PSA] test)

Skin cancer

Testicular cancer

Thyroid cancer

HEART AND VASCULAR DISEASES SCREENING

Abdominal aortic aneurysm

Carotid artery stenosis

Coronary heart disease

Hemoglobinopathies

Hypertension

Lip disorders

INFECTIOUS DISEASES SCREENING

Bacteriuria

Chlamydial infection

Gonorrhea

Hepatitis B virus infection

Hepatitis C

Human immunodeficiency virus (HIV) infection

Syphilis

Tuberculosis infection

MENTAL HEALTH CONDITIONS AND SUBSTANCE ABUSE SCREENING

Dementia

Depression

Drug abuse

Family violence

Problem drinking

Suicide risk

METABOLIC, NUTRITIONAL, AND ENDOCRINE CONDITIONS SCREENING

Anemia, iron deficiency

Dental and periodontal disease

Diabetes mellitus

Obesity in adults

Thyroid disease

MUSCULOSKELETAL DISORDERS SCREENING

Osteoporosis

OBSTETRIC AND GYNECOLOGIC CONDITIONS SCREENING

Bacterial vaginosis in pregnancy

Gestational diabetes mellitus

Home uterine activity monitoring

Neural tube defects

Preeclampsia

Rh incompatibility

Rubella

Ultrasonography in pregnancy

PEDIATRIC CONDITIONS SCREENING

Child developmental delay

Congenital hypothyroidism

Lead levels in childhood and pregnancy

Phenylketonuria

Scoliosis, adolescent idiopathic

VISION AND HEARING DISORDERS SCREENING

Glaucoma

Hearing impairment in older adults

Newborn hearing

Planning Tips

It is up to you to keep track of medical costs so that you can prove withdrawals from your HSA were used to pay qualified expenses. The financial institution with which you have your account won't ask you for any substantiation on your part. Neither will your employer if the account is set up through your company.

HSAs can be funded by a one-time transfer by an employer from a flexible spending account (FSA) or by a health reimbursement arrangement (HRA), to an employee's HSA or an IRA rollover. Transfers from FSAs and HRAs are limited (as explained earlier in this chapter). Rollovers from IRAs are not currently taxed.

HSAs can be funded by means of a direct deposit of a tax refund. For example, if you expect a refund for 2017 taxes and plan to contribute to an HSA, file your return early enough so that the IRS has time to process it and transfer your refund directly to the HSA (you must provide account information to make the transfer possible). Alternatively, use a 2017 refund to make a contribution to an HSA for 2018 if eligible to do so for that year (designate whether the refund is being used to fund a 2017 or 2018 contribution where possible).

Funds in the HSA can be used for retirement savings. Since there is no tax on earnings that the account is building up, the healthier you stay (and the less you need to use account funds for medical bills), the more you'll have in retirement to use for any purpose. While the withdrawals will be taxed, there is no penalty on withdrawals for nonmedical purposes once you reach age 65.

Pitfalls

If you take withdrawals to pay nonmedical expenses, the distribution is taxed as ordinary income, regardless of your age. In addition, if you are under age 65, you are also subject to a 20% penalty (unless you are disabled). Taxable income treatment and the 20% penalty applies if the IRS levies on the HSA to cover back taxes, even though the withdrawal is involuntary. There is no 20% penalty on distributions because of the account owner's death.

If you have a separate prescription drugs benefit plan that has no deductible (only copayments for each prescription), you cannot be an eligible individual for HSA purposes.

If you inherit an HSA and are not a surviving spouse of the account owner, you must take a complete distribution of the account and include all of the funds in your income. Check to see if you qualify for a deduction for federal estate tax on the HSA (see Chapter 16).

Where to Claim the Benefits

The deduction is figured on Form 8889, *Health Savings Accounts (HSAs)*. The deduction is then claimed as an above-the-line deduction in the "Adjusted Gross Income" section of Form 1040. You cannot claim the deduction if you file Form 1040A or 1040EZ.

If your employer contributes to an HSA on your behalf, this is a tax-free fringe benefit; no reporting is required.

Archer Medical Savings Accounts

Self-employed individuals and small employers had been able to set up Archer Medical Savings Accounts (MSAs) to save money for their health insurance costs by combining a "high-deductible" medical insurance policy with this special savings plan. The opportunity to set up new MSAs expired at the end of 2007, so contributions for 2017 can only be made to MSAs set up before 2008. If they have a policy that falls within parameters set by the tax law, then they (or their employees) can contribute a fixed amount to an IRA-like account. Contributions are deductible, earnings are not currently subject to tax, and withdrawals for medical purposes are tax free (i.e., contributions and earnings on contributions used to pay medical costs are never taxed). Archer MSAs are an alternative to HSAs for eligible taxpayers, although HSAs usually are more favorable.

Benefit

If you are self-employed or an employee of a small employer with a "high-deductible" health insurance policy (defined in "Conditions" section), you can contribute to a special savings account that can be tapped to cover unreimbursed medical expenses. There are several benefits to Archer MSAs:

- Contributions within set limits are deductible (or tax free if made by your employer).
- Interest or other earnings in the account are tax deferred.
- Withdrawals used to cover medical expenses are tax free.

Conditions

You must be self-employed or an employee of a "small employer" covered by a "high-deductible" health insurance policy. A small employer is an employer who had on average 50 or fewer employees during either of the 2 preceding calendar years. If the business is new, then the employer is treated as a small employer if it reasonably expects to employ 50 or fewer workers. If a business made contributions to an Archer MSA this year, it can continue to be treated as a small employer as long as it had no more than 200 employees each year after 1996.

A high-deductible policy is one that falls within certain limits on deductibles and out-of-pocket expenses required to be paid (other than premiums) before the policy kicks in. (See Table 2.5.)

TABLE 2.5 2017 Limits on Deductibles and Out-of-Pocket Expenses

Type of Coverage	Minimum Annual Deductible	Maximum Annual Deductible	Maximum Annual Out-of-Pocket Expenses
Individual (self-only policy)	$2,250	$3,350	$4,500
Family	$4,500	$6,750	$8,250

Example

In 2017, you are self-employed and have a self-only health insurance policy with an annual deductible of $2,250 and a limit on out-of-pocket expenses of $3,350. You had set up an MSA in 2006 and have been funding it annually. Assuming you meet other conditions, you have a high-deductible plan and can fund an Archer MSA in 2017.

You (or your spouse) cannot have any other health plan that is not a high-deductible plan. But coverage under certain other health plans will not prevent you from being able to fund an Archer MSA. Other coverage you may have *in addition* to a high-deductible plan includes insurance covering accidents, disability, dental care, vision care, long-term care, benefits related to workers' compensation, a specific illness or disease, or a fixed amount per day or other period of hospitalization.

Assuming you meet the conditions for claiming a deduction, the amount is limited to 65% of your annual deductible for self-only coverage or 75% of your annual deductible for family coverage.

Example

In 2017, you are self-employed and have a health insurance policy for family coverage with a $6,000 annual deductible. In 2017, you can contribute $4,500 to an Archer MSA ($6,000 × 75%) (assuming the account was set up prior to 2008).

If you have coverage for only part of the year, you must prorate the deduction.

Example

Same facts as in the preceding example but you end coverage on June 30, 2017, and maintain it for the balance of the year. You can contribute $2,250 to an Archer MSA ($6,000 × 75% ÷ 12 months × 6 months).

Contributions for 2017 must be made no later than April 17, 2018.

Planning Tips

You can roll over funds in an Archer MSA tax free to a Health Savings Account. This may be advisable because of the extensive availability of financial institutions offering HSAs compared with limited Archer MSA options.

You can fund an Archer MSA for 2017 or 2018 via a direct deposit of your 2017 tax refund. Just provide the IRS with the account information and your refund will be transferred directly to your account.

You can use an Archer MSA to provide retirement income. Money can be withdrawn for any purpose penalty-free after you attain age 65.

Pitfalls

If you are self-employed, you cannot contribute more than your net earnings from self-employment. Thus, if you have a loss year, you cannot fund an Archer MSA.

Example

You are 65 years old and, because you have stayed healthy, the funds in your account have accumulated to $10,000. You can withdraw this money to take a vacation. While you'll owe income tax on the withdrawal (because you are not using the funds for medical reasons), you are not subject to the 20% penalty (explained next).

If you withdraw funds from an Archer MSA for other than medical expenses before attaining age 65, the funds are subject to a 20% penalty unless you are disabled (or die).

WHEN YOU DIE

If you have an Archer MSA, you can name your spouse as the beneficiary of the account. Your spouse becomes the owner of the account when you die. If you designate any other person as your beneficiary, the account ceases to be an Archer MSA on your death and the funds remaining in the account are taxable to the beneficiary as income. If there is no designated beneficiary, the balance of your account is included as income on your final tax return.

Where to Claim the Benefits

The deduction is figured on Form 8853, *Archer MSAs and Long-Term Care Insurance Contracts*. The deduction is then claimed as an above-the-line deduction in the "Adjusted Gross Income" section of Form 1040. You cannot claim a deduction if you file Form 1040A or 1040EZ.

If your employer contributes to an Archer Medical Savings Account on your behalf, this is a tax-free fringe benefit; no reporting is required.

REPORTING INCOME

Withdrawals are reported to you (and the IRS) on Form 1099-SA, *Distributions from an HSA, Archer MSA, or Medicare Advantage MSA*. Funds withdrawn for anything other than medical expenses are taxable as ordinary income. Report the income on Form 1040 as other income.

If you owe a 20% penalty on withdrawals for nonmedical purposes before age 65, you report the penalty in the section for "Other Taxes" on Form 1040.

ABLE Accounts

Federal law enables states to create special accounts called Achieving a Better Life Experience (ABLE) accounts, which are designed to ease the financial burden of families with disabled children. At present, ABLE accounts are live in about half of the states, but more states are expected to support them in the future. These accounts generally do not adversely impact eligibility for means-tested government programs (e.g., Medicaid can continue regardless of the amount of assets in the account).

Benefit ✪

Contributions to an ABLE account are not tax deductible. However, earnings grow on a tax-deferred basis and withdrawals for qualified disability purposes are tax free.

The maximum contribution amount in 2017 is $14,000 per beneficiary.

Conditions

An ABLE account must be set up in the state in which the disabled child resides unless that state contracts with another to facilitate such an account. The beneficiary of the ABLE account must be either:

- Receiving Social Security disability payments on account of blindness or a disability that occurred before age 26
- Certified by a doctor that he or she is blind or disabled due to an impairment that began before age 26 and that is expected to result in death or last (or has lasted) for at least 12 months

The beneficiary can have only one ABLE account at a time.

Distributions from an ABLE account are excludable only if used for qualified disability expenses, which include:

- Assistive technology
- Education
- Employment training
- Funeral and burial expenses
- Health
- Housing
- Personal support services
- Prevention and wellness
- Transportation

Planning Tips

Investment choices can be changed up to 2 times per year.

A family that has been thinking of setting up a supplemental needs trust for a disabled child should consider whether an ABLE account can meet the family's objectives. Discuss the situation with a knowledgeable attorney.

While authorizing legislation has been done in the states, accounts can be opened on only a handful as yet. Check the map at the ABLE National Resource Center at www.ablenrc.org/state-review for information on your state. However, you do not have to open an account in your state; there is no residency requirement for having an ABLE account.

Pitfalls

While assets in an ABLE account do not prevent eligibility for Supplemental Support Income (SSI), once the account balance reaches $100,000, SSI benefits are suspended (but not terminated).

A distribution is comprised of a return of contributions (which are not taxed) and a receipt of earnings (which are taxed). This is figured on a pro rata basis. In addition, there is a 10% penalty on the taxable amount of the distribution (regardless of the beneficiary's age).

Where to Claim the Benefit

You do not report contributions you make to an ABLE account on your return (remember, they are not deductible). It does not matter which income tax return—Form 1040, 1040A, or 1040EZ—you file.

COBRA Coverage

The Consolidated Omnibus Budget Reconciliation Act of 1986, or COBRA for short, imposed a new requirement on certain employers who maintain health insurance coverage for workers: allow workers who leave the job to continue their company coverage for a period of time (at the workers' expense). The opportunity to continue under the company's health plan means that terminated workers and other eligible people pay for medical insurance at group rates.

Benefits

Under federal law, if you work for a company that regularly employs 20 or more workers and has group health insurance, you are entitled to continue under the employer's group plan even if you leave employment (voluntarily or are laid off for any reason other than gross misconduct) or your hours are reduced below the level entitling you to employer-paid coverage. This is referred to as COBRA continuation coverage, or simply COBRA. Your state may have its own "mini-COBRA" law, which may expand your rights (contact your state insurance department for details). For example, Massachusetts mini-COBRA requires employers with 2 to 19 employees to also offer continuation coverage. And there is a special second COBRA election period for certain qualifying individuals.

Being eligible for and electing COBRA coverage gives you 2 key benefits:

1. Health insurance at an affordable group rate.
2. A deduction for premium payments if you itemize your medical expenses. (The IRS has not yet ruled on whether you can deduct COBRA coverage as an adjustment to gross income if you are self-employed, although some experts argue that you can.)

You can continue COBRA coverage for up to 18 months or until you become eligible under a new employer's plan, you qualify for Medicare, or you fail to make your COBRA payments (there is usually a 30-day grace period). The coverage period can be extended to 29 months if you become disabled within the first 60 days of COBRA coverage. Your family can retain COBRA coverage for up to 36 months if their eligibility results from your death.

You usually must pay the full cost of coverage, plus up to 2% as an administrative fee (102% of the premiums). But you enjoy the group term rates, which may be less than what you could purchase on your own. Your payment of premiums under COBRA is a deductible medical expense (explained earlier).

If you are a displaced worker, you may be able to claim a tax credit for your COBRA premiums, as explained earlier in this chapter.

Conditions for Coverage

If your employer is subject to COBRA, you must notify the employer about a qualifying event and opt for coverage within 60 days of that event (no extensions are granted). A qualifying event includes:

- You terminate employment (voluntarily or involuntarily, as long as you are not terminated for fraud or other gross misconduct).
- Your parent has health insurance through his or her employer and you attain the age at which you no longer qualify (generally through age 26).
- Your spouse has health coverage through his or her employer and you divorce your spouse.

SECOND COBRA ELECTION PERIOD

To qualify, you must be receiving trade adjustment allowance (TAA) benefits (or would be but for the requirement that you first exhaust unemployment benefits), you lost health coverage because of termination of employment that resulted in TAA eligibility, and you did not elect COBRA during the regular COBRA election period.

Planning Tips

Before opting for COBRA, see if there are less costly health insurance options. For example, if your spouse is working, his or her employer may offer less expensive health coverage. Or you may be able to buy coverage through a professional or trade association or through the government Marketplace that is less expensive than COBRA.

If you obtain COBRA coverage with the federal subsidy, even if the subsidy is taxable to you, there is still a cost savings.

Pitfalls

COBRA may not be less costly than coverage you could obtain on an individual basis. You can reduce your current level of coverage under COBRA, but you can't increase it. For example, if you had dental coverage but now wish to eliminate it (and the expense) under COBRA, you can do so. But if you didn't have dental coverage, you can't add it under COBRA.

COBRA does not apply to long-term care insurance. You may be able to pick up the long-term care policy individually when you leave employment, but your employer is not required to offer you this coverage through COBRA.

If you leave employment and are at least 65 years old, Medicare is your primary carrier so apply for coverage. This is so even if you opt for COBRA coverage for medical costs not covered by Medicare.

Where to Claim the Deduction

COBRA payments are treated as a deductible medical expense (see earlier in this chapter).

Medicare

In 1965, Congress introduced a federally sponsored health insurance program as part of the Social Security Act. This program, called Medicare, is designed primarily to provide those age 65 and older with affordable comprehensive health coverage. Today, the program has grown to afford seniors various types of coverage options, from fee-based services to managed care programs. More than 55 million Americans are now covered by Medicare.

Benefit ⊜

If you are age 65 or older, are under age 65 and disabled for at least 2 years, or have end-stage renal disease, you are entitled to participate in Medicare. Your monthly premiums (whether paid directly by you or withheld from your Social Security benefits check), as well as your copayments and deductibles under Medicare, are qualified medical expenses that are deductible as miscellaneous itemized deductions to the extent your total exceeds 10% of adjusted gross income (see the general rules on deducting medical expenses, including medical insurance, discussed earlier in this chapter). You are not taxed on the benefits you receive through Medicare.

Part A, which covers hospitalization, is free (those who did not work a sufficient number of quarters can pay for this coverage). Part B, which covers doctors' charges and certain other expenses, requires you to pay a monthly premium. The premium is subtracted from your Social Security benefits if you are collecting benefits. Both Part A and Part B have certain copayments or deductibles for your covered medical expenses.

There is a Medicare prescription drug plan called Part D. There is a 49% discount on the total cost of generic drugs while in the "donut hole" when Part D doesn't provide coverage (your drug costs of $3,700 to $4,950 in 2017). Certain low-income beneficiaries qualify for additional assistance to pay for prescription drugs in what is called the Extra Help program. To be eligible, beneficiaries must have an annual income in 2017 below $17,820 if single or $24,030 if married and not be eligible for any other prescription drug coverage (including outpatient prescription drug coverage through Medicare managed care plans). Beneficiaries cannot have savings and resources (excluding a home, car, personal possessions, and a burial plot) exceeding $12,320 if single or $24,600 if married or living together. Details on the Medicare drug program can be found at www.medicare.gov.

Conditions

To be eligible for free coverage under Part A, you (or your spouse) must have at least 40 quarters of Medicare-covered employment. If you don't have the necessary number of quarters, you can pay for this coverage.

Part B is available to just about anyone age 65 or older (there are no minimum work requirements).

Part D is available to all Medicare beneficiaries.

Planning Tips

Medicare coverage generally isn't automatic; you must apply for it if you haven't yet applied for Social Security benefits. You should contact your local Social Security office to apply for Medicare 3 months before the date you reach your full retirement age so that coverage can start on time.

If you have been collecting Social Security benefits before your full retirement age (e.g., starting at age 62), you do not have to apply when you near full retirement age; enrollment in Medicare Part A (hospitalization insurance) in this case is automatic and free; however, you must then decide whether to also elect Medicare Part B (health insurance).

If you opt for traditional fee-for-service Medicare (rather than some managed care program within Medicare), you may want to purchase supplemental Medicare insurance ("Medigap" coverage). Medigap premiums are deductible as a qualified medical expense (explained earlier in this chapter).

Pitfalls

If you claim the standard deduction (including the additional amount for being age 65 or older), you cannot deduct your Medicare Part B payments since you do not itemize deductions.

If you wait too long to apply for Medicare Part B, your monthly premium will be increased. To obtain the lowest possible premium, you *must* apply either within a 7-month window extending from 3 months before to 4 months after your 65th birthday, or, if still employed and covered at work, within 8 months after that ends.

If you did not sign up for Medicare Part D but were eligible to do so, and you do not have other "creditable coverage" (e.g., employer or other coverage that is at least as good as Medicare), you are penalized 1% per month for each month you delay. For example, if you wait 15 months to sign up beyond the deadline, you pay 15% of the premium as a penalty when you enroll. If the premium is normally $40 per month, you'd pay $46 per month ($40 plus 15% penalty). The penalty percentage continues for the rest of your life.

Where to Claim the Deduction

You deduct premiums as well as your copayments and deductibles as itemized medical expenses (see earlier in this chapter). You must complete Schedule A and attach it to Form 1040.

Continuing Care Facilities and Nursing Homes

Elderly and infirm individuals may require round-the-clock care because of their age or condition. Comprehensive programs in special living arrangements are now used to care for these individuals. A portion of the cost may qualify as a deductible medical expense.

Benefit ⊜

Advanced age and/or chronic illness may require ongoing daily treatment. Payments for nursing homes, convalescent homes, and sanitariums may be treated as deductible medical expenses. The deduction generally is not limited to the portion covering medical care; it also includes lodging and meals if confinement is primarily for the purpose of medical treatment.

If the main reason for admission is not medical care, you can still treat the portion of monthly fees allocable to medical care as a deductible medical expense. Typically, this applies to fees to continuing care facilities—the portion of the fees for medical care is deductible but the portion covering lodging and meals is not.

Conditions

Admission to the facility must be *primarily* for medical treatment to deduct all charges and fees. You can prove this by showing that:

- Entry was on or at the direction of a doctor.
- Attendance or treatment at the facility has a direct therapeutic effect on the condition suffered by the patient.
- Attendance at the facility is for the treatment of a specific ailment and not merely for general good health.

Planning Tip

Generally, prepayments for future care are not currently deductible medical expenses. However, you can claim a current deduction if you can show there is a current obligation to pay and you can establish the portion of the prepayment allocated to medical care.

Example

You and your spouse enter a retirement home that requires the payment of an entrance fee of $50,000, plus monthly payments of $1,000, to cover your accommodations, meals, and medical care for life. The home estimates for you that 10% of the entrance fee and 15% of the monthly fee are used for medical care. If you leave the home, you are entitled to a refund of a portion of the founder's fee. On these facts, you can treat 10% of the entrance fee and 15% of the monthly fee paid in the year as deductible medical expenses.

Pitfall

If you claim the standard deduction (including the additional amount for being age 65 or older), you cannot deduct your payments for continuing care facilities or nursing homes since you do not itemize deductions. As a practical matter, however, if you are a resident in such a facility for a full year, the cost will generally result in a large enough medical deduction to warrant itemizing your deductions in lieu of claiming the standard deduction, even with the additional amount for age.

Where to Claim the Benefit

See itemized medical expenses earlier in this chapter.

Accelerated Death Benefits

Whoever thought that life insurance could be beneficial to the person insured? Today, policies intended to provide death benefits to heirs may be used for lifetime assistance to the insured under special circumstances. Congress acted in the wake of AIDS to allow proceeds from life insurance policies that are tapped during the insured's life to receive the same tax-free treatment as death proceeds in certain circumstances.

Benefit ⊗

If you own a life insurance policy with cash value and become terminally or chronically ill, you may be able to tap into that cash value on a tax-free basis to pay medical and other personal expenses.

There are 2 ways in which to use a life insurance policy to provide you with current cash on a tax-free basis:

1. Tap into the policy's cash surrender value under an accelerated death benefit clause if the policy contains such an option.
2. Sell the policy to a viatical settlement company (a company in the business of buying policies under these conditions).

Conditions

You must be terminally or chronically ill to qualify for the exclusion. You are considered to be terminally ill if a physician certifies that you suffer from an illness or physical condition that is reasonably expected to result in death within 24 months of the date of certification.

You are considered to be chronically ill if a licensed health care practitioner certifies that within the past 12 months you meet *either* of these conditions:

- You are unable for at least 90 days to perform at least 2 activities of daily living without substantial assistance, due to loss of functional capacity. Activities of daily living include eating, toileting, transferring, bathing, dressing, and continence.
- You require substantial supervision for your safety due to severe cognitive impairment.

LIMITS FOR THE CHRONICALLY ILL

While *all* payments received by someone who is terminally ill are fully excludable (whether or not such amounts are used for medical care), limits apply to those who are chronically but not terminally ill. The same limits for benefits received under a long-term care policy apply for this purpose. Thus, if accelerated death benefits are not more than the daily dollar limit ($360 in 2017) and do not exceed actual long-term care costs, they are fully excludable. But any excess amounts are taxable.

Planning Tip

To the extent you use accelerated death benefits for medical expenses, you reap a double tax benefit: The funds are tax-free income to you, and you can treat the payments you make as deductible medical expenses if you itemize your deductions.

Pitfall

To the extent you use your life insurance policy while you are alive, there is that much less for your beneficiaries after your death. If you have other options to cover your expenses, you might weigh your current needs against your beneficiaries' needs after your death in deciding whether to use accelerated death benefits.

Where to Claim the Benefit

If benefits are fully excludable, they need not be reported. However, if a chronically ill person receives benefits in excess of the limit ($360 per day in 2017), such amounts are reported as other income on Form 1040.

Decedent's Final Illness

There are no special deductions for someone who dies. But the tax law provides opportunities on the timing of deductions for the deceased. Those handling the affairs of a person who has died can choose how to handle medical deductions for optimum tax savings.

Benefit

Payments of medical expenses for a deceased spouse or dependent can be deducted as a medical expense in the year they are paid, even if this is before or after the person's death.

A decedent's personal representative (executor, administrator, etc.) has a choice of how to treat medical expenses—as an itemized deduction on the decedent's final income tax return (to the extent provided) or as a deduction on the estate tax return. Of course, if the decedent's estate is too small to require the filing of an estate tax return, there is no real choice; the deduction should automatically be treated as a deduction on the decedent's income tax return.

If the personal representative of a decedent's estate pays medical expenses within one year of death, an election can be made to treat the expenses as if they were paid by the decedent in the year the services were provided rather than the year in which they were paid. This may entitle the personal representative to file an amended return for the decedent for a prior year.

Example

In 2016, the decedent received treatment for a condition that eventually resulted in her death on May 1, 2017. At the time of death, payment for this treatment was outstanding. Assuming her personal representative pays any of her unreimbursed cost in February 2017, the personal representative may file an amended return for the decedent for 2016 to include the payment along with the decedent's other deductible medical expenses.

Condition

The decision on when and where to claim the decedent's medical expenses is made by the personal representative—the executor, administrator, or other person empowered by a court to act for the estate. This person can override a decision by a surviving spouse.

Planning Tip

Generally, if the decedent leaves an estate large enough to be subject to estate tax, it usually is preferable to claim the deduction on the estate tax return because the estate tax rate is 40%. What's more, *all* of the medical expenses can be deducted on the estate tax return; there is no 10%-of-AGI floor for this purpose. Of course, given the federal estate tax exemption of $5.49 million per person in 2017, most people who die in this period will not have any estate tax, so the costs of a final illness will probably be deducted on the final income tax return.

Pitfall

If the personal representative opts to deduct medical expenses on the decedent's income tax return, the portion that is not deductible because of the applicable percentage of AGI cannot be claimed on the estate tax return.

EXAMPLES OF NONDEDUCTIBLE EXPENSES FOR A DECEDENT

Burial fees

Cremation costs

Funeral expenses

Perpetual care for a grave or mausoleum

Where to Claim the Benefit

If the personal representative opts to deduct the medical expenses on the decedent's income tax return, a statement must be attached to the return agreeing *not* to claim the expenses as a deduction on the decedent's estate tax return.

Medical Insurance Rebates

Insurance companies must spend a set portion of premiums (called a medical loss ratio) on health services. If they fail to do so by overspending on salaries and other administrative costs, they are required to rebate premiums (in the form of cash or premium reductions) to policyholders. According to the Department of Health and Human Services, insurance companies rebated a total of $397 million in 2015, averaging $138 per family (statistics for 2016 are not known, but the amount of rebates has been declining year after year). Not everyone receives a rebate, but if you do, it may be tax free or taxable to you.

Benefit

If you claimed the standard deduction, any rebate is fully tax free. If you itemized deductions, the rebate is taxable to you according to the tax benefit rule (the same rule for tax refunds applies to medical insurance rebates so you can use Worksheet 16.1 to figure your taxable amount). Similarly, if you are self-employed and claimed a deduction for premiums from gross income, the rebate is taxable.

If, under an employer plan, you paid premiums through a salary reduction contribution using pretax dollars, the rebate is treated as additional compensation to you in 2017. If you used after-tax dollars, the rebate is taxed according to the tax benefit rule.

Where to Report the Rebate

If you determine that the 2016 rebate received in 2017 is taxable, do *not* amend your 2016 return. Instead report the taxable portion as "other income" on your 2017 Form 1040.

Education Costs

Alert

At the time this book was completed, Congress was considering important tax changes that could affect 2017 tax returns and planning for 2018. Check the online Supplement in February 2018 at www.jklasser.com or www.barbaraweltman.com to see what changes have been enacted and when they are effective.

N o one doubts the importance of education—for ourselves, our children, and our grandchildren—but obtaining it can be pricey. According to the Scholarship Workshop, the average cost of one year in a public university (in-state) for 2017–2018 is $35,674 and for a private college is $76,855, and the cost of higher education is increasing at nearly 7% annually (compared with an overall inflation rate of about 2% for 2017). Fortunately, the tax law provides many incentives to help you save for education and to pay for it on a tax-advantaged basis.

This chapter explains the tax deductions, credits, and other breaks you can claim with respect to education costs. For more information, see IRS Publication 970, *Tax Benefits for Education*.

FAFSA Submissions

If you want to apply for federal financial aid for yourself or your child, you must complete the Free Application for Federal Student Aid (FAFSA). The information on the application is based on your federal income tax return. The U.S. Department of Education made certain changes designed to ease the application process.

The deadline for submission is October 1 each year. In addition, the information on the application can be based on the *prior*-prior year's information (two years prior), instead of the prior year's information. This allows tax information from the prior-prior year to be readily available.

Example

The FAFSA form for aid in the 2018–2019 school year is based on your 2016 federal income tax return, which is filed no later than October 16, 2017 (assuming you obtained a filing extension).

You can retrieve your tax return information electronically if you e-filed your tax return. While this option has been available for a while, the new submission deadline makes it easier for you as well as more students and their parents to use the option. There have been some problems with the IRS Data Retrieval Tool, but the IRS said it would be online by October 1, 2017, to complete applications for 2018–2019.

Employer-Paid Courses

Companies want an educated workforce. Some are willing to underwrite the cost of additional education for their employees. The tax law not only allows companies to deduct the costs they pay on behalf of workers for higher education, but also workers can enjoy this fringe benefit tax free up to a set dollar amount each year.

Benefit ⊗

If your employer pays or reimburses you for the cost of higher education, you are not taxed on payments up to $5,250 annually. If the courses are job-related, there is no dollar limit to the exclusion from income for this employer-paid fringe benefit. This fringe benefit is not subject to Social Security and Medicare (FICA) taxes.

If you work for an educational institution and receive tuition reductions, such benefit may be excludable (see Conditions, next).

Conditions

Different conditions apply to employer-paid education under an education assistance plan and tuition reduction if you work for a college or university.

EMPLOYER-PAID EDUCATION

Employer-paid education must be furnished under an employer's education assistance plan that does not discriminate in favor of owners or highly paid employees.

The courses need *not* be job-related to qualify for the limited exclusion of $5,250 annually. For example, if you are currently a programmer and your employer pays for accounting courses, you can still exclude the benefit.

There is no dollar limit on the amount you can exclude from income if you meet the following 3 conditions:

1. The courses relate to your current job.
2. The courses do not qualify you for a new profession.
3. You have already met the job's minimum education standards.

For example, if you are a programmer who takes more programming courses, the value of this benefit is fully excludable.

TUITION REDUCTION

If you work for an educational institution, you are not taxed on tuition reductions for you, your spouse, and your dependents (as well as widows or widowers of deceased or former employees) if:

- The courses are undergraduate courses. However, if you are a graduate student who is a teaching or research assistant, you aren't taxed on tuition reduction as long as it is in addition to regular pay for your teaching or research activities.

- The benefit is *not* payment for teaching or other services. However, if you receive a scholarship under the National Health Services Corps Scholarship Program or the Armed Forces Health Professionals Scholarship Program, you can exclude any reduction despite your service requirements.

If you are eligible for tuition reduction, the benefit is not limited to courses taken at the school in which you work. You can exclude from your income the value of courses you take at any school covered by a tuition reduction agreement (area colleges and universities typically have reciprocal class agreements).

Planning Tip

If you are seeking a job and plan to pursue college or graduate courses while working, look for a company with an educational assistance plan. The value of this benefit can be substantial to you if you use it fully and should be factored into the salary being offered for the position.

Example

You are in the 28% tax bracket and in 2017 your employer pays for courses totaling $5,000. If you had to pay for these courses yourself, you would need to earn an additional $6,944 in income to have the funds to pay for the courses yourself (assuming you can't deduct them).

Pitfalls

Generally, you must attain a certain course grade for your employer to pay for the education. Make sure you understand what you must do to obtain reimbursement or have your course fully paid by your employer.

You cannot use any benefit received under an employer's plan as the basis for claiming a second tax benefit. For example, if your employer pays $2,000 for a course you take, you cannot claim an education credit for this amount.

Where to Claim the Exclusion

If employer-provided education is excludable from income, it is not reported on your return. You may find the amount of employer-paid education benefits reported on your Form W-2 for information purposes only; it is not added to your compensation.

Scholarships, Fellowships, and Grants

According to some estimates there are about $46 billion in scholarships available each year. This money is available through government programs, nonprofit organizations, and corporations that support education. Grants are made on the basis of need, scholastics, or special talents (such as athletics or music). The tax law enables you to receive this money on a tax-free basis under certain circumstances.

Benefit ⊗

If you are enrolled in a degree program at a school and receive a scholarship, fellowship, or grant, you can exclude the portion of the grant for tuition, course-related fees, books, supplies, and equipment. There is no dollar limit on this exclusion.

If you receive a Fulbright award, it is fully taxable (unless you can claim the foreign earned income exclusion explained in Chapter 14).

Condition

For tax-free treatment to apply, the grant must be for study in a degree program. A degree program includes:

- Primary and secondary school
- College or university degree programs
- Full-time or part-time scholarships for study at a school that provides an education program acceptable for full-time credit toward a degree or offers a program of training to prepare students for employment in a recognized occupation

Planning Tip

For education planning purposes, obtaining a scholarship, fellowship, or grant is the best way to finance learning. The award doesn't cost you anything and doesn't have to be repaid. Explore carefully any grants to which you, a spouse, or a dependent may be entitled.

Pitfalls

Scholarship amounts for room, board, and incidental expenses are taxable.

If you are a graduate student who receives payment (a stipend) for teaching, doing research, or providing other services as a condition of the grant, you are taxed on the payment. Such amount is reported on Form W-2 and is subject to income tax withholding.

Generally, no exclusion can be claimed if receipt of a federal grant is conditioned on your performing services in the future. For example, if you receive a scholarship that requires you to teach for at least 3 years as a condition of the grant, you cannot exclude this grant from your income.

Where to Claim the Exclusion

If the grant is excludable from income, you do not have to report it on your return.

If the grant is partially taxable (for example, you are not a degree candidate and so are taxed on the portion of the grant for housing), you report this as other income in the "Income" section of Form 1040 or Form 1040A. If you are a graduate student receiving a stipend for services, such amounts are reported as wages on your return, regardless of which type of return you file.

American Opportunity Credit

The tax law allows you to claim a limited tax credit, called the American opportunity credit, when you pay for higher education. The credit applies whether you pay out-of-pocket from savings or borrow the money. You may claim the credit each year you qualify for it.

Benefit

If you meet certain conditions and do not claim the lifetime learning credit discussed later, you can claim the American opportunity credit for higher education costs of up to $2,500 per student (100% of the first $2,000 of costs, plus 25% of the next $2,000 of costs). Thus, for example, if you have twins who are freshmen in college, you can qualify for a credit of up to $5,000.

In 2017, 40% of the credit is refundable in most situations (it can be repaid to you even though it is more than your tax liability).

Conditions

To claim the American opportunity credit, you must meet all 5 of these conditions:

1. Payments relate to the first 4 years of higher education.
2. Payments are made on behalf of an eligible student.
3. Payments are made to an eligible institution.
4. Payments cover qualified higher education costs.
5. Your modified adjusted gross income is not above a set limit.

FIRST 4 YEARS OF HIGHER EDUCATION

The credit applies for only the first 4 years of college or other postsecondary school. Thus, if a student takes 5 or more years to earn a college degree, the American opportunity credit applies only for study during the first 4 years of higher education.

Example

Your child started college in September 2014. Assuming you qualify, you can claim an American opportunity credit for tuition in 2017 because your child is still within the 4-year limit.

ELIGIBLE STUDENT

The credit may be claimed for you, your spouse, or your dependent for whom you claim an exemption on your return. The student must be enrolled for at least one academic period (a semester, trimester, or quarter) during the year.

No credit may be claimed if the student has a federal or state felony drug conviction on his or her record.

ELIGIBLE EDUCATIONAL INSTITUTION

Only payments to an eligible institution entitle you to claim the credit. This includes any accredited public, nonprofit, or proprietary postsecondary institution eligible to participate in the student aid programs administered by the U.S. Department of Education. Thus, enrollment in a foreign educational institution probably will not entitle you to claim this tax credit. Ask your school if it is eligible, or check www.studentaid.ed.gov.

Enrollment must lead to a degree, certificate, or other recognized educational credential.

QUALIFIED HIGHER EDUCATION COSTS

Qualified expenses include *only* tuition, related fees, and books, supplies, and required equipment. Related fees can include, for example, a student activity fee paid to the institution if it is required for all students and no portion of it covers personal expenses. Hobby or sports courses and noncredit courses do not qualify for the credit *unless* they are part of the student's degree program.

The following costs do *not* qualify for the credit:

- Any expenses paid with tax-free educational assistance
- Room and board (even if they are required to be paid to the institution as a condition of enrollment)
- Medical expenses
- Transportation
- Insurance
- Personal living expenses

The cost of a computer may qualify for the credit if it is needed for attendance at the school. Otherwise, it is viewed as a personal expense for which the credit cannot be taken.

As a practical matter, the institution furnishes the student with an information return showing qualified tuition and related expenses paid for the year. The return, Form 1098-T, *Tuition Payments Statement*, for 2017 is issued by January 31, 2018, and usually you need to have received the form in order to claim the credit.

If you prepay expenses for an academic period that begins within the first 3 months of 2018, you can include this amount when figuring your 2017 credit. You cannot choose to take the credit for the prepayment in 2018.

Example

In December 2017 you pay tuition for your child for the semester beginning February 2018. You can include the tuition payment as part of qualified expenses in figuring your 2017 credit.

MAGI LIMIT

The ability to claim the credit depends on your modified adjusted gross income (MAGI). MAGI for this purpose is adjusted gross income increased by the foreign earned income exclusion and other foreign items.

If your MAGI is below a phaseout range, then the full credit can be claimed; a partial credit is allowed for those with MAGI within the range. No credit can be claimed if MAGI exceeds the range. Table 3.1 shows the phaseout ranges for 2017.

Example

In 2017, you are single, with MAGI of $85,000. Your top credit is limited to $1,250 (one-half of the maximum credit of $2,500), since you are midway in the MAGI phaseout range. If your MAGI is $75,000, you can claim a credit up to $2,500; if your MAGI is over $100,000, you cannot claim any credit.

TABLE 3.1 2017 MAGI Phaseout Range for American Opportunity Credit

Filing Status	MAGI
Married filing jointly	$160,000–180,000
Other filing status*	$ 80,000–90,000

*No credit may be claimed for married filing separately.

Planning Tips

You can claim the credit even though eligible expenses are paid with the proceeds of a loan. You can also claim the credit if eligible expenses are paid by someone other than you, your spouse, or your dependent, such as the student's grandparent. The payment is treated as having been made by the student, and as your dependent, this entitles you to claim the credit if you are otherwise eligible to do so.

As the parent, if you pay the expenses but your MAGI is too high to permit you to claim the credit, you can waive your right to do so. This will allow your child to claim the credit on his or her own return (assuming the child has tax liability and can benefit from the credit). Your child can claim the credit even though you pay the expenses.

To allow your child to claim the credit you must forgo the dependency exemption for your child. To make the waiver, you do not have to file any special waiver forms or attach any statements to your return or to the child's return.

If your child cannot use the credit, consider taking the above-the-line deduction for tuition and fees if you are qualified to do so (explained later in this chapter). The tuition and fees deduction has a higher MAGI limit so you may qualify for this benefit even though your MAGI prevents you from claiming the credit.

Pitfalls

The credit must be coordinated with other education tax benefits you may be qualified to use. You can claim the credit in the same year in which you receive distributions from a Coverdell education savings account (ESA) or 529 plan. However, the expenses on which you base the credit cannot be the same expenses used to figure the tax-free portion of the distributions.

Example

Your child's college tuition bill for the year is $15,000. You pay $5,000 of this amount from a 529 plan. For purposes of figuring the credit, you can only take $10,000 of eligible expenses into account ($5,000 is used as a tax-free distribution from the 529 plan).

If you claim a credit and in a later year (after you have filed the return and claimed the credit) receive a refund of an amount that was used to figure the credit, you must recapture some or all of the credit. This means you must repay some or all of the credit. You treat the recaptured amount as additional tax liability for the year of recapture. Do not amend the return on which the credit was claimed.

> ### Example
>
> In 2017, you take an American opportunity credit of $2,500 based on $4,000 of tuition costs. In 2018, your child receives a grant reimbursing him for tuition of $1,000. You must recapture $250 (25% of $1,000). You report this recapture as "other income" on your 2018 return.

You may not claim the American opportunity credit if you claim the above-the-line deduction for tuition and fees for a student. You must choose which write-off gives you the greater benefit, assuming you qualify for each.

> ### Example
>
> You are a single parent with MAGI in 2017 of $40,000 and pay $5,000 in tuition for your child. You can claim an American opportunity credit of $2,500, which gives you a tax savings of $2,500. Or you can claim the above-the-line deduction for tuition of $4,000, which gives you a tax savings of $1,000 if you are in the 25% tax bracket ($4,000 × 25%) (assuming that the tuition deduction is extended for 2017). In this case, you'd choose the credit alternative.

You cannot claim the credit for expenses that are paid by tax-free scholarships, fellowships, grants, veterans' educational assistance, or employer-provided educational assistance.

Where to Claim the Credit

The American opportunity credit is figured on Form 8863, *Education Credits*. The credit is then entered in the "Tax and Credits" section of Form 1040, or in the "Tax, Credits, and Payments" section of Form 1040A.

You may not claim the credit if you file Form 1040EZ.

Lifetime Learning Credit

The tax law allows you to claim a limited tax credit, called the lifetime learning credit, when you pay for higher education and do not claim the American opportunity credit. The credit applies whether you pay out-of-pocket from savings or borrow the money. You may claim the credit each year you qualify for it.

Benefit

If certain conditions are met, you can claim a credit of up to $2,000 on your return for the payment of qualified higher education costs for you, your spouse, or your dependent. In contrast to the American opportunity credit, which is a per student credit, the lifetime learning credit is per taxpayer. So if you have 3 children in college, your lifetime learning credit for the year is limited to $2,000 (assuming you qualify to claim it).

Unlike the American opportunity credit, which applies only for the first 4 years of higher education, the lifetime learning credit can be claimed for any higher education, including graduate-level courses.

Conditions

Most of the conditions for the lifetime learning credit are the same as those for the American opportunity credit detailed earlier, unless otherwise noted here. Thus, the same planning tips and pitfalls also apply.

The ability to claim the lifetime learning credit depends on your modified adjusted gross income (MAGI). The limit for this credit is different from the limit applicable to the American opportunity credit. If your MAGI is below a phaseout range, then the full credit can be claimed; a partial credit is allowed for those with MAGI within the phaseout range. No credit can be claimed if MAGI exceeds the range. Table 3.2 shows the phaseout ranges for 2017.

ELIGIBLE STUDENT

There is no ban on claiming the lifetime learning credit for a student who has a felony drug conviction on his or her record, as there was for claiming the American opportunity credit.

HIGHER EDUCATION

Unlike the American opportunity credit, which can be claimed only for courses leading to a degree, the lifetime learning credit can be claimed for one or more courses at an eligible educational institution that are part of a postsecondary degree program or part of a nondegree program taken to acquire or improve

TABLE 3.2 2017 MAGI Phaseout Range for Lifetime Learning Credit

Filing Status	MAGI
Married filing jointly	$112,000–132,000
Other filing status*	$ 56,000–66,000

*No credit may be claimed for married filing separately.

job skills. In other words, the student does not need to be pursuing a degree or other recognized educational credential.

There is no limit on the number of years for which the lifetime learning credit may be claimed.

Planning Tip

Since the lifetime learning credit cannot be claimed for a student for whom an American opportunity credit is claimed, decide which credit produces the greater tax savings. Usually, this is the American opportunity credit because there is a higher credit limit ($2,500 versus a $2,000 limit for the lifetime learning credit). However, once a student is beyond 4 years of college, then there is no choice; only the lifetime learning credit can be claimed.

Pitfalls

The same pitfalls applicable to the American opportunity credit apply to the lifetime learning credit. Thus, you must receive Form 1098-T before claiming the credit.

Where to Claim the Credit

The lifetime learning credit is figured on Form 8863, *Education Credits*. The credit is then entered in the "Tax and Credits" section of Form 1040, or in the "Tax, Credits, and Payments" section of Form 1040A. You may not claim the credit if you file Form 1040EZ.

Job-Related Education

Americans are always trying to better themselves. Whether you are a teacher taking courses toward an advanced degree or a data processor learning the latest technology, you may be eligible to deduct your education costs.

Benefit

If you pay for education related to your current line of work, you may be able to deduct your expenses.

If you qualify for the deduction by meeting all of the conditions, you claim the deduction as a miscellaneous itemized deduction if you are an employee or as a business expense if you are self-employed. This means that if you are an employee, you can take the deduction only if your miscellaneous itemized deductions exceed 2% of your adjusted gross income. There is no dollar limit on this deduction. And if you are a high-income taxpayer, your deduction is subject to an additional reduction.

Conditions

To deduct education expenses, you must meet all 5 of these conditions:

1. You are an employee or self-employed.
2. You already meet the minimum job requirements for your work (as set by your employer or state law).
3. The courses maintain or improve your skills or you are required by your employer or by law to take the course to keep your current salary or position.
4. The courses do not lead to a new line of work.
5. You pay for eligible education expenses.

EMPLOYED OR SELF-EMPLOYED

You cannot deduct the cost of courses taken before you start to work.

Working for only a short period of time before beginning an MBA program may not establish you in a trade or business. For example, the Tax Court denied a deduction for the costs of an MBA to an individual who graduated from college in 2007 and started the MBA program in 2009 after holding only short-term positions, none of which required or even related to an MBA.

MINIMUM JOB REQUIREMENTS

Minimum job requirements are based on a review of your employer's standards, the laws and regulations of your state, and the standards of your profession or business. Just because you are currently employed doesn't automatically mean you meet minimum job requirements. You may be hired provisionally on the condition that you complete certain courses.

If job requirements change after you enter the job market or profession, any courses you take to meet the new standards are deductible.

Example

You graduated from college with a degree in physical therapy and start to work in your chosen occupation. Then state law is changed to require physical therapists to complete at least one year of graduate school to retain certification. You can deduct the cost of the additional year of schooling because you had already met your initial minimum job requirements.

MAINTAIN OR IMPROVE SKILLS REQUIRED BY EMPLOYER OR BY LAW

General education courses are not deductible. The courses must be designed to keep you up to date and qualified.

Courses that give you a specialty *within* your current line of work are deductible.

EXAMPLES OF DEDUCTIBLE COURSES

- Accounting manager who obtains an MBA.
- Attorney in practice who takes LLM courses to obtain a master's degree in taxation.
- Continuing education courses by professionals.
- Dentist who takes courses in orthodontics. This postgraduate schooling improves professional skills as a dentist.
- Practicing psychiatrist who takes courses at an accredited psychoanalytic institution.
- Psychiatrist who takes personal therapy sessions.
- Salesperson who is encouraged by his or her employer to pursue an MBA degree in order to move up in the company because the degree merely enhances his skills.
- Teachers may deduct courses taken for job changes within the teaching profession (e.g., elementary to secondary school, one classroom subject to another, classroom teacher to guidance counselor, and classroom teacher to principal).

NOT A NEW LINE OF WORK

If the courses enable you to follow a new line of work, they are not deductible.

EXAMPLES OF NONDEDUCTIBLE COURSES

- Software engineer who obtained an executive MBA.
- Law school (even by someone who intends to continue in his or her original line of work, such as accounting).
- Nurse who takes courses that qualify him to become a physician's assistant.
- NASA engineer who obtained a pilot's license (even though this helped with his engineering activities).

ELIGIBLE EDUCATION EXPENSES

If you qualify for the deduction, it is not limited to the cost of tuition and fees as is the case with many other types of education tax breaks. The deduction applies not only to the cost of courses but also to:

- Books and supplies.
- Local transportation expenses to and from the course, including bus, subway, or train fares. If you use your car, you can deduct mileage at the rate of 53.5¢ per mile in 2017, plus parking and tolls.

- Lodging, meals, and transportation. If you attend courses out of town, you can deduct away-from-home expenses. The deduction for meals is limited to 50% of actual cost.

Planning Tip

Check to see whether education expenses qualify for an education credit or the above-the-line tuition and fees deduction, which may provide a greater tax benefit for an employee than an itemized deduction subject to the 2% floor.

Pitfalls

As a practical matter, even if your costs for taking courses are eligible for the deduction, you may not achieve any meaningful tax benefit from claiming them. First, as mentioned earlier, the deduction is limited to amounts exceeding 2% of your adjusted gross income and is subject to the reduction on itemized deductions for high-income taxpayers. Thus, if your AGI is $50,000, your total miscellaneous itemized deductions must exceed $1,000 to claim any write-off; you lose the first $1,000 of deductions.

Second, if you are a high-income taxpayer, the allowable deduction is subject to the overall phaseout of itemized deductions. And third, claiming miscellaneous itemized deductions can trigger or increase the alternative minimum tax (AMT). The reason: Miscellaneous itemized deductions are *not* deductible for AMT purposes.

Where to Claim the Deduction

You must file Form 1040 to claim the deduction; you cannot claim the deduction if you file Form 1040A or 1040EZ.

If you are an employee, you complete Form 2106, *Employee Business Expenses*, or 2106-EZ, *Unreimbursed Employee Business Expenses*, to figure your unreimbursed employee expenses that are then deducted on Schedule A.

If you are self-employed, you deduct the expenses directly as a business expense on Schedule C.

Tuition and Fees Deduction

This tax deduction expired at the end of 2016 but could be extended for 2017. The following information is included in case of an extension. The tax law allowed you to claim a limited deduction when you pay for higher education. The deduction applied whether you paid out-of-pocket from savings or borrowed the money. You were able to claim the deduction each year you qualified for it.

Benefit ⬆

If you paid tuition and fees for higher education for you, your spouse, or a dependent, you may be able to deduct up to $4,000 as an adjustment to gross income, even if you don't itemize your other deductions.

Conditions

To claim the deduction for tuition and fees, you must meet all 4 of these conditions:

1. Be an eligible taxpayer.
2. Paid qualified expenses to an eligible educational institution.
3. Have MAGI below a set amount.
4. You do not claim an education credit.

ELIGIBLE TAXPAYER

You can claim the deduction for you, your spouse, or your dependent for whom you claim an exemption on your return.

You may not claim the deduction if you are married filing separately. You may not claim the deduction if you can be claimed as a dependent on another taxpayer's return.

ELIGIBLE EDUCATIONAL INSTITUTION

Only tuition and fees paid to an eligible educational institution qualify for the deduction. An eligible educational institution includes any college, university, vocational school, or postsecondary institution eligible to participate in the financial aid programs of the U.S. Department of Education.

QUALIFIED EXPENSES

The same expenses that qualify for the American opportunity credit discussed earlier qualify for the tuition and fees deduction. Student activity fees and even the cost of books can be treated as deductible fees if the cost is paid to the eligible educational institution. As a practical matter, the institution furnishes the student with an information return showing qualified tuition and related expenses paid for the year. The return, Form 1098-T, *Tuition Payments Statement*, for 2017 is issued by January 31, 2018, and usually you need the form in order to claim the deduction.

Qualified expenses do not include any amounts paid by tax-free scholarships, tax-free distributions from Coverdell education savings accounts or 529 plans, and excludable interest from the redemption of U.S. savings bonds.

TABLE 3.3 MAGI Limits for Tuition Deduction

Filing Status*	MAGI Limit for $4,000 Deduction	MAGI Limit for $2,000 Deduction
Married filing jointly	Not more than $130,000	More than $130,000 but not more than $160,000
Other taxpayers	Not more than $65,000	More than $65,000 but not more than $80,000

*You cannot claim the deduction if you are married filing separately.

Qualified expenses paid directly to the educational institution under a court-approved divorce decree are treated as paid by the student (not by the person making the payments), so only the student is eligible to claim the deduction. Remember that the student can claim the deduction only if he or she cannot be claimed as the dependent of another taxpayer.

The same treatment applies to qualified expenses paid by someone else (such as a grandparent). Again, the student is treated as making the payment, and the student is eligible to claim the deduction only if he or she cannot be claimed as the dependent of another taxpayer.

MAGI LIMIT

You can claim the deduction only if your MAGI is no more than the limit found in Table 3.3. MAGI for this purpose is adjusted gross income increased by the foreign earned income exclusion, income from Puerto Rico or American Samoa, and the foreign housing exclusion or deduction.

Example

You are married and file a joint return with your spouse. If your MAGI is:

- No more than $130,000, your deduction is $4,000.
- More than $130,000 but not more than $160,000, your deduction is $2,000.
- Over $160,000, your deduction is zero.

NO EDUCATION CREDIT

You cannot claim the deduction for a student's expenses for which you claim an American opportunity credit or lifetime learning credit (education credits). If you qualify for both the tuition and fees deduction and an education credit, you must choose the write-off that provides the greater benefit; generally this will be a credit.

Planning Tip

Compare the tax savings from claiming the deduction with the savings from an education credit. Remember that the amount of a credit equals the amount of your tax savings from claiming it. Usually the tax credit provides the greater benefit. Use the following worksheet to compare your tax savings:

Tuition and Fees Deduction		Education Credit	
Amount of deduction	$_____	Amount of credit	$_____
× your tax bracket	$_____		
Tax savings	$_____	Tax savings	$_____

Example

You are single and your MAGI permits you to claim either a $4,000 tuition and fees deduction or a $2,000 lifetime learning credit. You are in the 25% tax bracket. The deduction provides you with a $1,000 tax savings ($4,000 × 25%). The credit provides you with a $2,000 tax savings. But if your MAGI limited your lifetime learning credit to less than $1,000 (e.g., your MAGI is $50,000), you would reap a greater tax savings by claiming the deduction.

Pitfall

Even $1 over the MAGI limit prevents you from claiming a deduction. There is no phaseout of this deduction, as there is with many other deductions.

Where to Claim the Deduction

Figure the amount of the deduction on Form 8917, *Tuition and Fees Deduction*, if the deduction is extended for 2017. Then enter the deduction on Form 1040 or 1040A in the section called "Adjusted Gross Income." You cannot claim the deduction if you file Form 1040EZ.

Student Loan Interest

Millions of students must borrow money to pay for their education. Repayment of student loans runs between 5 and 30 years. Fortunately, the tax law allows interest on student loans to be deductible each year within limits.

Benefit ⬆

If you pay interest on student loans, you may be able to deduct up to $2,500 of interest as an adjustment to gross income (if your actual interest payment is more than $2,500, your deduction is limited to that amount). There is no limit on the number of years you can claim this deduction; as long as you continue to pay off the loan, you can deduct your interest if eligible to do so.

If the loan is canceled, you may qualify for tax-free treatment on the debt forgiveness (explained later in this chapter).

Conditions

There are a couple of conditions for claiming a deduction for student loan interest as an adjustment to gross income. You must meet both:

1. The loan must be a qualified loan.
2. Your modified adjusted gross income cannot exceed a set limit (there is a partial deduction allowed if MAGI falls within a phaseout range).

LOAN QUALIFICATIONS

To be treated as a student loan for which interest is deductible, the loan must have been taken out solely to pay qualified education expenses. Qualified education expenses relate to a qualified educational institution (virtually all accredited public, nonpublic, and proprietary postsecondary institutions are eligible educational institutions). Qualified education expenses include:

- Tuition and fees
- Room and board
- Books, supplies, and equipment
- Other necessary expenses (including transportation to and from school)

You cannot deduct interest on a loan from a related person or made under a qualified employer plan. Related persons include:

- Spouses
- Siblings and half-siblings
- Parents
- Grandparents
- Children
- Grandchildren
- Certain corporations, partnerships, trusts, and exempt organizations

The loan must be for you, your spouse, or your dependent (in the year you take out the loan). The loan must be taken for an eligible student, who is enrolled at least half-time in a degree program.

TABLE 3.4 2017 Phaseout Ranges for Student Interest Deduction

Filing Status*	MAGI
Unmarried (single), head of household, and surviving widow(er)	$ 65,000–80,000
Married filing jointly	$135,000–165,000

*You cannot claim the deduction if you are married filing separately.

You must be legally obligated to make payments on the loan. For example, if your child took out the loan and you are now helping her make the payments, you cannot deduct the interest because you are not the borrower (you are not legally responsible for the loan). However, your child can deduct the interest even if you make the payments (as long as your child is not your dependent).

If the loan is a revolving line of credit (e.g., credit card debt), interest qualifies as student loan interest only if funds on the line are used solely to pay qualified education expenses.

MAGI LIMITS

You can claim the full deduction if your modified adjusted gross income is below the phaseout range. A partial deduction is permitted if your MAGI is within the phaseout range. No deduction can be claimed if your MAGI exceeds the phaseout range, which is adjusted annually for inflation. Table 3.4 shows the 2017 phaseout ranges for claiming the student interest deduction.

Example

You are single and graduated from college in May 2017. You start to pay back your loans, paying interest in 2017 of $800. You can deduct this amount in full if your MAGI is under $65,000. If, however, you landed your dream job and earned $78,000 in just the 7 months remaining in 2017, you cannot deduct any of your student loan interest because your MAGI is above the limit for your filing status.

Planning Tips

If a student has taken the loan and parent, grandparent, or anyone else pays the debt, the student is treated as having made the payment and can take the student loan interest deduction (as long as the student is not a dependent and has MAGI below the threshold amount). In some instances, the cancellation of student loans can be tax free (usually the cancellation of debt is taxable). This is explained later in this chapter.

Today about 4% of employers are helping employees pay their student loan debt (e.g., PricewaterhouseCoopers gives $1,200 a year for up to 6 years to cover student loan repayment). Currently this is taxable compensation. However, there are bills pending in Congress to make this a tax-free fringe benefit (within limits). Check the Supplement for any update.

Pitfall

You cannot claim a double benefit for the same interest deduction. For example, if you take out a home equity loan to pay your child's college expenses, you cannot claim a student interest deduction if you deduct the mortgage interest as an itemized deduction. It is, of course, more favorable to treat the interest as student loan interest to the extent possible.

Where to Claim the Deduction

The deduction is claimed on Form 1040 or 1040A in the section called "Adjusted Gross Income." No special form or schedule is required. However, you can use a worksheet in the instructions to your return to figure your allowable deduction if your MAGI falls within the phaseout range.

You cannot claim the deduction if you file Form 1040EZ.

Interest on U.S. Savings Bonds

The first savings bonds, series A, were issued in 1935 at 75% of face value in denominations of $25 to $1,000, paying 2.9% accrued interest, and were sold through the U.S. Post Office. Since then savings bonds have become a permanent investment vehicle. Today, savings bonds can only be purchased online through TreasuryDirect.gov. Sales of savings bonds have dropped dramatically since the Treasury eliminated over-the-counter sales at banks. Nonetheless, you happen to be holding these bonds and decide to cash them in to pay for higher education costs, you may be eligible to receive the interest tax free.

Benefit ⊗

If you redeem U.S. savings bonds to pay for qualified higher education costs or to contribute to a 529 plan or Coverdell education savings account, you are not taxed on the interest as long as your modified adjusted gross income is below a set amount. There is no dollar limit to this benefit; if you qualify you can exclude from income all of the interest received on the redemption of the bonds.

Conditions

Assuming you have not been reporting interest on the savings bonds annually but deferring it, you can claim the exclusion if you meet all 4 of these conditions:

1. Eligible bonds.
2. Eligible taxpayer.
3. MAGI limit.
4. Qualified use of redemption proceeds.

ELIGIBLE BONDS

The exclusion applies only to series EE bonds issued after 1989 or series I bonds. You cannot claim the exclusion when redeeming older EE bonds or E bonds.

ELIGIBLE TAXPAYER

You must be the purchaser of the bond and hold it in your name or the joint name of you and your spouse. You must have been at least 24 years old when you purchased the bonds.

No exclusion can be claimed for interest on bonds held in the child's name or in the joint name of you and your child.

If you are married, you must file jointly to claim the exclusion.

MAGI LIMIT

To claim a full or partial exclusion you cannot have modified adjusted gross income (MAGI) over a fixed dollar limit (which is adjusted annually for inflation). MAGI for this purpose means AGI increased by the redeemed interest, the deductions for tuition and fees and for student loan interest, foreign earned income exclusion and other foreign items, and the exclusion for employer-paid adoption.

Table 3.5 shows the phaseout range for 2017. If your MAGI is below the start of the phaseout range, you can claim a full exclusion. If your MAGI is over the phaseout range, no exclusion can be claimed, even if all of the other conditions are met. If your MAGI is within the phaseout range, you can claim a partial exclusion.

TABLE 3.5 2017 Phaseout Ranges for Savings Bond Interest Exclusion

Filing Status	MAGI
Unmarried (single) and head of household	$ 78,150–93,150
Married filing jointly and surviving widow(er)	$117,250–147,250

Example

In 2017, you are married filing jointly with MAGI of $132,250. You redeem bonds with interest of $5,000, and you use all of the redemption proceeds for qualified higher education expenses. You can exclude $2,500 of the $5,000 interest because your MAGI is in the middle of the phaseout range.

QUALIFIED USE OF REDEMPTION PROCEEDS

The proceeds must be used only for a qualified purpose:

- Paying higher education costs (tuition and fees for a college, university, or vocational school that meets federal financial aid standards). The higher education expenses can be for you, your spouse, or a dependent.
- Funding a 529 plan or a Coverdell education savings account.

If the proceeds from the redemption exceed the amount used for a qualified purpose, you can exclude a portion of the interest based on the ratio of expenses (or funding) to the redemption amount.

Example

In 2017, you redeem bonds worth $10,000, using $5,000 to pay your child's qualified higher education costs. Interest on the bonds is $3,000. Since 1/2 of the proceeds were used for qualified expenses, half of the interest, or $1,500, is eligible for the exclusion (assuming the other conditions are met).

Planning Tips

If you are holding EE or I savings bonds and want to know how much they are worth today, you can check their redemption values at www.savingsbonds.gov.

The U.S. Treasury has changed the way in which interest on Series EE bonds is computed. Rather than adjusting the interest semiannually, these bonds now pay a fixed rate until redemption or maturity. As a result, Series I bonds may be a better option because their interest rate still adjusts semiannually for inflation.

You can purchase I bonds via a direct deposit of your tax refund into a TreasuryDirect account used for this purpose. Just provide the IRS with the account information, and your refund will be transferred directly to your account. Bonds can be purchased only in multiples of $50; there is a $5,000 limit on purchases using a tax refund.

Interest on savings bonds is *never* subject to state income tax (such interest is always exempt).

Pitfalls

You cannot use this exclusion to pay college expenses for your grandchild *unless* the grandchild is your dependent in the year in which the bonds are redeemed.

You cannot claim the exclusion if you are married and file a separate return from your spouse.

Where to Claim the Exclusion

If you claim the exclusion, you must complete Form 8815, *Exclusion of Interest from Series EE and I Bonds Issued after 1989*, and attach it to your return.

Coverdell Education Savings Accounts

Is the high cost of a prep school or college in your child or grandchild's future? If you decide to help save for this expense, consider doing so using a tax-advantaged savings account, called a Coverdell education savings account (ESA), designed for this purpose.

Benefit ⊗

You may be able to contribute up to $2,000 annually to a savings account for each beneficiary. The account is called a Coverdell education savings account (ESA) (it used to be called an education IRA). The account can have multiple contributors, but no more than $2,000 can be placed in the account for any one year.

Earnings on contributions accumulate tax deferred. If withdrawals from the account are used to pay qualified education expenses, the earnings become tax free.

Conditions

There are a couple of conditions for funding a Coverdell education savings account as well as for taking tax-free distributions.

1. For purposes of contributions, they can be made only on behalf of an eligible beneficiary (defined next) by a contributor whose modified adjusted gross income does not exceed set limits. Contributions must be made in cash, not property.

2. For purposes of tax-free distributions, funds must be used only for eligible expenses.

ELIGIBLE BENEFICIARY

Generally, a beneficiary is a person who is under the age of 18 at the time the contribution is made. Thus, for example, if a beneficiary attains the age of 18 on July 1, 2017, contributions can be made through June 30, 2017.

A beneficiary can also be a special needs person over the age of 18. A special needs beneficiary is one who requires additional time to complete his or her education because of a physical, mental, or emotional condition. This would include, for example, a person with a learning disability.

MAGI FOR CONTRIBUTORS

There is no familial requirement for contributors. Anyone can make a Coverdell education savings account contribution on behalf of an eligible beneficiary, as long as the contributor meets MAGI limits. Contributions can even be made by the beneficiary herself.

In order to contribute the full $2,000 to a Coverdell education savings account, your modified adjusted gross income cannot be more than a set limit. MAGI for this purpose means adjusted gross income increased by the foreign earned income exclusion, the foreign housing exclusion or deduction, the exclusion for income from American Samoa, or the exclusion for income from Puerto Rico.

A reduced contribution limit applies if your MAGI falls within a phaseout range. No contribution can be made if your MAGI exceeds the phaseout range, which is not adjusted annually for inflation. The MAGI phaseout range for Coverdell ESA contributors may be found in Table 3.6.

Example

In 2017, you are a single parent with MAGI of $80,000. You can make a $2,000 contribution on behalf of your 12-year-old child. But if your MAGI is between $95,000 and $110,000, only part of the $2,000 may be contributed (you figure the limit using a worksheet provided in IRS Publication 970).

CASH CONTRIBUTIONS

Contributions must be made in cash; you cannot contribute property to a Coverdell ESA. If you own stocks or mutual funds, you must sell the property and invest the proceeds. You may incur a capital gain on the sale of property.

TABLE 3.6 MAGI Phaseout Ranges for Coverdell ESA Contributors

Filing Status	MAGI Phaseout Range
Married filing jointly	$190,000–220,000
Other taxpayers	$ 95,000–110,000

ELIGIBLE EXPENSES

Unlike most other education tax breaks that are restricted to higher education, Coverdell education savings accounts can be used for education in grades K–12 and/or for higher education. Primary and secondary school can be public, private, or religious school.

The range of eligible expenses for which tax-free withdrawals can be made is quite broad. Just about anything related to education is a qualified expense.

EXAMPLES OF ELIGIBLE ELEMENTARY AND SECONDARY SCHOOL EXPENSES

Academic tutoring

Books

Computer and peripheral equipment; software only if it is predominantly educational in nature

Extended day programs required or provided by the school

Internet access

Special services for a special needs beneficiary

Supplies

Transportation

Uniforms

EXAMPLES OF ELIGIBLE HIGHER EDUCATION EXPENSES

Books, supplies, and equipment

Room and board

Tuition and fees

Planning Tips

You can open a Coverdell education savings account at any bank or other financial institution that has received IRS approval to offer Coverdell ESAs. You can then select the investments you prefer, from certificates of deposit to stocks and mutual funds (to the extent available from the institution you select).

Just like IRA contributions, contributions to Coverdell ESAs can be made up to the due date of the return for the year to which they relate. However, obtaining a filing extension does not extend the deadline for making contributions.

Example

Contributions for 2017 may be made only up to April 17, 2018, even if the contributor and/or the beneficiary has obtained a 6-month filing extension.

You can turn taxable custodial accounts into tax-free Coverdell education savings accounts by using the funds in the custodial account for contributions. However, only cash contributions are permitted to a Coverdell education savings account, so investments in the custodial accounts must first be sold so that the proceeds can be contributed.

Example

Junior has $5,000 in a custodial account that owns shares in a mutual fund, the earnings from which are reported annually as taxable income to Junior. He can opt to sell $2,000 from the mutual fund in his custodial account each year and contribute the proceeds to a Coverdell education savings account of which he is the designated beneficiary (assuming he meets the age and MAGI limits). The account can own shares in the same mutual fund, but now the earnings become tax deferred and, if funds are withdrawn for qualified expenses, they become tax free.

You can change accounts from one financial institution to another by means of a tax-free rollover. You may not be satisfied with the service or investment options you have at one financial institution and can switch by means of a rollover to another financial institution.

You can move money in a Coverdell ESA between certain beneficiaries on a tax-free basis. The amount withdrawn from a Coverdell ESA can be rolled over to the same or a new designated beneficiary who is a member of the original beneficiary's family (listed in the next section). The rollover must be completed within 60 days. There are no tax consequences to naming a new designated beneficiary (as long as such beneficiary is permissible).

You can fund contributions to a Coverdell ESA by means of a direct deposit of a tax refund. For example, say you are owed a refund on your 2017 return. Use the refund to contribute to a Coverdell ESA (assuming you meet eligibility requirements) by filing the return early enough for the IRS to process it and electronically transfer the refund to the Coverdell ESA by April 17, 2018, for a 2017 contribution (you can also use the 2017 tax refund to make a 2018 contribution if your income allows it and the beneficiary will not have aged out of eligibility).

Anyone who receives a military death gratuity or payment under the Servicemen's Group Life Insurance (SGLI) program can contribute this amount to a Coverdell ESA; the usual contribution limit and MAGI limit do not apply in this case.

Pitfalls

If you contribute more than $2,000 on behalf of a beneficiary within one year, the excess amount is subject to a 6% excise tax (this is a penalty). The penalty is paid by the beneficiary (not the contributor). But the penalty can be avoided by withdrawing the excess contribution, plus any earnings on the contribution, before the beginning of the 6th month following the year of the contribution (e.g., by May 31, 2018, for 2017 contributions).

> ### Example
>
> In 2017, Aunt Mary contributes $2,000 to a Coverdell ESA for Amy. Unaware of Aunt Mary's contribution, Uncle Ed also contributes $2,000 to a Coverdell ESA for Amy in 2017. Amy can avoid the 6% excise tax on the excess $2,000 contribution by withdrawing it, plus any earnings, by May 31, 2018. (Whether she chooses to give it back to Aunt Mary or Uncle Ed or split it between them is up to Amy.)

The 6% excise tax continues to apply each year in which excess contributions (and earnings on excess contributions) remain in the Coverdell ESA.

Taxable distributions, which are withdrawals made to pay for noneligible expenses, are not only taxed as ordinary income but are subject to a 10% additional tax. However, the 10% penalty does not apply to distributions that meet any of these conditions:

- Distributions are made to a beneficiary or to the estate of a designated beneficiary on or after the death of a designated beneficiary.
- Distributions are made because the designated beneficiary is disabled.
- Distributions are made because the designated beneficiary received a tax-free grant or educational assistance allowance that equals or exceeds the distribution.
- Distributions are taxable only because the qualified expenses are reduced by expenses taken into account in figuring an education credit.

Withdrawals from a Coverdell ESA can be made in the same year in which an education credit is claimed. However, the same expenses cannot be used for both benefits.

Withdrawals from both a Coverdell ESA and a 529 plan are permitted in the same year. But if total withdrawals exceed qualified higher education expenses, the expenses must be allocated between the Coverdell ESA and 529 plan to figure the taxable portion of the withdrawals. Generally, the allocation is based on the ratio of the Coverdell ESA withdrawals to the total withdrawals.

Example

In 2017, Henry begins college and withdraws $800 from a Coverdell ESA and $3,200 from a 529 plan to pay $3,000 of eligible expenses. Of the $800 withdrawn, $600 is tax free: $800 Coverdell ESA withdrawal ÷ $4,000 total withdrawals = 0.2; 0.2 × $3,000 qualified expenses = $600.

Funds remaining in the account become taxable to the beneficiary within 30 days of attaining age 30 (or within 30 days of death if the beneficiary dies before age 30). The 30-year age limit does not apply to a special needs beneficiary (defined earlier).

However, tax on the earnings in the account can be avoided if the balance in the account is transferred to another eligible beneficiary within 60 days of attaining age 30 (or death if earlier). An eligible beneficiary for this purpose includes members of the beneficiary's family:

- Spouse
- Child or stepchild
- Grandchild
- Brother, sister, half-brother, or half-sister
- Niece or nephew
- Parent or stepparent
- Grandparent
- In-laws and the spouses of any of the listed relatives

Where to Claim the Exclusion

Contributions to a Coverdell education savings account are not reported on the return of the contributor or the beneficiary. Similarly, withdrawals that are not taxable are not reported on any return.

If contributions are subject to the 6% excise tax, the beneficiary figures the excise tax in Part V of Form 5329, *Additional Taxes on Qualified Plans (Including IRAs) and Other Tax-Favored Accounts*, and report it as "Other Taxes" on Form 1040.

If withdrawals from a Coverdell ESA are taxable, they are reported on the beneficiary's return as "other income" on the return on Form 1040 or in the "Income" section on Form 1040A. If they are also subject to the 10% additional tax, this amount is figured in Part II of Form 5329, *Additional Taxes on Qualified Plans (Including IRAs) and Other Tax-Favored Accounts*.

Qualified Tuition Programs (529 Plans)

You can help save for the higher education expenses of your child or grandchild using a tax-advantaged account called a 529 plan. The 529 plan is a qualified tuition program offering federal (and in some cases state) tax incentives for savings.

Benefit

There are 2 types of qualified tuition programs (QTPs): a prepayment plan under which payments are guaranteed to cover (or partially cover) tuition, regardless of tuition increases, and a savings-type plan in which the funds you will have available to pay for higher education depend on the investment performance of your account. From a tax perspective, however, both types of plans are governed by the same tax rules under Section 529 of the Internal Revenue Code (hence the name "529 plans"), and both types of plans have the same benefits and conditions.

While contributions to qualified tuition programs do not generate a federal income tax deduction or credit, the long-term benefits are considerable:

- Earnings within the plan are tax deferred.
- If funds in the plan are used to pay qualified higher education costs, they are tax free (the earnings on the contributions are never taxed in this case).
- Unused amounts can be transferred tax free to another beneficiary if the original beneficiary does not go to college or otherwise need the funds.

There may be state income tax breaks for the contributions to qualified tuition programs as well. For example, if you are a resident in New York, you can deduct contributions to the New York 529 College Savings Program up to $5,000 per taxpayer per year on your New York state income tax return. Of the states with income taxes, only the following do not offer a deduction or credit for contributions: California, Delaware, Hawaii, Kentucky, Minnesota, New Jersey, and North Carolina.

Conditions

Most conditions and requirements are fixed by each state's own 529 plan. However, for tax purposes, there are a couple of key conditions to obtaining all of the benefits under a qualified tuition program:

1. Contributions can be made only to qualified tuition programs. There are no federal tax limits on annual or total contributions to a 529 plan. These

limits are fixed by each state's unique program (e.g., New York's plan has a $520,000 cap per beneficiary and no contributions can be made once the plan reaches this cap).

2. Distributions can be withdrawn only for qualified expenses.

QUALIFIED TUITION PROGRAMS

Contributions can be made only to state plans and IRS-approved private college/university plans. A personally devised plan, even one that mimics the investment strategies of the state plans, does not entitle you to these benefits.

At present, all states offer savings-type plans and nearly 2 dozen have prepaid tuition plans.

QUALIFIED EXPENSES

For distributions from qualified tuition programs to be tax free, they must be used only to pay for qualified expenses. These include tuition for higher education, fees, books, supplies, computers and technology (e.g., Internet access), and room and board (if the student is enrolled at least half time). Withdrawals from a 529 plan to pay for a computer, Internet access, or the like are not for qualified expenses, so they are taxable.

There is no set dollar limit on these expenses, including room and board. Thus, any reasonable amount for room and board (including expenses of off-campus housing) can qualify.

Planning Tips

The terms and conditions of qualified tuition programs vary considerably from state to state. You can learn about the investment options, fees, and other rules on state 529 plans at www.savingforcollege.com. For details on the private 529 plan created by a consortium of private colleges and universities (about 270 schools now participate), go to www.privatecollege529.com.

If you plan for your child to attend your alma mater on a legacy basis, ask the school whether it offers or plans to offer a tuition prepayment plan.

For purposes of the federal financial aid formula, funds in 529 plans are not considered to be the assets of the student.

Qualified tuition programs can be used effectively for estate planning purposes. For example, a wealthy grandparent can reduce the size of his or her estate while funding an education savings plan for a grandchild with little or no gift tax cost. If you plan to make sizable contributions in one year, you can elect to treat the contributions as made equally over 5 years. This will entitle you to apply the annual gift tax exclusion, which is $14,000 in 2017 ($28,000 for married persons making joint gifts) 5 times to avoid or reduce gift tax.

> **Example**
>
> In 2017, when the annual gift tax exclusion is $14,000 per beneficiary, you contribute $70,000 (or $140,000 per couple) to a state savings plan for your grandchild. Since you can treat the $70,000 as having been made ratably over 5 years, there is no taxable gift in this transfer. The transfer is fully offset by the annual gift tax exclusion ($14,000 × 5).

If the contribution exceeds this limit, the excess amount is treated as a gift in the year the contribution is made.

Amounts in a 529 plan can be transferred to a new beneficiary or rolled over tax free within 60 days of a distribution. There is a limit of one transfer or rollover per year. However, a beneficiary can be changed without making a transfer or rollover; the new name is substituted for the old one on the same account. This option applies only if the new beneficiary is a member of the old beneficiary's family, which includes:

- Child or grandchild
- Stepson or stepdaughter
- Sibling or stepsibling
- Parent or grandparent
- Stepparent
- Aunt or uncle
- Niece or nephew
- Son-in-law, daughter-in-law, father-in-law, mother-in-law, brother-in-law, or sister-in-law
- The spouse of any relative on this list
- First cousin

In the case of a savings-type 529 plan, if the account declines in value from the amount contributed, the loss can be recognized when all of the funds in the account are distributed. The IRS says that the loss is claimed as a miscellaneous itemized deduction on Schedule A of Form 1040, which is deductible to the extent total miscellaneous itemized deductions exceed 2% of adjusted gross income, and is subject to the reduction of itemized deductions for high-income taxpayers. Some tax experts believe that the loss is simply claimed as an ordinary loss. This theory has yet to be tested in court.

You can change investment selections once a year, and whenever there is a change in beneficiary.

Funds within 529 plans offer asset protection in case of bankruptcy. Contributions to the plan made at least one year but less than 2 years before filing for bankruptcy are protected up to $5,000. Contributions made 2 years or more before filing for bankruptcy are fully protected (no dollar limit applies). All contributions made within one year of filing for bankruptcy are at risk.

Pitfalls

If funds are withdrawn from a 529 plan and *not* used for qualified education expenses, earnings on the distribution are taxable. For example, if part of a distribution is used for spending money or travel expenses, the earnings on this portion of the distribution are taxable.

Example

If $25,000 is withdrawn and $20,000 is used for qualified expenses while $5,000 is used for spending and travel money, earnings on the $5,000 portion of the distribution are taxable.

In addition, the portion of the distribution representing earnings on contributions is subject to a 10% penalty. However, both the tax and the penalty on a refund made by the institution (e.g., because the student receives a scholarship) can be avoided by redepositing the funds in the 529 plan within 60 days of receipt.

Withdrawals from a 529 plan can be made in the same year in which an education credit is claimed, but the same expenses cannot be used for both benefits.

If withdrawals are made from a 529 plan and Coverdell ESA in the same year and the total withdrawal exceeds qualified education expenses, a portion of the withdrawal is taxable. How to figure the taxable portion was explained earlier in the Coverdell Education Savings Accounts section, under "Pitfalls."

Where to Claim the Exclusion

Contributions to qualified tuition programs need not be reported on the return of the contributor or the return of the beneficiary.

Distributions from qualified tuition programs need not be reported if they are tax free. To figure the tax-free portion of distributions, you can use a worksheet for this purpose in IRS Publication 970. For any year in which distributions are made, the 529 plan must send you (and the IRS) an information return, Form 1099-Q, *Qualified Tuition Program*. For distributions in 2017, the return must be issued no later than January 31, 2018.

ABLE Accounts

If you have a disabled child or are under age 26 and meet certain eligibility conditions, you can have a special savings account that generally does not adversely impact eligibility for means-tested government programs (e.g., Medicaid). The ABLE account is similar to a 529 savings plan (discussed earlier in this chapter), but differs in several ways. An ABLE account can be used on a tax-free basis for education and job training, as well as other qualified disability expenses. See details in Chapter 2.

Seminars

You've seen the ads: Attend a seminar to learn all about this subject or that. While some seminars are free of charge, others can cost hundreds or even thousands of dollars. From a tax standpoint, the cost of seminars is deductible only under limited circumstances.

Benefit ⬟

Job-related seminars may be deducted if the conditions for job-related education discussed earlier in this chapter are met.

No deduction can be claimed for seminars on self-improvement that are not job-related. No deduction can be claimed for investment seminars.

Where on the Return to Claim the Deduction

See job-related education discussed earlier in this chapter.

Educational Travel

Saint Augustine said, "The world is a book, and those who do not travel read only a page." Taxwise, the cost of travel usually is a nondeductible personal expense. But there are exceptions for which the cost of travel may be deductible.

Benefit ⬟

They say travel is broadening (a century ago, wealthy young men and women used to "take the grand tour" as a coming-of-age lesson). From a tax perspective, however, a deduction for educational travel is extremely limited. As a general rule, no deduction can be claimed for educational travel. However, this ban does not apply to overseas courses and lectures, the cost of which may qualify for a job-related education deduction.

Conditions

To be deductible as job-related education, travel must meet all of the conditions discussed earlier in this chapter.

Planning Tip

Overseas courses need not be taken for credit to qualify for a deduction. For example, an English teacher who took a course on Greek myths in Greece taught by university professors was allowed a deduction for her travel expenses and course registration fees even though she did not take the courses for credit.

Pitfall

No deduction can be claimed for travel that is merely beneficial. For example, an architect who travels to Europe to view cathedrals there cannot deduct the cost of the trip as an education expense.

Where to Claim the Deduction

See job-related education earlier in this chapter.

Cancellation of a Student Loan

If you are facing mountains of debt from student loans and have opted to get out from under by taking a particular job, you may be able to not only have your loans canceled, but have them canceled without any tax cost to you.

Benefit ⊗

Normally, the cancellation of a loan results in taxable income to the borrower. But under certain conditions, the cancellation of a student loan can be tax free. There is no dollar limit to this benefit.

Example

You take out a government loan to obtain your teaching license. The loan is forgiven if you work for 5 years as a teacher on a Native American reservation. This debt forgiveness is *not* income to you if you complete the required years of work.

Conditions

You can exclude the debt forgiveness on your student loan from income if you are required to work for a set period of time in a certain profession (e.g., nursing, medicine, or law) for any of a broad class of employers.

The loan must have been made by a qualified lender, which includes:

- The government (federal, state, or local government or an agency of the government)
- A tax-exempt public benefit corporation
- An educational institution if the loan is made under an agreement with the government or a tax-exempt public benefit corporation or under a program designed to encourage students to serve in occupations or areas with unmet needs

Under health care reform, as a way to encourage more health care professionals to work in underserved areas, the exclusion has been expanded to repayments under other state loan repayment or forgiveness programs and is intended to increase health care services to areas with shortages of health care professionals.

Planning Tips

Make sure you fully understand your work obligation in order to secure tax-free treatment for cancellation of your student loan.

NOTE

Congress is considering various student loan relief measures; see the Supplement for any update.

Those who are totally and permanently disabled (e.g., having a service-connected disability) can receive a discharge of certain types of student loans. However, this debt discharge is not tax free, although it is not part of "modified adjusted gross income" for purposes of Medicaid. The amount discharged is includible in gross income for federal income tax purposes. To reduce or avoid this tax, a disabled person may want to request an offer in compromise for the tax bill.

Pitfall

If you satisfy only part of the required work and a portion of the loan is forgiven anyway, you must include that portion in income.

Where to Claim the Benefit

If the loan forgiveness is tax free, you do not report anything on your return. If cancellation of your student loan is not tax free, you must include the debt forgiveness in income on your return. Report it as "other income." Generally, debt forgiveness that is not tax free is reported to you (and to the IRS) on Form 1099-C, *Cancellation of Debt*.

Penalty-Free Withdrawals from IRAs

Distributions can be taken from an IRA before age 59$^1/_2$ if the funds are used to pay qualified higher education costs for yourself, your spouse, or dependent. The Tax Court has said that funds used to buy a computer are *not* a qualified expense where its use is not required for any course and access to computer-posted course syllabi can be done through school computers in the library.

Withdrawals can be taken penalty-free only in the year in which you pay the expenses.

Government Reimbursements

If you have a disabled child who cannot receive adequate education in your school district and you are reimbursed by your school district for the costs of special education, you are *not* taxed on this reimbursement. Since federal law requires schools to provide special education, you are treated as if you incur the costs on behalf of the school district.

Internships and Apprenticeships

If you're paid while learning on the job, your wages are includible in gross, but the value of your training is not taxable. The U.S. Department of Labor estimates that the value of training through a registered apprenticeship program is $40,000 to $150,000.

Your Home

Alert

At the time this book was completed, Congress was considering important tax changes that could affect 2017 tax returns and planning for 2018. Check the online Supplement in February 2018 at www.jklasser.com or www.barbaraweltman.com to see what changes have been enacted and when they are effective.

Home ownership is part of the American dream. According to the U.S. Census Bureau, 63.7% of Americans owned their own homes in the second quarter of 2017. There are many reasons that we want to own rather than rent a home—for example, as a way to build up equity. But there are also sound tax reasons favoring home ownership. Certain expenses of home ownership are deductible. And when you sell your home, some or all of your profit may be tax free. If you had problems with your mortgage or lost your home to foreclosure, there may be special tax breaks for you.

This chapter explains the tax breaks you can claim with respect to your home. Casualties and disasters that can befall your home, and the deductions you can claim for them, are explained in Chapter 13. The home office deduction for using a portion of your home for business is explained in Chapter 15.

For more information, see IRS Publication 521, *Moving Expenses*; IRS Publication 523, *Selling Your Home*; IRS Publication 530, *Tax Information for First-Time Homeowners*; IRS Publication 936, *Home Mortgage Interest Deduction*; and IRS Publication 4681, *Canceled Debts, Foreclosures, Repossessions, and Abandonments*.

Mortgages

Mortgages are a way to leverage yourself into home ownership: The bank or other lender (called the mortgagee) lends you the funds needed to buy your home over and above your out-of-pocket investment. You become the mortgagor and each month repay a portion of the principal (the money you borrowed), plus interest. While your repayment of principal is *never* deductible, you may be able to deduct your interest payments.

Benefit

Interest on your home mortgage may be fully deductible as an itemized deduction. There is no dollar limit on the amount of interest you can deduct annually, but there are limits on the size of the mortgage on which the interest is claimed. The mortgage interest rule applies to both fixed and adjustable rate mortgages.

You may deduct interest on so-called acquisition indebtedness up to $1 million (or any amount for loans obtained before October 14, 1987). In addition, you can deduct interest on home equity debt up to $100,000 (discussed later in this chapter). Thus, you can deduct interest on total home debt up to $1.1 million (one-half these dollar limits if married filing separately, even if the other spouse does not claim any deduction for mortgage interest). According to one appellate court, the dollar limits apply per residence(s), so if unmarried co-owners jointly own a home, each can use the $1.1 million total home debt limit. The IRS has agreed to follow this appellate court decision. You can use this rule for your main home plus one additional residence of yours that you designate as your second home.

A special limitation applies to distressed homeowners, as explained later.

Conditions

For interest to be fully deductible, you must meet 4 conditions:

1. Acquisition indebtedness (which is usually a mortgage used to buy or build your home) cannot exceed $1 million. However, this dollar limit does not apply to a mortgage obtained before October 14, 1987.
2. The debt must be secured by the residence.
3. You deduct interest on no more than 2 residences.
4. You are personally obligated for repayment of the debt.

ACQUISITION INDEBTEDNESS

Acquisition indebtedness is usually a mortgage obtained to buy, build, or substantially improve a home (subject to the 2-residence limit). If you use the funds to construct your home, only interest paid during the 24-month period starting with the month in which construction begins is deductible. Interest paid before or after this 24-month period is not acquisition indebtedness; it is treated as nondeductible personal interest.

Example

In May 2017, you buy land to build your dream home and obtain a construction loan in June. Construction begins in September 2017, and the home is completed in June 2018. On your 2017 return, you may deduct interest on the loan starting with interest in September 2017, the month in which construction began. Since the home is completed within 24 months, interest for January 2018 through the end of construction is deductible on your 2017 return.

If a loan is taken out within 90 days after construction is completed, it may still qualify in full as acquisition indebtedness. It qualifies as acquisition indebtedness to the extent of construction expenses incurred within the last 24 months before the completion of the home, plus expenses through the date of the loan.

Example

Same as the preceding example, except that in July 2017 you refinance the loan. Since the loan is obtained within 90 days after building completion, it qualifies as acquisition indebtedness, and interest is deductible.

How much renovation is required to be considered a substantial improvement to the home? There is no clear rule. Generally, if you add a room, convert an attic, garage, or basement to living space, or renovate a kitchen, you can safely treat interest on the loan as acquisition indebtedness. Just about any type of capital improvement that adds to the basis of your home constitutes a substantial improvement; a repair is not a capital improvement, and a loan to make repairs is not acquisition indebtedness.

A home for this purpose isn't limited to a single-family dwelling. It also includes a condominium or cooperative unit, houseboat, mobile home, or house trailer as long as it has sleeping, cooking, and toilet facilities.

The $1 million limit applies to total acquisition indebtedness; it does not apply on a per-home basis.

DEBT SECURED BY THE HOME

The loan must be secured by your main or second home in order for interest on the loan to be deductible. "Secured" means that the loan is recorded in your city, town, or county recording office or the loan satisfies similar requirements under your state's law that gives the lender the right to foreclose against your home if you fail to repay the loan.

TWO-RESIDENCE LIMIT

A deduction for mortgage interest is limited to 2 residences: your main home and a second residence. If you have more than 2 homes, you can select which of the additional homes to designate as your second residence for interest deduction purposes. Obviously, it pays to designate the home with the larger interest payments. You can change your designation from year to year.

If a married couple files jointly, they can designate a second residence as a home even if it is owned or used by one of them. But if they file separately, each spouse generally may deduct interest on debt secured by one home unless they agree in writing to allow one spouse to deduct interest on the main home plus a second residence.

If you rent out a home during the year but use it for personal (nonrental) purposes for more than 14 days or 10% of the rental days, you can treat the home as a personal residence for which the interest is deductible. In counting rental days, include any days that the home is held for rental. In counting personal days, include any days your home is used by close family members.

Example

In addition to your main home, you own a beachfront condominium that you rent out through a rental agency 2 weeks each year at the start of the summer

(Continued)

(Continued)

season. You spend the balance of the summer at your unit, so your personal use is sufficient for your home to be treated as a personal residence despite the rental. You can designate your condo as your second residence and deduct interest on the mortgage on the condo.

PERSONAL LIABILITY

To deduct interest on a home mortgage you must be personally obligated for its repayment. If, for example, you are financially unable to obtain a mortgage so your parents help you out by obtaining the loan, you cannot deduct mortgage interest (even if you pay the lender directly rather than repaying your parents). Only they can deduct the interest.

One case did allow a homeowner to deduct interest on a loan obtained by a brother because the homeowner had a poor credit rating, but the facts in the case were unique; the homeowner was contractually obligated to his brother to pay off the mortgage.

DISTRESSED HOMEOWNERS

A distressed homeowner is someone who is at risk of foreclosure because of delinquent mortgage payments. Such a homeowner may obtain certain mortgage assistance, such as a reduction or suspension of payments or a loan modification to reduce the outstanding balance (and in turn, the amount of monthly payments). The IRS has created a safe harbor for determining the amount of mortgage interest a distressed homeowner can claim. The safe harbor runs through 2021. More specifically, such a homeowner may deduct the lesser of:

- Actual home mortgage interest payments to the mortgage servicer or the state housing finance agency (HFA)
- Amounts shown on Form 1098 for mortgage interest received, real property taxes, and mortgage insurance premiums (if otherwise deductible by the homeowner)

Planning Tips

Think hard about the type and amount of mortgage you want to take out when you buy your home. Once you have purchased your home, additional financing generally doesn't qualify as acquisition indebtedness.

When you sell your home, look at the settlement papers to determine the interest charged up to the date of sale so that you don't overlook any interest deduction you may be entitled to claim.

Pitfalls

You cannot deduct your interest if you claim the standard deduction; you must itemize deductions to claim this benefit.

You cannot deduct mortgage fees that you paid to obtain the loan, such as the cost of an appraisal, a credit report, or loan assumption fees. But points paid to obtain the mortgage may be deductible, as discussed later.

You cannot deduct interest on mortgage assistance payments made on your behalf under Section 234 of the National Housing Act.

The IRS has a good idea about what your initial mortgage was because the outstanding mortgage balance at the start of the year and the loan origination date are reported by the lender to the IRS and you on Form 1098. A married person filing separately has an interest deduction limit on borrowing up to $550,000 ($500,000 for acquisition indebtedness plus $50,000 home equity debt), even if the other spouse does not claim *any* mortgage interest deduction.

Where to Claim the Deduction

You deduct home mortgage interest on Schedule A of Form 1040. You cannot claim the deduction if you file Form 1040A or Form 1040EZ. The amount of mortgage interest is reported annually to you by the lender on Form 1098, *Mortgage Interest Statement*.

Mortgage Interest Tax Credit

The government's policy is to encourage home ownership. To help low-income people become homeowners, the government offers certain assistance, including the opportunity to claim a tax credit for mortgage interest.

Benefit ✚

Even better than deducting your mortgage interest, you may be eligible for a tax credit of up to $2,000 of home mortgage interest paid through mortgage interest certificates. These certificates are issued to certain homeowners as a means of encouraging home ownership. The credit may be claimed regardless of whether you itemize your personal deductions or claim the standard deduction.

If you received a mortgage credit certificate from your state or local government in connection with the purchase or renovation of your main home, you may be entitled to claim a tax credit with respect to your mortgage interest. The amount of the credit is the percentage shown on your mortgage credit certificate multiplied by the lesser of:

- Interest you paid during the year on your actual loan amount
- Interest you paid on the loan amount shown on your mortgage credit certificate

The credit cannot be more than $2,000 if the percentage shown on your mortgage credit certificate is 20% or more.

You must reduce your deduction for home mortgage interest by the amount of any credit you claim.

Conditions

You can claim this tax credit only if you meet 2 conditions:

1. You have received a mortgage credit certificate from your state or local government ("qualified mortgage credit certificate").
2. Your home meets certain requirements ("qualified home").

QUALIFIED MORTGAGE CREDIT CERTIFICATE

Qualified mortgage interest certificates are issued by a state or local government or agency under a qualified mortgage credit certificate program designed to help low- and moderate-income people become homeowners. You qualify for the credit only if you receive a qualified mortgage credit certificate (MCC). Certificates issued by the Federal Housing Administration, the Department of Veterans Affairs, and the Farmers Home Administration as well as Homestead Staff Exemption Certificates do not qualify.

QUALIFIED HOME

The home must be your main home. The value of your home cannot exceed a certain value:

- A value of 90% of the average area purchase price
- A value of 110% of the average area purchase price in certain targeted areas

Planning Tips

If you are thinking about buying a home but do not know if you can afford the payments, you may be able to swing a deal if you qualify for this type of government assistance. For information about special financing programs, visit the U.S. Department of Housing and Urban Development at www.hud.gov/buying/insured.cfm.

To find out whether you are eligible for a mortgage credit certificate, contact your local housing or redevelopment agency or ask your local real estate agent for information.

If you qualify for the credit and it exceeds your tax liability without regard to other tax credits, you do not lose the credit. Instead, you can carry the excess amount forward to be used in a future year if you are also eligible for the credit in that year.

If you refinance your mortgage, you do not lose your eligibility to claim the credit if your certificate is reissued and the reissued certificate meets 5 conditions:

1. It must be issued to the original holder of the existing certificate for the same property.
2. It must entirely replace the existing certificate (you cannot retain any portion of the outstanding balance of the existing certificate).
3. The certified indebtedness on the reissued certificate cannot be more than the outstanding balance on the existing certificate.
4. The credit rate of the reissued certificate cannot be more than the credit rate of the existing certificate.
5. The reissued certificate cannot result in a larger amount of interest than is otherwise allowable under the existing certificate for any year.

Pitfalls

You must reduce your deduction for home mortgage interest by the amount of the credit.

If you own your home jointly with a person who is not your spouse, you must divide the credit between the two of you according to your respective ownership interests. If you each own a 50% interest in the home, then you are each entitled to one-half of the credit.

If you buy a home using a mortgage credit certificate and sell it within 9 years, you may have to repay some of the credit.

Where to Claim the Credit

You figure the credit on Form 8396, *Mortgage Interest Certificate*, and enter the amount of the credit in the "Tax and Credits" section of Form 1040.

You cannot claim the credit if you file Form 1040A or 1040EZ.

If you are subject to recapture of the credit because you sold your home within 9 years of using the mortgage credit certificate, you must complete Form 8828, *Recapture of Federal Mortgage Subsidy*. You report the recaptured amount in the "Other Payments" section of Form 1040. You must file Form 1040 and cannot file Form 1040A or 1040EZ.

Home Equity Loans

Equity is the amount of money you would receive, over and above any outstanding mortgage, if you were to sell your home today. Equity is built up in 2 ways: by paying down a mortgage on the home and by appreciation in property values. As your equity increases, you may be able to tap into it *without* selling the home by using a home equity loan. This loan may be the only loan on the property or it may be a second or even third loan in addition to any other home mortgage. The tax law allows interest on home equity loans to be deductible under certain conditions.

Benefit

You may deduct interest on home equity loans up to $100,000 if you itemize your deductions ($50,000 if married filing separately). There is no dollar limit on the amount of interest you can deduct (the limit applies to the amount of borrowing).

The rules for deducting interest on home equity loans apply to any type of home equity loan: a fixed home equity loan or a home equity line of credit with an adjustable interest rate. The deduction applies regardless of how you spend the proceeds (i.e., you don't have to use them for the home and can spend them in any way you desire, including paying off credit card debt).

Conditions

The same 4 conditions discussed for mortgage interest earlier (except for a smaller maximum amount) apply to deducting interest on home equity loans in full.

1. Total home equity debt cannot exceed $100,000. In measuring the $100,000 limit, take into account only the amount you've borrowed, not your potential borrowing under a home equity line of credit loan. The $100,000 home equity limit is figured separately from the $1 million home acquisition limit discussed earlier in this chapter, so that interest is deductible on total borrowing up to $1.1 million ($1 million acquisition debt and $100,000 home equity debt). Married persons filing separately must use one-half of these dollar limits, even if one spouse does not claim any mortgage interest deduction.
2. The debt must be secured by the residence.
3. The debt can apply to your main or second home.
4. You are personally obligated for repayment of the debt.

Planning Tips

If the amount of a home equity loan exceeds the $100,000 limit, you treat the interest on the first $100,000 as fully deductible mortgage interest. Interest on the balance of the debt may still be deductible under a tax rule other than home mortgage interest. The treatment of this portion of interest depends on what you use the proceeds for:

- If you use the proceeds to pay personal expenses (e.g., a vacation or credit card debt), it is nondeductible.
- If you use the proceeds to purchase investments (other than tax-exempt securities), you can treat it as investment interest. The rules on deducting investment interest are explained in Chapter 8.
- If you use the proceeds for your business, interest may qualify as fully deductible business interest, as explained in Chapter 15.

Pitfalls

Watch the amount of interest you report on a home equity loan because the IRS has a good idea about the amount of the loan. The amount of the outstanding mortgage principal at the start of the year, as well as the loan origination date, are reported on Form 1098.

In the case of a reverse mortgage, where a homeowner who is at least age 62 borrows against the equity in the home to pay personal living expenses and does not make mortgage payments (the lender recoups what is owed when the homeowner sells the home or dies), interest is deductible only when the loan is repaid. No deduction can be taken as the interest accrues each month on the outstanding loan.

While interest on home equity debt up to $100,000 is fully deductible for regular tax purposes regardless of what the loan proceeds are used for, such interest is deductible for purposes of the alternative minimum tax only if the proceeds are used to improve your main or second home.

Where to Claim the Deduction

You deduct interest on home equity debt on Schedule A of Form 1040. The amount of mortgage interest is reported annually to you by the lender on Form 1098, *Mortgage Interest Statement*.

You cannot claim the deduction if you file Form 1040A or Form 1040EZ.

Points

"Points" are additional charges for acquiring a loan. Each point is 1% of the loan amount. In general, the more points you pay, the lower your interest rate on the loan. Points generally are deductible; the only question is *when* they can be deducted.

Benefit

When you take out a mortgage, you may pay points to the lender. Points paid to obtain a home mortgage are deductible as part of your itemized interest deduction. However, points in some cases are deductible in full in the year in which they are paid while in other cases they must be amortized (deducted ratably) over the term of the loan.

Conditions

First determine whether the payment qualifies as "points" (defined next). Then see if the points can be deducted in full in the year of payment or must be deducted over the term of the mortgage.

IMMEDIATE DEDUCTIBILITY

If the loan is taken to buy, build, or substantially improve your main home, you may deduct the points in the year of payment if you meet the following conditions:

- Points are charged for interest and not for services performed by the lender. The designation of the payment, as points, loan origination fees, or otherwise, is not controlling of the tax treatment; it is the purpose for which the money is charged that governs whether you can treat points as interest.
- The loan is secured by your main home. If the loan relates to a second home, you cannot fully deduct the points in the year of payment.
- The charging of points is an established business practice in the geographical area in which you are located.
- The amount of points is computed as a percentage of the loan and specifically earmarked on the loan closing statement as points, loan origination fees, or loan discount.
- You pay the points directly to the lender. Points withheld from the loan proceeds used to buy your main home are treated as having been paid directly to the lender. Points withheld from loan proceeds used to substantially improve your main home are not immediately deductible; you must pay the points with other funds to secure a full deduction in the year of payment. Points paid by the seller are not treated as paid directly to the lender but rather are viewed as an adjustment to the purchase price of the home.

DEDUCTIBLE OVER THE TERM OF THE LOAN

As long as the payments meet the definition of points (e.g., are not fees for services performed by the lender), but cannot be deducted in full in the year of payment (or you opt not to deduct them in full), they are deducted over the term of the loan.

Example

In January 2017, you pay points of $3,600 to obtain a 30-year mortgage for your vacation home. You must amortize the points over 360 months and can deduct $10 per month each year until you've deducted all of the points or pay off the mortgage.

The following are situations in which you amortize the points rather than fully deduct them in the year of payment:

- To buy a second home.
- To substantially improve your main home but the points are withheld from the mortgage.
- To refinance an existing mortgage.
- To buy your main home but you elect to amortize the points.

Planning Tips

If you pay points to buy your main home, you are not required to deduct them in full in the year of payment. You can opt to amortize them over the term of the loan. You may wish to make this election if you can't benefit from the deduction in the year of payment. This might occur if you buy your home late in the year and your total itemized deductions do not exceed your standard deduction amount.

When you are financing a mortgage and are faced with the option of paying higher interest with little or no points or a lower interest rate but some or substantial points, which option should you select? The answer usually depends on how long you plan to remain in the home (how long you will be paying the mortgage). To help you make this decision based on your circumstances, use a mortgage points calculator (you can find one at www.dinkytown.net/java/MortgagePoints.html).

Pitfall

If you refinance your loan with a new lender and have been amortizing points over the term of a previous loan (for example, this is your second or third refinance), be sure to deduct the remaining balance of the unamortized points.

Example

In January 2016, when rates had declined below your original mortgage rate, you refinanced your outstanding balance for a new 15-year mortgage, paying

(Continued)

(Continued)

$1,800 in points. In July 2017, you refinance again. On your 2017 return, be sure to deduct the unamortized points of $1,260: $1,800 ÷ 180 months = $10 per month; 4 years, 6 months × $10 = $540; $1,800 − $540 = $1,260.

Where to Claim the Deduction

You deduct points along with your home mortgage interest on Schedule A of Form 1040. There is a separate line on Schedule A to list your points if they are not included on Form 1098 with your other home mortgage interest.

You cannot claim the deduction if you file Form 1040A or Form 1040EZ.

Refinancing

When interest rates decline or a personal credit rating improves, homeowners with existing mortgages can obtain more favorable terms by refinancing. Generally, this means getting a new mortgage to replace the old one. But you may borrow more than you owe on your old loan if the equity in your home allows for such borrowing—to add a room, replace a roof, pay off credit card debt, fund a child's education, or take a vacation. Under the tax law, the treatment of interest depends on what you use the excess funds for.

Benefit

With interest rates still relatively low, refinancing is a highly popular strategy to reduce monthly mortgage payments or to obtain additional cash for various purposes. If your home has appreciated in value and/or you have paid down your mortgage, you may be sitting on substantial equity that you can tap by refinancing. You are not taxed on the equity you receive when you refinance your mortgage—the proceeds are tax free.

Example

You bought your home 10 years ago for $100,000, using an $80,000 mortgage, which you've paid down to $72,000. Today your home is worth $225,000. If you refinance for $175,000 and use $72,000 of the proceeds to pay off the old mortgage, you can put $103,000 in your pocket tax free.

Whether and when interest on refinanced debt, as well as points to obtain the new loan, are deductible depend on the purpose of the refinancing (these rules are explained next).

Conditions

Your purpose in refinancing the outstanding debt on your home determines the tax treatment of the interest.

If you refinance your existing acquisition indebtedness, the new loan continues to be treated as acquisition indebtedness so that the interest is fully deductible (assuming the mortgage does not exceed $1 million). It does not matter whether you shorten or lengthen the term of the loan.

If you refinance your existing mortgage to take out equity you've accumulated in your home, deductibility of the interest on a new mortgage depends on what you do with the proceeds in excess of amounts used to simply refinance the existing debt.

If you use the excess proceeds to pay off credit card debt or other personal expenses, this portion of the debt is treated as home equity debt subject to the $100,000 limit. If the excess debt used for personal purposes exceeds this amount, a portion of your interest is nondeductible.

Example

Your home today is worth $500,000 and the remaining balance of your old mortgage is $200,000. If you refinance for $350,000 and use $50,000 of the proceeds to buy a personal car, take a vacation, and pay off some credit card debt, you can deduct interest on only $300,000 ($200,000 of acquisition indebtedness and $100,000 of home equity debt).

If you use the excess proceeds to substantially improve your home, such as remodel the kitchen or add a family room, interest on this portion of the debt, as well as the portion used to pay off the existing mortgage, is treated as acquisition indebtedness, which is fully deductible if the total does not exceed $1 million.

Example

Same as the preceding example except you use the $50,000 to add a family room to your home. Now you can deduct all of the interest on the new loan ($250,000 of acquisition indebtedness and $100,000 of home equity debt).

Planning Tip

If this is a subsequent refinancing (you've already refinanced your original acquisition indebtedness at least once), points paid on the prior refinancing become fully deductible in the year of your latest refinancing.

> **Example**
>
> In January 2013, you refinanced your original mortgage from 2011 and paid $3,600 for a 30-year loan. In January 2017, when interest rates have again declined, you refinance the outstanding balance of the 2013 loan. Of the points paid in 2011, you have already deducted $480 ($120 for 2013, 2014, 2015, and 2016). On your 2017 return you can deduct $3,120, the remaining amount of points on your 2013 refinancing.

Pitfall

If you refinance, consider what term you want for the new loan. If, for example, you have been paying off a 30-year mortgage and have only 22 years remaining, when you refinance, do you want to start the clock over again with a new 30-year mortgage? Maybe the answer is yes just to keep monthly payments as low as possible. But you may opt for a shorter term, such as 15, 20, or 25 years, so that you will pay off the mortgage at or about the same time as you had originally planned.

Where to Claim the Benefits

Since the equity you receive on refinancing for more than your old mortgage is not taxable income, you do not have to report it on your return.

You deduct home mortgage interest (including home equity debt and points) on Schedule A of Form 1040. The amount of mortgage interest is reported annually to you by the lender on Form 1098, *Mortgage Interest Statement.*

You cannot claim the deduction if you file Form 1040A or Form 1040EZ.

Prepayment Penalties

It costs a lender money to make a loan, which it expects to recoup through interest collected during the term of the loan. But if a borrower pays off a loan within a short time of obtaining it (generally under 2 years), the lender has not had time to recoup its lending costs. To protect the lender against a quick payoff, prepayment penalties may be owed. The prepayment penalties are spelled out in the mortgage note at the time of obtaining the mortgage. From the borrower's perspective, the tax law looks favorably on prepayment penalties, allowing them to be deductible if certain conditions are met.

Benefit

If you pay off your mortgage or home equity debt before you are required to, there may be a prepayment penalty as specified in your mortgage papers.

Prepayment penalties are treated as deductible interest. They are a set amount of interest: for example, 6 months of interest on 80% of your outstanding loan balance if you pay off the mortgage before a set term (usually one to 2 years). For the rules on deducting interest on your home or second home, see earlier in this chapter.

Conditions

There are no special conditions to meet for deducting prepayment penalties. Simply refer to the rules discussed earlier in this chapter on how to treat mortgage interest.

Planning Tip

Think ahead. When taking out a mortgage, check whether there are any potential prepayment penalties. You may be able to get the lender to delete these from the loan agreement. This is important because you may have to relocate before you had planned and do not want to incur this needless cost.

Pitfall

Don't sign any mortgage loan agreement before finding out if there are prepayment penalties. One common scam by unscrupulous lenders is nondisclosure of prepayment penalties, which can run as much as 6 months of interest on up to 80% of the outstanding loan balance. Such a high penalty can keep you locked into a mortgage when you otherwise could have refinanced for a lower mortgage rate.

Where to Claim the Deduction

Assuming that the prepayment payment penalty is deductible, you claim it with your home mortgage interest on Schedule A of Form 1040. The amount of mortgage interest is reported annually to you by the lender on Form 1098, *Mortgage Interest Statement*.

You cannot claim the deduction if you file Form 1040A or Form 1040EZ.

Late Payment Penalties

Under the terms of a loan, if a payment is late for any reason the borrower may owe additional amounts called late payment penalties. There are different types of late payment penalties: a flat fee, such as $25, charged without regard to the amount of the late payment or how long it is outstanding, and a percentage fee, fixed with regard to the late payment. The percentage fee continues to be assessed each month that a payment remains delinquent. Only late payment penalties qualifying as "interest" may be deductible.

Benefit

If you are late in making a payment, you may be charged a penalty by the lender. Generally, penalties for delinquent payments are treated as deductible interest, which can be written off if you itemize your deductions.

> ### Example
>
> Your monthly mortgage payment is $1,000, which is subject to a 2% late payment penalty. Due to unexpected financial reverses, you fail to make your payment for June, July, and August. In September, you're back on your feet and pay up all outstanding amounts, including the late payment penalties of $120 (June payment: 2% of $1,000 × 3 months; July payment: 2% of $1,000 × 2 months; August payment: 2% of $1,000 × 1 month). Since the late payment penalties are an interest charge, they are deductible.

Condition

Late payment penalties are treated as deductible interest as long as they are not imposed for a specific service provided by the lender. If they are a flat charge imposed regardless of how late the delinquency may be, they are viewed as a nondeductible service charge rather than as deductible interest.

Planning Tip

Even though late payment penalties can be deductible, you should try to avoid them if possible. The deduction does not fully offset your payment. One way to do so is to arrange for mortgage payments to be debited automatically from your checking account.

Pitfall

Being late on making your mortgage payments can cost you more than late payment penalties. Being late can adversely affect your credit rating and hurt your ability to obtain a loan or even get a job within 2 years or so of the late payment. Usually if your payment is no more than 30 days late, it will not show up on your credit report. But anything later will be reported by the lender to the major credit reporting bureaus and can affect your creditworthiness for about 2 years.

Where to Claim the Deduction

Assuming that the late payment penalty is deductible, you claim it with your home mortgage interest on Schedule A of Form 1040. The amount of mortgage interest is reported annually to you by the lender on Form 1098, *Mortgage Interest Statement*.

You cannot claim the deduction if you file Form 1040A or Form 1040EZ.

Mortgage Insurance

The deduction for mortgage insurance expired at the end of 2016 but could be extended for 2017. If extended, then the following information applies to 2017. If you put less than 20% down to purchase your home, you may be required to carry private mortgage insurance (PMI) or mortgage insurance from a government agency on the shortfall to protect the lender from a default. The cost of PMI typically runs from 0.6% to 0.8% of the loan amount. Payments of mortgage insurance may result in a tax deduction.

Benefit ⊜

Premiums for PMI paid can be deducted as mortgage interest by those with adjusted gross income below a threshold amount. There is no dollar limit on the amount of the deduction for this expense.

Conditions

To qualify for this itemized deduction, 2 conditions must be met:

1. The insurance must be first obtained after 2006 and through 2017 (if this deduction is extended for 2017, so check the Supplement). This insurance is available through commercial insurers as well as through federal loan programs such as the Veterans Administration (VA), the Rural Housing Administration (RHA), and the Federal Housing Administration (FHA).

2. To claim the full deduction, your adjusted gross income cannot exceed $100,000 ($50,000 for married persons filing separate returns). Any deduction is reduced by $1 for each dollar in excess of the AGI limit; no deduction is allowed if AGI exceeds $109,000 ($54,500 for married persons filing separate returns).

Planning Tip

PMI may be a way to help you buy a home even though you haven't yet saved the full down payment.

Once the equity in your home, from making payments on your mortgage as well as appreciation in property value, reaches 20%, cancel the mortgage insurance.

Pitfall

There is no downside to claiming this deduction.

Where to Claim the Deduction

The deduction is reported on Schedule A of Form 1040. You cannot claim the deduction if you file Form 1040A or Form 1040EZ.

Reverse Mortgages

Homeowners who are at least 62 years old and have little or no mortgage left on their primary residence can access the equity that has built up in their home over the years by obtaining a reverse mortgage. As the name implies, you receive money from a lender but do not have to repay it immediately; usually repayment is postponed until you move from your home or die. Proceeds of the mortgage can be made to you in a lump sum, as monthly payments, or as a line of credit that you can draw on to the extent needed.

Benefit

Proceeds received from a reverse mortgage are tax free. There are no dollar limits on the amount that is tax free, but there are limits on how much of a reverse mortgage you can obtain, based on your age, the current interest rate, and the appraised value of your home.

Conditions

To qualify for a reverse mortgage, you must be at least 62 years old and own a primary residence. There are no income limits on eligibility.

Planning Tip

To learn more about reverse mortgages from the U.S. Department of Housing and Urban Development (HUD), go to www.consumer.ftc.gov/articles/0192-reverse-mortgages.

Pitfall

Even though interest accrues on funds borrowed under a reverse mortgage, no deduction can be claimed until repayment is made.

Where to Claim the Benefit

You do not have any tax reporting with a reverse mortgage when you obtain the loan proceeds. You report (and deduct) interest only when you actually pay it. Reporting rules on mortgage interest are explained earlier in this chapter.

Cancellation of Mortgage Debt

This tax break expired at the end of 2016 but could be extended for 2017. If extended, then the following information applies to 2017. During the subprime mortgage debacle, thousands of Americans lost their homes. Homeowners are usually personally liable for the amount of the mortgage, even though the lender can foreclose, sell the home, and use the sale proceeds to pay down the debt. Unfortunately, the borrower may still owe money on the loan after foreclosure (the home sale may not cover what's due). Generally, when the lender forgives a portion of the outstanding mortgage, a practice that lets the borrower off the hook, this debt forgiveness is considered to be ordinary income for tax purposes. However, under a special law, forgiven debt on a main home may not be taxable.

Benefit ⊗

If you are not personally liable on the mortgage debt, then forgiveness of debt does not result in any income. There are more than a dozen states with anti-deficiency laws that make the forgiven debt to a homeowner not recourse and, therefore, nontaxable.

If you are personally liable on the debt, forgiveness is treated as tax-free income within the limits that follow, provided that Congress extends this tax break.

Conditions

There are 2 conditions for tax-free treatment:

1. The forgiven debt must have been used to buy, build, or substantially improve your main home and the debt must have been secured by the home. If a debt has been refinanced, the amount qualifying for this tax break is limited to the mortgage principal immediately before the refinancing.
2. The limit on qualifying debt is $2 million ($1 million for a married person filing separately).

Planning Tip

Debt forgiveness can apply to a so-called short sale, which occurs when the amount of the outstanding debt is greater than the value of the home (what a lender would realize if the home were sold). The short sale avoids the need for foreclosure. Also, some lenders will work with a homeowner to reduce the mortgage balance or change the terms of the loan so the homeowner can stay in his or her home. If there is any cancellation of debt, it can be tax free to the same extent as cancellation related to a foreclosure.

Pitfalls

The tax break on forgiven debt does not apply to a second home, rental property, or business property. You may still have to recognize gain if the home was foreclosed upon and the amount realized on the sale is greater than your basis in the home. The fair market value of the property (reported to the borrower in Box 7 of Form 1099-C, *Cancellation of Debt*) is treated as the amount realized on the sale. If you sell your home at a loss, you cannot deduct the loss; it is a nondeductible personal loss.

However, if any part of the mortgage is forgiven in conjunction with the sale, the resulting income can be excluded if the conditions stated earlier apply.

Where to Claim the Benefit

Forgiven debt is reported to you by the lender on Form 1099-C. To claim the exclusion, complete Form 982, *Reduction of Tax Attributes Due to Discharge of Indebtedness* (instructions to the form point out the specific lines applicable to home mortgage debt forgiveness). There is no income from debt cancellation to report on the return; just attach the completed Form 982 to the return.

Penalty-Free IRA Withdrawals for Home-Buying Expenses

If you thought IRAs were for retirement only, you'd be wrong. The tax law lets you tap into your IRA for certain special reasons without incurring any penalty (although withdrawals are subject to tax). One of those reasons is to buy a home.

Benefit

You may be able to use money in your IRA toward the cost of buying a home without incurring an early distribution penalty from your IRA. The withdrawal is subject to regular income tax, but you avoid the 10% early distribution penalty on withdrawals before age 59½.

Condition

You can withdraw only up to $10,000 free from penalty from your IRA. This is a once-in-a-lifetime opportunity. If you have already used this break to buy a previous home, you can't use it again.

You must spend the $10,000 on qualified first-time home-buying expenses, such as a down payment to purchase a home. These are expenses used to buy, build, or rehabilitate a main home for yourself, your spouse, child, grandchild, or ancestor (parent or grandparent) of you or your spouse. Such person cannot have had an ownership interest in a principal residence within 2 years before the purchase, construction, or renovation of the new home.

Planning Tip

Use this tax break only as a last resort. Once you withdraw the funds from the IRA and spend them on home-buying expenses, you cannot replace the funds in your retirement savings account. In effect, you lose the opportunity to build up your retirement savings.

Pitfalls

If you take a withdrawal from your IRA with the intention of using the money to buy a home but the sale falls through, you become taxed on the money unless you redeposit it back in the IRA. You have 120 days from your initial withdrawal to redeposit the funds. And, if you're under age 59¹/₂, the distribution is also subject to a 10% penalty.

When a couple is buying a home together, each must be a first-time home-buyer for the penalty exception to apply.

Where to Claim the Benefit

If you take money from your IRA, you must file Form 5329, *Additional Taxes on Qualified Plans (Including IRAs) and Other Tax-Favored Accounts*. You report total early distributions from your IRA. You can then subtract those exempt from the 10% penalty because you used them for qualified first-time home-buying expenses. You must indicate on the appropriate line on the form which exception to the 10% penalty you are relying on (a number is assigned to each exception, and these numbers are listed in the instructions to this form).

Since you do not have any penalty on the distribution, you do not report anything in the section of Form 1040 for "Additional Taxes."

If you take money out of your IRA, you *must* file Form 1040 even if you are not subject to a penalty; you cannot file Form 1040A or 1040EZ.

Real Estate Taxes

Property owners are charged real estate taxes to cover government services related to the property. Local property taxes may include city, town, and/or county taxes; school taxes; and even other charges (such as fire or sewer district taxes). Fortunately, the tax law allows property owners to deduct these taxes as an itemized deduction.

Benefit

Your burden of paying local property taxes, including city, town, and/or county taxes and school taxes, can be eased somewhat by deducting your payments.

If you itemize deductions, you can deduct real estate taxes you pay on your main home and any other home you own. There are no limits on the dollar amount of real estate taxes you can deduct. There are no limits on the number of homes for which you can claim the deduction. The deduction for real estate taxes on your residence and vacation homes is claimed as an itemized deduction (you cannot use this benefit if you claim the standard deduction).

If you pay real estate taxes on a rental property, it is deductible against your rental income, regardless of whether you itemize your personal deductions.

Conditions

You must be the owner of the home so that you are obligated for the payment of the tax. If you buy the property at a tax sale, you cannot start to deduct property taxes until you receive title to the property under state law (typically following a redemption period).

If you pay the seller's unpaid back taxes when you purchase the home, you cannot deduct this payment as your taxes. You can add the payment to your basis in the home used for figuring gain or loss when you sell it.

In the year that property is sold, real estate taxes must be allocated between the buyer and the seller. (Generally this allocation is reflected in your closing papers.)

- The seller can deduct taxes for the portion of the year through the day before the date of sale.
- The buyer can deduct taxes for the portion of the year commencing with the date of sale.

Generally, if you rent rather than own your home, you cannot deduct the portion of the rent that the landlord uses to pay the property taxes. However, in Hawaii you can do so if the lease runs for 15 years or more. Also, as a tenant in California you can deduct your payments if you have your name placed on the tax rolls and agree to pay the tax directly to the taxing authority.

Planning Tips

Consider prepaying an upcoming tax bill before the end of the year to increase your current deductions. For example, you can pay your January 2018 property tax bill in December 2017 to increase your deductions for 2017 (and likely obtain a discount for paying early).

Ask your city or town whether you qualify for any property tax reductions or rebates. Some areas provide them on the basis of age (reduction for seniors), veteran status, or for some other reason. Some locations even suspend real estate taxes for seniors entirely until the home is sold (e.g., when the owner dies or relocates). Generally, a reduction or rebate is not automatic; the homeowner must apply for it. The amount saved because of a property tax reduction or rebate is *not* treated as income; it merely lowers the amount you pay for real estate taxes and, in turn, the amount of your itemized deduction for real estate taxes.

Pitfalls

If you make payments to the lender that are held in escrow and disbursed to the taxing authority, you can only deduct real estate taxes when the lender makes the disbursements (not when you pay the lender).

If the title to your home is in the name of one spouse and the other spouse pays the real estate tax bill, the deduction can be claimed only if you file a joint return. Since the party paying the tax isn't the legal owner of the home, the tax may not be deducted on a separate return.

Special assessments by homeowners associations for the purpose of maintaining common areas or special assessments by municipalities for certain government services (water, sewage, or garbage collection) are not deductible as real estate taxes.

Do not prepay real estate taxes if you are subject to the alternative minimum tax (AMT). Since taxes are not deductible for AMT purposes, prepaying them can trigger or increase your AMT liability. You effectively lose the benefit of claiming the deduction.

If you receive a homestead tax credit from your state based on a percentage of your real estate taxes, the IRS says that the credit is treated for federal tax purposes as a reduction in your state income tax. This limits the amount of state income tax you can claim as an itemized deduction on your federal income tax return; it doesn't change your deduction for real property taxes.

Where to Claim the Deduction

You deduct your payment of real estate taxes on your residence and vacation homes as an itemized deduction on Schedule A of Form 1040. You deduct real estate taxes on rental properties on Schedule E of Form 1040.

You cannot deduct property taxes on a personal residence or rental property if you file Form 1040A or 1040EZ.

In the year you sell property, if your share of real estate taxes is paid in advance by the buyer, the lender or real estate broker will generally include this information on Form 1099-S, *Proceeds from Real Estate Transactions*. But this form is not required to be filed for all sales, so you should keep track of this information (check your settlement papers).

Each year that you own property you do *not* receive any official information return notifying you of the amount of taxes you paid during the year. As a practical matter, if you make payments to a commercial lender to cover real estate taxes, your annual tax payments will be detailed in a year-end statement sent to you by the lender.

Cooperative Housing

Cooperative housing, also called a co-op, is a form of home ownership. You become a tenant-stockholder in a cooperative housing corporation (CHC) that owns and runs a multiunit housing complex. Your shares entitle you to exclusive use of your housing unit, plus access to common areas. There are tax breaks unique to this form of home ownership.

Benefits

You may experience 2 levels of deductions—one that is allocated to you from the CHC and the other that you obtain through your direct payments. For example, you may incur 2 interest deductions—one for your share of interest on debt of the CHC (e.g., for common areas) and one for the purchase of your unit that you financed through a bank. This section discusses only your allocated deduction; deductions for your direct payments are included in other sections of this chapter (e.g., home mortgage interest).

Condition

The only condition for claiming a deduction for CHC expenses allocated to you is ownership of shares in the CHC.

Planning Tip

Tenant-stockholders in cooperative housing corporations are treated the same in the tax law as homeowners of condominiums and single-family homes.

Pitfall

While a tenant-shareholder of an apartment in a cooperative housing corporation can deduct his/her share of the co-op's real estate taxes, a federal appeals court has decided that these taxes are *not* deductible for purposes of the alternative minimum tax (AMT). Even though the AMT rules do not specifically bar a deduction, these taxes are treated in the same manner as if the taxes had been paid directly by the owner of a single-family home.

Where to Claim the Deduction

You claim a deduction for your share of the CHC's mortgage interest and real estate taxes allocated to you on Schedule A of Form 1040 as a "Miscellaneous Itemized Deduction." This deduction is not subject to the 2% of AGI limitation but is subject to the reduction in itemized deductions for high-income taxpayers.

You cannot deduct your allocated mortgage interest and real estate taxes if you file Form 1040A or 1040EZ.

The CHC should provide you with Form 1098, *Mortgage Interest Statement*, to show your share of these expenses.

Minister's Housing Allowance

Members of the clergy of any recognized faith or denomination who receive assistance with their housing costs, through free use of a home or payments toward these living costs, may qualify for a tax break. Their housing allowance, sometimes referred to as a parsonage allowance, may be a nontaxable fringe benefit of their job. An estimated 44,000 ministers, rabbis, imams, priests, and others take advantage of this tax break. One U.S. district court ruled that this tax break is unconstitutional because it violates the Establishment Clause in the U.S. Constitution, but an appellate court dismissed the matter for lack of standing (none of those who brought the suit had tried to claim the housing allowance and been denied). In April 2016, another lawsuit was filed to challenge the constitutionality of the exclusion for this housing allowance. The court dismissed the part of the challenge to the tax-free "in kind" housing (i.e., use a parsonage or other housing provided by the church or other religious group at no cost) but allowed the challenge to the exclusion for the housing allowance to continue. Check the Supplement for any update.

Benefit ⊗

You are not taxed on the rental value of a home provided to you by your religious institution—this is tax-free income to you. If you receive an allowance for housing, you can exclude the amount used to pay rent, make a down payment to buy a house, or make mortgage payments, or for utilities, real estate taxes, or repairs to the home. There is no dollar limit on this exclusion.

Conditions

You must be a duly ordained minister and acting in that capacity. A rabbi or cantor is treated as a minister for purposes of this exclusion. Retired ministers can qualify for the exclusion if the housing allowance is made in recognition of past services. A minister acting as a teacher or an administrator of a parochial school or seminary qualifies for the exclusion if the school is an integral part of a church organization.

Church officers who are not ordained cannot qualify for the exclusion. Ordained ministers who are working as executives of nonreligious organizations cannot claim the exclusion even if they perform religious duties. For example, a minister-administrator of an old age home not under church authority could not claim the exclusion.

The religious institution (e.g., church or local congregation) must designate the part of your compensation that is the housing allowance. This designation must be made in advance of the payments to you. Designation can be made in an employment contract, minutes, a resolution, or a budget allowance.

Planning Tip

If you pay mortgage interest and/or real estate taxes, you can claim deductions for these payments even if you finance them with the tax-free housing allowance. You must itemize your deductions to write off mortgage interest and real estate taxes on your home, as explained in this chapter.

Pitfalls

Even though the housing exclusion is not subject to income tax, it is treated as self-employment income for purposes of Social Security and Medicare taxes. If you use a church-provided home tax free, figure the rental value for purposes of self-employment taxes at what you would pay for similar quarters in your area, including utilities and garage or parking space, if any.

Claiming the housing allowance can have an adverse impact on your business deductions. The portion of business deductions allocable to the tax-free housing allowance is not deductible.

Example

Your salary as a minister is $25,000. You also receive a $25,000 housing allowance. Your work-related expenses are $6,000. You can deduct only $3,000. Since half of your income is tax free, only half of the expenses are deductible.

Where to Claim the Exclusion

If you can exclude the benefit, you do not have to report anything on your return. If you receive an allowance in excess of the amounts used for housing expenses, you must include the excess as part of your salary reported on your income tax return. You can do so on Form 1040, 1040A, or 1040EZ.

Home Sale Exclusion

Homeowners are highly favored under the tax law. Not only can they deduct certain costs of home ownership, such as mortgage interest and property taxes, but they can also receive tax-free income when they sell their homes. A special rule permits a limited amount of gain from the sale of a main home to escape federal income tax. And this tax break can be used over and over again within certain limits.

Benefit ⊗

If you sell your home for a profit, you may avoid tax on some or all of your gain as long as you meet certain conditions. More specifically, you do not pay any tax on a gain up to $250,000 from the sale of your home ($500,000 on a joint return or by a surviving spouse if the sale is within 2 years of the other spouse's death) if you owned and used the home as your main residence for at least 2 of the 5 years preceding the date of sale. The amount you exclude is tax-free income to you.

Conditions

To be eligible to use the full exclusion amount of $250,000 ($500,000 on a joint return or for a surviving spouse), you must meet all 3 conditions:

1. The home must be your main home ("principal residence").
2. You owned your home for at least 2 years prior to the sale.
3. You used your home as your main home for at least 2 years prior to the sale.

If you acquired your home in a tax-free exchange, the ownership and use periods must be 5 full years (instead of 2 of 5 years) before qualifying for the exclusion.

If you are a member of the uniformed services, Foreign Service, or intelligence community, or are a Peace Corps volunteer, you can elect to suspend the 5-year testing period for the ownership and use tests for up to 10 years.

MAIN HOME

Your main home is the one in which you primarily dwell. If you own 2 or more homes, you must determine which one is your primary residence. This determination is usually based on which one you live in for the greater part of the year. However, this isn't a bright line test; you can use other factors to show that the home you used less of the time is your main home. Such factors include:

- Where you work or own a business
- Where your family members reside
- The address you use for your federal and state income tax returns
- The address you use for your bills and correspondence
- Where you have your driver's license and voter registration
- The location of religious institutions and clubs you belong to

Your main home isn't limited to a single-family dwelling. You can treat as your main home a mobile home, trailer, houseboat, or condominium apartment used as your primary residence. Even stock in a cooperative housing corporation is subject to this rule as long as you live in the cooperative apartment or house as your main home.

If you change the title to your home, you don't necessarily lose the opportunity to claim the exclusion.

- If you transfer ownership of your home to a grantor trust, one in which you are treated as the owner of the trust and report all of the trust's income on your personal tax return, the trust can use the exclusion provided you meet the ownership and use tests.
- If you transfer ownership of your home to a single-member limited liability company, again, the LLC can use the exclusion provided you meet the ownership and use tests. The LLC is treated as a "disregarded entity" for tax purposes so you report all of the LLC's income on your personal tax return.
- If you divorce and the title to the home is changed from your spouse's name or joint name to your name alone, you can include the period of your spouse's ownership in meeting the ownership test.
- If you are a surviving spouse, you can use the $500,000 exclusion amount if you sell the home within 2 years after your spouse's death. But if you sell in a later year, you are limited to the $250,000 exclusion.

OWNERSHIP TEST

You must own your home for at least 2 years in the aggregate prior to the date of sale. This means that you owned the home for a full 24 months or 730 days (365×2) during the 5-year period that ends on the date of sale. The periods of ownership and use need not be continuous or identical.

If you are married and file a joint return, only 1 spouse is required to meet the ownership test to qualify for the exclusion as long as both satisfy the use test.

USE TEST

You must use your home as your primary residence for at least 2 years in the aggregate prior to the date of sale. This means that you lived in the home for a full 24 months or 730 days (365×2) during the 5-year period that ends on the date of sale. The periods of ownership and use need not be continuous or identical.

Example

In November 2013, you purchased your home and lived there until September 2015, when you took a 1-year sabbatical overseas. You returned to your home in September 2016 and lived there until you sold the home in December 2017. You meet the use test because you lived in your home for 26 months (10 months before the sabbatical and 16 months after it).

Temporary absences (for example, a 3-week vacation) are ignored. This is true even if you rent out your home while you are away.

If a homeowner becomes incapacitated before meeting the 2-year use test and resides in a licensed care facility, the full home sale exclusion can be used as long as the homeowner used the home for at least one year prior to moving from the home and meets the 2-year ownership test.

PARTIAL EXCLUSION

Even if you sell before meeting the full 2-year ownership and use tests, you may be eligible to use a prorated exclusion amount for the period of your ownership and use. A partial exclusion is allowed if you sell early because of:

- *Change in jobs.* If you relocate for a new job or a new business (if self-employed), you automatically are treated as having a qualified change in jobs if the distance test used for the moving expense deduction (explained later in this chapter) is met. The distance between your new job location and your former home must be at least 50 miles greater than the distance between your old job location and your former home. If your spouse, co-owner, or person who resides with you has a change of jobs, you can qualify for the exclusion.

- *Health reasons.* The change must be medically motivated (for example, your doctor recommends a change so you can receive medical or personal care for an illness or injury). A change that is merely beneficial to your health (for example, moving to a warmer climate) isn't viewed as a health reason for purposes of using the partial exclusion. Again, the health of your spouse, co-owner, or person who resides with you can be taken into account in determining your eligibility for the partial exclusion.

- *Unforeseen circumstances.* If you are forced to sell because of events beyond your control, you can use the partial exclusion. Such events include, but are not limited to: Your home is destroyed through acts of war or terrorism, someone in your household dies or goes on unemployment benefits, you become unable to pay basic living expenses because of a change in employment (e.g., being furloughed for 6 months) or self-employment, there is a legal divorce or separation, you have multiple births resulting from the same pregnancy, you must have a larger home to meet adoption agency requirements, you received death threats at the current address, you must leave a senior retirement home so your young grandchild can live with you, you must move to a home that can accommodate your paralyzed mother's disability, you are forced to sell because of pressure from neighbors, you experience excessive airport noise that was not disclosed by the seller, or you become part of a blended family or have additional children that cannot be accommodated in your current home.

Planning Tips

If you have owned your home for a long time and paid down the mortgage, your gain may exceed your exclusion amount. You can minimize your gain by adding to the basis of your home any capital improvements you've made to it.

EXAMPLES OF CAPITAL IMPROVEMENTS

Addition of a deck, garage, porch, or room

Appliances

Duct work

Fencing

Heating and cooling systems

Kitchen and bathroom modernization

New roof

Paving the driveway

Retaining wall

Satellite dish

Security system

Septic system

Soft-water system

Storm doors and windows

Walkway

Well

Wiring upgrade

If you subdivide your property, selling off vacant land separately from the parcel on which the home is situated, you can claim the exclusion for the sale of the vacant land and the sale of the home provided they occur within 2 years of each other. However, only one exclusion amount applies to both sales.

Example

You are single in 2017 and subdivide your property and sell the vacant land for a profit of $100,000 (you must allocate the basis in your home between the vacant land and the parcel with the home to determine your gain on the sale of each parcel). You can exclude this gain on your 2017 return. In 2018, you sell the parcel containing your home for a profit of $200,000. You can exclude

$150,000 of this $200,000 gain on your 2018 return (you already used $100,000 of the exclusion on your 2017 return). You must report and pay tax on the remaining $50,000 profit.

If you have been claiming a home office deduction for a portion of the home, you can still apply the exclusion to the home office portion as long as both the personal and business portions are part of the same dwelling.

You can use the exclusion over and over again. As long as you meet the 2-year ownership and use tests for each residence, you can avoid tax on gains from each one. One exclusion can be claimed every 2 years.

If your home is destroyed by a casualty, and insurance proceeds exceed the basis of your home, resulting in a taxable gain, the transaction may qualify as a home sale for purposes of the home sale exclusion. The damage to the home must be sufficient to constitute a "destruction."

Pitfalls

The home sale exclusion applies only to "qualified use" of a residence. "Non-qualified use" includes any period after December 31, 2008, in which the home is not used as a principal residence. Thus, if you stop using the home as your main home and use it only as vacation property, or if you rent it out, gain related to this period does not qualify for the home sale exclusion. Temporary absences are not treated as nonqualified use; they're disregarded.

If you have been claiming a home office deduction for a portion of your home, you must recapture depreciation you have claimed for the office after May 6, 1997. This is so even though you can use the exclusion for gain on this part of the home. "Recapture" means you pay tax on all the depreciation claimed after May 6, 1997, at the rate of 25% (assuming your tax bracket is at or above this rate). Home office deduction rules are discussed in Chapter 15.

You must reduce the basis of your home by the amount of any energy credit claimed. For example, if you claimed a $1,500 tax credit in 2010 for installing new storm doors and windows, you must subtract $1,500 from the basis of your home. The same is true if you claimed a $500 tax credit in 2016 for adding attic insulation.

If you fail the 2-year ownership and use test, you cannot claim a partial home sale exclusion based on unforeseen circumstances merely because a job promotion, house appreciation, or winning the lottery enables you to buy a bigger home.

Where to Claim the Exclusion

If your gain is fully excludable, you do not have to report the sale of your home on your return. If, however, some of the gain is taxable because it exceeds the exclusion amount (or all of your gain is taxable because you opt *not* to use the exclusion), you report the sale on Form 8949, *Sales and Other Dispositions of Capital Assets*, of Form 1040.

You can use a worksheet in IRS Publication 523 to figure your gain and whether any portion of the gain is excludable.

Moving Expenses

According to the U.S. Census Bureau, 11.2% of Americans moved in 2016. It's estimated that individuals will move 11.4 times during their lives. The American Moving and Storage Association says the average cost of an interstate move is about $4,300 while it's only $2,300 intrastate (both assuming 7,400 pounds). The cost of a move may be even higher—$13,000 or more (depending on distance and the amount of furniture and household goods to be moved). From a tax perspective, deductibility of moving costs depends on the reason for the move and satisfying certain conditions.

Benefit

When you move your things to a new residence because of a change in your work location, you may be able to deduct moving expenses as an adjustment to gross income, even if you don't itemize your other deductions. There is no dollar limit on this benefit.

Deductible amounts include amounts paid to pack, crate, and move your household goods and personal effects. Storage and insurance costs can be treated as deductible expenses for any period within 30 days after the items were moved from your old home but before they were delivered to your new home. If you move overseas, there is no limit on storage and insurance costs while you work at your overseas location. The cost of connecting or disconnecting household appliances is a deductible moving expense, but the cost of installing a telephone in your new home is not deductible.

Deductible amounts also include travel expenses for you and members of your household.

EXAMPLES OF DEDUCTIBLE TRAVEL EXPENSES FOR THE MOVING DEDUCTION

- Lodging en route from the old home to the new home. Include the cost of lodging before you depart for one day after your old residence is unusable as well as lodging for the day of arrival at your new location before you move into your home. However, the cost of meals is not deductible.
- Transportation from the old home to the new home. You and members of your household do not have to travel together; simply add up the costs for each person.

- Your car expenses at 17¢ per mile for travel in 2017, or your actual out-of-pocket costs for oil, gas, and repairs, if any, for the move. You can also deduct parking and tolls, regardless of which deduction method you use.

- The cost of moving your pets. Pets are viewed as household items, not as members of your family.

If your employer pays to relocate you, reimbursements or employer payments on your behalf are not income if you would have been able to deduct the expenses had you paid for them yourself (i.e., you meet the deduction conditions given next). Such reimbursement need not be included on your Form W-2 if the benefit is excludable. Of course, reimbursements for nondeductible expenses, such as premove house-hunting expenses, are reported on your W-2 and taxable to you as income.

Conditions

To be treated as a deductible expense (or to qualify as a tax-free fringe benefit if paid by the employer), the expense must meet 2 tests:

1. A distance test
2. A time test

DISTANCE TEST

The distance from your new workplace must be at least 50 miles farther from your old home than your old workplace was. The location of the new home does not affect the distance test. If you relocate to a distant city or across the country, there's no question that you satisfy the distance test. But if you relocate within the same general area, make sure that the move meets the distance test.

> **Example**
>
> Your old workplace was 5 miles from your old home. Your new workplace is 75 miles from your old home. Since the difference is more than 50 miles, you meet the distance test.

If you are a member of the armed forces, you do not have to meet the distance test if the move is due to a permanent change of station. A permanent change of station includes a move in connection with retirement or termination of active duty if it is within one year of such retirement or termination.

TIME TEST

If you are an employee, you must work full time in the area of your new workplace for at least 39 weeks during the 12-month period following your move. If you change from being self-employed to being an employee, you must meet the 39-week test as an employee and cannot use any weeks of self-employment for this purpose.

If you are self-employed, you must work full time in the area of your new workplace for 78 weeks during the 24-month period following your move. If you change from being an employee to being self-employed, you can include any weeks of employment for purposes of the 78-week test.

On a joint return, only one spouse is required to meet the time test.

If you expect to satisfy the time test, you can claim the deduction on your return even though you have not yet satisfied it.

Example

You move in August 2017 to a job in another state. By the end of 2017, you have completed only 20 weeks of full-time work in your new workplace. You can deduct your moving expenses on your 2017 return as long as you anticipate staying on the job for at least another 19 weeks.

If you don't claim the deduction in the year of the move, you must then file an amended return to claim the moving expense deduction. But if you claim the deduction on your return for the year of the move but later fail to satisfy the time test, you can either:

- Amend your return, eliminating the deduction you had claimed.
- Report as income the deduction you claimed on the earlier return.

If you expected to meet the time test, you don't have to report the deduction as income if the failure was due to:

- Disability that results in job termination.
- Job termination because you are laid off or fired for a reason other than willful misconduct.
- A permanent change of station if you are in the armed forces.
- Being a retiree or survivor of a person living outside the United States. If your old workplace and old home were both outside the United States, a move home is deductible (you don't have to meet any time test). Similarly, if you are the spouse or dependent of someone whose principal workplace was outside the United States at the time of his or her death, your moving costs are deductible without regard to the time test if the move begins within 6 months of the death and you lived with the person at the time of his or her death.

- Death. In other words, if someone claimed a moving expense deduction but died before meeting the time test, there is no income recapture of the benefit.

Planning Tip

Even though you can deduct your moving costs, it still makes sense to keep them as low as possible. When planning a move, to get a rough idea of moving costs, use The Moving Calculator from Realtor.com (www.homefair.com/home fair/calc/moveclacin.html). Be sure to get several binding quotes from reputable moving companies before contracting with one of them. Finally, put everything you agree to in writing and include adequate insurance for loss, breakage, and other damage. Learn about moving, including how to insure the move, in *The Moving Guide* from MovingGuru (www.movingguru.com).

Pitfalls

You cannot claim a moving expense deduction if you are relocating because of retirement (other than in the case of the armed forces). For example, if you sell your business in New York and retire to Florida, the cost of the move is a nondeductible personal expense.

You cannot deduct the costs of a move to start your first job after you've completed your education unless the place of work is at least 50 miles from your former home. The same rule applies if you've been out of work for a long time and are returning to the workplace; you must meet this 50-mile test.

Not every move-related expense is deductible.

EXAMPLES OF NONDEDUCTIBLE MOVING EXPENSES

- Any part of the purchase price of a new home
- Car registration tags
- Driver's license
- Expenses of buying or selling a home
- Expenses of getting or breaking a lease (lease cancellation fee)
- Home improvements to sell your home
- Losses from disposing of club memberships
- Meal expenses
- Mortgage penalties (but they may be deductible as an itemized mortgage interest expense as explained earlier in this chapter)
- Premove house-hunting expenses
- Real estate taxes (but they may be deductible as an itemized expense)
- Refitting of carpets and draperies

- Security deposits forfeited
- Storage charges except those incurred in transit and for foreign moves
- Temporary living expenses

Where to Claim the Deduction

If your employer pays your moving costs and you are eligible to exclude this benefit from your income, you do not report them on your return.

If you deduct your expenses, figure the deduction on Form 3903, *Moving Expenses*, which you attach to your return. Enter the deductible amount in the "Adjusted Gross Income" section of Form 1040.

You cannot claim a moving expense deduction if you file Form 1040A or Form 1040EZ.

Energy Improvements

The nonbusiness energy credit expired at the end of 2016 but could be extended for 2017. If extended, then the following information applies to 2017. Homeowners can claim various tax credits for making certain energy-saving improvements. In view of currently high energy costs, consider taking advantage of tax breaks to save money on taxes and energy costs.

Benefit ⊕

There are 2 tax credits that a homeowner may claim for making certain energy improvements to the home. These include a 10% credit for adding qualified energy efficiency improvements (nonbusiness energy property credit if extended for 2017) and a 30% credit for solar energy and fuel cell power plants (the 30% credit for solar energy is reduced after 2019).

Conditions

The law requires that these improvements meet certain energy-saving standards and cannot exceed certain dollar limits. Different requirements apply to energy improvements and to solar energy and fuel cell power plants.

The qualified improvements must be made to an existing home, not a home that is being constructed. The home must be your principal residence and not vacation property.

ENERGY IMPROVEMENTS

The nonbusiness energy credit expired at the end of 2016 but could be extended for 2017. If extended, then the following information applies to 2017. To qualify for the 10% nonbusiness energy property credit energy improvements must meet or exceed the criteria set for January 1, 2009, building standards and must be installed in your main home in the United States. Exterior windows, exterior doors, and skylights must meet Energy Star program requirements. You can rely on a manufacturer's certification in writing that a product is qualified residential energy property. Don't attach the certification to your return, but keep it with your records.

ELIGIBLE ITEMS

These include:

- Insulation systems that reduce heat loss/gain
- Exterior windows (including skylights)
- Exterior doors
- Metal roofs treated with special paint (meeting applicable Energy Star requirements) and certain asphalt roofs
- Advanced main air-circulating fan
- Qualified natural gas, propane, or oil furnace or hot water heater

These items are listed in the law, but they are not the only ones to qualify for the credit; other items meeting certain energy standards can also qualify. It is up to the manufacturer to obtain certification for its products. For example, certification has been obtained for a qualifying wood or pellet stove, fireplace, and fireplace insert by various manufacturers. Other items meeting certain energy standards include central air conditioners.

LIMITATIONS

The credit is 10% of the cost of expenditures, up to a maximum credit of $500.

Special limits. Certain expenditures are capped at low dollar amounts, so the $500 cap may not apply to them:

- $300 for approved electric and geothermal heat pumps; central air-conditioning systems; and natural gas, propane, or oil water heaters
- $200 for new windows
- $150 for a natural gas, propane, or oil furnace or hot water boiler
- $50 for an advanced main air-circulating fan

Lifetime limit. The $500 limit for the credit must be reduced by any nonbusiness energy property credit claimed after 2005.

SOLAR POWER AND FUEL CELLS

To qualify for the 30% residential alternative energy credit, solar panels, solar water heating equipment, a geothermal heat pump, a small wind property, or a fuel cell power plant must be added to your main home in the United States.

In general, a qualified fuel cell power plant converts a fuel into electricity using electrochemical means, has an electricity-only generation efficiency of more than 30%, and generates at least 0.5 kilowatts of electricity.

You can claim one credit equal to 30% of the qualified investment in a solar panel and another equivalent credit for investing in a solar water heating system.

Additionally, you are allowed a 30% tax credit for the purchase of qualified fuel cell power plants. The credit may not exceed $500 for each 0.5 kilowatt of capacity.

Planning Tips

How can you know whether improvements to your home will qualify for these tax credits? Obtain a manufacturer's certificate that the item has been approved by the IRS as qualifying for the credit. You can find helpful information at www.EnergyStar.gov.

The residential alternative energy credit can be claimed even for expenditures made with funds obtained from subsidized energy financing. The value of any subsidy provided by a public utility is excluded from gross income, but this must be used to reduce the basis of the energy improvement for purposes of figuring the credit.

Low- and middle-income homeowners who receive payments from the state to help pay for energy-efficient boilers and furnaces are not taxed on these payments (the state is not required to report them on Form 1099).

If you can't fully use the credit for alternative energy improvements in the current year, you can carry the unused credit forward; there is no limit on this carryforward period.

Check with your utility company to learn whether there are any grants or rebates for making energy improvements to your home.

Pitfalls

Not every energy-saving measure qualifies for a credit. For purposes of the energy improvements credit, insulated vinyl siding does not qualify. For purposes of the solar or fuel cell power plant credit, no part of either system can be used to heat a pool or hot tub.

You must reduce the basis of your home by the amount of any energy credit claimed. For example, if you claim a $500 tax credit in 2013 for installing new storm doors, you must subtract $500 from the basis of your home.

Where to Claim the Credits

You figure the credit on Form 5965, *Residential Energy Credits*. The credit is then entered in the "Tax and Credits" section of Form 1040, or in the

"Tax, Credits, and Payments" section of Form 1040A. You may not claim the credit if you file Form 1040EZ.

ABLE Accounts

If you have a disabled child or are under age 26 and meet certain eligibility conditions, you can have a special savings account that generally does not adversely impact eligibility for means-tested government programs (e.g., Medicaid). An ABLE account can be used on a tax-free basis for housing, as well as other qualified disability expenses. See details in Chapter 2.

Retirement Savings

Alert

At the time this book was completed, Congress was considering important tax changes that could affect 2017 tax returns and planning for 2018. Check the online Supplement in February 2018 at www.jklasser.com or www.barbaraweltman.com to see what changes have been enacted and when they are effective.

Your Social Security benefits alone, or even retirement benefits derived from employer contributions to retirement plans on your behalf, won't provide you with the financial security you want for your retirement years. You need to save so that you'll have the assets to generate income after you stop working.

Fortunately, the tax law provides important incentives to encourage your personal savings in special retirement accounts. You may be able to write off your savings (contributions) as well as qualify for special treatment when you start drawing from these savings. There are many different types of retirement plans that you may be able to use to save for your future. Contributions are subject to limits; if your income is high enough, it may bar you from contributing to some plans but not to others.

This chapter explains the tax breaks you may be entitled to when you save for retirement using tax-advantaged ways. If you are an employer, you may be eligible for a tax credit for starting a qualified retirement plan for your business. This credit is explained in Chapter 15.

For more information, see IRS Publication 560, *Retirement Plans for Small Business*; IRS Publication 575, *Pension and Annuity Income*; IRS Publication 590-A, *Contributions to Individual Retirement Arrangements (IRAs)*; IRS Publication 590-B, *Distributions from Individual Retirement Arrangements (IRAs)*; and IRS Publication 4333, *SEP Retirement Plans for Small Businesses*.

Traditional IRAs

The Employee Retirement Income Security Act of 1974 (referred to as ERISA) created individual retirement accounts (IRAs) to enable taxpayers to save for their own retirement largely because company pensions could no longer be relied upon for retirement income. With an IRA, the government effectively contributes to your retirement savings by permitting a tax deduction for contributions if certain conditions are met. The tax savings are the government's contribution. For example, if you are in the 33% tax bracket, the government contributes almost one-third of your contributions to a traditional (deductible) IRA—your tax savings from the total contribution amount; you only have to come up with about two-thirds of the contribution.

Benefit

If you work as an employee or have net earnings from self-employment, you can contribute to an IRA. The contribution limit for 2017 is $5,500, or $6,500 if you are age 50 or older by the end of 2017, as long as you earn at least this dollar amount.

Example
If you are single, under age 50, and earn at least $5,500, you can make a full contribution. If you work part-time and earn only $2,000, your contribution is limited to $2,000.

If you have a spouse who does not work for compensation, you can contribute to an IRA for your spouse based on your own earnings. The IRA for a nonworking spouse is called the Kay Bailey Hutchison Spousal IRA. The same dollar limit of $5,500 (or $6,500 if age 50 by the end of 2017) applies to a spousal IRA. This means that if you have sufficient earnings and both you and your spouse are under age 50, you can contribute up to $11,000 ($5,500 for yourself and $5,500 for your spouse) for 2017.

If you do not participate in another qualified retirement plan, such as a 401(k) plan, or if you do participate but your income is below a set amount, you can deduct your contributions. The deduction is claimed as an adjustment to gross income; you claim it regardless of whether you itemize your other deductions.

Earnings on IRA contributions build up on a tax-deferred basis (no tax is owed annually on the earnings of an IRA). However, you are required to take certain withdrawals from the IRA starting at age 70½. If you fail to take these required amounts (called required minimum distributions, which are not discussed further in this book), you may be subject to a whopping 50% penalty of the amount you should have taken.

Conditions for Making Contributions

There are 3 conditions for making a contribution:

1. Earned income
2. Under age 70½
3. Cash contributions

EARNED INCOME

Earned income for purposes of making IRA contributions means taxable wages (including tips, commissions, bonuses, and jury duty fees) and net earnings from self-employment. Earned income for purposes of making IRA contributions also includes taxable alimony and tax-free combat pay.

You must earn the income. If you live in a community property state where one-half of your spouse's earnings is viewed as income, you cannot use your share of your spouse's income as the basis for making your IRA contribution.

Earned income does *not* include:

- Conservation Reserve Program (CRP) payments even though they are reported as income for self-employment tax purposes.
- Deferred compensation, pensions, or annuities.
- Investment income, such as dividends or interest.

- Income earned abroad for which the foreign earned income exclusion has been claimed.
- Partnership income from a business for which you do not provide services that are a material income-producing factor.
- Social Security benefits.
- Unemployment compensation.

UNDER AGE 70^1/$_2$

There is no *minimum* age requirement for making an IRA contribution. Thus, if your 12-year-old child has a newspaper delivery route, he or she can make IRA contributions based on earnings from this job.

However, no contributions are permitted starting for the year in which you turn age 70^1/$_2$.

Example

You were born in March 1947. Since you attain age 70^1/$_2$ in 2017, no IRA contributions can be made for 2017. If you were born in September 1947, you attain age 70^1/$_2$ in 2018, so you can still make an IRA contribution for 2017.

If you continue to work past this age, you may still contribute on behalf of a nonworking spouse who is under age 70^1/$_2$.

CASH CONTRIBUTIONS

All contributions must be made in cash (which includes payments by check). If you currently own investments that you want to use as your contributions, you must first liquidate them. Your IRA can then reacquire the same investments (provided they are not prohibited investments discussed later).

Condition for Claiming a Deduction

Just because you meet all the conditions for making an IRA contribution does not mean that you can claim a deduction for the contribution. Even if you qualify to make contributions, there is an additional condition in order to deduct your contributions.

To deduct contributions you must not participate in another qualified retirement plan or if you are an active participant in a qualified retirement plan, your modified adjusted gross income (MAGI) cannot exceed a phaseout range. The deduction amount phases out for MAGI within the phaseout range. No deduction can be claimed if MAGI exceeds the phaseout range. MAGI for this purpose is adjusted gross income, increased by exclusions for interest on U.S. savings

TABLE 5.1 2017 MAGI Phaseout Range for Active Participants Deducting IRA Contributions

Filing Status*	MAGI
Married filing jointly	$99,000–119,000
Other taxpayers (other than married filing separately)	$ 62,000–72,000

*A married person filing a separate return has a zero limit so that no deduction can be claimed if the person is an active participant.

bonds used for higher education, employer-paid adoption assistance, and foreign earned income as well as deductions for interest on student loans and higher education tuition and fees. Table 5.1 shows the phaseout ranges for 2017.

Example

You are single, age 42, and participate in your company's 401(k) plan. If your AGI is $50,000, you can fully deduct your IRA contributions. If your AGI is $67,000, your basic deduction is limited to $2,750 ($1/2$ of $5,500). If your AGI is $72,000 or more, you cannot deduct your IRA contributions.

If one spouse is an active participant, the other spouse is permitted to make a deductible IRA contribution only if the couple's MAGI is below a set limit. For 2017, the MAGI limit in this case is $186,000. The nonactive participant's spouse's contribution is reduced when the couple's MAGI exceeds $186,000; it is fully phased out when MAGI reaches $196,000.

Planning Tips

You have until the deadline for filing the return to make an IRA contribution. For example, you have until April 17, 2018, to make an IRA contribution for 2017. But even if you obtain a filing extension, you do not gain any additional time to make your annual contribution.

Just because you have more time to act doesn't mean it's a good idea to delay. The earlier in the year you make your contribution, the sooner you begin to earn tax-deferred income. For example, if you make your 2017 contribution on January 15, 2017, rather than on April 17, 2018, you gain an additional 15 months of tax-deferred investment buildup in the IRA.

You can help your child jump-start his or her retirement savings by providing the funds for an IRA contribution. As long as your child has earned income (e.g., from a part-time or summer job), you can make a gift of the contribution amount to your child.

Example

Your child earns $1,800 from a summer job and uses her earnings as spending money for the year. You can give your child $1,800 to make an IRA contribution.

The basic IRA contribution limit can be increased for inflation in $500 increments, so check the Supplement for any changes for 2018. The additional limit for those age 50 and older remains at $1,000. If, in the course of a marital dissolution, and IRA is awarded to a spouse or former spouse, the IRA owner can avoid tax on the transfer by retitling the account in the spouse's name or making a direct trustee-to-trustee transfer. A distribution followed by a transfer to the spouse is taxable to the owner.

Pitfalls

IRAs are designed to be long-term investments for you. Don't make contributions if you know you'll need the funds within a short time (say, this year or next); early withdrawals may trigger a tax penalty and possibly an investment-related penalty (such as bank charges for cashing in a certificate of deposit before maturity). Early distribution penalties and the exceptions to them are discussed next.

Also, use care in figuring how much you can put into the IRA each year and how much you may be required to withdraw annually. Again, there are penalties for putting in too much or taking out too little under certain circumstances (discussed later).

You cannot treat reinvestments in your IRA as additional contributions and claim a deduction for them. Dividend reinvestments are merely investment returns on your contributions.

EARLY DISTRIBUTION PENALTIES

If you need funds from your IRA before you retire, you may be subject to a 10% early distribution penalty. This penalty applies if you take money out before age $59\frac{1}{2}$, unless you meet one of the following exceptions to the penalty:

- You become disabled (or die and your heirs take out the money).
- You take the money in a series of substantially equal periodic payments. This essentially means you take withdrawals in even amounts for at least 5 years or until you attain age $59\frac{1}{2}$, whichever is later.
- You use the money to pay medical expenses exceeding 10% of your adjusted gross income.

- You are unemployed and receiving unemployment benefits for at least 12 consecutive weeks (or if you had been self-employed, you would have received such benefits due to lack of work).
- You use the money to pay higher education expenses (this exception to the 10% penalty is explained more fully in Chapter 3).
- You take out no more than $10,000 and use it to pay first-time home-buying expenses (this exception to the 10% penalty is explained more fully in Chapter 4).
- The IRS places levies on your IRA for back taxes.
- You are a reservist called to active duty.

There is no exception to the early distribution penalty for withdrawals on account of financial hardship (e.g., to pay your mortgage in order to keep your home out of foreclosure). There is no exception to the penalty for paying income taxes, even if this is done to avoid a levy on the IRA (which is a penalty exception).

EXCESS CONTRIBUTIONS PENALTY

If you are an active participant who contributed to an IRA but after the close of the year you find out your AGI is too high for a deductible contribution, you have several options to correct the contribution and avoid a 6% excise tax on excess contributions. The 6% excise tax applies each year until you correct the excess contribution.

You can treat the contributions as nondeductible IRA contributions. Alternatively, you can withdraw the excess contribution (plus any earnings on it) by the due date of your return (plus extensions). If you miss this deadline, you can limit the tax penalty to one year by withdrawing the excess by December 31 of the year following the year of the contribution.

Example

In 2017, you are 48 years old and an active participant in a qualified retirement plan. You anticipate your AGI for the year to be low enough to make a deductible IRA contribution. You contribute $5,500 to your IRA on November 15, 2017, intending to take a deduction for it on your 2017 return. In December you receive unexpected income (e.g., a year-end bonus, a large distribution from a mutual fund) that makes your AGI exceed the limit for making a deductible contribution in 2017. You can treat the contribution as a nondeductible IRA for 2017. You can withdraw the contribution (and earnings on it) by April 17, 2018, and avoid the penalty. You can withdraw the contribution (and earnings on it) by December 31, 2018; you'll owe the penalty for 2018.

If you contribute to an IRA but later determine that your income prevents you from claiming the IRA deduction reported on your return (for example, you are an active plan participant and a later IRS audit increases your MAGI above the phaseout range), you are subject to a 6% excise tax, called an excess contributions penalty. This tax continues to apply every year in which the excess contribution (and earnings on such contribution) remains in the IRA.

You can, however, designate that the excess contribution be treated as your IRA contribution in a subsequent year.

Example

In 2017, you deduct your $5,500 IRA contribution on your return. In 2019, the IRS audits your return and increases your MAGI to an amount that makes your contribution nondeductible. You were not eligible for a deductible contribution in 2018 but can make a fully deductible contribution in 2018. Designate the 2017 contribution as your 2019 deductible contribution to limit the 6% penalty to 2017 and 2018.

PENALTY FOR INSUFFICIENT WITHDRAWALS

Starting in the year in which you attain age 70$\frac{1}{2}$, you must take required minimum distributions (RMDs). If you don't take RMDs, you can be subject to a 50% penalty on the amount you failed to take. RMDs are based on IRS tables found in IRS Publication 590-B. Use the table in Appendix C that fits your situation:

- If you inherit an IRA (and you are not a spouse who made a rollover to your own IRA), then you must take RMDs based on Table I in Appendix C.
- If you are married and the beneficiary of your IRA is your spouse, who is more than 10 years younger than you, use Table II.
- All other IRA owners use Table III (uniform lifetime).

You are not limited, however, to RMDs and can withdraw more or all of the funds in the account at any time.

INVESTMENT LIMITATIONS

You can invest your IRA contributions in a wide array of investment vehicles, including certificates of deposit, stocks, bonds, and mutual funds. You can even invest in real estate if you avoid self-dealing and other prohibited transaction rules.

However, the law places certain limits on the types of things you can invest in. If you opt to invest in a prohibited vehicle, you are treated as having taken a distribution; you are taxed on the amount and, if under age 59$\frac{1}{2}$, subject to a

10% penalty. You are prohibited from putting your IRA money into collectibles, which include:

- Antiques
- Art works
- Coins (other than state-issued coins or certain U.S. minted gold, silver, or platinum coins)
- Gems
- Guns
- Metals (other than gold, silver, platinum, or palladium bullion held by your IRA trustee)
- Stamps

Technically, you are permitted to own realty in an IRA. However, you must do so through a self-directed IRA that permits such investment, and you cannot mortgage the property (IRAs are barred from any borrowing, as explained later).

Also, even though there is no law preventing you, it makes no sense to put IRA money into tax-exempt municipal bonds. Since the IRA is already tax deferred, you don't gain any benefit from the tax-free interest on the bonds. And when you take distributions from the IRA, they will all be treated as ordinary income (even though the underlying investment producing the earnings was tax-exempt bonds).

It may also be advisable to avoid foreign investments because foreign taxes paid from the IRA do not qualify for a deduction or credit; they only reduce the funds within the account.

BORROWING LIMITATIONS

You are prohibited from borrowing from your IRA or using it as collateral for a loan. If you do so, the amount borrowed or used as collateral is treated as a taxable distribution to you (and can be subject to penalty if you are under age 59½). If you take a loan from the IRA, the value of the entire account as of the first day of the year in which the loan is taken is includible in your income. If you pledge part of the account, that part of the account is includible in your income.

But you can have access to the funds for a short time without any adverse tax consequences. You can take a distribution and use it for 60 days; as long as the funds are replaced by the end of 60 days, there is no taxable distribution.

ACCOUNT LOSSES

If your investments turn out to be unsound and you lose money, you generally can't deduct the loss. For example, if you put $5,500 of your IRA money into a mutual fund that declines in value to $800, you cannot deduct your $4,700 loss, even if the IRA sells the fund.

The only way to deduct a loss with respect to an IRA is if you made nondeductible IRA contributions and then liquidate all of your IRAs or spend all of the funds. In this case, if the total amount you receive is less than what you contributed to the nondeductible IRA, you can claim a loss on your return for the year of liquidation or account depletion.

Where to Claim the Deduction

You deduct your IRA contributions in the "Adjusted Gross Income" section of Form 1040 or 1040A. No special form or schedule is required to report your deductible contribution. However, because the receipt of Social Security benefits in a year in which IRA contributions are made can impact the deductible amount, there is a special worksheet in IRS Publication 590 for figuring the IRA deduction in this case. You cannot claim an IRA deduction if you file Form 1040EZ.

If you are treating the contribution as a nondeductible IRA, you must complete Form 8606, *Nondeductible IRAs*. The purpose of this form is to help you keep track of your contributions so that when distributions are later taken, you won't pay tax on these after-tax contributions.

If you are subject to the 10% penalty on early withdrawals from the IRA, you must file Form 5329, *Additional Taxes on Qualified Plans (including IRAs) and Other Tax-Favored Accounts*, and enter the penalty in the "Other Taxes" section of Form 1040; you cannot file Form 1040A if you are subject to this penalty.

Roth IRAs

Roth IRAs (named after U.S. Senator William Roth, who sponsored the law) are an alternative personal retirement savings account that debuted in 1998. While these accounts offer no immediate tax break since contributions are not deductible, they offer long-term tax savings.

Benefit

You can contribute a limited amount to a special type of retirement savings account that allows you to build up tax-free income. (Contribution limits for Roth IRAs are the same as for deductible IRAs discussed earlier in this chapter.) While there is no current tax deduction for your contributions, you have access to your contributions and can withdraw them at any time tax free (after all, you made those contributions with after-tax dollars). But you can also withdraw earnings on those contributions tax free after 5 years if certain conditions discussed later are met.

CONVERSION

You can also convert your existing traditional IRA to a Roth IRA; there is no dollar limit on the amount you can convert. You must pay income tax on the account, just like you would if you had taken a distribution. But there's no 10% early distribution penalty if you are under age 59½ as long as the funds remain in the Roth IRA for at least 5 years. Income from 2017 conversions is reported in full on 2017 returns.

Conditions for Making Roth IRA Contributions

To be eligible to make contributions to a Roth IRA, you must meet 2 conditions:

1. You must have earned income (as explained earlier under traditional IRAs).
2. Your modified adjusted gross income (MAGI) cannot exceed a set limit.

MAGI LIMIT

Your MAGI in 2017 cannot be more than $118,000 if you are unmarried, or $186,000 if you are married filing jointly. A partial contribution is allowed if your MAGI is between $118,000 and $133,000 if you are unmarried, or $186,000 and $196,000 if you are married filing jointly. No contribution is permitted if your MAGI exceeds $133,000 if you are unmarried, or $196,000 if you are married filing jointly.

> ### Example
>
> You are single, age 40, with MAGI in 2017 of $75,000. You can contribute up to $5,500 to a Roth IRA in 2017. If your MAGI is over $133,000, no contribution is allowed, even if your company doesn't have any qualified retirement plan. If your MAGI falls within the phaseout range, you can make a partial contribution. You figure your allowable limit using Worksheet 5.1, adapted from IRS Publication 590-A.

This MAGI limit applies whether or not you participate in another qualified retirement plan.

One important condition that applies to traditional IRAs does not apply to Roth IRAs: There is no age limit for making contributions. If you continue to work past age 70½, you can continue to put money into a Roth IRA (assuming your MAGI is below the limit).

WORKSHEET 5.1 Reduced Roth IRA Contribution Limit for 2017

1. Enter your MAGI.	1. _____
2. Enter: • $186,000 if you file a joint return or are a qualifying widow(er). • $0 if you are married filing a separate return and you live with your spouse at any time during the year. • $118,000 for all other taxpayers.	2. _____
3. Subtract line 2 from line 1.	3. _____
4. Enter: • $10,000 if you file a joint return or are a qualifying widow(er). • $15,000 for all other taxpayers.	4. _____
5. Divide line 3 by line 4. Enter the result as a decimal (carried to 3 places). If the result is 1.000 or more, enter 1.000.	5. _____
6. Enter the lesser of: • $5,500 ($6,500 if 50 or older), or • Your taxable compensation.	6. _____
7. Multiply line 5 by line 6.	7. _____
8. Subtract line 7 from line 6. Round the result up to the nearest $10. If the result is less than $200, enter $200.	8. _____
9. Enter contributions for the year to other IRAs.	9. _____
10. Subtract line 9 from line 6.	10. _____
11. Enter the lesser of line 8 or line 10. *This is your reduced Roth IRA contribution limit.*	11. _____

Conditions for Converting a Traditional IRA or 401(k) to Roths

If you want the opportunity for your retirement savings to build up on a tax-free basis, consider converting your existing IRA, 401(k), or similar plan account to a Roth IRA or convert your 401(k) to a designated Roth account that is part of that plan. There are no adjusted gross income limits on eligibility to convert to a Roth IRA.

You can choose to convert some or all of your retirement plan account or IRAs at a time. Consider the impact that additional income from the conversion will have on the amount of Social Security benefits to be included in income if you receive such benefits or whether the additional income puts you into a higher tax bracket, subjects you to additional Medicare Parts B and D premiums, and, perhaps, makes you subject to the phaseout of itemized deductions and personal exemptions. You must report all of the resulting income on your 2017 return.

Conversions from traditional 401(k) plans to a designated Roth account (if the plan allows for such conversions) are called in-plan rollovers. However, they are essentially the same as conversions to Roth IRAs. The conversion amounts are currently taxable, with no early distribution penalty even if you are under age 59½ at the time of the conversion. But once you make an in-plan rollover, it cannot be undone (as can a conversion to a Roth IRA).

You cannot convert your required minimum distribution for the year; you must take it and then convert from the amount remaining in your account.

Conditions for Tax-Free Income Withdrawals

You can withdraw earnings on your contributions tax free after 5 years if you meet *any* of the following 3 conditions:

1. You are over age 59½.
2. You become disabled.
3. You withdraw no more than $10,000 and use the money for qualified first-time home-buying expenses. (Qualified first-time home-buying expenses are explained in Chapter 4.)

For contributory Roth IRAs, the 5-year period runs from the first day of the year to which your contributions relate. For example, if you contribute $5,000 to a Roth IRA for 2017 on April 17, 2018, the 5-year period commences on January 1, 2017. For Roth IRAs established through conversions, the 5-year period used to determine whether the 10% penalty applies if you are under age 59½ at the time of the conversion, the period starts on the first day of the year in which the conversion is made.

Example

On April 15, 2013, you contributed $4,000 to a Roth IRA for 2012. If you are at least 59½ in 2017, you can now withdraw the earnings you have built up in the account completely tax free—no income tax and no early distribution penalty. The 5-year period began on January 1, 2012. If, instead, you converted the Roth IRA on April 15, 2013, the 5-year period would have begun on January 1, 2013.

Planning Tips

The deadline for 2017 Roth IRA contributions is April 17, 2018. This is the same deadline for traditional IRAs discussed earlier in this chapter.

Assuming your income gives you the option of choosing between making a deductible IRA contribution or a nondeductible Roth IRA contribution, which alternative makes more sense for you? In most cases, choosing to make the Roth

IRA contribution is wiser because the value of the IRA deduction you are forgoing is much smaller than the value of receiving tax-free income from the Roth IRA in the future.

Example

You are eligible to make either a deductible IRA contribution or a Roth IRA contribution. Assuming you are in the 28% tax bracket, a $5,500 deduction to a deductible IRA would save you $1,540 this year. But let's also assume that a $5,500 contribution can quadruple in the next 25 years to $22,000 (of which $16,500 is earnings on your contribution). If you opt for the Roth IRA, then when you withdraw the funds (assuming you are over age 59½), you won't pay any income tax on the earnings—a $4,620 tax savings if you are still in the 28% tax bracket.

Survivors of military personnel who died from injuries on or after June 17, 2008, can contribute the proceeds from Servicemembers' Group Life Insurance (SGLI) to a Roth IRA without regard to the annual contribution limit and without regard to the MAGI limit. This contribution is treated as a rollover contribution and must be made no later than one year after receipt of the SGLI proceeds.

Should you convert an existing traditional IRA or 401(k) plan account to a Roth IRA? There is no fixed answer; it depends on your situation. Factors to consider are your age (the younger you are, the longer you will have to build up tax-free income, but there is no age limit on making a conversion); your income (the more modest your income, the less the tax on the conversion); and whether you have the funds to pay the tax resulting from the conversion. If you decide you want to convert your 401(k) or similar account to a Roth IRA, be sure to do so using a direct rollover (the plan administrator will transfer the funds directly to your Roth IRA) so you avoid the mandatory 20% withholding tax that applies to qualified retirement plan distributions.

Contributions you make to a designated Roth account within a 401(k) plan have no impact on your ability to contribute to a Roth IRA. For example, say in 2017, you contribute $18,000 to a designated Roth account 401(k) within your employer's plan (you're not 50 years old or older). You can also contribute $5,500 to a Roth IRA (assuming your income does not exceed the limits).

Making a Roth IRA conversion for the year does not automatically prevent you from also making a Roth IRA contribution if you are otherwise eligible to do so. Of course, income resulting from the conversion can impact your eligibility by increasing your MAGI.

This decision to convert isn't an all-or-nothing proposition. You can convert part of your IRA to a Roth IRA. In fact, you can do this every year in which you are eligible to make a conversion.

Pitfalls

You should have the cash on hand to pay the tax resulting from the conversion. If you convert part of an IRA and use part of it to pay the tax, the portion used to pay the tax cannot later be placed in the Roth IRA. In effect, you lose out on an important retirement savings opportunity. What's more, if you are under age 59½, the portion used to pay the tax is subject to a 10% penalty.

Example

In 2017, when you are 40 years old, you opt to convert your $100,000 IRA to a Roth IRA. Assuming you are in the 28% tax bracket, the conversion costs you $28,000. If you use $28,000 of the $100,000 to pay the tax, then you have only $72,000 in your Roth IRA. And the $28,000 not converted to the Roth IRA is subject to a 10% penalty, for an additional tax of $2,800.

Don't confuse a Roth IRA with a Roth 401(k) (called a designated Roth account). The rules for a designated Roth account are separate and distinct from the rules for a Roth IRA.

Where to Claim the Benefit

You do not report contributions you make to a Roth IRA on your return (remember, they are not deductible). It does not matter which income tax return—Form 1040, 1040A, or 1040EZ—you file.

If you convert your traditional IRA to a Roth IRA, you must report the income resulting from the conversion in the "Income" section of Form 1040 or Form 1040A. You cannot file Form 1040EZ to report a conversion. If you use a portion of your IRA to pay the tax on the conversion and are subject to the 10% penalty on this amount, you must file Form 5329, *Additional Taxes on Qualified Retirement Plans (Including IRAs) and Other Tax Favored Accounts*, and enter the penalty in the "Other Taxes" section of Form 1040; you cannot file Form 1040A if you are subject to this penalty.

If you make excess contributions to the Roth IRA (by contribution or conversion), you are subject to a 6% excise tax and must file Form 5329, *Additional Taxes on Qualified Plans (Including IRAs) and Other Tax-Favored Accounts*. Enter the excise tax in the "Other Taxes" section of Form 1040; you cannot file Form 1040A if you are subject to this tax.

IRA Rollovers

IRAs are highly portable—they can be transferred from one investment company to another with no immediate tax consequences if certain conditions are met. This allows taxpayers to move accounts from a bank to a mutual fund or from one brokerage firm to another.

Benefit ⊗

You can transfer funds from one IRA to another without any current tax. There are no dollar limits on the amount you can roll over each year.

There are 2 ways in which to make the transfer:

1. *Direct transfers.* You can instruct the custodian or trustee of your IRA to transfer funds directly to the custodian or trustee of another IRA.
2. *Distribution and reinvestment.* You can take a withdrawal of funds from your IRA and replace the funds within 60 days.

Conditions

The transfer method you use determines the conditions you must meet to achieve tax-free treatment.

DIRECT TRANSFERS

You instruct the custodian or trustee of your IRAs to complete the action; you cannot receive any funds that are part of the transfer. There is no time requirement for your fiduciaries to complete the transaction. There is no limit on the number of direct transfers you can make each year.

DISTRIBUTION AND REINVESTMENT

You must complete the transaction within 60 days. Generally, the IRS cannot extend this period. But you may qualify for a waiver of the 60-day deadline in limited circumstances detailed later under "Pitfalls."

You are permitted to make only one rollover per 12-month period (this rule is called the one-rollover-per-year rule even though technically it's a 12-month period). This rule applies per taxpayer, so only one rollover can be made within the period, regardless of how many separate IRA accounts you may have.

Note: Regardless of which method you select, rollovers are handled separately from annual contributions to IRAs and Roth IRAs. Thus, for example, you may make a rollover even if you also make a deductible IRA contribution for the year.

Planning Tips

You can use funds in your IRA as a short-term loan. While borrowing against an IRA is not permitted, you can take a distribution and avoid current tax if you replace the funds within 60 days.

If you try to complete the rollover on time but outside events prevent you from doing so, you may be able to obtain an extension to the 60-day limit. The limit is automatically extended if the account is frozen, if you are serving in a combat zone, are in a federal disaster area, or a victim of terrorist or military action. The limit is also extended if you meet all of the following conditions:

1. You were not previously denied a waiver request for a rollover by the IRS.
2. Your reason for missing the 60-day deadline is one of the following:
   - Your financial institution made an error.
   - You misplaced the distribution check and never cashed it.
   - You deposited the distribution in an account you thought was an eligible retirement plan.
   - Your principal residence was severely damaged.
   - A member of your family died.
   - A member of your family was seriously ill.
   - You were incarcerated.
   - You were subject to restrictions imposed by a foreign country.
   - There was a postal error.
   - The distribution was made on account of an IRS levy and the proceeds have been returned to you.
   - The party making the distribution delayed providing information required by the receiving plan or IRA despite your best efforts to obtain it.
3. You complete the rollover as soon as practical. There is a 30-day safe harbor, which means doing so within 30-days after the occurrence of the condition that prevented the rollover.

If you qualify for this self-certification, send a written letter to the plan administrator or IRA trustee stating that you satisfy the conditions for relief. There's a sample letter for this purpose in the Appendix to Revenue Procedure 2016–47.

Even if you can't use the self-certification process, you may still obtain relief for missing the 60-day rollover deadline in some situations. For example, the Tax Court allowed more time for a person suffering from depression to complete a rollover.

Pitfall

If you take a distribution and plan to reinvest within 60 days, make sure to watch the calendar closely. If you miss the deadline by even one day (and don't qualify for relief explained earlier), the entire distribution becomes taxable to you.

Where to Claim the Benefit

IRA rollovers that are distributed to you are reported to you (and the IRS) on Form 1099-R, *Distributions from Pensions, Annuities, Retirement or Profit-Sharing Plans, IRAs, Insurance Contracts, Etc.*

You must report the distribution on your return, but if you successfully completed the transfer within 60 days, enter only zero on the income line for IRA distributions in the "Income" section of Form 1040 or Form 1040A. You cannot file Form 1040EZ in this case.

MyRAs

By Presidential memorandum, MyRAs were created in 2014 to give low- and moderate-income workers a retirement savings option if there is no qualified retirement plan at their place of employment. Think of MyRAs as mini-Roth IRAs in terms of nondeductible contributions and tax-free distribution treatment. The Treasury announced in mid-2017 that it was phasing out the MyRA program due to lack of demand. Since the program stated, only about 30,000 people set up accounts, and only 20,000 actually funded them. When this book was prepared, some details about the phaseout were not yet released. Check the Supplement for any updates.

Here is what is known so far about the phaseout of MyRAs.

- MyRA accounts that were opened but had a zero balance as of September 15, 2017, were automatically closed. No further action on the part of the owner is required.

- If you have been funding a MyRA with payroll withholding, notify your employers to end withholding. (The Treasury has yet to provide specific dates for this action.)

- If you have been funding a MyRA with direct deposits from your bank, you do not have to take any action. The Treasury will notify your bank to stop any debits of funds.

- You are advised to begin shopping around for Roth IRA providers. The funds in the MyRA can be transferred to a bank, brokerage firm, mutual fund, or other financial institution that acts as a custodian or trustee for Roth IRAs. Once the Roth IRA is opened, funds in the MyRA can be transferred directly to the new account with no taxation to you. Alternatively, you can take a distribution and avoid immediate tax by rolling it over to the new account within 60 days.

401(k) and Similar Plans

Pensions used to be the responsibility of employers, but for the past quarter of a century that responsibility has shifted to employees. To make it easier for employees to pay for their own retirement savings, the tax law has created special retirement plans. Companies set up the plans, but employees fund them (in whole or in part) by contributing a portion of their salary each year. Employees decide how their contributions are to be invested by selecting from a menu of investment options provided by the employer. The tax law encourages employee contributions by allowing them to escape immediate taxation.

Benefit

If you are eligible to participate in your employer's 401(k) or similar plan, you can agree each year to contribute a portion of your salary as your contribution to the plan. You can change your contribution from year to year; you may also be able to reduce it within a year.

Your contribution is called an elective deferral or salary reduction amount. This amount is *not* treated as compensation to you for the year; you do not pay income tax on your elective deferral (you do pay Social Security and Medicare taxes on the elective deferral). For example, if your wages this year are $45,000 and you contribute $8,000 to your company's 401(k) plan, only $37,000 of your wages for purposes of income taxes is reported on your Form W-2; you only pay income taxes on $37,000 this year.

Note: Contributions to a designated Roth account within a 401(k) plan are not treated as elective deferrals; they must be made with after-tax contributions. A designated Roth account is similar but not identical to a Roth IRA.

Conditions

Eligibility requirements to make elective deferrals are spelled out in your company's plan. You should receive a summary of the plan from your employer and be given an opportunity to designate your elective deferrals for the year (typically within a month or so before the start of a new year or upon becoming eligible to participate in your company's plan).

ELECTIVE DEFERRAL LIMITS

The law fixes the *maximum* elective deferral limits for each year. Your plan may place other restrictions or limits on how much you can contribute annually to the plan.

The law allows you to contribute up to 100% of your earnings to the plan, up to a dollar limit on contributions. For 2017, the dollar limit is $18,000 (or $24,000 if you are age 50 or older by the end of 2017).

Example

In 2017, you are 28 years old and earn $30,000. Your maximum contribution is $18,000 (although your plan may restrict contributions to a percentage of your compensation).

Planning Tips

If you are pressed for funds and find it difficult to take full advantage of the elective deferral opportunity, at least contribute what is necessary to obtain your employer's matching contribution if available. Your employer's matching contribution is, in effect, "free money" to you, and it would be unwise to ignore it.

Example

In 2017, you are permitted under the plan to contribute $18,000 through elective deferrals. Your employer will match 50% of your contributions up to 6% of your compensation. If you earn $30,000, you must contribute at least $3,600 to obtain your employer's top contribution on your behalf of $1,800.

If you are self-employed and have no employees, you can set up a solo 401(k) to maximize your retirement plan contributions. You effectively make both employee and employer contributions (even though you are self-employed). This means you can contribute a total of up to $55,000 ($60,000 if you are age 50 or older by the end of 2017).

401(k) plans can offer a designated Roth option. If your plan allows it, you can choose to make after-tax contributions to a designated Roth account so that withdrawals can become tax free (like withdrawals from Roth IRAs). Contributions to a traditional and/or designated Roth cannot exceed the annual limit (which is $18,000, or $24,000 for those age 50 or older by December 31, 2017). You can choose to split your contribution between a regular 401(k) and a designated Roth account—for example, $10,000 to a regular 401(k) and $8,000 to a designated Roth account; total contributions cannot exceed annual limits.

Keep in mind that taxes are only the tail that wags the investment dog. If you have a 401(k), be sure to monitor investment performance as well as fees for investment choices to optimize your retirement savings.

Pitfalls

Once you have made your elective deferral contributions, access to your money is limited by the terms of the plan and the tax law. Generally, you can't receive the funds until you retire from the company. However, you may be permitted to withdraw funds. There is a 10% penalty for distributions before age 59½ unless a penalty exception applies. Exceptions include:

- Death
- Disability
- Series of substantially equal periodic payments
- Payments under a qualified domestic relations order (QDRO)

- Payment of unreimbursed medical expenses exceeding your applicable AGI threshold
- Separation from service during or after the year you become age 55 (age 50 for public safety employees)
- Certain distributions to qualified military reservists called to active duty
- IRS levy

You may be able to borrow from the plan or take a "hardship distribution." These withdrawal options are discussed in Chapter 12.

Even though you are not taxed on your elective deferral amount (it is subtracted from your taxable compensation), such amount is still subject to Social Security and Medicare taxes, which are withheld from your pay.

Where to Claim the Benefit

You do not have to report anything on your tax return. You will note that your elective deferral amount is subtracted from your pay so that only the reduced amount is reported as taxable compensation to you on Form W-2, which you then report as wages on whichever tax return you file (Form 1040, 1040A, or 1040EZ).

Self-Employed Retirement Plans

In 1962, self-employed individuals for the first time were given the opportunity to set up tax-qualified retirement plans similar to those available to corporations. Initially referred to as HR 10 plans (after the number of the tax bill creating them) or Keogh plans (after the senator sponsoring the bill), these plans have evolved over the years into the same retirement savings plans as are open to corporations. The tax law today calls them self-employed retirement plans.

Benefit 🔼

If you are a sole proprietor or independent contractor and have a profitable year, you can contribute to a qualified retirement plan. There are 2 main types of plans:

1. *Defined contribution plan.* The funds you have on retirement are based solely on what you've contributed and how well your investments have performed. A profit-sharing plan is a defined contribution plan.
2. *Defined benefit plan.* At retirement, you receive a pension based on your earnings (each year before retirement your contribution is determined by an actuary to be sufficient to pay this pension at a specific age, assuming a certain return on your investments).

WORKSHEET 5.2 Figuring Your 2017 Contribution to a Defined Contribution Plan

1. Enter your net earnings from self-employment.	1. _____
2. Enter your deduction for self-employment tax (employer equivalent portion of the tax).	2. _____
3. Subtract line 2 from line 1.	3. _____
4. Enter your effective contribution rate (no more than 20%).	4. _____
5. Multiply line 3 by line 4.	5. _____
6. Multiply $270,000 by your actual contribution rate (no more than 25%).	6. _____
7. Enter the smaller of line 5 or line 6.	7. _____
8. Contribution dollar limit.	8. $54,000
9. Enter the smaller of line 7 or line 8. *This is your contribution.*	9. _____

You claim a deduction for your contribution. For a defined contribution plan in 2017, you can deduct 25% of compensation or $54,000, whichever is less. However, for self-employed individuals, net earnings from self-employment (the figure on which contributions are based) must be reduced by the contribution itself, so that the effective contribution rate is only 20% (not 25%). Also, you must reduce your net earnings from self-employment by the employer equivalent portion of your self-employment taxes. It may sound complicated to figure your allowable deduction, but you can use Worksheet 5.2, adapted from IRS Publication 560, to guide you (if you use tax preparation software, this is done automatically for you).

For a defined benefit plan, your deduction is based on what is actuarially required to fund the promised pension. You need the actuary to tell you what your contribution is, based on plan assumptions (e.g., at what age you expect to retire).

Conditions

There are many conditions for starting and maintaining a qualified retirement plan. Some are highly complex and well beyond the scope of this book. But here are some things to watch out for:

- The plan must be set up before the end of the year. Even though you have until the due date of your return (including extensions) to make contributions, the plan must be in existence (you must sign the paperwork) before the end of the year.

Example

In 2017, you are self-employed and profitable. You want to contribute to a profit-sharing plan for the year. You must set up the plan by December 31, 2017. You have until April 17, 2018, (or later if you obtain a filing extension) to actually put your contribution into the plan.

- You must cover employees if they meet certain requirements. This raises the cost of having a plan. But you deduct contributions on behalf of your employees from your business income, reducing your net earnings from self-employment.
- You *may* have to file an annual information return with the U.S. Department of Labor. Generally, all qualified plans must file an information return, even if you are the only plan participant. However, if assets at the end of the plan are no more than $250,000, you don't have to file anything if you (or you and your spouse) are the only participants. A simplified annual return is used for plans covering fewer than 25 participants.

Example

In 2017, you have net earnings from self-employment (your profits on Schedule C) of $80,000 and your plan sets a contribution limit of 25%. Your contribution for 2017 on your behalf is $14,870, figured as follows:

1. Enter your net earnings from self-employment.	1.	$80,000
2. Enter your deduction for self-employment tax (employer equivalent portion of the tax).	2.	5,652
3. Subtract line 2 from line 1.	3.	74,348
4. Enter your effective contribution rate (no more than 20%).	4.	20%
5. Multiply line 3 by line 4.	5.	$14,870
6. Multiply $270,000 by your actual contribution rate (no more 20%, which is the plan contribution limit of 25%).	6.	54,000
7. Enter the smaller of line 5 or line 6.	7.	14,870
8. Contribution dollar limit.	8.	$54,000
9. Enter the smaller of line 7 or line 8. *This is your contribution.*	9.	$14,870

Planning Tip

You may want to consult with a benefits expert to help you decide which type of retirement plan is best for you, based on your profitability, age, the nature of your business, and other factors, including your desire to optimize contributions.

Pitfalls

Having a qualified retirement plan means you are subject to annual reporting requirements referred to earlier; the government wants to know some details about your plan.

Generally, for the 2017 plan year, you must file Form 5500-EZ, *Annual Return of One Participant (Owners and Their Spouses)*. But you are exempt from filing if you have a one-participant plan (the only participant is you or your spouse) and plan assets at the end of the year do not exceed $250,000. However, a return must be filed for the final year of a plan, even if assets are below the $250,000 limit.

If you are required to file, you cannot download the form from the Internet like most other tax forms because Form 5500-EZ is a scannable form that must be obtained by mail or at an IRS office. Usually it is sent to you automatically if you have filed one in the past; otherwise, you can request one from the IRS by calling 800-829-FORM. One-participant plans may file Form 5500-SF electronically in place of a paper-only Form 5500-EZ.

Either way, the form usually must be filed under the ERISA Filing Acceptance System (EFAST2) (www.efast.dol.gov). The form is due by the last day of the seventh month following the close of the plan year (e.g., July 31, 2018, for the 2017 year of a calendar-year plan). You can obtain an automatic extension to October 15, 2018 (the same extended due date for federal income tax returns on extension) by filing Form 5558, *Application for Extension of Time To File Certain Employee Plan Returns*. If you obtain an automatic extension of time to file your 2017 income tax return, then you don't have to file Form 5558; you get an automatic extension for your Form 5500-EZ to October 15, 2018, as long as you and your plan have the same taxable year (retain a copy of Form 4868 used to obtain the income tax filing extension with your records for your qualified retirement plan).

If you are delinquent in filing Form 5500-EZ, you may obtain relief from penalties that would otherwise apply. Follow the steps in Revenue Procedure 2015–32.

Where to Claim the Benefit

You deduct contributions to the plan for your employees on Schedule C (such contributions are a business expense). You deduct your own contributions in the section for "Adjusted Gross Income" on Form 1040. No special form or schedule is required for figuring your deduction.

You cannot deduct contributions if you file Form 1040A or 1040EZ.

SEPs

A simplified employee pension (SEP) is a type of IRA that any business, whether self-employed or incorporated, can use for retirement savings. It is "simplified" because it is easy to set up and there are few administrative requirements (for example, there is no annual reporting to the government as is the case with most other company-sponsored retirement plans). The business sets up the plan and makes tax-deductible contributions to participant accounts.

Benefit

If you are self-employed (sole proprietor, independent contractor, partner, or limited liability company member) and have a profitable year, you can make deductible contributions to a simplified employee pension plan, or SEP. This is a type of IRA to which you can contribute more to than a traditional IRA. The same rules that apply to sole proprietors also apply to partners and LLC members.

You claim a deduction for the contribution on your behalf as an adjustment to gross income (not as a business expense). For 2017, the top deduction is 25% of your compensation or $54,000, whichever is less. Compensation if you are self-employed means your net earnings from self-employment, reduced by the employer equivalent portion of self-employment tax and by the contribution for yourself; your effective percentage rate becomes 20% in this case.

Example

In 2017, you are a consultant (sole proprietor) and have net earnings from self-employment of $50,000 (after reduction for the employer equivalent portion of self-employment tax). Your maximum deductible contribution is $10,000 ($50,000 × 20%).

Unlike qualified retirement plans, there is no annual reporting requirement for SEPs.

Conditions

You must meet 2 conditions to deduct your SEP contributions:

1. You must have profits if you are self-employed or receive a salary if you are an S corporation.
2. You must include your employees within the plan if they (1) are at least age 21, (2) earn more than $600 in 2017, and (3) have worked for you at least 3 of the past 5 years. If they are included in the plan, you must make contributions on their behalf based on their compensation.

Even though a SEP is a type of IRA, you can continue to make contributions on your behalf beyond the age of 70½ as long as you continue to work. However, you must still commence your required minimum distributions at age 70½ (even though you are still working). You cannot postpone taking distributions until retirement because you own more than 5% of the business.

Planning Tips

If you failed to set up a qualified retirement plan by the end of the year, you can still set up and contribute to a SEP up to the extended due date of your return.

Example

You are an independent contractor in 2017 but did not set up a profit-sharing plan before the end of the year. You can set up and make your contributions to a SEP through April 17, 2018, or if you obtain an automatic 6-month filing extension for your 2017 return, to October 16, 2018.

You can convert a SEP to a Roth IRA if you meet the eligibility requirements discussed earlier in this chapter. Conversion allows all future earnings on the money to become tax free when you take withdrawals from the Roth IRA (but you must now pay a tax on the converted amount).

Pitfall

You cannot contribute to a SEP if you also have a self-employed qualified retirement plan; you must choose which plan is more favorable to you. Excess contributions are subject to the same penalties discussed earlier under IRAs.

Where to Claim the Benefit

You deduct contributions to the plan for your employees on Schedule C (such contributions are a business expense). You deduct your own contributions in the section for "Adjusted Gross Income" on Form 1040. No special form or schedule is required to figure your deduction.

You cannot deduct contributions if you file Form 1040A or 1040EZ.

SIMPLEs

Savings incentive match plans for employees, or SIMPLEs, are a type of retirement plan that allows businesses to share the cost of funding retirement savings. The company sets up the plan and employees are given the option of contributing, within set limits, a portion of their salaries to the plan. The company must make certain contributions according to a formula fixed by the tax law. The reason this type of retirement plan is SIMPLE lies in the ease of setting it up and administering it.

Benefit ⬆

If you are self-employed or a shareholder in a corporation, the business can set up a SIMPLE plan that allows you (and your employees) to make elective deferrals (salary reduction contributions) to the plan. Such amounts are excluded from your income. As an employer, you must contribute a set amount for each plan participant; you deduct your employer contribution as a business expense.

Whether you are the owner of the business or merely a rank-and-file employee, you can make elective deferral contributions to the plan. Like 401(k) plans discussed earlier, the portion of your compensation that you treat as your elective deferral is not included in your income for the year. (Limits on elective deferrals and required employer contributions are explained next under "Conditions.")

Earnings on contributions build up on a tax-deferred basis.

A SIMPLE can be set up as either a SIMPLE-IRA or a SIMPLE-401(k) plan. For purposes of the following discussion, only the SIMPLE-IRA, the more popular type, is examined.

Conditions

There are only 2 key conditions for setting up a SIMPLE plan:

1. You must be a "small employer." You must have had 100 or fewer employees who received $5,000 or more in compensation from you in the preceding year. If you set up the plan but in a later year exceed the 100-employee limit, you have 2 more years to continue the SIMPLE plan; after 2 years, you no longer qualify for a SIMPLE plan because you are no longer a small employer. You can also set up a plan if you are self-employed (even though you don't have any employees).

2. You do not maintain any other qualified plan. If, for example, you already have a profit-sharing plan, you can't also have a SIMPLE plan.

ELECTIVE DEFERRAL LIMIT

Whether you are the owner of the business or just an ordinary employee who is eligible to participate, you can agree to contribute a portion of your annual compensation to the SIMPLE plan. Your contribution, or elective deferral amount, is limited in 2017 to $12,500, or $15,500 if you are age 50 or older by the end of 2017. However, your contribution cannot exceed 100% of your compensation.

In 2017, you are under age 50; you can contribute $12,500 whether your wages are $12,500, $30,000, or even $100,000. You can contribute up to 100% of your compensation, but no more than $12,500.

REQUIRED EMPLOYER CONTRIBUTION

Like other retirement plans, you must meet certain nondiscrimination requirements; your plan cannot favor you as the owner and other highly paid employees. However, SIMPLE plans don't have any complicated nondiscrimination formulas. Instead, if you make the required employer contribution on behalf of each employee who is eligible to participate, your plan is viewed as nondiscriminatory.

You must adopt one of these 2 contribution formulas and make contributions accordingly:

1. Employer matching contribution on a dollar-for-dollar basis
2. Nonelective contributions of 2% of compensation

In an employer matching contribution arrangement, you match employee contributions on a dollar-for-dollar basis up to 3% of employee compensation. If an employee does not make an elective deferral, you do not have to contribute anything on behalf of the employee.

Example

Your employee makes an elective deferral contribution to the SIMPLE of $5,000. Her annual compensation is $40,000. You must contribute $1,200 on behalf of this employee (matching her contribution of $5,000 up to 3% of $40,000).

Example

You make an elective deferral of $12,500, the maximum permitted in 2017. Your compensation is $420,000. Your matching contribution in this case is $12,500 (matching your contribution of $12,500, which is less than 3% of $420,000, or $12,600).

If the formula requires nonelective contributions of 2% of compensation, these contributions must be made without regard to any employee elective deferrals. Thus, even if the employee makes no elective deferral, you must still contribute 2% on the employee's behalf if the employee is eligible to participate in the SIMPLE plan. No more than $270,000 of compensation can be taken into account in figuring nonelective contributions.

Example

Your employee makes an elective deferral contribution to the SIMPLE of $5,000. Her annual compensation is $40,000. You must contribute $800 (2% of $40,000).

Example

You make an elective deferral of $12,500, the maximum permitted in 2017. Your compensation is $280,000. Your nonelective contribution in this case is $5,300 (2% of $265,000).

Planning Tips

SIMPLEs may enable you to make the largest contribution possible (compared with self-employed retirement plans and SEPs) if your self-employment income is modest. SIMPLEs may also be the most cost-effective plan to use if you have employees. Discuss your retirement plan options with a benefits expert.

If you have made contributions to a SIMPLE-IRA, you can convert it to a Roth IRA (see earlier in this chapter). But you must wait at least 2 years following the contribution to make the conversion or be subject to a 25% early distribution penalty if you are under age 59½.

The basic limit ($12,500) and the additional limit for those age 50 and older ($3,000) can be adjusted annually for inflation.

Pitfalls

Distributions from SIMPLE-IRAs before age 59½ are subject to a higher early distribution penalty than the penalty imposed on traditional IRAs. Instead of the usual 10% early distribution penalty, you may be subject to a penalty of 25% for distributions within 2 years of SIMPLE-IRA participation if you are under age 59½.

Where to Claim the Deduction

You deduct contributions to the plan for your employees on Schedule C of Form 1040 (such contributions are a business expense). You deduct your own contributions in the section of Form 1040 marked "Adjusted Gross Income." You do not have to complete any form or schedule to claim the deduction.

You cannot deduct contributions to a SIMPLE if you file Form 1040A or 1040EZ.

Retirement Saver's Credit

A worker's wages just don't seem to stretch far enough to pay the bills *and* save for retirement. The tax law tries to encourage those having the most difficulty—low-income taxpayers—to make retirement plan contributions by offering a special tax credit. Those qualifying for this credit also enjoy other tax benefits from making the contributions, such as a deduction for IRA contributions. This is one of the few instances in the tax law where you get to "double dip" with a tax deduction or exclusion, plus a tax credit, for the same action (your retirement plan contribution). At the end of the road, taxpayers taking advantage of these breaks have not only enjoyed current tax savings but have also built up their personal retirement savings.

Benefit ✚

If you contribute to a retirement plan through your company or to an IRA, you may be eligible to claim a tax credit of up to 50% of contributions up to $2,000, for a top credit of $1,000. This credit is in addition to any other benefit to which you may be entitled, such as salary reduction for a 401(k) plan contribution or a deduction for an IRA contribution.

Conditions

There are 3 conditions for claiming the retirement saver's credit. In order to claim the credit you must:

1. Have qualified retirement savings contributions for the year
2. Be an eligible individual
3. Have adjusted gross income below a set amount

QUALIFIED RETIREMENT SAVINGS CONTRIBUTIONS

Retirement savings can come from several sources; you total your contributions to all of the following:

- IRA contributions (whether they are deductible or nondeductible)
- Roth IRA contributions
- MyRA contributions

- Elective deferrals (salary reduction contributions) to 401(k) plans, 403(b) annuities, or 457 plans
- Voluntary contributions to any qualified retirement plan of your employer

You must reduce your qualified contributions and elective deferrals by distributions included in your income that you receive from any qualified retirement plan of your employer or from a deferred compensation plan of your employer (if your employer is a state or local government or tax-exempt organization). You must also reduce your qualified contributions and elective deferrals by distributions from Roth IRAs during the 5 years following your contributions to such accounts or from a rollover to a Roth IRA. You must include not only distributions in the current year, but also those made in the 2 preceding years and in the period after the year for which you are figuring the credit up to the due date of the return (including extensions).

Example

You want to claim the retirement saver's credit for 2017. In determining your eligible contributions and elective deferrals for 2017, you must look to distributions taken in 2015 and 2016, plus any distributions you take in 2017 and up to April 17, 2018, (assuming you file your return by this deadline).

You don't have to reduce your qualified contributions and elective deferrals by the following distributions:

- Amounts treated as loans from a qualified plan
- Excess contributions
- Deductions for dividends paid on certain employer securities
- Contributions returned to you before the due date of your return
- IRA accounts rolled over to a Roth IRA

ELIGIBLE INDIVIDUAL

To be eligible to claim the credit you must:

- Be at least 18 years old by the close of the year. Thus, even though someone who is 14 can contribute to an IRA, he or she isn't old enough to claim this credit.
- Not be claimed as a dependent on another taxpayer's return.
- Not be a full-time student (someone who is enrolled full time for at least 5 calendar months during the year).

TABLE 5.2 MAGI Limits in 2017 for Retirement Saver's Credit

Modified Adjusted Gross Income						Applicable Percentage
Joint Return		Head of Household		All Others		
Over	Not Over	Over	Not Over	Over	Not Over	
$ 0	$37,000	$ 0	$27,750	$ 0	$18,500	50%
37,000	40,000	27,500	30,000	18,500	20,000	20
40,000	62,000	30,000	46,500	20,000	31,000	10
62,000		46,500		31,000		0

MAGI LIMIT

To claim the top credit, your modified adjusted gross income must be below a set amount. If your MAGI is more modest, you may be entitled to a smaller credit. No credit can be claimed if your MAGI in 2017 exceeds a set limit, detailed in Table 5.2. MAGI for this purpose is your adjusted gross income increased by the foreign earned income exclusion, the foreign housing exclusion, or the exclusion for income from U.S. possessions or Puerto Rico.

Example

In 2017, you are single with MAGI of $26,000. Your elective deferral to your company's 401(k) plan for the year is $3,000. You may claim a tax credit of $200 (10% of $2,000, the maximum contribution taken into account in figuring the credit).

Planning Tip

The credit can be claimed in addition to other benefits that contributions entitle you to. For example, even though you excluded your 401(k) plan contributions from income, you can still claim the credit with respect to those same contributions. Similarly, even though you deducted your IRA contributions, you can also base the credit on the same contributions.

Pitfalls

Even though you meet all conditions for claiming the credit, you may lose out on the opportunity to use it if you claim certain other credits that offset your tax liability. The retirement saver's credit cannot be in excess of your regular tax liability, plus your alternative minimum tax liability, reduced by the sum of all credits to which you may also be entitled other than the child tax credit, the adoption credit, and the foreign tax credit. You cannot receive a refund from the retirement saver's credit, and you cannot carry forward the unused amount to a future year.

Lower-income individuals who qualify for the 50% credit may not have sufficient tax liability to use the entire credit (even assuming they can afford to make retirement plan contributions). For example, a married couple with MAGI of $30,000 is entitled to a maximum credit of $1,000 (50% of $2,000). However, their tax liability is only $920 (10% of [$30,000 MAGI – $12,700 standard deduction – $8,100 for 2 exemptions]).

Where to Claim the Credit

To claim the retirement saver's credit, you must file Form 1040; you cannot claim this credit if you file Form 1040A or Form 1040EZ.

You figure the credit on Form 8880, *Credit for Qualified Retirement Savings Contributions*, which you attach to the return. You enter the amount of your credit in the "Tax and Credits" section of Form 1040.

Custodial/Trustee Fees

Having an IRA isn't necessarily free—there may be charges for maintaining an account with a brokerage firm or mutual fund that acts as the IRA's custodian or trustee. Following the imposition of the Department of Labor's "fiduciary rule" on June 9, 2017, which requires investment advisors to act in your best interest, many financial institutions have begun to charge a fee based on a percentage of the value of assets in the account (e.g., 1% or more; lower for "robo advisors" providing computerized plans but no investment advice). Some firms, however, continue to charge only for trades that you make in the account. Fortunately, these fees may be deductible if certain conditions are met.

Benefit ⊜

You can deduct your payments of custodial or trustee fees to maintain your IRA. There is no dollar limit on what you can deduct.

This deduction is claimed as a miscellaneous itemized deduction, which is subject to a 2% floor (only miscellaneous expenses over 2% of your adjusted gross income are deductible). You cannot claim this deduction if you use the standard deduction.

Conditions

You must pay the custodial or trustee fees directly. You cannot have them debited from your IRA account.

Planning Tip

Since you must pay the custodial or trustee fees directly in order to claim a deduction, talk to your custodian or trustee to make sure the fees are separately billed to you and not automatically debited from the account. For example, if you're charged a flat fee for having a managed account at a brokerage firm, ask that you be billed for this fee. Payment by check will ensure that you have adequate proof for your deduction.

Pitfall

As a practical matter, you may not obtain any tax benefit from the payment of custodial or trustee fees. If your miscellaneous itemized deductions, including the payment of IRA custodial fees, are not more than 2% of your adjusted gross income, then you cannot use the deductible expense. But if you pay the fees separately rather than having them deducted from your IRA, then at least the IRA fund will not be diminished by the fees.

Where to Claim the Deduction

You claim the deduction as a miscellaneous itemized deduction on Schedule A of Form 1040. Note in the "Miscellaneous Deductions" section of Schedule A (or on a separate statement attached to the schedule) that your expense is "custodial/trustee fees." You do not have to complete any other form or schedule to claim this deduction.

You cannot claim the deduction for custodial fees if you file Form 1040A or Form1040EZ.

Employer-Paid Retirement Planning Advice

Retirement planning is a difficult and confusing subject. Employees nearing the end of their careers often must make important decisions regarding their company retirement plans and their personal retirement savings in order to maximize their retirement income and minimize their taxes. Companies may step in to assist these employees by bringing in outside professional assistance to provide retirement planning advice. Employees taking advantage of this expertise may enjoy the fringe benefit tax free.

Benefit ⊗

You are not taxed on the value of retirement planning advice you (and your spouse) receive through your employer. You can exclude this benefit from your income. There is no dollar limit on what you can exclude.

Conditions

This fringe benefit must be provided to you by your employer on a nondiscriminatory basis (i.e., the benefit cannot be limited to owners and highly paid employees). Whether the benefit is discriminatory is something determined by your employer, not by you.

The tax-free benefit is limited to employer-paid retirement education services that you can use to make more informed investment decisions for your retirement plan contributions as well as decisions regarding distributions upon termination of employment. You may not exclude the value of related services, such as tax-preparation, accounting, legal, or brokerage services.

Planning Tip

Many companies are now offering free online investment information related to their retirement plans; take advantage of any advice offered.

Pitfall

There is no downside to taking full advantage of any advice and information your employer offers you. If, however, you believe the advice you have received is not suitable or helpful, then talk to your own retirement-planning adviser.

Where to Claim the Benefit

Since the benefit is not included in your income, you do not have to report it on your return or complete any form or schedule to claim it.

Charitable Transfers of IRA Distributions

There is a special tax break that allows those age 70½ and older to make tax-free transfers from their IRAs to a public charity. Technically, the transfer is called a qualified charitable distribution (QCD). It is a way for individuals who do not itemize as well as itemizers to benefit their favorite charities while obtaining a tax break (the exclusion from income for the transfer).

Benefit ⊗

You can exclude up to $100,000 per year for a direct transfer from your IRA to a public charity. You can make such transfers year after year if you desire. The contribution can count toward your required minimum distribution for the year.

Example

Your RMD for 2017 is $6,680. You instruct your IRA custodian to transfer $6,500 to the American Red Cross. Of the $6,680 RMD, $6,500 is tax free; the balance is taxable as ordinary income.

Conditions

There are 3 conditions for a QCD:

1. You must be at least age 70$\frac{1}{2}$.
2. You must be the owner of the IRA (i.e., not a beneficiary who inherited the IRA).
3. The funds must be transferred to a qualified charity by December 31. This is a public charity. Donor-advised funds and supporting organizations are not eligible recipients for a QCD.

Planning Tips

If you made nondeductible contributions to your IRA, a special rule treats amounts distributed to charities as coming first from taxable funds, instead of proportionately from taxable and nontaxable funds, as would be the case with regular IRA distributions.

If you want to make a QCD, contact your IRA custodian or trustee to determine what steps you must take. Some financial institutions require an IRA owner to submit written instructions for a QCD; others will make a transfer based on oral instructions.

Pitfalls

A QCD can only be made from an IRA or a Roth IRA (although there is no tax reason to transfer funds from a Roth IRA). You cannot make a QCD from IRA-like retirement plans such as a SIMPLE-IRA or a SEP-IRA.

You cannot take a charitable contribution deduction for a QCD. The tax benefit is the exclusion from income for the IRA transfer.

Where to Claim the Exclusion

You will receive Form 1099-R reporting your QCD. The full amount of the QCD is shown on Line 15a of Form 1040 or line 11a of Form 1040A. Do not enter any of these amounts on Line 15b of Form 1040 or line 11b of Form 1040B, but write "QCD" next to that line. You cannot file Form 1040EZ when taking any IRA distributions.

Loans from Retirement Plans

You may be able to borrow from your 401(k) plan account or other qualified retirement plan. The loan is not taxable to you. You cannot borrow from your IRA; if you do, the value of the account is treated as a taxable distribution to you as of the first day of the year in which the loan occurs. Loans from qualified retirement plans are discussed in Chapter 12.

Charitable Giving

Alert

At the time this book was completed, Congress was considering important tax changes that could affect 2017 tax returns and planning for 2018. Check the online Supplement in February 2018 at www.jklasser.com or www.barbaraweltman.com to see what changes have been enacted and when they are effective.

Americans are very generous people. Aside from the good feeling you get from following your philanthropic nature, the tax laws reward you for making donations. Americans donated $390.1 billion to charities in 2016 (according to estimates by the Giving USA group) and nearly 25% did volunteer work for charities.

This chapter covers the basic rules for claiming charitable contribution deductions, including the limits on different types of contributions and the substantiation required to support the deductions. This chapter also contains a record keeper that you can use to track your cash contributions throughout the year.

For more information, see IRS Publication 526, *Charitable Contributions*; IRS Publication 561, *Determining the Value of Donated Property*; IRS Publication 1771, *Charitable Contributions—Substantiation and Disclosure Requirements*; IRS Publication 3833, *Disaster Relief: Providing Assistance through Charitable Organizations*; and IRS Publication 4303, *A Donor's Guide to Vehicle Donations*.

Cash Donations

Donations by cash, check, or credit card to charities or government bodies are deductible within set limits if certain conditions are met. The impact of this deduction is that Uncle Sam becomes your partner in making contributions. For example, if you are in the 33% tax bracket, the government is effectively making almost $\frac{1}{3}$ of your contribution through the tax savings you enjoy from the donation.

Benefit ⬄

You can deduct the cash donations you make to tax-exempt organizations and the government. Generally, you can annually write off your cash donations up to 50% of your adjusted gross income (AGI), if you itemize your deductions. There is no dollar limit on your annual deduction; you are merely limited by your AGI.

Donations in excess of 50% of your AGI can be carried forward for up to 5 years.

Example

If your AGI is $30,000, you can deduct cash donations of only $15,000. If you actually donated $20,000, you can deduct $15,000 this year and carry the $5,000 excess amount forward to next year (if it is deductible next year, depending on your AGI).

Conditions

To claim a deduction for your cash contributions to charity, you must meet all 3 conditions:

1. Donations must be made to a qualified charity.
2. You cannot deduct donations exceeding 50% of your adjusted gross income.
3. You must have proof of your donations.

QUALIFIED CHARITY

Just because a charity calls itself one does not mean it is tax-qualified; it must receive IRS approval to be a tax-exempt organization to which contributions are tax deductible. The charity must be a domestic nonprofit organization, trust, community chest, fund, or foundation that is operated exclusively for one of the following purposes:

- Charitable purposes
- Fostering amateur sports competition
- Prevention of cruelty to children or animals
- Religious purposes
- Scientific, literary, and educational purposes

Other organizations or places to which you can make tax-deductible contributions are:

- Domestic fraternal groups operating under a lodge system
- Domestic nonprofit veterans' organizations or auxiliary units
- Legal services corporations set up under the Legal Services Corporation Act
- Nonprofit cemetery and burial companies (as long as voluntary contributions benefit the whole cemetery and not merely your plot)
- U.S. government; government of a U.S. possession, state, city, or town; or Indian tribal government

Certain well-known charities, such as the American Red Cross, the United Way, the Boy Scouts and Girl Scouts, and the Salvation Army, are clearly authorized to accept tax-deductible contributions. Some charities may be less known, and the IRS warns taxpayers to beware of scams that pop up following disasters, such as Hurricane Harvey in August 2017. If you have any question about an organization's status, ask about its status or check with the IRS, which maintains an online database in IRS Publication 78, *Cumulative List of Organizations*, at www.irs.gov/charities-non-profits/exempt-organizations-select-check.

Once you determine that an organization is eligible to receive a tax-deductible contribution, you may want to check whether the organization is worthy. You can see how much of your contribution goes to the purpose you intend versus being used for administrative costs (e.g., advertising, salaries) of the organization at Charity Navigator at www.charitynavigator.org.

AGI LIMIT

Your deduction generally is limited to 50% of your adjusted gross income (AGI), which is explained more thoroughly in the introduction to this book.

Note: There are some organizations to which donations are limited to 30%, but this is not the usual case. To find out more about so-called "30% charities," see IRS Publication 526, *Charitable Contributions*, at www.irs.gov.

SUBSTANTIATION

You must have proof of your donations in the event your return is questioned. The tax law is very specific about the type of proof (called substantiation in the tax law) that is recognized by the IRS.

Donations in *any* amount must be substantiated by a written acknowledgment from the charity or a bank statement. Formerly, you may have deducted cash donations to the weekly collection plate or the Salvation Army's red kettle during holiday time; such unsubstantiated donations are no longer allowed. Organizations that accept weekly cash donations may make arrangements to substantiate these donations, such as providing you with a monthly acknowledgment of total donations for the period.

Charitable donations through payroll deductions are treated as substantiated by a variety of means, including pay stubs, W-2 forms, or other written statements from an employer.

If the donation is more than $75, get a disclosure statement from the charity stating the value of any benefit received. Donations of $250 or more require a written acknowledgment from the charity; a canceled check is not enough proof in this case. More details on this statement may be found later in this chapter.

EXAMPLES OF DEDUCTIBLE CONTRIBUTIONS
- Checks payable to charity
- Collection plate contributions substantiated by the charity
- Credit card donations
- Rebates applied through credit card programs
- Withholding from wages for charitable purposes
- License plate fee above the normal plate cost if the state gives the extra amount to a qualified charity

- Voluntary contributions to a qualified charity made in the space provided on your state income tax return (you effectively make the donation by increasing your state income tax payment or reducing your income tax refund)

Planning Tips

You can use the record keeper at the end of this chapter to track your total distributions for the year. Be sure to obtain substantiation for all donations.

TIMING ISSUES

You can deduct contributions made up to the last day of the year. In making year-end contributions, keep these points in mind:

- Contributions by credit card are deductible in the year you charge them, not in the year you pay your credit card bill. If you charge the gift by December 31, 2017, it is deductible in 2017 even though you pay the credit card company in 2018.
- Contributions by check that are mailed before December 31 are deductible in the year of mailing even though the charity receives the check and cashes it in the following year.
- A pledge to make a charitable contribution is not deductible until you pay the pledge.
- Contributions made through a pay-by-phone bank account are not deductible when you make the call but rather as of the payment date on the bank statement.

If you have not received a written acknowledgment from the charity by the deadline for filing your return, obtain a filing extension. This will allow you to meet substantiation requirements.

AGI PLANNING

Generally, tax planning dictates that you try to *reduce* your adjusted gross income to boost your deductions for medical and miscellaneous expenses as well as eligibility for certain exclusions and credits. But if you make sizable donations, you may not want or need to adopt strategies to reduce your AGI. By claiming your charitable deduction, you effectively reduce or eliminate the tax on your income.

Example

In 2017, you donate $25,000. Your AGI is $60,000. You can try to reduce your AGI, but don't do so below $50,000 (the AGI that entitles you to fully deduct your contribution this year).

Pitfalls

Despite your generous nature and good intentions, you can easily slip up on technicalities that can prevent you from claiming a deduction. For example, an owner of a nationally well-known tax preparation company donated stock to charity. Since the value of the donation was never in question, he never bothered to obtain a qualified appraisal as required by the tax law. This tax-savvy taxpayer lost out on a sizable deduction for his stock donation because he overlooked a basic requirement for claiming it and the IRS caught him.

High-income taxpayers lose some of the benefit of their contributions because of their reduction in itemized deductions (see the Introduction to this book).

NONQUALIFIED ORGANIZATIONS

An organization may seem like a charity and still not be one. Don't assume that a hospital or school is automatically qualified to accept deductible donations. If it is operated for profit, your contributions are not deductible.

You may not deduct donations to foreign charities unless allowed by international treaties (for example, donations to charities in Mexico and Canada can be deductible). However, a domestic charity set up to distribute funds abroad may be a qualified organization under the rules discussed earlier.

Other organizations that are nonqualified include:

- Sororities and fraternities.
- Civic leagues, chambers of commerce, business leagues, or labor unions. However, you may be able to treat contributions to these organizations as deductible business expenses (see Chapter 15).
- Professional associations of attorneys, doctors, and accountants. However, some unrestricted gifts to state bar associations may be deductible (the bar association reports to you the portion of annual dues treated as charitable contributions).
- Foreign organizations other than certain Canadian, Israeli, or Mexican charitable organizations.
- Homeowners' associations.
- Political organizations and candidates.

You cannot deduct a donation you make directly to an individual, no matter how worthy the person is. For example, suppose your neighbor's house was severely damaged by a fire and you give your neighbor $1,000 to help him through the days following the fire. Your generosity does not warrant a tax deduction.

You cannot deduct a qualified charitable distribution from your IRA (discussed later in this chapter).

EXPIRATION OF CARRYOVER

Unlike other carryovers in the tax law that run indefinitely, the carryover of excess charitable contributions is limited to 5 years. If you have such carryovers, don't let the 5 years expire causing you to waste potential write-offs. Consider realizing sufficient income to allow you to use up your carryovers.

Where to Claim the Deduction

If you itemize your deductions, report your charitable deduction for your cash donations on Schedule A of Form 1040. If you make only cash donations, you do not need any additional form or schedule other than Schedule A to report your charitable contributions. You cannot claim a deduction for donations if you file Form 1040A or Form 1040EZ.

Appreciated Property Donations

The government encourages donations of appreciated property held for more than one year by allowing tax deductions at the property's value (rather than limiting them to the donor's cost or other tax basis) as long as certain conditions are met. Even though cuts in the tax rates diminish the value of such contributions from a tax-savings perspective, philanthropic-minded individuals can still enjoy considerable tax breaks while benefiting their favorite causes.

Benefit

You can claim a charitable contribution deduction *and* avoid capital gains by donating appreciated property to charity. As long as the property has been held for more than one year, the charity is qualified, and other conditions are met, the donation is based on the property's value.

Example

You own stock you bought years ago for $2,000 that is now worth $10,000. If you donate it to a tax-exempt organization, you can claim a charitable contribution deduction of $10,000, the current value of the stock. What's more, you don't have to pay capital gains tax on your $8,000 of appreciation ($10,000 − $2,000), which would have cost you $1,200 ($8,000 × 15%). If you are in the 28% tax bracket, your deduction saves you $2,800 in taxes ($10,000 × 28%). Your total savings from your generosity is $4,000 ($1,200 capital gains tax saved plus $2,800 tax savings from the deduction).

Donations of appreciated property are limited to 30% of your adjusted gross income for the year, in most cases. Donations in excess of this limit can be carried forward for up to 5 years.

Donations of appreciated property that do not meet the conditions listed next are deductible only to the extent of your cost. In the case of donations of tangible personal property that do not meet the conditions, donations are based on basis (generally, cost) rather than value, but can be claimed up to 50% of your adjusted gross income.

Conditions

To claim a deduction for the value of the property you donate to charity, you must meet all 4 conditions:

1. The property must be held long-term ("holding period").
2. If the property is tangible personal property, such as artwork, cars, and equipment, the charity must put the property to use in its exempt purpose ("tangible property used in the charity's exempt purpose").
3. The property cannot be "ordinary income property" (which is property that would generate ordinary income rather than capital gain if it were sold instead of donated).
4. You must comply with substantiation requirements.

Remember that donations to only a qualified charity produce a tax deduction for you. Which organizations are qualified charities, and which are not, is discussed earlier in the chapter under "Cash Donations."

HOLDING PERIOD

To meet the long-term holding period, you must own the property for more than one year prior to the date of the donation.

TANGIBLE PROPERTY USED IN THE CHARITY EXEMPT PURPOSE

If you give property other than securities or real estate, you are giving tangible personal property. Items commonly donated in this category include works of art, books, antiques, furniture, equipment, and collectibles.

Use of the property in the charity's exempt purpose means that the use serves a function related to the charity's exemption. For example, if you donate art to a school and the school displays the work in the library or school museum so that students can study it, the property is being used in the charity's exempt purpose.

If the charity sells the property you donate, you don't meet the related use test even though the proceeds certainly serve the charity's exempt purpose.

The tax law treats the sale as an unrelated purpose (see "Planning Tips" for protection).

PROPERTY IS NOT ORDINARY INCOME PROPERTY

If you donate appreciated property that would produce ordinary income if it were sold rather than donated, you cannot deduct the property's value; your donation is limited to your cost. Examples of ordinary income property include inventory, stock in trade, farm crops, and works of art, books, and memoranda donated by the person who created them. For example, businesses, whether or not incorporated, can claim an enhanced charitable contribution for donations of food inventory.

SUBSTANTIATION REQUIREMENTS

If the total deduction claimed for your property donations is more than $500, you *must* attach Form 8283, *Noncash Charitable Contributions*, to your return.

If you make a donation exceeding $5,000 (one item or a collection), you must obtain a written appraisal for your donation. An appraisal is also required for a donation of used clothing or a household item valued at over $500 that is not in good used condition or better. The appraisal is summarized on the form.

You do not need a written appraisal if the donation is:

- Publicly traded securities—you simply use the market value on the date of the donation.
- Nonpublicly traded stock (stock in a private corporation) if valued at $10,000 or less. You do need an appraisal if the value exceeds this amount.

In addition to obtaining the appraisal, the charity must acknowledge on Form 8283 that it received your donation (so leave enough time to obtain this acknowledgment before filing your return).

If you donate art valued at $20,000 or more, you must attach the written appraisal to the return, along with a color photo or slide, if the IRS asks for it.

If you are required by the tax law to obtain an appraisal for your property donation, you must use a qualified appraiser (a person with the right credentials). Obtain the appraisal no earlier than 60 days before you make the donation. You must have the appraisal in hand by the time you file your return (including extensions).

Planning Tips

If you are concerned that the charity may sell the tangible property you donated, which would limit your deduction to your cost, ask the charity for a letter stipulating that it has no immediate intentions of selling. Then your deduction for the value of the property would be protected even if the charity later changes its intentions and sells your donation.

Donations of collectibles can yield even greater tax savings than donations of securities. The reason: Gain on a sale of collectibles is taxed up to 28%, compared with a top 15% (or 20% for those in the top tax bracket) rate on gain from a sale of securities. Donations avoid the capital gains tax entirely.

ELECTION TO CHANGE AGI LIMIT

If you qualify to deduct the market value of your property, you can elect to reduce the gift by its appreciation and instead use the 50% AGI limit (instead of the 30% AGI limit that is usually required). This election makes sense when there is little appreciation on the property, and opting to reduce the deduction by appreciation still gives you a greater write-off.

> ### Example
>
> You donate stock valued at $100,000 that cost you $90,000. Your AGI is $180,000. If you do nothing, your deduction for your $100,000 is limited to $54,000 (30% of $180,000). But if you make the election to reduce the deduction by its appreciation so that it is limited to your cost of $90,000, you can deduct it in full; your limit in this case is 50% of AGI or $90,000.

You make the election simply by attaching your own statement to your return explaining that you are making the election; no special IRS form or schedule is required. But you can't change your mind later unless your election was based on a material mistake; you can't change your mind simply because you later reconsider the situation and prefer to carry forward the unused deduction that you could have claimed.

IRS APPRAISAL

If you are donating very expensive works of art valued at $50,000 or more, you can protect your deduction from IRS questioning by obtaining an advance valuation of the art from the IRS's Art Advisory Panel. If the IRS agrees to give you this advance valuation, you'll receive an IRS Statement of Value (SOV) that you attach to your return to support your deduction. There is a fee of $5,700 for one to 3 items, and $290 for each additional item, and obtaining an SOV can take as long as a year. The good news is that an SOV avoids hassles with the IRS over valuation later on. But the bad news is that if you don't agree with the SOV, you are left with no alternative but to litigate the issue (you still must attach it to your return, even if you claim a higher deduction than the SOV).

Pitfalls

Donations of appreciated property can produce important tax savings for you, but here are some things to watch out for.

PENALTY FOR OVERVALUATIONS

Valuing property isn't an exact science. When making charitable donations, you hope that the property is valued as highly as possible to boost your deduction. But don't be too generous in your estimations; substantial overvaluations of charitable donations resulting in a tax underpayment exceeding $5,000 can lead to a penalty.

- If the value claimed is 200% or more of the correct value (and results in an underpayment exceeding $5,000), the penalty is 20% of the underpayment.
- If the value claimed is 400% or more of the correct value (and results in an underpayment exceeding $5,000), the penalty is 40% of the underpayment.

Example

You donate an oil painting to charity and estimate that its value is $35,000. In truth, it is actually worth only $10,000. Since the value claimed is more than 200% of the correct value and your valuation results in your underpaying tax by more than $5,000, you are subject to a 20% penalty of the resulting underpayment of tax. In this case, for example, if you had been in the 28% tax bracket, there would have been a $7,000 underpayment ([$35,000 − $10,000] × 28%) so your penalty would be $1,400 ($7,000 × 20%). If you had valued the painting at $40,000, your penalty would have been 40% of the underpayment.

The penalty is applied on an item-by-item basis. So, for example, if you donate 2 objects, overvaluing one item and undervaluing the other, you cannot offset the undervaluation by the overvaluation.

DONATIONS OF PROPERTY THAT HAS DECLINED IN VALUE

If you donate property that meets all of the conditions discussed, your tax deduction is based on the value of the property, even if you paid more for it. In effect, you get no benefit from the loss in value.

Unless the charity has a specific need for your item, it is advisable to sell the property rather than donate it if you can claim a tax deduction for your loss (for example, the property is investment property on which a capital loss can be claimed). You can then donate the proceeds so that the charity receives the same benefit. But selling the property will allow you to take a tax loss on the sale.

You own stock you paid $10,000 for years ago. It is now worth $2,000. If you donate the stock, your deduction is limited to $2,000. If you sell the stock and donate the proceeds, the charity receives the same $2,000. However, you can claim a tax loss of $8,000 ($10,000 − $2,000). You can use this loss to offset your capital gains and then up to $3,000 of your ordinary income; excess capital losses can be carried forward indefinitely and used in future years.

This strategy, however, does not apply to personal (noninvestment or non-business) items, such as your personal car, because you cannot take a capital loss deduction on their sale.

Where to Claim the Deduction

Like cash donations, you report property donations on Schedule A of Form 1040; you cannot claim the deduction if you file Form 1040A or 1040EZ.

But you may also have to complete Form 8283, *Noncash Charitable Contributions*, as explained earlier under "Substantiation."

Used Clothing and Car Donations

Clothing that no longer fits, appliances and sporting equipment that are no longer used, and cars being replaced may be of great benefit to someone else. The tax law rewards donations of these items to charities that can put them to continued good use by permitting a tax deduction if certain conditions are met.

Benefit

Your old clothing, linens, toys, cars, and other items can be of benefit to others. Consider donating them to charity and taking a tax deduction for your efforts. A deduction of these items is generally subject to the 50% of adjusted gross income limit. This means that donations of these items are included along with your cash contributions to determine your annual limit.

Conditions

The items must be donated to a qualified charity (see the explanation of a qualified charity under "Cash Donations" earlier in this chapter).

You cannot claim a deduction if you donate items directly to an individual, no matter how much in need that person may be. For example, if a fire destroys a neighbor's home and you provide your neighbor with clothing and other items, you cannot claim a charitable contribution deduction for your generosity.

For donations of used clothing and household items, no deduction can be claimed unless the items are in "good used condition or better." However, if a single item is appraised at over $500, it can be deducted even though it is not in good used condition (although condition certainly affects its value).

Special substantiation rules apply to donations of cars, boats, and planes valued at over $500. You must obtain a written acknowledgment, Form 1098-C, *Contributions of Motor Vehicles, Boats, and Airplanes*, within 30 days of the date of contribution or the date that the organization sells the vehicle without using it in any significant way (e.g., driving a car to deliver meals to the needy for one year). If the organization sells the vehicle without using it in a significant way in its charitable activities or making any improvements to the vehicle, your donation is limited to the sale proceeds that the organization receives from a sale. Information about the sale is provided to the IRS. Use of Form 1098-C is mandatory for these donations; a thank-you letter from the charity is no substitute.

If you value a car over $250 but not over $500 and the charity sells it, you can deduct the actual fair market value (you are not limited to the sales proceeds). But if you value the car over $500 and the charity sells it for less than $500, your maximum deduction is $500. For example, if you value the car at $650 and the charity sells it for $450, you can deduct $500.

Planning Tips

Don't know what your used items are worth? Here are some resources you can turn to for help:

- Used cars: Kelley Blue Book at www.kbb.com provides free online prices for used cars, based on the vehicle's mileage, condition, and other factors.
- Used clothing and household items: The Salvation Army's Valuation Guide at https://satruck.org/Home/DonationValueGuide is a free online guide to valuing used clothing, appliances, furniture, and other household items. The Valuation Guide for Goodwill Donor at www.goodwill.org/wp-content/uploads/2010/12/donation_valuation_guide.pdf is another free online guide. Bankrate.com also has an online valuation guide at www.bankrate.com/finance/money-guides/tax-guide-for-donated-goods.aspx.
- Used computers, smartphones, and other electronics: Gadget Value at www.gadgetvalue.com provides values for old PCs.

In one case, a court allowed a donation for used clothing valued at $25 per bag.
There are some apps to help with valuation, such as TurboTax's ItsDeductible Donation Tracker, which is free. There are also a number of apps, such as

DonationApp and IGiveItFree, that you can use for valuation purposes (check the fees for using an app). You can use your smartphone to take photos of the donated items to keep with your records.

Pitfalls

Don't expect the charity to provide you with a valuation of your donation. It's up to you to assess the value of the items you donate; the charity merely confirms that you actually made the donation.

Don't include in the amount of your charitable contribution any appraisal fees or the cost of packing and shipping you incur when making property donations. These costs are separately deductible as a miscellaneous itemized deduction (see later in this chapter).

Where to Claim the Deduction

For information about where to claim a deduction for your donation, see the rules under "Appreciated Property Donations" earlier in this chapter, including the rules on substantiation and filing Form 8283, *Noncash Charitable Contributions*. Also attach Form 1098-C, *Contributions of Motor Vehicles, Boats, and Airplanes*, if you donated such an item valued at over $500.

Intellectual Property Donations

If you give a patent, a certain copyright, or other intellectual property to charity, you can not only deduct the initial contribution, but can also claim deductions in future years for a percentage of the income that the charity derives from the property.

Benefit

You can claim an itemized deduction for donations of intellectual property to charity of:

- The fair market value of the donation in the year of the donation for intellectual property that you did not create (or, for self-created property, the amount that would have been ordinary income had you sold it rather than donated it).
- A percentage of the income derived from the property for up to 10 years following the year of the donation. The percentage is based on Table 6.1.

Conditions

At the time of the donation, you must tell the charity that you intend to claim the additional deductions. This is done by providing the charity with your

TABLE 6.1 Deduction for Income from Intellectual Property Donations

Year Ending after Date of Contribution	Applicable Percentage
1st	100%
2nd	100
3rd	90
4th	80
5th	70
6th	60
7th	50
8th	40
9th	30
10th	20
11th	10
12th	10

personal written statement of your intention to treat the contribution as a qualified intellectual contribution. This statement must also describe the property and the date of the donation.

Planning Tip

The additional deduction applies to all types of intellectual property donated after June 3, 2004. This includes not only patents and certain copyrights, but also trademarks, trade names, trade secrets, know-how, certain software, and certain applications or registrations of this property.

Pitfall

The additional deductions can be claimed only for up to 10 years following the year of the intellectual property donation.

If the life of the property is shorter than 10 years, you cannot claim additional deductions beyond this life.

The additional deduction does not apply to donations of intellectual property to a private foundation other than an operating private foundation.

Where to Claim the Deduction

Each year the charity informs you (and the IRS) of the income derived from your donation on Form 8899, *Notice of Income from Donated Intellectual Property*.

To claim a charitable contribution deduction, complete Schedule A of Form 1040. You may also have to complete Form 8283, *Noncash Charitable*

Contributions, as explained earlier in this chapter under "Substantiation Requirements" for appreciated property donations.

You cannot claim the initial or additional deductions if you file Form 1040EZ or 1040A.

Real Estate Donated for Conservation Purposes

Real estate development has gobbled up open spaces and turned them into houses, shopping malls, and office buildings. But the government wants to encourage the maintenance of green spaces and does so by permitting tax deductions for donations of certain property interests for this purpose.

Benefit

Certain donations of partial interests in real property to government agencies or publicly supported charities for exclusively conservation purposes may entitle you to a deduction. Such donations include:

- Your entire interest in real property other than retained rights to subsurface oil, gas, or other minerals. For example, you own land and donate it to your town, retaining these mineral rights.

- A remainder interest in real property. For example, you own land. You keep the right to use it for the rest of your life, giving your town the remainder interest in the property. You do this by deeding the remainder interest to the town.

- An easement, restrictive covenant, or similar property restrictions granted in perpetuity (meaning forever). For example, you own property but give your town an easement limiting the use of a portion of it for a bird sanctuary forever. Even if you later sell the property, the new owner must continue to respect the easement and keep the use as a bird sanctuary.

Conditions

Only donations for qualified conservation purposes entitle you to a deduction. Qualified conservation purposes include:

- The preservation of land areas for outdoor recreation, education, or scenic enjoyment.

- Preservation of historically important land areas or structures.

- Protection of plant, fish, and wildlife habitats or similar natural ecosystems.

For a conservation easement contribution that relates to a building in a registered historic district, there is a $500 filing fee if the claimed deduction is more than $10,000. This payment is accompanied by Form 8283-V, *Voucher for Filing Fee Under Sec. 170(f)(13)*.

Planning Tips

To make the donation of an easement on your property, you may need to pay an attorney to handle the legal work involved.

Donations are deductible up to 50% of the contribution base (which is essentially adjusted gross income), instead of the usual 30% limit (provided the use of the donated property does not prevent farming or ranching). Farmers and ranchers have a 100% limit. Unused contributions because of this limit can be carried forward for up to 15 years.

Pitfalls

Once you give away this interest, you can't change your mind and get it back. As explained earlier, the donation must be in perpetuity (forever). Here is a list of actions that run counter to the rule about perpetuity and can cost you a deduction for any conservation easement donation:

- Failing to subordinate a mortgage to the easement (making the interests of the lender secondary to those of the easement, which requires the consent of the lender)
- Making a conservation easement in North Dakota, which limits the term of an easement to 99 years
- Providing (even informally) that the property be returned if the IRS denies a tax deduction
- Retaining the right to substitute property (even though no property is ever returned to you)

The IRS has designated syndicated conservation easements, which allow investors to deduct more than their economic outlays, as a listed transaction. Anyone entering one on or after January 1, 2010, must disclose this on his or her tax return. The failure to make this disclosure can result in penalties.

Where to Claim the Deduction

For information about where to claim a deduction for your donation, see the rules under "Appreciated Property Donations," earlier in this chapter, including the rules on substantiation and filing Form 8283.

Bargain Sales

Taxpayers can have their cake and eat it, too—recoup their investments in property while obtaining tax deductions to boot—by making bargain sales of property to charity. It's a bargain because the charity is paying only a portion of the property's actual value, typically the donor's original cost for the property. It's a sale because the donor is receiving payment for the transaction and not merely donating the entire value of the property. Even so, a partial tax deduction is permitted under certain conditions.

Benefit

If you have appreciated property, you can recoup your investment while obtaining a tax deduction when you make a bargain sale to charity. In effect, the donation is viewed as 2 transactions: part sale and part gift.

You figure your gain on the sale by allocating the basis between the sale and the gift part as follows:

Step 1: Divide the sales proceeds by the fair market value of the property (include any outstanding debt as sales proceeds).

Step 2: Apply the percentage in Step 1 to the adjusted basis of the property to find the portion of the basis allocated to the sale.

Step 3: Subtract the resulting basis of Step 2 from the sales proceeds to find your gain.

Example

You sell property to your favorite charity for what you paid for it ($12,000). At the time of the donation, it is worth $20,000. Under Step 1, divide $12,000 by $20,000, which is 0.6 or 60%. Apply 60% to the adjusted basis of $12,000, which is $7,200, the basis allocated to the sale. Your gain is $4,800, the difference between your sales proceeds of $12,000 and this basis of $7,200. By making the donation, you have obtained a charitable contribution deduction of $8,000 (the appreciation on the property), while recouping your initial investment, so you are out-of-pocket nothing. Had you sold the property to someone other than a charity, you would have paid capital gains tax on the gain of $8,000 ($20,000 − $12,000), or $1,200 at a 15% capital gain rate (assuming you are not in the 39.6% tax bracket).

Conditions

The same conditions apply to bargain sales as to other charitable contributions (for example, the charity must be an IRS-approved organization). For conditions, see earlier in this chapter.

Planning Tip

A bargain sale can enable you to recover your cost (investment in the property) while also obtaining a deduction for any increased value in the property. Donating the property through a bargain sale saves you the time and expense of selling it to a third party in order to raise the funds to make the donation you would make if you keep your initial investment.

Pitfall

If the property you donate is not the type of property that entitles you to a donation of the appreciation (for example, you didn't own it for more than one year), then the bargain sale doesn't produce any charitable contribution deduction. Of course, the charity still obtains the item at a bargain price.

You must allocate the basis of the property on a bargain sale even if the annual AGI limit prevents you from claiming a charitable contribution deduction.

Where to Claim the Deduction

You report the bargain sale on 2 schedules on Form 1040: Use Schedule D to report the sale portion and Schedule A to report the gift portion.

Details on reporting gifts of appreciated property are explained earlier in this chapter.

Volunteer Expenses

During Hurricane Harvey and its aftermath, the efforts of volunteers were widespread and dramatic. The U.S. Department of Labor, Bureau of Labor Statistics, says that between September 2014 and September 2015 (which are the latest statistics) about 62.6 million Americans did some volunteer work, and some organizations suggest the number is even higher. While individuals bear the burden of the time and effort they put in, the government helps defray any actual out-of-pocket costs through a deduction that can be claimed if certain conditions are met.

Benefit ⬚

If you incur out-of-pocket expenses in serving your favorite charity, you can deduct these costs as part of your itemized deduction for charitable donations.

If you use your vehicle for charitable purposes, including attending meetings of organizations you serve, you can deduct your actual vehicle expenses for gas and oil or mileage at the rate of 14¢ per mile. The 14¢ per mile rate is fixed by law (unchanged since 1997); it cannot be increased by the IRS and so has remained constant for many years. Whichever method you select, you can also write off parking and tolls.

Conditions

As long as you incur out-of-pocket costs for a qualified charity (explained earlier in this chapter under "Cash Donations"), your costs are deductible.

EXAMPLES OF DEDUCTIBLE UNREIMBURSED EXPENSES

Materials and supplies you furnish (e.g., stamps)

Related costs of hosting a fund-raiser (e.g., invitations, food, and beverages)

Telephone calls

Travel expenses, including meals and lodging for overnight trips away from home to serve as an official delegate to a convention of a church, charitable, veteran, or other similar organization

Travel expenses to work for a charitable organization (such as Habitat for Humanity)

Uniforms required in serving the organization

Planning Tip

Keep track of your mileage and out-of-pocket expenses on behalf of the charity. In a diary or logbook, note the odometer readings for every charity-related trip for which your car is used.

Pitfall

Just because you are not compensated by the charity for your efforts doesn't automatically mean that every cost you incur on behalf of the charity is deductible. You *cannot* deduct:

- The value of your time and energy. Even if you perform work for the charity, you cannot deduct what you would have charged for your expertise.

Example

You are an attorney who does pro bono work for a local charity. You cannot deduct your usual hourly rate for the time spent on this charitable activity.

- The rental value of your home or vacation home that you allow the charity to use in its fund-raising activities.

Example

You own a vacation home and let the charity raffle off a 1-week stay there. You cannot deduct the fair rental value of that 1 week's use of your vacation home.

- Babysitting expenses you paid to enable you to put in time for your charity.
- Travel costs to attend a convention for a nonprofit organization if you are not a delegate.
- Travel costs to work on a project for a nonprofit organization if there is a significant element of personal pleasure, recreation, or vacation involved.

You *must* substantiate your out-of-pocket expenses in order to deduct them. If total expenses are $250 or more, you must obtain a written acknowledgment from the charity for your activities. Without this substantiation, a deduction is limited to $249, provided there are credit card statements, canceled checks, or other documentation.

Where to Claim the Deduction

To claim a charitable deduction for your unreimbursed expenses, you must complete Schedule A of Form 1040. You cannot deduct donations if you file Form 1040A or Form 1040EZ.

Tickets to Fund-Raisers, Raffles, and Sporting Events

Who hasn't bought a ticket to a fund-raising event or activity, such as a raffle dinner dance, to benefit a charity? Just because the check is written out to a charity doesn't automatically entitle taxpayers to a deduction. Special rules govern the extent, if any, to which the cost of fund-raising tickets may be deductible.

Benefit ⊜

You can deduct the purchase price for raffle tickets and charity-sponsored events in excess of the regular admission price or other benefit you receive.

Example

You pay $100 for a ticket to an evening sponsored by your favorite charity that includes dinner and a show. The value of the dinner and show (what you would have paid regularly) is $75. You can deduct $25 (the excess cost over the regular price).

SPECIAL LIMIT FOR TICKETS TO SCHOOL ATHLETIC EVENTS

If you contribute to a public or nonprofit college or university and receive the right to buy preferential seating at the school's athletic facilities, your deduction is fixed at 80% of your contribution. The cost of the tickets themselves is not deductible. If you receive a ticket when you make your donation, first reduce the contribution by the price of the ticket and then apply the 80% limit.

> **Example**
>
> You make a sizable donation to your alma mater and receive season's tickets worth $250. Subtract $250 from your donation and then multiply the result by 80% to find your deduction amount.

Condition

If you pay more than $75, the charity must supply you with a written explanation of the value of the benefit you receive so that you can figure your deduction, if any.

Planning Tip

If your donation entitles you to a ticket to a charity event but you do not want to attend, you can refuse to accept the ticket. In this case you can deduct your entire contribution (provided you meet other conditions such as substantiation). Make sure that an acknowledgment you receive from the charity reflects your refusal to accept the ticket.

Pitfall

You cannot deduct any of the cost of Girl Scout cookies you buy for your own consumption. The cost of the cookies is treated as their fair market value so you haven't made any gift. But if you leave the cookies with the troop, you may treat your payment as a deduction. Similarly, if you donate the cookies to a charity, you can deduct your cost (not the estimated retail value).

Where to Claim the Deduction

To claim a charitable deduction for your donations in connection with tickets, raffles, or other fund-raisers, you must complete Schedule A of Form 1040. You do not have to attach the written explanation for your donations to your return; save them for your records with the copy of your return.

If you do not make donations of property, you do not need any additional form or schedule other than Schedule A to report your charitable contributions.

You cannot deduct your donations if you file Form 1040A or Form 1040EZ.

Membership Fees to Nonprofit Organizations

Anthropologist Margaret Mead said, "Never doubt that a small group of thoughtful, committed citizens can change the world. Indeed it is the only thing that ever has." Perhaps that's why so many Americans belong to organizations of all kinds, including religious, civic, and fraternal organizations. Belonging is rewarded taxwise to a certain extent by permitting the cost of dues to be deductible, within certain limits.

Benefit

If you pay dues to nonprofit organizations, you can treat the payments as cash contributions subject to the rules discussed earlier in this chapter. Examples of membership fees that are deductible include payments to religious organizations (e.g., your church) and fraternal organizations operating under a lodge system (e.g., Elks Club).

You must reduce your deduction, however, by the value of any benefits (other than token amounts) you receive, such as monthly journals.

Example

You donate $100 to your local public broadcasting station during its annual fund drive. You receive a videocassette of one of its programs. Your deduction is limited to the donation in excess of the value of the videocassette (the station should supply you with this information).

You do *not* have to reduce your donation by these tokens distributed by the charity in gratitude for your gift:

- Items costing no more than $10.70 if your gift is at least $53.50 in 2017 (these figures are adjusted annually for inflation)
- Items worth no more than $2.14 (2% of $107) in 2017, regardless of the amount of your gift

If you pay $75 or less for membership that entitles you to benefits, you can fully deduct your dues if either of these alternatives applies:

- You receive membership privileges that can be exercised frequently (e.g., free or discounted parking or admission) or discounts on gift shop or mail order items.
- Your membership entitles you to admission to members-only events and the cost of each event is no more than $10.70 in 2017.

If you pay more than $75, you can exclude only those benefits that you would have excluded had you paid $75 or less; more expensive benefits are not excludable.

Student Exchange Program

Individuals who open their homes to students, serving as hosts under special programs, may be eligible for a tax break that helps to defray the cost of hospitality. To claim this tax benefit (which hasn't changed since 1960), certain conditions must be met.

Benefit

If you support a student in your home, you may deduct up to $50 per month as a charitable contribution deduction as long as you itemize your deductions and meet certain conditions. If the student is in your home for at least 15 days of a month, you can treat it as an entire month.

Conditions

To claim a deduction for supporting a student in your home, you must meet all 3 of these conditions:

1. The student must be in elementary or high school.
2. The placement in your home must be arranged under an educational program by a charitable organization and is documented by a written agreement.
3. You have records showing what you spend on the student's food, clothing, medical care, schooling, and recreation.

Planning Tip

Supporting a student in your home may entitle your child to spend time in another family's home. For example, if you accept a foreign exchange student into your home, you may not only obtain a tax deduction for that foreign student, but in addition, your child may be able to go abroad and there is no tax cost to this benefit—to you or to your child. While you may have to pay out-of-pocket for airfare, your child's living expenses abroad may be provided for free.

Pitfall

You usually cannot deduct any payments made where you receive money from the charity for the student's maintenance. For example, if the charity reimburses you for medical expenses you pay for the student, you cannot deduct the medical expenses you paid. However, you are permitted to deduct your prepayment of a one-time expense, such as a medical bill or vacation for the student at the request of the student's parents or sponsoring organization for which you are later reimbursed for part of the cost.

Where to Claim the Deduction

See under "Cash Donations" earlier in this chapter.

Special Inventory Donations

Business owners may enjoy an enhanced charitable contribution deduction for donations by sole proprietors and any other businesses to public charities. The food must be apparently wholesome and meet all federal quality and labeling standards. The deduction is the lesser of (1) the item's basis in inventory plus $1/2$ of its appreciation, or (2) 2 times the item's basis.

Donor-Advised Funds

You've heard the old saying "buy now, pay later." Well, you can donate now and deduct the contribution now, even though money is not disbursed to a charity until later. Using a donor-advised fund, you make contributions to the fund and *suggest* which charity should benefit from them. The fund usually follows your recommendation, although it is not required to. You claim the deduction when money or property goes into the fund.

Benefit

You can deduct the money and property donated to the fund (see earlier in this chapter for rules on cash donations and donations of appreciated property).

Conditions

You cannot *require* the fund to disburse the money to a charity of your choice. You can only make suggestions. For example, if you have $15,000 in your fund account, you can ask that $5,000 be disbursed to the American Red Cross; the fund will usually follow your request, but does not have to.

Planning Tip

Wealthy individuals can set up private foundations or use other charitable vehicles to direct funds to the charities of their choice. If you do not have sufficient funds to create a private foundation, you can use a commercial fund (minimum contributions start at $5,000), such as:

- Fidelity Investments Charitable Gift Fund (www.fidelitycharitable.org) ($5,000 initial contribution)
- Franklin Templeton Charitable Giving Fund (www.franklintempleton.com and search "donor advised fund") ($5,000 initial contribution)

- Schwab Charitable Fund (www.schwabcharitable.org) ($5,000 initial contribution)
- The Vanguard Charitable Endowment Fund (www.vanguardcharitable .org/) ($25,000 initial contribution)

Some large charities and trusts offer donor-advised funds, which you can find through a web search.

Pitfall

No deduction can be claimed for a contribution to a donor-advised fund if the sponsoring organization is a war veterans organization, a fraternal society, or a nonprofit cemetery company.

Where to Claim the Deduction

See "Cash Contributions" earlier in this chapter.

Appraisal Fees and Other Costs

When donating property, how can one know how much to deduct? The answer for certain donations depends on what the property is worth, and it's not always easy to determine this value. You may want, or in some cases need, the assistance of a professional appraiser to determine property value. The fees paid to appraisers may be deductible under certain circumstances. Similarly, you may pay packing, shipping, and insurance costs to send donated items to a charitable organization. These costs may also be deductible.

Benefit

When you donate property to charity, you may pay appraisal fees to determine the property's value. You may also pay to pack up and ship a painting or other item donated to charity. You may deduct these fees and costs incurred for the purpose of claiming a charitable contribution deduction as a miscellaneous itemized deduction. You do *not* include them as part of the donation.

The deduction is part of miscellaneous itemized expenses, which are deductible only to the extent the total exceeds 2% of your adjusted gross income.

Conditions

There are no specific conditions to meet in order to deduct your appraisal fees and other costs. Simply retain proof of this cost (keep it with copies of your tax return).

Planning Tip

Find the right appraiser for the item you are donating. For example, those qualified to appraise real estate may not be the best choice if you are donating art or closely held stock.

In general, to find a qualified appraiser, see:

- American Society of Appraisers (www.appraisers.org)
- Appraisers Association of America (www.appraisersassoc.org)
- International Society of Appraisers (www.isa-appraisers.org)

Pitfall

If your miscellaneous itemized deductions do not exceed 2% of your adjusted gross income, you do not receive any benefit from the write-off of appraisal fees. In effect, the deduction is lost forever.

TABLE 6.2 Record Keeper for Your Cash Donations

Date	Name of Charity	Amount of Donation
		$
		$
		$
		$
		$
		$
		$
		$
		$
		$
		$
		$
		$
		$
		$
		$
		$

Where to Claim the Deduction

You claim the deduction for appraisal fees and other costs as a miscellaneous itemized deduction on Schedule A of Form 1040. You cannot claim the deduction if you file Form 1040A or 1040EZ.

IRA Transfers to Charity

Individuals age 70½ and older can make direct transfers from their IRAs to public charities up to $100,000. No charitable contribution deduction can be claimed for the transfer, but the distribution is not taxable. The rules for IRA transfers to charity are explained in greater detail in Chapter 5. This transfer option may be especially appealing to seniors who want to benefit their favorite charity but who do not itemize their deductions and could not claim a charitable deduction in any event. For details about doing this, see Chapter 5.

Leave-Based Donation Programs

If your employer has a leave-based donation program that typically is used to help co-workers who need help when out because of illness or other event, you may be eligible for a special break in 2017. If you forgo vacation, sick, or personal leave in exchange for cash payments that your employer makes to a charity providing disaster relief to victims of Hurricanes Harvey and Irma, you are not taxed on the donated leave.

Record Keeper for Your Charitable Giving

Use the record keeper in Table 6.2 to note cash contributions you make throughout the year. Include in this record your weekly donations in the church plate and similar donations. Obtain a written acknowledgment from the charity for these donations.

Your Car

Alert

At the time this book was completed, Congress was considering important tax changes that could affect 2017 tax returns and planning for 2018. Check the online Supplement in February 2018 at www.jklasser.com or www.barbaraweltman.com to see what changes have been enacted and when they are effective.

Americans love their cars. According to the U.S. Department of Transportation, there were more than 263.6 million registered cars registered in the U.S. as of 2015 (the most recent year for statistics). Cars can be expensive to buy or lease and to operate, especially with today's high fuel prices. But the tax law provides some relief for your car use by way of tax write-offs.

This chapter explains the tax breaks you can take for your car (the term may also cover light trucks and vans for certain purposes as explained later).

Deducting the use of your car for medical-related travel is discussed in Chapter 2. Deducting the use of your car for a job-related move is discussed in Chapter 4. Deducting the use of your car when working as a volunteer for charity is discussed in Chapter 6.

For more information, see IRS Publication 463, *Travel, Entertainment, Gifts, and Car Expenses*; IRS Publication 535, *Business Expenses*; IRS Publication 547, *Casualties, Disasters, and Thefts (Business and Nonbusiness)*; and IRS Publication 584, *Casualty, Disaster, and Theft Loss Workbook (Personal-Use Property)*.

Business Use of Your Personal Car

According to the U.S. Department of Transportation's Federal Highway Administration, Americans drive their cars on average 13,500 miles each year. The cost of driving can be high when you factor in gasoline, insurance, and other costs. But the tax law lets a portion of the cost of this mileage be deductible under certain circumstances.

Benefit

If you use your personal car for business and do not receive any reimbursement for such use by your employer or you are self-employed, you can deduct expenses related to the business use of your car.

There is a choice of methods for claiming your deduction: You can deduct your actual expenses, including an allowance for depreciation if you own your car or lease payments if you lease it ("actual expense method"), or you can claim the IRS standard mileage rate.

The IRS standard mileage rate is 53.5¢ per mile for business driving in 2017. Whichever method you select, you can also deduct parking and tolls that are business expenses (and not for personal commuting).

There is no dollar limit on what you can deduct for your car use each year. However, if you own your car and use the actual expense method, there are dollar limits on how much you can deduct for depreciation or first-year expensing (unless your car weighs more than 6,000 pounds).

If your employer reimburses you for business use of your car under an "accountable plan," you do not have to report the reimbursements as income (the reimbursements are not even included on your Form W-2). But you cannot claim a deduction for your car use. Ask your employer if reimbursements are made under an accountable plan, or check your W-2 form.

If your employer reimburses you for business use of your car under a nonaccountable plan, such reimbursement is treated as additional compensation to you; it is included on your Form W-2. You can then deduct business use as a miscellaneous itemized deduction (subject to a 2%-of-AGI floor and the reduction in itemized deductions for high-income taxpayers).

Conditions

To claim write-offs for business use of your personal car you merely have to keep good records, as explained later. However, *what* you can deduct may be limited by certain conditions.

STANDARD MILEAGE RATE

You can use the IRS standard mileage rate whether you own or lease your car. The standard mileage rate takes the place of separately deducting gas, oil, repairs, new tires, vehicle registration fees, insurance, and depreciation if you own the car, or lease payments if you lease the car.

However, you cannot base your car deduction on the standard mileage rate if you have depreciated your car or claimed first-year expensing. This would have occurred if you owned your car in a previous year and claimed the actual expense method.

DEPRECIATION

If you own your car and use the actual expense method, you can claim an allowance for depreciation (including bonus depreciation) or elect first-year expensing. Cars are treated as 5-year property; for depreciation purposes they have a 5-year recovery period. Because of a special rule, however, a part of the depreciation allowance is limited in the first year so that the balance must be claimed in a sixth year if you still own the car at that time. (Remember, you apply depreciation only to the business-use portion of the car, and you can use accelerated depreciation only if the car is used more than 50% for business; if business use is 50% or less, you are limited to straight-line depreciation.)

If you use accelerated depreciation (and are not subject to a special rule called the midquarter convention, which applies if you place more than 40% of all of your depreciable property in service in the last quarter of the year), your depreciation rates are:

- Year 1 (the year the car is placed in service): 20%
- Year 2: 32%
- Year 3: 19.2%
- Year 4: 11.52%
- Year 5: 11.52%
- Year 6: 5.76%

Example

In January 2017, you buy a car for $28,000 and use it 60% for business and 40% for personal purposes. You do not use first-year expensing. Assume that your business-personal use percentages remain constant so that the business-use portion of the car for depreciation purposes is $16,800 ($28,000 × 60%). Here is your depreciation amount for each year (subject to the dollar limits discussed later).

Year 1: $3,360

Year 2: $5,338

Year 3: $3,226

Year 4: $1,935

Year 5: $1,935

Year 6: $968

Instead of depreciating the business-use portion of your car, you can elect to expense it in the year it is bought and placed in service. However, like depreciation, this option may be restricted to a dollar limit, explained next.

DOLLAR LIMIT

Unless your car weighs more than 6,000 pounds, your allowance for depreciation or first-year expensing is limited to a dollar amount fixed by the IRS. Table 7.1 shows the dollar limits for gas-powered cars (higher limits not included here apply to electric vehicles).

Example

In November 2017, you buy a used car costing $24,000 and use it 60% for business and 40% for personal purposes. Your dollar limit is $1,896 (60% of $3,160).

TABLE 7.1 Dollar Limit on Depreciation of Passenger Cars

Date Car Placed in Service	1st Year	2nd Year	3rd Year	4th and Later Years
2012 through 2017	$11,160*	$5,100	$3,050	$1,875
2010 and 2011	11,060**	4,900	2,950	1,775
2008 and 2009	10,960***	4,800	2,850	1,775

*$3,160 if the car does not qualify for bonus depreciation (i.e., it is a used car).
**$3,060 if the car does not qualify for bonus depreciation (i.e., it is a used car).
***$2,960 if the car does not qualify for bonus depreciation (i.e., it is a used car).

The full amount of the dollar limit on depreciation applies only if the car is used 100% for business. If the car is used partly for business, you must allocate the dollar limit.

If the vehicle weighs more than 6,000 pounds but not more than 14,000 pounds, as is the case for a heavy SUV used in business, you can elect to expense its cost up to $25,000; the dollar limits in Table 7.1 do not apply in this case (although Congress may eliminate this SUV loophole). In addition, you can claim normal depreciation for the vehicle without applying the dollar limits. Normal depreciation rates are 20% for the first year, 32% for the second year, 19.2% for the third year, 11.52% for the fourth and fifth years, and 5.76% for the sixth year.

Special dollar limits apply to light trucks and vans (those weighing 6,000 pounds gross weight or less). For these limits, see IRS Publication 463, *Travel, Entertainment, Gift, and Car Expenses*.

Vans and trucks that are not suitable for personal use (e.g., they have permanent shelving, a front jump seat, or a permanent business sign) can be depreciated or expensed without any dollar limit.

SUBSTANTIATION

You *must* keep good records to back up your deduction for business use of your car. If you fail to do so, you can lose some or all of your deduction. Here's what your records should show:

- Mileage (your odometer reading at the start and end of each trip for business purposes). A court has indicated that you cannot merely note the length of the trip (e.g., 10 miles) but must record the actual odometer readings for the trip.
- Date, destination, and purpose for the trip (when you used your car, the customers or clients you visited, and the reason for taking the trip).
- Costs for gas, oil, and other car-related expenses. *Note:* If you claim the standard mileage rate, you do not have to keep track of these costs.

Planning Tips

At the start and end of the year, note your odometer reading in your records. Then use a diary, logbook, handheld computer, or other device to record your business mileage throughout the year. Knowing your annual mileage and what part of it represents your business mileage will allow you to properly allocate your car expenses.

You can simplify your recordkeeping for car use with a method called "sampling." This allows you to keep records for only a part of the year and then extrapolate the business mileage for the entire year. You can use this method *only* if the portion of the year in which you kept records (e.g., the first quarter of the year) is representative of car use throughout the year.

Special dollar limits not discussed here apply to light trucks and vans. For details, see Revenue Procedure 2017-29.

For more details and strategies for deducting the expenses of using your car for business, see *J.K. Lasser's Small Business Taxes 2018*.

Pitfalls

If you own your car and you want to use the IRS standard mileage rate, you must elect to do so in the first year of use. Otherwise you are limited to deducting your actual expenses. For example, if you bought and used your car for business in 2016 and used the actual expense method for claiming a deduction for business use, you cannot use the IRS standard mileage rate in 2017 for this car.

If you lease your car and claim a deduction under the actual expense method, you may have to include a phantom amount in income. This is called the inclusion amount and is designed to equate write-offs for leased cars with those that are purchased. The inclusion amount is generally a modest figure that you take from an IRS table created for this purpose. You include only the portion of the inclusion amount related to your car use. For example, if you use your car only 25% for business, you include only 25% of the applicable inclusion amount. Table 7.2 shows you some sample inclusion amounts for passenger cars (different amounts apply to light trucks and vans that you lease).

Inclusion amounts for vehicles leased prior to 2017 can be found in IRS Publication 463, *Travel, Entertainment, Gifts, and Car Expenses*.

Where to Claim the Benefit

Where you claim write-offs for business use of your personal car depends on whether you are an employee or a self-employed person.

TABLE 7.2 Sample Inclusion Amounts for Cars First Leased in 2017*

Fair Market Value		Tax Year during Lease				
Over	Not Over	1	2	3	4	Later
$19,000	$19,500	$ 6	$ 14	$ 20	$ 23	$ 27
20,000	20,500	8	18	26	30	35
22,000	23,000	12	27	39	47	53
25,000	26,000	18	38	58	68	78
30,000	31,000	27	58	87	104	118
35,000	36,000	36	79	116	140	160
40,000	41,000	44	99	146	175	202
50,000	51,000	63	139	206	246	284
60,000	62,000	82	181	268	321	371
70,000	72,000	101	221	327	393	453

*Figures from Rev. Proc. 2017-29 at https://www.irs.gov/pub/irs-drop/rp-17-29.pdf.

EMPLOYEE

If you use your own car for business and are not reimbursed for such use by your employer, you can deduct your car use as a miscellaneous itemized deduction on Schedule A of Form 1040.

You must complete Part II of Form 2106, *Employee Business Expenses*, or Part II of Form 2106-EZ, *Unreimbursed Employee Business Expenses*, to figure the deduction for car use. Be sure to answer the questions about whether you have written evidence of your car use. *Note:* If you opt to use Form 2106-EZ, you are limited to using the standard mileage rate; you cannot claim depreciation on the vehicle.

SELF-EMPLOYED PERSON

If you use your car for both business and personal purposes, you can deduct expenses related to your business use on Schedule C of Form 1040.

If you own your car and are required to file Form 4562, *Depreciation and Amortization* (you are claiming depreciation on property placed in service in 2017), complete Part V of the form. Be sure to answer the question about whether you have written evidence of your claimed use.

If you are not required to file Form 4562, you must answer the questions about your car use in Part IV of Schedule C or in Part III of Schedule C-EZ. These questions concern your mileage for business and personal use and whether you have written evidence to support your deduction.

Since you are self-employed, you must file Form 1040; you cannot use Form 1040A or 1040EZ.

Employer-Provided Car

Perhaps one of the most helpful employee benefits is the so-called company car, which means that the business pays for a car you are allowed to use not only for business travel but also for personal purposes. The extent, if any, to which you are taxed on use of a company car depends on several factors, including *how* you are using the car.

Benefit

If you use a company-owned car *only* on company business, you are not taxed on this use of the company car because it is for business (it is tax-free income to you). Similarly, if you use a certain type of company vehicle for personal use, you are not taxed on this benefit because the IRS views you as having limited personal use (it is tax-free income to you). Such vehicles include: ambulances; hearses; flatbed trucks; dump, garbage, and refrigerated trucks; one-passenger delivery trucks (even if there is a folding jump seat); tractors and other farm equipment; and forklifts. The same exclusion from income applies to vehicles where personal use is restricted or authorized only by a government authority: school buses, passenger buses, moving vans, and police and fire vehicles (including unmarked cars).

If you are given unfettered use of a company-owned car and it is not used only for business but also for personal purposes, you are taxed on your personal use. The tax can be figured in several ways (a complete discussion of which is beyond the scope of this chapter). One way is by reference to an IRS table on the annual lease value of the car (determined by the fair market value of the car). But the income resulting from personal use of a company car may be substantially less than it would cost you to own or lease a car for your personal use. Thus, even though you may have income from using the company car, it is still a tax benefit because of your out-of-pocket savings (what you would have had to pay if the company had not provided you with a car for personal use).

Example

In 2017, your employer allows you to use a company car for personal purposes and you do so 25% of the time the car is used (the rest of the use is strictly for business). Assuming the car's value is $20,000, your employer includes in your income $1,400 ($5,600 annual lease value of the car × 25%). If you are in the 28% tax bracket, this added income results in additional tax of $392. In effect, it costs you just $392 to use your company's car for personal purposes for the year.

Your employer must figure the value of your personal use of a company car using one of several alternatives and report this amount to you on your Form W-2. However, your employer may opt to report the full value of the car's use for the year (not merely your personal use); this is based on the car's lease value. In this case, you may deduct your business use of the company car as an unreimbursed employee business expense (explained earlier in this chapter) if you itemize your deductions.

If you are a full-time car salesperson who is allowed to use demonstration cars for personal use, you are not taxed on this benefit (it is tax-free income to you), provided there are restrictions on personal use. For example, personal use after normal business hours might be restricted to a 75-mile radius of the dealer's sales office or you might not be allowed to drive family members or use the car for vacation trips.

Condition

To fully exclude the value of using a company car, your personal use must be restricted or the company vehicle must be one of those listed earlier.

Planning Tip

Your employer is *not* required to withhold income taxes on your personal use of a company car. If there is no withholding for car use and you have not paid enough taxes throughout the year by means of withholding or estimated tax payments, you may wind up owing taxes at the end of the year. You may wish to voluntarily increase your withholding if you know that your employer will not withhold taxes for your car use to avoid the problem.

Pitfalls

As mentioned earlier, your employer is not limited to reporting as income only your personal use of the company car; your employer may opt to include *all* use—both business and personal—as income to you. The amount of this income may be figured by reference to the car's annual lease value, which is a figure taken from an IRS table based on the car's fair market value (or some other IRS-approved method for valuing car use).

Example

Your employer opts to report as income to you all use of a company car valued at $20,000. The annual lease value from the IRS table is $5,600, so this amount is reported as income to you.

If your employer reports the full value of the car as income on your W-2 form (as in the preceding example), you can claim a deduction for your business use (as explained earlier in this chapter). However, your deduction is subject to the 2% of AGI floor and the reduction in itemized deductions for high-income tax-payers. This means that if you don't have other miscellaneous itemized deductions, you effectively lose write-offs equal to 2% of your adjusted gross income and are taxed on business use of the company car.

Where to Claim the Benefit

If you are not taxed on using the company car (i.e., your employer does not report it on your Form W-2), you do not have to report anything on your return.

If your employer reports only the actual value of your personal use of a company car, again you do not have to do anything on your return. This income is included in your compensation and reported as such on your return, whichever type of return you file.

If your employer reports 100% of the car's lease value as income to you on your Form W-2 and you used the car part of the time for business, you must complete Part II of Form 2106, *Employee Business Expenses*, or Part II of Form 2106-EZ,

Unreimbursed Employee Business Expenses, to figure the deduction for the business use of the car. Be sure to answer the questions about whether you have written evidence of your car use. *Note:* If you opt to use Form 2106-EZ, you are limited to using the standard mileage rate; you cannot claim depreciation on the vehicle.

You then report the deductible amount of unreimbursed employee business expenses as a miscellaneous itemized deduction on Schedule A of Form 1040. You cannot claim a deduction if you file Form 1040A or 1040EZ.

Vehicle Registration Fees

One way in which states raise revenues is through the fees they charge for certain activities, including registering cars and other vehicles. The cost of registration, however, may be deductible under certain conditions.

Benefit

The state registration fees you pay for your vehicle may be deductible. If your car is used only for personal purposes, you can deduct auto registration fees based on the value of the car as a state personal property tax if certain conditions are met. You must itemize your deductions to be able to deduct this expense.

Conditions

To deduct auto registration fees as a state personal property tax, you must meet all 3 requirements:

1. The fee is an ad valorem tax. This means the fee is based on a percentage of the car's value, for example, 1% of the value. Table 7.3 lists the states that satisfy this requirement.

2. The fee is imposed on an annual basis, even though it is collected more or less frequently.

3. The fee is imposed on personal property.

If the tax or fee is based on weight, model, year, or horsepower, it is not deductible. But if the tax is based on *both* value and another factor, the portion based on value is deductible.

Example

Your vehicle registration fee is 1% of the car's value, plus 40¢ per hundredweight. You can deduct the 1% portion as a personal property tax.

TABLE 7.3 States with Ad Valorem Taxes*

Alabama	Michigan
Arizona	Minnesota
California	Mississippi
Colorado	Montana
Connecticut	Nebraska
Georgia**	Nevada
Indiana	New Hampshire
Iowa	North Carolina
Kansas	South Carolina
Kentucky	Virginia
Maine	Wyoming
Massachusetts	

*In Louisiana, Missouri, and Virginia there may be county-imposed ad valorem taxes.
**One-time title ad valorem tax.

Planning Tip

If you have questions about whether your state's registration fee is deductible in whole or in part, contact your state tax authority.

Pitfall

There is no downside to deducting auto registration fees as a personal property tax if you are eligible to do so.

Where to Claim the Benefit

If you are deducting auto registration fees on your personal car as a state personal property tax, you must file Schedule A of Form 1040.

You cannot claim the deduction if you file Form 1040A or 1040EZ.

Car Accidents and Other Car-Related Problems

According to the U.S. Department of Transportation, there were about 6.3 million motor vehicle accidents in the United States in 2015 (the most recent year for statistics). Whether a car is partially damaged or totaled, an owner may have out-of-pocket costs. These may be limited to the deductible or may be a greater amount. The tax law may allow for a write-off, even if the car is used exclusively for personal reasons and not at all for business.

Benefit ⊜

If your personal car is damaged or destroyed in an accident and the damages are not fully covered by insurance or other reimbursement, you can deduct your loss as a casualty loss, provided you itemize your deductions. The same rules apply if your car is stolen.

There is no dollar limit on how much you can deduct.

Conditions

To claim a deduction for your loss arising from a car accident or other car-related problems, you must meet 4 conditions:

1. Prove that the loss arose from a casualty or theft.
2. Establish the amount of your loss.
3. Reduce your loss by $100 if your car is used for personal purposes.
4. Reduce your total losses for the year by 10% of your adjusted gross income if your car is used for personal purposes.

CASUALTY EVENT

Unless it is stolen, you must show that the damage to your car resulted from a casualty, which is a sudden, unexpected event such as an accident. Generally, this does not pose any problem since car accidents are clearly casualty events. Similarly, if a tree falls on your car during a hurricane or the car is washed away during a flood, the damage can be viewed as arising from a casualty because the triggering event is sudden and unexpected.

However, you cannot treat damage resulting from your failure to winterize your car as a casualty. The damage in this case results from your personal neglect and not from an accident or other destructive force.

ESTABLISH THE AMOUNT OF LOSS

Just because an accident has occurred does not mean you have a tax-deductible loss. You must show that a loss occurred and that you didn't receive compensation from insurance or another source.

You measure your loss by comparing the value of the car before and after the casualty. However, your loss for tax purposes cannot exceed your basis in the car.

Example

You paid $8,000 for a used car that you purchased from a friend who gave you a break (the car was actually worth $9,000). Shortly thereafter, the car is totaled in an accident that is not covered by insurance. The value of the car before the accident is $9,000 and its value after the accident is scrap of $500, for a difference of $8,500. However, your loss for tax purposes cannot exceed $8,000, which is your adjusted basis in the car.

You can use the cost of repairs to the car to show your loss if the cost is not excessive and the repair merely restores the car to its preaccident condition.

Example

You bought your car new for $20,000 a few years ago. In 2017, it is damaged in a collision that is not covered by your insurance. You pay the repair shop $3,000 to fix the damage. You can treat this amount as your loss (assuming that this amount is not excessive and the repair fixes only the damage).

You must reduce your loss by any insurance or other reimbursement you receive. For example, if your car is hit by another driver who prefers to pay you rather than go through his insurance company, this is a reimbursement and you must reduce your loss by the amount you receive.

APPLYING THE $100 FLOOR

If your car is for personal use, you must reduce your loss for tax purposes by $100 per occurrence in 2017. If, by some bad twist of fate, your car is in 2 accidents within the same year, you would have to subtract $100 from each loss (for a total of $200 for the year).

If your car is used exclusively for business, you do not apply the $100 floor to your loss.

10% OF AGI FLOOR

You can deduct casualty and theft losses for the year only to the extent that total losses are more than 10% of your adjusted gross income.

Example

In 2017, you suffer a $6,000 loss in a car accident and have a $12,000 theft loss from your home (after reducing each occurrence by $100), for total losses

(Continued)

(*Continued*)

of $18,000. Your adjusted gross income is $70,000. Your deduction for 2017 is limited to amounts in excess of $7,000 (10% of $70,000), which in this case is $11,000—you can never deduct the first 10%, or $7,000.

If your car is used exclusively for business, you do not apply the 10% of AGI floor to your loss.

Planning Tips

Retain proof of the accident to support your deduction. Helpful proof includes:

- Appraisals of the car's value before the accident. You can rely on automotive "blue books" for this purpose (e.g., Kelley Blue Book at www.kbb.com).
- Canceled checks, bills, receipts, and vouchers for expenses of restoring the car to its condition before the accident.
- Photos of the damaged car (yours or newspaper clippings of the accident).

If you are married and one spouse owns the car that is damaged, consider filing separate returns rather than filing jointly. If the owner-spouse has the lower income, that spouse may be able to deduct a greater portion of the loss because of the AGI floor. However, there are other situations that benefit from filing jointly, so it is advisable to run the numbers using both filing statuses and choose the one that results in the lower overall tax.

Since the tax deduction for your car accident will not fully compensate you for your loss, it is advisable that you carry enough car insurance to cover any future accidents. While many financial experts advise against continuing collision coverage after the car is old, you must weigh the cost of insurance against what you could lose if your car is damaged, even through no fault of your own.

The deduction for casualty losses, while subject to a 10%-of-AGI threshold, is *not* subject to the reduction in itemized deductions for high-income taxpayers.

Pitfalls

You may not deduct your loss if damage resulted from your willful conduct. For example, if you crash your car while under the influence of alcohol, you cannot claim a tax loss for your car damage.

Certain car accidents and related costs are *not* deductible. These include:

- Costs you pay for damaging another person's vehicle. However, if the damage arose in the course of your business (for example, you were driving between 2 business locations), then the loss is deductible as a business loss.

- Legal fees or court costs you may pay to defend an action resulting from your negligence in operating the car for personal purposes (including commuting to or from work).
- Personal injuries to you or other people arising out of the accident.
- Towing charges.

Where to Claim the Deduction

You must complete Form 4684, *Casualties and Thefts*, to figure your loss. The form takes you line-by-line through the process, including how to apply the $100 limit and 10% of AGI floor to a loss on your personal car.

You report your deduction on Schedule A of Form 1040. You cannot claim a loss if you file Form 1040A or 1040EZ.

Donating Your Car

If you donate your car to a tax-exempt organization, you may be entitled to claim a deduction for the car's fair market value. For more details, see Chapter 6.

Credit for Electric Drive Vehicles

You can claim a tax credit for buying a plug-in electric drive vehicle in 2017. The credit applies whether you use the vehicle for personal driving, business driving, or a combination of both. The credit applies to 4-wheel vehicles. The credit had applied to 2-wheel vehicles, but it expired at the end of 2016 and will not apply for 2017 unless extended by Congress.

Benefit

You can reduce your tax bill by claiming a tax credit of between $2,500 and $7,500 for the purchase of a 4-wheel plug-in electric vehicle. The amount of the credit does not depend on the weight of the vehicle. Instead, it depends on battery power. A minimum credit of $2,500 applies to a vehicle with a battery capacity of 4 but less than 5 kilowatt hours. The base credit amount of $2,500 is increased by $417 for a vehicle drawing propulsion energy from a battery with at least 5 kilowatt hours of capacity, plus $417 for each additional kilowatt hour of capacity in excess of 5 kilowatt hours, up to a maximum of $5,000 (for a total credit limit of $7,500). If the credit is extended for 2017, then a 2-wheel plug-in electric vehicle (motorcycle), the credit is based on the cost of the vehicle. The credit is 10% of the cost, up to a maximum credit of $2,500.

Conditions

The credit applies to vehicles with a minimum of 4 wheels manufactured for use on public streets (i.e., have a speed of at least 35 mph and require state tags) and roads that are propelled by a battery having a capacity of at least 4 kilowatt hours. The vehicle must weigh less than 14,000 pounds. Two-wheel vehicles must have a minimum top speed of 45 mph (if the credit is extended).

Planning Tips

The tax credit can be used to offset both the regular tax and the alternative minimum tax.

In addition to this federal income tax credit, you may be eligible for state-level tax breaks on sales and income taxes. Check with your state tax department for details or go to www.afdc.energy.gov/afdc/incentives_laws.html and click on your state.

When a manufacturer sells more than 200,000 4-wheel plug-in vehicles for use in the United States after 2009, the credit limit will be phased out (50% credit in the 2 quarters after the 200,000 vehicle limit is reached and 25% in the next 2 quarters). Thus, anyone interested in purchasing a plug-in electric vehicle should monitor these sales figures (the dealer should be able to provide information) and not miss the opportunity to claim the full credit. At the time this book was published, no manufacturer had yet achieved this sales threshold; check the Supplement for any update.

For links and resources for plug-in electric vehicles, go to FuelEconomy.gov (www.fueleconomy.gov/feg/taxevb.shtml).

Pitfall

The credit for 2-wheel plug-in electric drive vehicles expired at the end of 2016 and does not apply for 2017 unless Congress again extends this break.

Where to Claim the Credit

If the vehicle is used for personal driving, then the credit is reported on Form 8834. *Qualified Plug-in Electric and Electric Vehicle Credit*, and entered in the Tax and Credits section of Form 1040. The credit cannot be claimed on Form 1040A or 1040EZ.

If the vehicle is used for business driving, then the credit is part of the general business credit and subject to limitations. The same form is used and then the business portion is entered on Form 3800, *General Business Credit*; the net general business credit is then entered in the Tax and Credits section of Form 1040.

Investing

Alert

At the time this book was completed, Congress was considering important tax changes that could affect 2017 tax returns and planning for 2018. Check the online Supplement in February 2018 at www.jklasser.com or www.barbaraweltman.com to see what changes have been enacted and when they are effective.

Putting money aside for that proverbial rainy day is an admirable and necessary goal but it can be a difficult proposition, especially when your paycheck doesn't seem to stretch far enough. Still, savings and investing are essential to your financial well-being, and Americans are saving at a growing rate. According to Federal Reserve Bank of St. Louis, the personal savings rate in the U.S. was 3.5% as of July 2017, up from a low of 1.9% in July 2005. Fortunately, the tax laws can help you to make the most of your efforts. It also provides tax breaks if your investments don't work out.

This chapter deals with tax breaks for so-called *taxable accounts* and other investments that are not held in tax-favored retirement accounts. The tax breaks for IRAs and qualified retirement accounts can be found in Chapter 5. For more information, see IRS Publication 514, *Foreign Tax Credit for Individuals*; IRS Publication 525, *Taxable and Nontaxable Income*; IRS Publication 544, *Sales and Other Dispositions of Assets*; IRS Publication 550, *Investment Income and Expenses*; IRS Publication 551, *Basis of Assets*; IRS Publication 564, *Mutual Fund Distributions*; and IRS Publication 575, *Pension and Annuity Income*.

Penalty on Early Withdrawal of Savings

Time deposit accounts and certificates of deposit are fixed for a set term. These savings vehicles generally pay a higher rate of interest than money-market and passbook accounts. But if they are cashed in before maturity, a bank penalty is imposed. The penalty usually is forfeiture of some interest and, in some cases, even principal. The penalty is tax deductible.

Benefit ⬆

If you cash in a certificate of deposit (CD) or savings account before its fixed maturity date for any reason (such as you need the money to pay personal expenses or you can obtain a higher interest rate if you move the money), you may be forced to pay a penalty. The penalty is subtracted from the funds you receive.

You can deduct this penalty, which may be a forfeiture of interest and/or principal (if the penalty exceeds the interest), even though you do not itemize your other deductions. In the case of savings certificates with fixed maturities of longer than one year, your deduction is based on the forfeiture of original issue discount (which is nothing more than a way of figuring interest). Regardless of the maturity involved, this deduction is called a penalty on early withdrawal of savings. There is no dollar limit on this deduction.

Conditions

There are no conditions or requirements to meet. As long as you take money out of a savings certificate before the specified maturity date and are subject to a penalty, you can deduct the penalty in full.

Planning Tip

When putting money into time-savings vehicles, such as certificates of deposit, don't extend the investment period beyond the time you *may* need the funds so that you can avoid early withdrawal penalties if you *do* need the money then. Consider splitting your savings into multiple savings certificates with different maturity dates so that you can readily have access to some funds penalty free.

Example

You have $10,000 for savings. Instead of putting $10,000 into a single CD for 5 years, consider putting only $5,000 in for 5 years and putting the other $5,000 into a renewable 12-month CD. Each year you know that you can obtain at least $5,000 penalty free. This will also allow some of the funds to be reinvested for higher interest rates should rates rise (but, conversely, you may lose out on your interest rate if rates decline).

Pitfalls

You cannot net the penalty against the interest you receive and eliminate the need to separately deduct the penalty. You must report all of the interest on the savings certificate and then separately deduct the early withdrawal penalty.

The above-the-line deduction for the penalty on early withdrawals from savings accounts does not apply to the 10% early distribution penalty imposed on withdrawals from IRAs before age 59½.

Where to Claim the Benefit

The forfeited amount is reported to you (and the IRS) on Form 1099-INT if the certificate of deposit is for one year or less, or on Form 1099-OID if the certificate of deposit is for longer than one year. You deduct this amount in the "Adjusted Gross Income" section of Form 1040.

You cannot deduct the penalty if you file Form 1040A or 1040EZ.

Loss on Bank Deposits

During the Great Depression, there was a run on the banks; depositors rushed to withdraw their money, forcing many banks to go under. Today, there are many protections in place (such as state-mandated funding requirements and Dodd-Frank, a federal law) to ensure the integrity of banks. But despite these protections, some banks still fail. Losses suffered by depositors of failed banks that are not insured by the Federal Deposit Insurance Corporation (FDIC) or funds not covered by FDIC protection may be tax deductible under certain conditions.

Benefit

If your bank goes under and your account is not covered in whole or in part by FDIC insurance, you can deduct your loss.

There are different ways to treat your loss (each of which is explained in the next section):

- Bad debt deduction
- Casualty loss
- Ordinary loss

Choose the method that results in the greatest write-off.

Conditions

The conditions for deducting your loss on bank deposits are simple: The bank must be insolvent or bankrupt so that there is no reasonable prospect of recovering your money, and your deposits must not be covered by FDIC or state insurance. Additional conditions and limits, however, may apply to the deduction method you select.

BAD DEBT

You can opt to treat your loss as a bad debt, which is classified for tax purposes as a short-term capital loss (regardless of how long your money was on deposit). This means you can deduct your loss against capital gains. If you do not have capital gains or if these losses are greater than your capital gains, you can only deduct up to $3,000 against your ordinary income. Any unused amount of the loss can be carried forward and used in a future year.

There is one condition for selecting this deduction method: There must be no reasonable prospect of recovery from the insolvent or bankrupt bank. You must wait until the year in which your nonrecovery becomes clear.

The rules for bad debts are explained more fully in Chapter 12.

CASUALTY LOSS

You can opt to treat your loss as a casualty loss, which means you must itemize deductions to claim the loss. The amount of your loss is reduced by $100 right off the top—the $100 subtraction is a feature in the tax law for claiming a casualty loss deduction.

Casualty losses (after the $100 reduction) are deductible only to the extent they exceed 10% of your adjusted gross income, another condition in the tax law.

Once you choose the option to treat your loss on bank deposits as a casualty loss, it's irrevocable and must be used for any additional losses you incur from the same financial institution.

You can use this option if you have an estimated loss. You do not have to wait until there is no reasonable prospect of recovery to claim a casualty loss deduction. If, by some reason, you eventually receive some or all of your money, you must report the recovery as income in the year you receive it to the extent your original deduction produced a tax benefit.

This option is *not* open to stockholders of the bank who own more than a 1% interest. Similarly, this option cannot be used by the bank's officers or relatives of officers or stockholders.

The rules for casualty losses are explained more fully in Chapter 13.

ORDINARY LOSS

You can opt to deduct up to $20,000 ($10,000 if you are married and file a separate return) as a miscellaneous itemized deduction, which is subject to the 2% of AGI floor and the reduction in itemized deductions for high-income taxpayers. The dollar limit applies per institution, not per account. For example, if you have 2 accounts at the same insolvent bank, each for $15,000, your total deduction is limited to $20,000. But if you have those accounts at 2 separate insolvent banks, you could deduct a total of $30,000 ($15,000 for each account since this does not exceed the $20,000 per-bank limit) in the same year.

There is one condition for selecting this option: None of your deposits were federally insured.

Planning Tips

If you qualify to select any of the 3 deduction options, which one should you choose? There is no single answer; it depends on the amount of your loss and your other income. Keep these factors in mind and run the numbers on each of your options.

Choose the bad debt deduction option if your loss can be fully used in the current year (you have capital gains to offset the loss or no more than $3,000 of bad debt in excess of your capital gains). If you suffered a deposit loss years ago but didn't know about it, it may be too late to claim an ordinary or casualty loss but not too late for a bad debt deduction. Generally, you have 7 years from the due date of your return for the year of the loss to amend it and report the bad debt deduction.

Choose the casualty loss option if you already have casualty or theft losses for the year that offset the 10% of AGI floor.

> **Example**
>
> In 2017, your car was damaged in an accident and you did not have collision insurance. Your loss on this incident was $6,000. You also have an uninsured loss on your bank deposit of $10,000. Assuming your adjusted gross income is $60,000 or less, you can then fully use the $10,000 bank deposit loss. But if the bank deposit loss was your only loss for the year, using the casualty loss method means you cannot benefit from the first $6,000 of your $10,000 loss because of the 10% of AGI floor.

Choose the ordinary loss option if your loss is under the dollar limit and you already have miscellaneous itemized deductions that offset the 2% of AGI floor and are *not* subject to the alternative minimum tax (AMT).

> **Example**
>
> In 2017, you have an uninsured bank loss of $15,000. Your adjusted gross income is $60,000 and you also have $1,200 or more of other miscellaneous itemized deductions. You can fully deduct your $15,000 loss. But if you are subject to the alternative minimum tax, selecting this option may increase your liability because miscellaneous itemized deductions are not deductible for AMT purposes.

But why rely on tax write-offs to make you whole? The best option is to make sure that your deposits are adequately covered by FDIC insurance. Understand your FDIC limits so you don't expose your savings to potential loss, especially when you have accounts in separate institutions that have merged or been taken over.

The rules on FDIC coverage and a listing of the banks with this insurance protection may be found at www.fdic.gov. You can also use the Electronic Deposit Insurance Estimator (EDIE) at www.fdic.gov/edie/ to see where you stand in terms of FDIC coverage for your checking and savings accounts, money market accounts, and certificates of deposit.

Pitfall

The biggest problem with bank losses is knowing exactly what your losses really are. You may recover something when the bank's finances are settled, even if it is only pennies on the dollar. Generally the trustees of a troubled bank will give you an estimate of your expected recovery and loss.

Where to Claim the Benefit

If you opt to treat the loss as a bad debt, report it on Form 8949. Be sure that your loss is entered in parentheses to indicate a loss amount.

If you treat the loss as a casualty loss, you must file Form 4684, *Casualties and Thefts*, to report the loss, which is then entered on Schedule A.

If you claim the loss as an ordinary loss, you must file Schedule A to report the loss.

Regardless of which option you select, you can claim a loss on bank deposits only if you file Form 1040. You cannot claim the loss if you file Form 1040A or 1040EZ.

Capital Losses

Wouldn't it be great if every investment turned out to be profitable? Unfortunately, this isn't the way things work—despite our best efforts, investments may decline in value. A mere drop in an asset's value isn't a tax loss; there must be an actual transaction that fixes the loss. If a sale produces a loss, it may be tax deductible.

Benefit 🔼

In today's volatile stock market, it's not uncommon to have losses. Capital losses are deductible in full (there is no dollar limit) as an offset to your capital gains for the year. If your capital losses exceed your gains, up to $3,000 of capital losses can be used to offset ordinary income, such as salary and interest income. If your capital losses are more than this $3,000 limit, you can carry the excess forward indefinitely to be used in a future year. The $3,000 limit has not been increased since 1978.

Understand what capital losses are so that you can plan wisely to get the greatest tax benefit from your losses. Capital losses generally arise on the sale or other disposition of capital assets, such as stocks, collectibles, or real estate. Your loss is the difference between what you receive on the sale and your adjusted basis in the property (usually what you paid for it).

Example

In 2014, you bought 100 shares of X Corporation for $10,000. In December 2017, you sell those shares for $6,000. You have a $4,000 capital loss ($10,000 basis – $6,000 proceeds on the sale). If this is your only capital transaction for the year, you can deduct $3,000 in the current year as an offset to ordinary income and carry forward $1,000 ($4,000 – $3,000) to the next year.

There are 2 classes of capital losses: short-term losses resulting from assets held one year or less and long-term losses resulting from assets held more than one year. As a practical matter, while complex rules govern the order in which capital losses are used to offset different categories of capital gains, in the end capital losses can be used to fully offset capital gains.

Conditions

You must sell or otherwise dispose of an asset to have a deductible loss. A mere decline in the value of an asset you continue to hold does not entitle you to claim a loss. There are exceptions to the disposition requirement (e.g., a bad debt is treated as a short-term capital loss even though the debt is not sold or otherwise disposed of).

As mentioned earlier, the loss must be with respect to a capital asset. And this asset must be held for investment or business purposes. You cannot deduct a capital loss on an asset held primarily for personal purposes (such as your home, personal car, or boat).

Planning Tips

Don't overlook basis adjustments that may increase your loss (by increasing your basis). Take into account:

- Stock dividends you reinvested in the same company
- Brokers' commissions
- Acquisition costs (e.g., attorney's fees to handle the purchase of real estate)
- Selling costs (e.g., real estate broker's fees)

At year-end, review your investment portfolio to see if there are capital losses you want to harvest for tax advantage. But always temper your tax planning with investment considerations. Don't sell only to generate losses; let your investment decisions be driven primarily by economics (e.g., you think the investment will never recover or there are better places to put your investment dollars).

Pitfalls

While you may have an economic loss on a transaction, do not automatically assume it qualifies for capital loss treatment for tax purposes. Certain pitfalls may trip you up.

WASH SALE RULE

You cannot claim a loss if you acquire substantially identical securities within 30 days before or after the date of sale. Under this "wash sale rule," you do not lose the loss entirely. Instead, you adjust the basis of the newly acquired securities to reflect the loss you could not take. This will enable you to claim the loss when you later sell the newly acquired securities in a transaction that is not subject to the wash sale rule.

What is a substantially identical security? If you sell Facebook stock at a loss on March 14, 2017, and purchase Facebook stock on April 10, 2017, you are subject to the wash sale rule. But if you sell Facebook stock at a loss on March 14 and buy Twitter on April 10, the wash sale rule does not apply because these are different companies and their stocks are not substantially identical securities.

If you sell a Netflix bond at a loss on March 14, 2017, bearing an interest rate of 4.375% payable in 2026, and purchase a Netflix bond on April 10, 2017, bearing an interest rate of 5.75% payable in 2025, you are *not* subject to the wash sale rule. The differences in the coupon rates and maturities of these bonds make them different securities.

Also, if you sell stock at a loss in your personal investment account and then you cause your IRA or other tax-advantaged account to buy the identical stock within the wash sale period, you cannot take the loss.

OTHER PITFALLS

You cannot claim a capital loss on the sale or other disposition of all property. Some types of property are not classified as capital assets so they do not qualify for capital loss treatment:

- Business inventory and property held for sale to customers
- Depreciable business property and rental property
- Copyrights, literary compositions, letters, or other such property that you created, that you acquired by gifts from the persons who created them, or that were created for you
- Government publications

If a spouse incurs the capital loss and dies, it can be used only in the year of death. Excess capital losses cannot be carried forward and used by a surviving spouse in a later year.

Also, as mentioned earlier, you may not claim a loss on your personal property, such as on the sale of your residence, vacation property, or personal car. You can claim a loss only on assets held for investment and which are not otherwise excluded from capital loss treatment. While you may view your home as an investment (perhaps your greatest investment), the tax law does not.

INHERITED PROPERTY

As explained earlier, the capital losses you can deduct are the difference between what you receive on the sale or other disposition and your tax basis (usually what you paid for the items). In the case of inherited property that was part of an estate that filed a federal estate tax return, your tax basis for an item of property is reported to you on Form 8971. If you don't receive this form (e.g., the estate is too small to be required to file a federal estate tax return), your tax basis is the value of the property on the date of the decedent's death.

Where to Claim the Loss

To claim capital losses, you must file Form 8949, *Sales and Other Dispositions of Capital Assets*, and Schedule D to figure the deductible amount. Short-term transactions are entered in Part I of Form 8949; long-term transactions are entered in Part II of Form 8949. The form has 3 different ways to determine basis: transactions listed on Form 1099-B with basis included, transactions listed on Form 1099-B without basis included, and transactions not reported on Form 1099-B. You must use a separate Form 8949 for each type of basis determination. Gains and losses are netted in each of these parts and then short-term gains or losses are carried over to Parts I and II of Schedule D and then netted against long-term gains or losses in Part III of Schedule D. Make sure that the amount of any loss entered in column (f) of Schedule D is within parentheses to indicate a loss amount.

You enter the amount of your net capital loss from Part III of Schedule D onto Form 1040.

You cannot claim capital losses if you file Form 1040A or 1040EZ.

Capital Gains and Qualified Dividends

During the tough economy, investments may not necessarily have paid off. However, you may still have realized some capital gains or received a capital gains distribution from a mutual fund; you may also have received dividends from stocks and equity mutual funds. Normally, net capital gains, capital gains distributions, and qualified dividends are taxed at a top rate of 15% (20% for those in the 39.6% tax bracket). However, those in the 10% or 15% tax bracket pay *no* tax on this income.

Benefit

If you qualify, you pay *no* tax on net capital gains (net long-term capital gains in excess of net short-term capital losses), capital gain distributions from certain mutual funds, and qualified dividends.

Conditions

To qualify for the zero tax rate, you must be in the 10% or 15% tax bracket. Table 8.1 shows the upper limit for taxable income that you can receive and

TABLE 8.1 2017 Ceiling on Taxable Income for Zero Tax Rate

Filing Status	Taxable Income Limit
Single	$37,950
Head of household	50,800
Married filing jointly and surviving spouse	75,900
Married filing separately	37,950

still be in the 15% tax bracket. The potential zero-tax income (e.g., qualified dividends) is taken into account in determining whether you fall within these tax brackets.

Taxable income is adjusted gross income reduced by exemptions and the standard deduction or itemized deductions; it does not take tax credits into account.

The gains must be from property held long term (usually more than one year). Capital gains distributions and qualified dividends are identified as such on Form 1099-DIV.

Planning Tip

Just because you are in a tax bracket above 15% does not mean you lose out entirely on the zero tax rate. Depending on your filing status, taxable income, and qualified dividends and capital gains, you may be able to use the zero rate for some of your dividends and capital gains.

Pitfalls

Receiving too much income in capital gains can push you into a higher tax bracket and void the use of the zero tax rate. For example, say you are single and you estimate that your taxable income for the year will be $35,000. You sell property you've held for years at a profit of $10,000. This gain will put you over the $37,950 cap on the 15% tax bracket, preventing your gain from being fully tax free.

Net capital gains of a child subject to the "kiddie tax" are taxed to the child at the parent's capital gain rate if that rate is higher than the child's rate.

Where to Claim the Benefit

Dividends and capital gains must be reported on the return, even though they may be tax free because of the zero tax rate. Dividends are reported on Schedule B of Form 1040 (or Schedule 1 of Form 1040A) if they exceed $1,500 or directly on the tax return if below this amount. Capital gains distributions and capital gains must be reported on Schedule D of Form 1040 (capital gains distributions can be reported directly on Form 1040A, but this form cannot be used if there are any capital gains). Form 1040EZ cannot be used to report dividends in excess of $1,500 or any capital gains distributions or capital gains.

Worthless Securities

Investments in a corporation—stocks or bonds—are made with the intention of collecting income and/or making a profit. But some corporations go under and investors are left holding the bag. The tax law allows a deduction for worthless securities. Special rules for losses resulting from Ponzi schemes are discussed later in this chapter.

Benefit ⬆

If you hold stocks or bonds issued with coupons or in registered form that become worthless, you can deduct your investment. Worthless securities are treated as becoming worthless on the last day of the year in which they actually become worthless. This date governs whether the loss is treated as a short-term loss (if you held the security no more than one year prior to December 31) or a long-term loss (if you held the security more than one year prior to December 31).

The loss is treated as a capital loss (discussed earlier in this chapter), even though there is no sale involved. However, if the loss relates to Section 1244 stock (discussed later in this chapter), the loss is treated as an ordinary loss up to $50,000 ($100,000 on a joint return).

Conditions

There are 2 conditions you must meet to write off your investment in worthless securities:

1. The security must have had some value at the end of the prior year.
2. The security must have become *totally* worthless.

VALUE IN THE PRIOR YEAR

To claim a loss in 2017, you must show that the stock or bond had some value on December 31, 2016. Generally, you can learn whether the stock has any value by checking your year-end statements from brokerage firms holding your investment. If you hold publicly traded stock in your own name rather than in the brokerage firm's name ("street name"), check newspapers for December 31 to see if the stock is listed in the financial section (only stock with a value is listed in the papers). For example, Enron stock officially became worthless on November 17, 2004 (so the loss was claimed on December 31, 2004), even though the corporation filed for bankruptcy in 2001. Similarly, Radio Shack filed for bankruptcy in 2015, but the company said the stock would have no value when the bankruptcy was completed (there is no indication when this will occur).

TOTALLY WORTHLESS

The stock or bond must have *no* value by the end of the year in which you claim the loss. Just because a bond has stopped paying interest or a stock has been delisted does not mean it is totally worthless. Hostess (maker of Twinkies and Ding Dongs) filed for bankruptcy under Chapter 11 in 2012 (a reorganization); it emerged from bankruptcy and was relisted on the New York Stock Exchange (NYSE) in 2016; its stock never became totally worthless. Similarly, a number of energy companies that had been in reorganization have emerged from bankruptcy and are now relisted on the NYSE or NASDAQ. Be prepared to present facts showing your security is worthless. You can assume that it is worthless if the company issuing it:

- Goes into bankruptcy that results in a liquidation of the company
- Ceases to do business
- Becomes insolvent

However, don't assume that a security is worthless if the company has plans to reorganize in bankruptcy.

Planning Tips

If you hold a security that is partially but not wholly worthless, sell it to nail down your loss. For example, if you think a company is on the brink of bankruptcy, try to sell the security so that you can fix the loss. Typically, your brokerage firm will buy it for a nominal amount, enabling you to claim a loss for the difference between your basis (usually what you paid for it) and what you received for it. Or you can abandon the security, which means that you permanently surrender and relinquish all rights in the security and receive no consideration in exchange for the security.

Bonds not issued with interest coupons or in registered form that become worthless result in a bad debt deduction (discussed earlier under "Loss on Bank Deposits").

You can claim a loss only in the year in which the security becomes totally worthless, but you have 7 years to discover that a security has become worthless. This is because the statute of limitations on amending your return to claim the loss for a worthless security is 7 years rather than the usual 3 years from the due date of your return.

> **Example**
>
> In 2017, you discover that a stock you held became completely worthless in 2010. You have until April 17, 2018, to file an amended return for 2010 (which was due on April 15, 2011) to report the loss.

If you are unsure in which year to claim the loss, it is generally advisable to report it in the earliest year you suspect that the worthlessness occurred and then to renew your claim in each subsequent year when the earliest year proves to be incorrect. This requires that you file amended returns to eliminate the loss from the earliest return and report it on a subsequent return.

Pitfalls

Don't let time pass you by. Once the 7-year period for filing an amended return has passed, your loss can never be claimed. Each year, make sure to check on the status of any questionable securities to make sure you don't overlook a loss write-off you are entitled to claim.

The amount you can write off for worthless securities is limited to your basis in the stocks or bonds. Even though you may have witnessed soaring prices only to be followed by the wipeout, you cannot benefit in any way from those record highs; your tax loss is limited to your basis, which is usually what you paid for the securities.

Where to Claim the Loss

You report worthless securities on Form 8949, *Sales and Other Distributions of Capital Assets*, of Form 1040 (in Part I if the securities were held for no more than one year; Part II if they were held more than one year). In columns (c) and (d) write "Worthless." Then, in column (f), be sure to enter the amount of your loss in parentheses.

You cannot deduct a loss for worthless securities if you file Form 1040A or 1040EZ.

Loss on Section 1244 Stock

Typically, losses on stock are treated as capital losses, which are deductible to the extent of capital gains for the year, plus up to $3,000 of ordinary income. But losses on a special type of stock, called Section 1244 stock after the section in the Internal Revenue Code defining it, can be treated as ordinary losses within set limits.

Benefit 🛈

If you own stock that qualifies as Section 1244 stock, you can claim an ordinary loss on the sale or worthlessness of the stock. The ordinary loss is limited to $50,000 ($100,000 on a joint return).

Conditions

To be able to treat your loss as an ordinary loss, you must meet the following 2 conditions:

1. The stock must qualify as Section 1244 stock.
2. The amount of your loss cannot exceed the dollar limit.

SECTION 1244 REQUIREMENTS

The issuing corporation can be a C or an S corporation. The stock can be common or preferred (provided the preferred stock was issued after July 18, 1984). But all 4 of these conditions must be met:

1. The corporation's equity cannot be greater than $1 million at the time the stock is issued (including amounts received for the stock).
2. The stock must be issued for money or property (other than securities). If you inherited the stock or acquired it for services rendered to the corporation, you cannot treat your loss as an ordinary loss.
3. The corporation must have derived more than half of its gross receipts during the 5-year period before your loss from business operations (and not from passive income such as investments, rents, or royalties). If the corporation is in business less than 5 years, then it must have derived more than half of its gross receipts from business operations in all of its years in existence.
4. You must be the original owner of the stock (you cannot have purchased it from the original owner or someone else).

DOLLAR LIMIT

You can treat only the first $50,000 of the loss as an ordinary loss. The limit on a joint return is $100,000, even if one spouse owned the stock in his or her sole name. Losses in excess of this dollar limit may be treated as capital losses (discussed earlier in this chapter).

Planning Tip

You can claim a Section 1244 loss regardless of how you suffer the loss. Whether you sell your stock at a loss or the company goes under, ordinary loss treatment applies if you meet the conditions discussed earlier.

You (and the corporation) must keep certain records and make them available for IRS inspection, if requested. The records should show that the corporation met the qualifications for the stock to be classified as Section 1244 stock. The corporation should keep records on its gross receipts data for 5 years, and you should keep records on what you paid for the stock. If you don't keep these records, you risk losing your ordinary loss deduction.

Pitfall

If you own stock in an S corporation that holds small business stock, the portion of any loss on such stock passed through to you does *not* qualify as an ordinary loss on Section 1244 stock. Under the technical language of the tax law, only individuals and partnerships can claim Section 1244 losses. Even though S corporations are pass-through entities like partnerships, they are not eligible to claim Section 1244 losses.

Where to Claim the Loss

An ordinary loss on Section 1244 stock is reported on Form 4797, *Sales of Business Property*, which you attach to Form 1040. This form is used whether the loss arises from the sale of the stock or from its becoming worthless so that no sale takes place.

If the amount of the loss exceeds your dollar limit, you treat the excess loss as a capital loss (discussed earlier).

You cannot claim a Section 1244 loss if you file Form 1040A or 1040EZ.

Margin Interest and Other Investment-Related Borrowing

Interest paid to borrow money for the purpose of making investments is viewed as "investment interest." The tax law sets strict limits on when and the extent to which investment interest may be deductible.

Benefit

You can deduct interest on borrowing from a brokerage firm that uses your brokerage account as collateral if the money is used for investment purposes. This is called margin interest, and the brokerage firm sets the limits on borrowing, interest rate, and other terms of the loan. You can also deduct interest on other loans used to make investments as an itemized deduction to the extent of your net investment income. If your investment interest is more than your net investment income for the year, you can carry the excess interest forward indefinitely and use it in a future year.

Conditions

There are 2 important conditions:

1. The funds borrowed must be used for investment purposes.
2. For full deductibility of the interest, you must have net investment income to offset it.

BORROWING FOR INVESTMENT PURPOSES

It is not the source of the borrowing that determines the treatment of the interest but the purpose for which you use the proceeds from the loan. For example, margin interest is not automatically deductible. If you use the loan to buy a personal car, you cannot deduct the margin interest even though the loan arises from your investment account.

If you borrow money to buy stock in a business, interest on the loan is treated as investment interest, not business interest. In contrast, if you buy the assets of a business, the interest is treated as fully deductible business interest, not investment interest limited to the extent of net investment income.

NET INVESTMENT INCOME

Your investment interest is deductible only to the extent of your net investment income for the year. Investment income includes:

- Interest income
- Annuities
- Royalties

Interest from passive activities that is not classified by the activities as "portfolio income" is not treated as investment income. This includes interest on rental real estate or interest passed through to you from investments in limited partnerships or other pass-through entities in which you do not materially participate. Property subject to a net lease is not treated as investment property (it is treated as a passive activity). As a practical matter, you simply look at the Schedule K-1 sent to you by the investment to see how to classify the passed-through interest.

You must reduce investment income by investment expenses for the year to arrive at your net investment income. Investment expenses are expenses directly connected with the production of investment income *after* applying the 2% of AGI floor. Examples of other investment expenses are found throughout this chapter. (If you have both investment expenses and miscellaneous itemized expenses, the tax law assumes that the 2% floor offsets those other deductions before your investment expenses.)

Planning Tip

You can opt to treat capital gains and/or qualified dividends as investment income. If you make this election, your capital gains and/or dividends are not eligible for preferential tax rates and are instead included as ordinary income.

Generally it is *not* advisable to make this election because doing so effectively converts income that would otherwise be taxed at no more than 15% to income taxed at up to 35% (for those in the top tax bracket, it would mean income otherwise taxed at 20% would be taxed at 39.6%). But the election can make sense in some situations; only running the numbers can determine when this is so.

> ### Example
>
> You are in the 33% tax bracket and have $3,000 of capital losses for the year and $6,000 of capital gains. You also have investment interest of $3,000 and no other investment income. If you don't make the election, $3,000 of your capital gains is taxed at 15%, but you can't deduct any of your investment interest this year. If you do make the election, then your capital losses become deductible against ordinary income so that only $3,000 of your capital gains is exposed to ordinary income, while all of your investment interest becomes deductible.

Pitfall

You cannot deduct interest, regardless of the source of the loan, if you use the money to buy or carry municipal bonds (for example, you need to raise cash and you sell your taxable investments while holding on to your municipal bonds).

Where to Claim the Deduction

You figure your investment interest limitation on Form 4952, *Investment Interest Expense Deduction*. You then enter the deductible amount on Schedule A, which is filed with Form 1040.

You cannot deduct investment interest if you file Form 1040A or 1040EZ.

Safe-Deposit Box Rental Fee

Where do you store your valuables? There's no tax break for keeping them under the mattress. But if you rent a safe-deposit box, you may be able to deduct your annual costs.

Benefit

If you rent a safe-deposit box in a bank or company specializing in safe-deposit box rentals in order to store your investments, you can deduct the fee as a miscellaneous itemized deduction. The deduction for investment expenses is subject to the 2% of AGI floor discussed earlier in this chapter, as well as the reduction in itemized deductions for high-income taxpayers.

Conditions

To claim the deduction, the use of the safe-deposit box must be investment-related. For example, you use the safe-deposit box to store your stock certificates or gold coins.

If you use it to store your personal items, such as your will, the expense is not a deductible investment expense.

Planning Tip

If all you keep in a safe-deposit box is securities, you can eliminate the need for the box and save the rental fee by putting the securities in street name. This means giving physical custody of your stock and bond certificates to your brokerage firm, which then transfers title into its name. You continue to see your holdings on your monthly statements.

Pitfall

Claiming a deduction for a safe-deposit box on your return alerts the IRS to the fact that you have investments and/or other property stored away. Are you reporting investment income on your tax return? A negative answer to this question may prompt the IRS to question your deduction for the safe-deposit box.

Where to Claim the Deduction

You report the safe-deposit box rental fee as a miscellaneous itemized deduction on Schedule A of Form 1040.

You cannot claim a deduction for safe-deposit box rental fees as an investment expense if you file Form 1040A or 1040EZ.

Subscriptions to Investment Newsletters, Online Services, and Apps

Investors need to stay up to date with developments in the economy and the stock market in order to make sound investment decisions. There are many ways to stay current—investment newsletters, magazines, web-based services, and apps. The cost of keeping on top of financial developments may be tax deductible.

Benefit

If you subscribe to investment newspapers, newsletters, online services, or apps, you can deduct the expenses as a miscellaneous itemized deduction. The deduction for investment expenses is subject to the 2% of AGI floor discussed earlier in this chapter as well as the reduction of itemized deductions for high-income taxpayers explained in the Introduction to this book.

Conditions

The purpose for the expense must be investment-related. If you are using online services for personal purposes, your outlays are not deductible.

If you use your purchases for both investment and personal purposes, you should allocate your costs and deduct only the portion related to investments.

Example

You pay $240 annually for your Internet access. You estimate that you spend half your time online tracking your investments and the other half pursuing personal interests. You allocate $1/2$ of the expense, or $120, to investment purposes. This is your deductible amount.

Planning Tip

If you pay for multiple-year subscriptions and deduct only a portion of the cost for this year, be sure to keep records so you won't overlook the opportunity to deduct another portion next year.

Pitfall

There is no downside to claiming a deduction for these subscription costs if you are eligible to so do.

Where to Claim the Deduction

You report the costs of investment newsletters and other investment-related expenses as a miscellaneous itemized deduction on Schedule A of Form 1040.

You cannot claim a deduction for these investment-related expenses if you file Form 1040A or 1040EZ.

Computers and Tablets Used for Investments

Laptops, desktops, and tablets can be used for more than just posting to social media, e-mailing relatives, or reading the news. This technology can be used for investment activities, including research and recordkeeping. Depending on how the computer is used, some costs may be deductible.

Benefit

If you buy or lease a computer or tablet to monitor your investments, you can deduct expenses for the computer as a miscellaneous itemized deduction. The deduction for investment expenses is subject to the 2% of AGI floor discussed earlier in this chapter as well as the reduction of itemized deductions for high-income taxpayers explained in the Introduction to this book.

If you buy the item, you depreciate its cost over its recovery period, a fixed time in the tax law (you cannot deduct the entire cost in the year you buy the item because first-year expensing is a write-off limited to business property, as explained in Chapter 15). The computer or tablet is treated as 5-year property. However, since the item is not used more than 50% in business (presumably you use it entirely for your investments, or only incidentally for personal purposes), you must use straightline depreciation.

Example

In 2017, you pay $600 for a tablet used to track your investments. In 2017, you can claim an allowance for depreciation of $60 (10% of $600). During each of the next 5 years you may deduct $120 (20% of $600). In the 6th year, assuming you still have the same tablet, you can again deduct $60 (10% of its cost).

Instead of spreading depreciation deductions for the computer over a number of years, you can use bonus depreciation.

Example

Same facts as in the preceding example. Instead of claiming only $60 in 2017, you can deduct $300 (using 50% bonus depreciation). However, you can opt *not* to use bonus depreciation and instead rely on the basic depreciation rules.

If you lease the item for investment-related purposes, you can deduct your annual lease payments. However, while doable, leasing or renting the item is highly unusual.

Conditions

The use of the item must be investment-related. If you use it primarily for personal purposes and only incidentally for investment purposes, your outlays are not deductible.

If you use your item for both investment and personal purposes, you should allocate your costs and deduct only the portion related to investments.

Example

You pay $732 annually to rent a computer under a rent-to-own plan. You estimate that you spend half your time on the computer tracking your investments and the other half pursuing personal interests. You allocate $1/2$ of the expense, or $366, to investment purposes. This is your deductible amount.

Planning Tips

You cannot claim first-year expensing for a computer or tablet used for monitoring your investments. Only business assets qualify for the expensing write-off.

If you use an item for business as well as investment purposes, different rules may apply. See Chapters 14 and 15 for details.

Pitfall

If you qualify to depreciate the item, you effectively can't opt *not* to claim the write-off. While you do not have to subtract your depreciation allowance, you must reduce the basis of the computer by the depreciation you were entitled to claim. This means that if you later sell the item, you may have a gain (because of the reduction to basis from depreciation), even though its value has declined.

Where to Claim the Deduction

To claim depreciation, you must file Form 4562, *Depreciation and Amortization*. You enter your depreciation allowance in Part III of the form (Part II if you use bonus depreciation). The deductible amount is then entered on Schedule A of Form 1040, miscellaneous itemized deductions. If you lease the computer, lease payments are entered directly on Schedule A.

You cannot claim a deduction for a home computer if you file Form 1040A or 1040EZ.

Fees for Financial Advice

When it comes to investments, it's helpful to turn to experts for assistance. Financial experts may be compensated for their services in different ways. Stockbrokers, for example, are paid through commissions on the investments they sell or by charging a management fee (a percentage of assets under management).

Some financial advisers are paid on a fee basis; some receive both fees and commissions. Commissions are not a deductible expense (they are added to the cost basis of the investments purchased). But fees may be deductible.

Benefit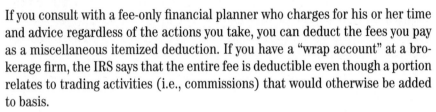

If you consult with a fee-only financial planner who charges for his or her time and advice regardless of the actions you take, you can deduct the fees you pay as a miscellaneous itemized deduction. If you have a "wrap account" at a brokerage firm, the IRS says that the entire fee is deductible even though a portion relates to trading activities (i.e., commissions) that would otherwise be added to basis.

Conditions

You can deduct only fees that are separately paid. If you consult with a financial planner who charges you both a fee plus commissions, you can deduct only the fee portion.

If you consult with an attorney who prepares a will for you while providing estate planning advice, you can deduct the portion of the attorney's fee for estate planning services if such amount is itemized on the attorney's invoice.

Planning Tips

Fee-only financial planners charge you an hourly rate or a flat fee for a specific service, such as creating a comprehensive financial plan. If you have the planner monitor your assets throughout the year, you may also be charged a fee based on a percentage of these assets. Usually, fee-only planners are in the best position to give you objective financial advice because they do not stand to gain or lose by your subsequent actions.

If you pay fees on your IRA, you can also deduct them as long as they are separately billed (i.e., not merely subtracted from your account).

Pitfall

If you consult a commission-based financial planner who does not charge you a fee for advice, but includes commissions or charges on investments he or she sells you, you cannot deduct these costs. Instead, add commissions or other costs to the basis of the assets you acquire to reduce your gain (or increase your loss) on a subsequent sale.

Where to Claim the Deduction

You report the fees paid to financial planners as a miscellaneous itemized deduction on Schedule A of Form 1040.

You cannot claim a deduction for fees to financial planners as an investment expense if you file Form 1040A or 1040EZ.

Amortization of Bond Premium

If you buy a bond at a price greater than its stated principal (or face) amount, the excess is called bond premium. You may opt to amortize the premium on taxable bonds; in some cases you *must* amortize bond premium (you don't have any choice).

Benefit

If you buy a taxable bond, such as a corporate bond, you can elect in the year of the purchase to begin amortizing the bond premium. This means that each year you own the bond, you can offset the taxable interest received on the bond by the amortizable premium amount.

> **Example**
>
> In 2017, you buy a $5,000 corporate bond for $5,500. Your bond premium is $500. Assuming the bond has 5 years left to maturity, you can amortize the $500 premium over 5 years. This means you can use $100 ($500 ÷ 5 years) to offset interest from the bond.

If you buy a tax-exempt bond, such as a municipal bond, at a premium, you *must* amortize the bond premium. You cannot deduct the amortized premium amount. Instead, you reduce the basis of the bond by the amortization for the year.

> **Example**
>
> Same as the preceding example except the bond is a tax-free municipal bond. If you sell the bond at the end of the third year, the basis in the bond is $5,200 ($5,500 − $300). If the sale price of the bond is $5,200, you have no gain or loss on the transaction. If the price is higher than $5,200, you have a taxable gain; if the price is lower, you have a taxable loss.
>
> Alternatively, you could *not* amortize the premium, leaving the bond's basis at $5,500. Then, when the bond is redeemed in 5 years, you will have a $500 loss ($10,000 − $10,500).

Conditions

To amortize the bond premium on a taxable bond, you must meet the following 2 conditions:

1. You elect amortization.

2. You figure amortization using the constant yield method for bonds issued after September 27, 1985 (other amortization methods apply for earlier bond issues). This is a 3-step process under which you determine your yield, the accrual periods to use in figuring amortization, and the bond premium. The computation is rather complicated. For more details, see Chapter 3 of IRS Publication 550, *Investment Income and Expenses*.

Planning Tips

It is usually advisable to elect amortization so you can offset current interest income from the bond. If you do not make the election, you will probably realize a capital loss when the bond is redeemed at par or you sell it for less than you paid for it.

You do not have to elect amortization for taxable bonds held in IRAs or qualified retirement plans. Since the interest is not currently deductible, no offset is necessary.

Pitfall

If you want to amortize bond premiums on taxable bonds, you generally must elect to do so by attaching your own statement to the return indicating this choice. The election applies to all taxable bonds you own and to those you buy in later years.

Once you have made your choice, you can't change it unless you receive the written approval of the IRS. To request a change, you must file Form 3115, *Application for Change in Accounting Method*.

Where to Claim the Deduction

The amortizable amount of a premium is not a separate deduction. Instead, it is an adjustment to the interest reported on Schedule B of Form 1040. Report the bond's interest and on the line below it subtract the amortization, noting "ABP Adjustment" next to it.

If the amortization exceeds the amount of interest reported, the excess can be deducted as a miscellaneous itemized deduction on Schedule A of Form 1040. This deduction is not subject to the 2% of adjusted gross income floor but is subject to the reduction in itemized deductions for high-income taxpayers.

You cannot deduct amortization of bond premiums if you file Form 1040A or 1040EZ.

Municipal Bonds

States, local governments, and their agencies raise money to operate through the sale of bonds. They pay interest on the bonds as inducements to investors to buy the bonds (i.e., lend them money). The federal government generally exempts this interest from taxes; there may or may not be any state income tax breaks as well. Special rules apply to Build American bonds discussed in the Planning Tips.

Benefit ⊗

Interest on municipal bonds is not subject to federal income tax. You may fully exclude this interest from income. There is no dollar limit.

The exclusion applies to both interest on individual bonds and interest from mutual funds holding municipal bonds.

Conditions

Interest is classified as municipal bond interest only if the bond is issued by a state or local government or government agency.

Planning Tip

Interest on municipal bonds may also be exempt from state income taxes. Table 8.2 shows you how the states treat municipal bond interest. The U.S. Supreme Court has decided that it is permissible for a state to tax the interest earned on out-of-state bonds while exempting the interest from in-state bonds.

Pitfalls

Municipal bond interest can affect the amount of taxes you pay on your Social Security benefits. Municipal bond interest, while exempt from federal income tax, is taken into account in determining your provisional income, the figure used to fix the taxable portion of Social Security benefits at 85%, 50%, or zero.

Interest on private activity bonds issued after August 6, 1986, while excluded from income for regular tax purposes, is subject to the alternative minimum tax (AMT) (the interest on such bonds issued in 2009 and 2010 continues to be exempt from AMT). These bonds generally pay a slightly higher interest rate than other municipal bonds. However, if you know you will be subject to AMT, it is advisable when making bond investments to forgo the additional interest in favor of municipal bonds not subject to AMT.

Even though interest on municipal bonds is tax free, gain on the sale of the bonds is taxable. For instance, you purchase a bond at par value and sell it 2 years later for $2,000 more than you paid. You have a $2,000 gain that is taxable.

TABLE 8.2 State Income Tax Treatment of Municipal Bond Interest

State	State Income Tax Treatment
Alaska, Florida, Nevada, South Dakota, Texas, Washington, and Wyoming	No state income tax (so interest on municipal bonds is not taxed).
Alabama, Arizona, Arkansas, California, Colorado, Connecticut, Delaware, Georgia, Hawaii, Idaho, Indiana, Kentucky, Louisiana, Maine, Maryland, Massachusetts, Michigan, Minnesota, Mississippi, Missouri, Montana, Nebraska, New Hampshire, New Jersey, New Mexico, New York, North Carolina, North Dakota, Ohio, Oregon, Pennsylvania, Rhode Island, South Carolina, Tennessee, Vermont, Virginia, and West Virginia	Interest is exempt from state income tax if the bond is issued by the state in which you file your return (or by Puerto Rico, U.S. Virgin Islands, or American Samoa).
District of Columbia and Utah	Interest is tax free regardless of the state of issuance (in Utah interest on out-of-state bonds is tax free only if the other state does not tax interest on Utah bonds).
Illinois, Iowa, Kansas, Oklahoma, and Wisconsin	Interest is fully taxable for state income tax purposes regardless of the state of issuance.

Where to Claim the Exclusion

Even though the interest is fully excludable, you are required to report tax-exempt interest on your return. You report this interest on the line provided for it on Form 1040 or Form 1040A.

You do not have to report this income if you file Form 1040EZ. However, you cannot use this form if you have Social Security benefits.

Savings Bonds

United States savings bonds were first sold by the federal government in World War I and again in World War II as a way to raise money. Today, these bonds have become a permanent savings vehicle for the millions of Americans who own them. They can only be purchased online at www.treasurydirect.gov.

Benefit

Tax on the interest on series E, EE, and I bonds can be deferred until the bonds are cashed in or reach their final maturity dates.

Conditions

Deferral is automatic; you don't have to take any action to receive this tax treatment. You simply do not report the interest annually on your return.

Planning Tips

You can opt to report interest on these savings bonds annually instead of using deferral. This option may make sense when the bondholder has little or no other income so that the interest is taxed at a low rate, if at all.

Example

A child receives a series EE bond at her birth with a face value of $1,000. Since these bonds are sold at a 50% discount (the $1,000 bond costs only $500), any increase in the bond's value over $500 is treated as interest. If the child has no other income, the interest is effectively tax free provided that an election is made to report the interest annually. This election is made simply by including the interest on a tax return filed for the child. File a return to establish this reporting even though the child is otherwise not required to file because his or her income is below the filing threshold.

The U.S. Treasury has changed the way in which interest on series EE bonds is computed. Rather than adjusting the interest semiannually, bonds sold on or after May 1, 2005, now pay a fixed rate until redemption or maturity (e.g., 0.10% for bonds purchased from May 1, 2017, to October 31, 2017). As a result, Series I bonds may be a better option because their interest rate still adjusts semiannually for inflation. For example, I bonds purchased from May 1, 2017, through October 31, 2017, pay a variable rate of 0.98% plus a fixed rate of 0.00%, for a total rate of 1.96%.

Interest *may* be tax free if bonds are redeemed to pay certain higher education costs and other conditions are met (see Chapter 3).

Interest is *never* subject to state and local income taxes.

You can use a federal tax refund to purchase up to $5,000 in series I savings bonds. Purchases must be made in multiples of $50. You can request up to 3 different savings bond registrations (e.g., in your name, in your spouse's name, or for someone else). See the instructions to Form 8888, *Allocation of Refund (Including Savings Bond Purchases)*, for details.

Pitfalls

Do not continue to hold a bond beyond its final maturity date. No interest is paid after this date. As of December 31, 2016, the value of unredeemed bonds that had reached their final maturity date was more than $23.3 billion. Bonds reach final maturity in 30 years for series EE and I bonds. E bonds used to have maturies of 30 years or 40 years; the last E bond reached its final maturity in June 2010.

In the past, you could have continued deferral beyond a bond's maturity date by rolling it over into a series HH bond. However, these bonds ceased being issued as of August 31, 2004 (previously issued series HH bonds continue to earn interest).

You cannot redeem an EE or I bond until 12 months after its purchase *unless* your county has been declared a disaster area. There is a 3-month interest penalty for bonds redeemed before 5 years.

Where to Claim the Benefit

You do not have to report interest if you want to defer it; no special form or schedule needs to be filed.

Gain on the Sale of Small Business Stock

The government wants to encourage investments in small businesses. To do so, it has created certain tax breaks should these investments turn out to be profitable.

Benefit ⊗

If you have a gain on the sale of small business stock, you have 2 options for favorable tax treatment:

1. You can roll over the proceeds into other small business stock to defer the gain. You must reinvest your proceeds from the sale within 60 days of the date of sale to complete the rollover. If you roll over less than all of the proceeds, you must report gain on the portion of the proceeds not rolled over.

2. You can do nothing and exclude a percentage of the gain from income (called a Section 1202 exclusion). The portion of the gain that is not excluded is subject to a 28% capital gain rate (unless your tax bracket is below this rate so that the tax rate is limited to your bracket, which is what you would pay on ordinary income). The amount of the exclusion depends on when the stock was acquired. The exclusion is 50% of the gain on stock acquired before February 18, 2009; 75% of the gain for stock acquired after February 17, 2009, and before September 28, 2010; and 100% for stock acquired after September 27, 2010. The exclusion was 60% for the stock of a small corporation located in an empowerment zone; this special exclusion

expired but continues to apply to stock acquired there after December 21, 2000, and sold before 2017 (this rule may also be extended, which matters only for stock acquired before February 18, 2009).

Conditions

To qualify for rollover treatment or to exclude a percentage of the gain from income, the stock must qualify as small business stock and you must meet a holding period requirement.

SMALL BUSINESS STOCK

There are 5 conditions for qualifying as a small business stock:

1. The issuing corporation must be a C corporation (an S corporation cannot issue small business stock for purposes of rollover or exclusion treatment).
2. The stock must have been originally issued after August 10, 1993.
3. The gross assets of the business cannot be more than $50 million when the stock is issued.
4. The corporation must be an active business (and not a holding or investment company). This requires that at least 80% of the corporation's assets are used in the active conduct of a qualified business. A qualified business is one involved in other than the practice of law, medicine, architecture, engineering, health, performing arts, consulting, actuarial science, financial services, brokerage services, banking, insurance, leasing, farming, hotel or motel management, restaurants, or similar businesses. This means that eligible businesses are in such fields as technology, manufacturing, retail, and wholesale.
5. You must have acquired the stock for cash or other property or as pay for services. You cannot treat inherited or gifted stock as small business stock.

HOLDING PERIOD

For rollover treatment, you must have held the stock more than 6 months before the date of sale.

For the special exclusion, you must have held the stock more than 5 years before the date of sale.

Planning Tips

Assuming you qualify for rollover treatment and the exclusion, which one should you use? Generally, if you reinvest in small business stock, opt for the rollover treatment, which allows you to defer your gain. At some future time when you do not reinvest in small business stock in a timely fashion, you can use the exclusion.

If you have losses on other investments during the year, you may prefer *not* to use deferral or the exclusion but instead report the gain. Losses can offset your gains to eliminate any tax due on these gains.

Pitfall

If you defer gain on the sale of small business stock, understand that eventually you may pay tax on the gain. You must reduce the basis in the small business stock acquired during the 60-day period by the amount of the deferred gain. When you sell this stock, the reduction will effectively increase your gain.

Example

In 2017, you sell small business stock and acquire new stock within 60 days. The gain from the sale is $10,000. You pay $25,000 for the new stock. Your basis in the new stock is $15,000 ($25,000 – $10,000 deferred gain). Later, when the value of the new stock has increased to $35,000, you sell (and there is no additional deferral or exclusion). At this time you have a taxable gain of $20,000 ($35,000 – $15,000).

Where to Claim the Rollover or Exclusion

If you elect rollover treatment, you must do so by reporting the entire gain on Form 8949, *Sales and Other Dispositions of Capital Assets*, of Form 1040, and then on the line immediately below the line on which you reported gain write "Section 1045 rollover" and enter the amount rolled over as a loss (in parentheses) in column (f).

If you exclude a portion or all of your gain, report the entire gain on Form 8949, completing all the columns on that line. Then immediately below the line on which you reported gain in column (a) write "Section 1202 exclusion" and in column (g) enter the amount of the exclusion as a loss (in parentheses). If you have net capital gains for the year, then enter the exclusion as a positive number on line 2 of the 28% Rate Gain Worksheet in the IRS instructions to Schedule D.

If you have any gain on the sale of small business stock, you cannot file Form 1040A or 1040EZ.

Gain on Empowerment Zone Assets

Empowerment zone designations and the tax breaks for them expired at the end of 2016, but could be extended for 2017. The following information is provided in case of an extension. There are about 180 empowerment zones (EZs) in the United States; urban EZs fall under the jurisdiction of the U.S. Department of Housing and Urban Development (HUD). Rural EZs are overseen by the U.S. Department of Agriculture-Office of Community Development (USDA-OCD). You can find these designated areas at www.hud.gov/crlocator.

If you invest in government-designated economically disadvantaged areas, any gain you realize on the sale of assets in these areas is eligible for special treatment.

Benefit ⊗

If you have a gain on the sale of empowerment zone assets, there are 2 favorable options that you may qualify for:

1. You can roll over part or all of the gain from empowerment zone assets held more than one year.
2. You can exclude all of the gain from assets held more than 5 years in the District of Columbia enterprise zone for assets if they were acquired before January 1, 2012. In effect, you are not taxed when you sell these qualified assets.

Conditions

Separate conditions apply to each benefit.

ROLLOVER OF GAIN FROM EMPOWERMENT ZONE ASSETS

There are 4 conditions to qualify for rollover treatment:

1. Both the assets you sold and the assets you acquired as replacement property must be qualified empowerment zone assets, which are tangible property acquired after December 21, 2000, and used in the zone with you as the original owner, or stock in a domestic corporation or capital or profits interest in a domestic partnership acquired after December 21, 2000, if the business is operated in the zone.
2. You must have held the assets that were sold for more than one year.
3. You must acquire other empowerment zone asset(s) as replacement property.
4. You must reduce the basis of the replacement property by the amount of postponed gain.

EXCLUSION OF GAIN FROM DC ZONE ASSETS

There are 3 conditions for excluding gain on property acquired before January 1, 2012:

1. The property must be a District of Columbia enterprise zone (DC zone) asset, which includes DC zone business stock, DC zone partnership interest,

and DC zone business property (including real or other property integral to a DC zone business).

2. You must have acquired the DC zone assets before January 1, 2012, and held them for more than 5 years before the sale.

3. The gain may not be otherwise treated as recapture income or gain from a sale to a related party.

Planning Tips

To determine whether you own property in a qualified zone, see IRS Publication 954, *Tax Incentives for Distressed Communities*.

If you own a business that employs people in a qualified zone, you may be eligible for a special employment tax credit (see Chapter 15).

Pitfall

The election to postpone gain from empowerment zone assets by making a rollover is irrevocable without IRS consent to change your mind.

Where to Claim the Benefit

To report a rollover of gain from empowerment zone assets, enter on line 8 of Schedule D "Section 1397B Rollover" in column (a) and enter a loss in column (g); enter the gain in Part II of Form 8949, *Sales and Other Dispositions of Capital Assets*.

To report the exclusion of DC zone assets, enter on line 3 of Form 8949 "DC Zone Asset" in column (b).

Foreign Taxes on Investments

Investors in foreign companies may pay taxes overseas to other governments. To provide a break so that these investors aren't taxed twice, for federal income tax purposes a deduction or tax credit can be claimed if certain conditions are met.

Benefit

If you hold investments in foreign countries, including stocks or mutual funds, you may pay taxes abroad. You can write off foreign taxes you pay in one of 2 ways:

1. Deduct the taxes as an itemized deduction.

2. Claim a tax credit for the foreign taxes.

Either way, there is no dollar limit to the benefit you can claim.

Conditions

The foreign tax must be a tax on income similar to U.S. tax. However, you cannot write off any tax imposed by a country designated by the U.S. government as engaging in terrorist activities. These countries are listed in IRS Publication 514, *Foreign Tax Credit for Individuals*.

Planning Tips

Generally, claiming the credit is more valuable than deducting the foreign taxes. The credit reduces your tax liability dollar for dollar. You do not have to be an itemizer if you claim the credit. And, if you do itemize deductions but are subject to a reduction in your itemized deductions because you are a high-income taxpayer, claiming the credit avoids this additional limit.

If you opt to claim the credit and the amount of the credit you can use in the current year is limited because of your tax liability, you can carry the excess credit back to the 2 preceding years and then forward for up to 5 succeeding years until it is used up. You can only use a carryback or carryover in a year in which you have income from foreign sources.

You have 10 years in which to change your choice from deduction to credit or credit to deduction. You can file an amended return for a period of up to 10 years to change the treatment of the write-off on your return.

Example

For the past 15 years, you have been claiming a deduction for foreign taxes you paid with respect to a mutual fund. In March 2018, you discover that it would have been preferable to claim the credit. You can amend returns from 2007 onward. The 10-year period for the 2007 return ends on April 17, 2018, 10 years from the due date of that 2007 return.

Pitfalls

You cannot elect to treat some foreign taxes as a deduction while treating others as a credit within the same year. You must opt to use one write-off method for all your foreign taxes. But you can change your choice from year to year.

You get no benefit for foreign taxes paid on investments held by an IRA. Since the IRA is not a taxpayer, it cannot claim a deduction or credit for the foreign taxes paid by it. This means the funds in your IRA are reduced by these taxes with no offsetting benefit. You may wish to reconsider investments subject to foreign taxes being held in an IRA.

If you are subject to the alternative minimum tax (a shadow tax system to ensure that taxpayers who successfully reduce their regular tax will at least pay some income tax), you lose the benefit of an itemized deduction for foreign taxes, which are not deductible for AMT purposes.

You may have to complete Form 8938, *Statement of Specified Foreign Financial Assets*, and file it with your personal tax return if the value of foreign accounts exceeds certain thresholds (e.g., more than $50,000 at the end of the year if you're single). This is referred to as FATCA because the reporting obligation was created by the Foreign Account Tax Compliance Act. Check the instructions to this form and IRS guidance at www.irs.gov/Businesses/Corporations/Basic -Questions-and-Answers-on-Form-8938 for more details about the foreign assets to which the form applies.

If you own or have authority over a foreign financial account, including a bank account, brokerage account, mutual fund, unit trust, or other type of financial account, with a value exceeding $10,000 at any time during the year, you may be required to file a Report of Foreign Bank and Financial Accounts (FBAR) annually. FinCEN Form 114 is used for this purpose and must be filed for 2017 by April 17, 2018 (the same deadline as the one for your federal income tax return) with a 6-month filing extension (this extension is automatic). Filing Form 8938 does not relieve you of the obligation to file the FBAR form. If you failed to file for prior years, you may be able to come into compliance with reduced penalties under the Voluntary Offshore Compliance Program at www.irs.gov/uac/2012-Offshore-Voluntary-Disclosure-Program.

Where to Claim the Deduction or Credit

Foreign taxes you pay on investments are reported to you (and the IRS) on Form 1099-INT or Form 1099-DIV. Use this figure for claiming your deduction or credit.

If you are claiming a deduction for foreign taxes, you must file Schedule A. Your deduction is part of your itemized deductions entered on Form 1040. You cannot claim a deduction if you file Form 1040A or 1040EZ.

If you are claiming the foreign tax credit related to your investments, you may qualify to report it directly on Form 1040 (without having to complete an additional form). This simplified filing option applies if the amount of the foreign tax credit is not more than $300 ($600 on a joint return). You report the credit in the "Tax and Credits" section of Form 1040. You cannot claim the foreign tax credit if you file Form 1040A or 1040EZ.

If your foreign tax credit is more than this limit, you must complete Form 1116, *Foreign Tax Credit (Individual, Estate, or Trust)*, and then follow the filing instructions given earlier.

Exercise of Incentive Stock Options

Employees may receive special options, called incentive stock options (ISOs), to buy company stock at attractive prices. The exercise of ISOs is not taxable for regular tax purposes, although the spread between the exercise price and stock price is an adjustment for the alternative minimum tax (AMT) and can result in AMT liability.

Benefit

There is no regular tax on the exercise of incentive stock options.

Conditions

Incentive stock options (ISOs) are a type of compensation that must be granted in connection with employment. An ISO gives an employee the right to buy employer stock at a set price (called the strike price) within a set time period, after the ISO vests (i.e., cannot be taken from the employee unless he or she leaves employment). If the strike price is less than the market price, an employee exercising the option buys the stock at a bargain; the spread between the strike price and market price at the time the ISO is exercised is not subject to regular income tax if the following 2 conditions are met:

1. You must hold the stock acquired through the ISO for more than 2 years from the date the ISO was granted and more than one year after the ISO was exercised.
2. You must have been continuously employed by the employer granting the ISO from the date of the grant up to 3 months prior to the date on which you exercise the ISO.

If the stock acquired through the ISO is sold prior to the required holding period, then there is taxable compensation and immediate capital gain or loss recognition. The rules are complex; see IRS Publication 525, *Taxable and Nontaxable Income.*

Planning Tip

If you hold ISOs, determine how many to exercise this year, factoring in their expiration date and the impact on alternative minimum tax.

Pitfall

While there is no *regular* tax on the exercise of an ISO if certain conditions are met, the spread between the strike price and market price is treated as an adjustment for the alternative minimum tax (AMT). Thus, exercising ISOs can generate or increase AMT liability.

Where to Claim the Benefit

The exercise of the ISO is not reported on Form 1040, except to the extent it is included on Form 6251, *Alternative Minimum Tax—Individuals*.

Losses from Investment Ponzi Schemes

During the financial meltdown in 2008 and 2009, some investors discovered that their money had been lost through Ponzi schemes. Unscrupulous moneymen collected funds from investors and used new investments to pay off old investors; this worked until they were unable to bring in new investors and the scheme was exposed. While Bernard Madoff, a Ponzi scheme king, is serving a 150-year prison sentence for these crimes, new schemes continue to come to light. The IRS has provided some relief to make it easier for affected investors to recoup at least some of their losses through tax write-offs.

Benefit

Under the safe harbor deduction, an investor in a Ponzi scheme can deduct 95% of the "qualified investment" if he or she isn't pursuing any third-party recovery, or 75% if pursuing or intending to pursue a third-party recovery.

The "qualified investment" is the sum of cash and the basis of property invested in the arrangement over the years, plus income (even so-called phantom income) derived from the arrangement that was included for federal tax purposes in the investor's income, minus any cash or property withdrawn by the investor from the arrangement. After applying the 95%/75%, the deductible amount is then reduced by any actual or potential insurance or SIPC recovery.

Conditions

If you are an eligible investor, you can use this safe harbor deduction in the year of discovery, which is usually the year in which the lead figure is indicted.

Planning Tip

Because the loss is treated as a theft loss (not subject to the $100 and 10% of adjusted gross income limits usually applied to casualty and theft losses), amounts that can't be used in the current year can be carried back to offset income in prior years.

Pitfall

This safe harbor rule applies only if the investment was made in a taxable account; it cannot help an investor's losses in an IRA or other tax-deferred account in most cases. The reason: There is usually no tax basis that can be recouped from a tax-deferred account.

This safe harbor rule applies only to direct investors (those who gave money directly to the lead figure); it does not apply to investors who gave money to other money managers.

Where to Claim the Deduction

The deduction is claimed as a casualty and theft loss deduction on Schedule A of Form 1040; you can't claim the deduction on Form 1040A or 1040EZ.

Attach to the return for the year of discovery a form found in Appendix A of Revenue Procedure 2009-20. The form has lines to complete for the computation of the deduction, as well as required statements and declarations to rely on the safe harbor.

Also, because the loss is technically treated as a theft loss, Form 4684 must be used to report the theft loss. Section C of this form is specifically for reporting losses from Ponzi-like investment schemes.

Travel

Alert

At the time this book was completed, Congress was considering important tax changes that could affect 2017 tax returns and planning for 2018. Check the online Supplement in February 2018 at www.jklasser.com or www.barbaraweltman.com to see what changes have been enacted and when they are effective.

We live in a highly mobile age—we are always on the go for work, play, or other activities. We travel by car, airplane, train, ship, bus, and taxi. We spend a lot of money annually on getting around. The tax laws can help to defray some of your travel costs in certain situations.

This chapter explains the types of travel expenses you can deduct. You will find an explanation of recordkeeping rules for travel expenses as well as some forms you can use to comply with these rules.

For more information, see IRS Publication 463, *Travel, Entertainment, Gift, and Car Expenses*; and IRS Publication 1542, *Per Diem Rates*.

Business Travel

Americans travel quite a lot for business. According to the U.S. Travel Association, U.S. residents logged 459 million person-trips (one person one way on a trip away from home) for business in 2015, with 37% for meetings and events. The costs of travel, including transportation, lodging, and meals, that are related to business may be fully or partially tax deductible if certain conditions are met.

Benefit

Whether you are self-employed or an employee whose company-related travel costs are not covered by an accountable plan, business travel is a deductible expense. As an employee, it can be deducted to the extent miscellaneous itemized expenses exceed 2% of adjusted gross income and is subject to the reduction of itemized deductions for high-income taxpayers. An accountable plan is a reimbursement arrangement under which you are required to account for your expenses to your employer within a set time and refund to your employer any excess advances or reimbursements.

If, however, your employer has an accountable plan that reimburses you for travel expenses, you are not taxed on the reimbursements, so you do not get to deduct the expenses (your employer claims the deduction).

If you are self-employed, the deduction for business expenses is *not* limited by 2% of your adjusted gross income. These costs are fully deductible to the extent otherwise allowed. There is no overall dollar limit on what you can deduct.

Conditions

Business travel costs are deductible if they are ordinary and necessary business expenses. In other words, the travel costs must be business-related and not for personal reasons.

Also, as a condition for claiming a deduction, you must maintain good records (discussed later).

EXAMPLES OF BUSINESS TRAVEL EXPENSES

Airfare

Bus fare

Car expenses (explained in Chapter 7)

Cab fare

Convention costs (explained later in this chapter)

Educational travel, if work-related (explained later in this chapter)

Fax service charges

Job-hunting travel costs in the same line of work

Laundry and dry cleaning during trips

Lodging

Lodging taxes

Meals away from home

Out-of-town expenses while working on a temporary job assignment (explained later in this chapter)

Subway and train fare

Telephone calls

You cannot deduct travel expenses if you are looking for your first job or changing your line of work. For example, if you fly from Los Angeles to Houston to interview for a new position in your same line of work, you can deduct your airfare and local transportation costs as a business expense. But if this travel is for your first job out of college, it is not deductible.

LOCAL OVERNIGHT STAYS

The IRS has liberalized the rules for deducting the cost of local overnight stays. As long as this is not a compensatory benefit but done for a business purpose, you are not taxed on the overnight stay(s) paid by your employer. If you paid the cost, you can deduct it. For example, your company requires you to stay at a local hotel for the bona fide purpose of facilitating training or team building directly connected with the employer's trade or business.

PART-BUSINESS TRIPS WITHIN THE UNITED STATES

If you combine business with pleasure, you can deduct your travel costs, such as airfare, as a business expense if the *primary* purpose of the trip is for business. But you can deduct hotel costs only for the business portion of the trip.

Example

You live and work in New Haven and fly to San Francisco for a 5-day business trip. You extend your stay for 2 extra days to sightsee. You can fully deduct your

(Continued)

> (*Continued*)
>
> **airfare as a business expense since the primary purpose of your trip is business. Your lodging is deductible only for the 5 days on business (the cost of lodging for your 2 personal days are nondeductible).**

If you extend your stay over the weekend to obtain more favorable airfare that requires a Saturday night stay-over, this time is treated as business time, not personal time, even if you spend the weekend on personal activities.

If the primary purpose of your trip is for personal activities, you can deduct only local transportation costs to and from business locations as a business expense.

Example

You live and work in New Haven and fly to San Francisco to attend your niece's wedding. Family activities take up 4 days of your trip. On the 5th day you see a client and then fly home. Only local transportation costs from your hotel to the client and from the client to the airport are deductible.

PART-BUSINESS TRIPS ABROAD

If you combine business with pleasure on a trip outside the United States, different rules apply to determine if and the extent to which airfare can be treated as a deductible business expense.

If you are an employee who does not have control over scheduling business trips, you can deduct all of your expenses, including airfare, lodging, and 50% of meal costs if the primary purpose of the trip is business. Taking some time out to sightsee does not change this result.

If you are a managing executive, a more than 10% owner of the business, or a self-employed person with control over scheduling, you can deduct airfare, lodging, and 50% of meal costs only if you fall within one of these categories:

- The trip lasts a week or less (not counting the day you left the United States but counting the day of your return).
- The trip lasts more than one week, but less than 25% of time (counting both the day of departure and arrival) is spent on personal activities.
- In planning the trip, major emphasis was not placed on personal activities.

If a trip lasts more than one week and you spend 25% or more on personal activities (and cannot show that major emphasis was not placed on these activities), then you can deduct only the portion of expenses related to business. This requires that you allocate costs between business and personal time. Divide the total number of days of the trip by the days spent on business activities to find the deductible portion of your costs.

> ### Example
>
> On Sunday you fly from New York to London for a 10-day stay. You spend Monday through Friday on business and the balance of the trip sightseeing. You can deduct $1/2$ of your airfare, lodging, and meal costs as a business expense ($5 \div 10$).

If you have business meetings scheduled before or after a weekend or holiday, you can treat the days in between the meetings as business days, even though you spend the time on personal activities.

PER DIEM RATES

Instead of keeping track of your actual costs for lodging, meals, and incidental expenses away from home on business, you can rely on government-set standard rates. (Incidental expenses include tips for porters, baggage carriers, bellhops, and hotel maids.) You have 2 options for rates:

1. *Maximum federal per diem rate*—an allowance for lodging and for meals and incidental expenses (M&IE) for travel within the continental United States (CONUS). The rate you use depends on the location you are in and the time of travel. Federal per diem rates may be found at www.gsa.gov (click on Per Diem Rates).

2. *High-low substantiation rate*—an IRS-set rate for lodging and for meals and incidental expenses for business travel within CONUS. One rate applies for IRS-designated high-cost areas while the other rate applies to all other areas in CONUS. The rates for October 1, 2016, through September 30, 2017, can be found in IRS Notice 2016-58. The rates for October 1, 2017, and beyond will be listed in the Supplement to this book.

Even though you use a standard per diem rate, you must still apply a 50% limitation to the M&IE portion of the allowance. The 50% limitation is explained in Chapter 10.

If you incur incidental expenses on any travel day for which you do not have deductible meals, you can deduct these expenses at a flat $5 per day.

Planning Tips

If you plan a business trip that is canceled, you can deduct the costs you can't recoup. These costs may include a hotel charge that is nonrefundable or an airline fee to reschedule a flight.

You *must* keep good records of your business travel in order to claim a deduction. The tax law requires substantiation of business travel expenses as a condition of claiming the deduction. You generally need 2 types of records: written information and documentary evidence such as receipts or credit card statements.

You must note certain information in a diary, logbook, account statement, handheld computer, or other record keeper. The type of information to record and a sample weekly travel expense form that you can use for this purpose are included at the end of this chapter.

If you are an employee whose employer has an accountable plan, you are required to provide recordkeeping information to your employer. If not, you should generally retain these records along with copies of your tax return for at least 3 years from the date you filed the return on which you claimed a deduction for business travel. This will allow you to back up your deduction if your return is questioned by the IRS.

You do not have to retain receipts for travel costs (other than lodging) of less than $75. Thus, for example, you do not need receipts for taxi fares under $75.

If you fail to maintain the necessary records or if they are destroyed by events beyond your control, such as a flood or fire, you *may* be able to prove your entitlement to a deduction through your own written or oral statement and other supporting evidence. But it may be difficult to establish the full amount of expenses, and you can lose out on a deduction you are otherwise entitled to claim.

In some situations, especially when records are destroyed through no fault of the taxpayer, courts have allowed taxpayers to estimate their expenses. This is called the *Cohan rule*, named after the famous entertainer George M. Cohan, who convinced a court of his entitlement to a business deduction despite the lack of records.

Pitfall

Generally the cost of commuting to and from work is not deductible; it is a personal expense. This is so even if you are forced to use your car because there is no public transportation or you must travel great distances. You cannot convert nondeductible commuting costs to deductible expenses merely by using your cell phone on business or putting a sign with your business logo on the side of your car. Nondeductible commuting costs include:

- Carpooling expenses, even if you discuss business with your fellow passengers
- Emergency travel between home and work
- Travel from a union hall to a job site

However, there are certain situations in which commuting costs can be treated as deductible business expenses.

- If you incur additional costs to transport tools to and from work you can treat the added cost as a deductible expense.
- You commute to a temporary work location.
- You work from home and claim a home office deduction. The cost of travel between your home and any business location, such as customers' offices, is deductible.
- You work at temporary locations. For example, if you are an accountant or other professional who travels to client work sites for a few days or a week or 2, you can deduct the costs of travel between home and these sites as business travel, *provided* you have a regular work office.

Where to Claim the Deduction

If you are an employee whose job-related travel costs are covered by an employer's accountable plan, you do not have to do anything. Reimbursements for this travel are *not* included on your Form W-2. You do not have to deduct anything (your employer claims the deduction for your travel costs).

If you are an employee whose job-related travel costs are *not* covered by an accountable plan, you first figure your deductible travel costs in Part I of Form 2106 or 2106-EZ. Your deductible expenses are then entered on Schedule A of Form 1040.

If you are self-employed, you deduct your business travel costs on Schedule C or C-EZ.

You cannot claim a deduction for business travel expenses if you file Form 1040A or 1040EZ.

Temporary Work Assignments

Not everyone who works does so from a fixed location. Some people are stationed at various work locations for a few days, a few months, or even longer. Living away from home means paying for additional housing and travel expenses between home and work. In recognition of the burden these additional costs can place on workers, the tax law allows what might be viewed as personal expenses to become deductible if certain conditions are met.

Benefit

If you work at a temporary location, your travel costs between home and this location are deductible.

If the temporary location is out of town, you can deduct not only your travel costs but also your living expenses, including lodging and 50% of meals. There is no dollar limit on what you can deduct.

Conditions

There are 2 key conditions for deducting expenses related to temporary work assignments:

1. The assignment must be temporary.
2. You must have a regular place of business to deduct travel costs between home and work or be away from home on business to deduct travel and living costs.

DEFINITION OF TEMPORARY WORK ASSIGNMENTS

For travel expenses to be deductible, the work assignment must be temporary. This means that the assignment is expected to last no more than one year and does in fact end within this time. A work assignment is *not* considered temporary if it is expected to last:

- For more than one year even if it in fact ends within the year
- For no more than one year but runs beyond this time (although expenses for the period up to one year are deductible in this case)

REGULAR PLACE OF BUSINESS

You must maintain a regular place of business outside of your home, or have a home office that is your principal place of business.

If all of your work takes place at temporary assignments outside of the metropolitan area in which you live, you do not have a regular place of business and cannot deduct your travel costs.

AWAY FROM HOME

You must maintain a tax home from which you are away on business to deduct travel and living costs. Your tax home is your place of employment or business, regardless of where you or your family live. It may be one and the same place if you live and work in the same area.

Example

You live and work in Trenton, New Jersey. You travel to Boston for 2 weeks of business. You can deduct your travel and living expenses on this trip.

Example

You live in Trenton, New Jersey, and work in Washington, D.C. Washington, D.C., not Trenton, is your tax home. You cannot deduct your travel costs between Trenton and D.C. But if you travel for 2 weeks to Dallas, Texas, you can deduct your travel costs between D.C. and Dallas, as well as your living costs in Dallas.

If you are constantly on the road, moving from job to job so that you do not work within any particular locality, you may not deduct your living costs. The reason: You are not away from home on business.

Your residence can be treated as your tax home so that if you travel away from home on business your costs are deductible if you meet 3 conditions:

1. You do *some* work in the vicinity of your residence.
2. You have mortgage expenses or pay rent for the residence while you are on the road.
3. You or a member of your immediate family has lived in the area of your residence for a long time.

If you meet 2 of the 3 conditions, you *may* be able to use your residence as your tax home, but if you meet only one condition, you cannot do so. A member of the armed forces who maintains a home cannot treat the home as his or her tax home if he or she has a permanent duty station elsewhere.

If you regularly work in 2 or more locations, your tax home is the area of your *principal* work location. This is usually determined by the time spent in each location, the degree of business activity in each place, what income you receive from each place, where you have your home, and whether either location is temporary. You can't use any single factor to decide which of the 2 locations is your tax home.

Planning Tips

When you travel away from home, be sure to keep accurate and complete records of your travel and living expenses.

If you are in the armed forces and your ship or squadron is away from your home port or base, you may be able to deduct travel expenses while away. However, you are not treated as being "away" if you are at your permanent duty station or you are a naval officer assigned to permanent duty aboard a ship.

Pitfall

Spouses who live and work in different cities can have different tax homes. Just because they are treated as domiciled within the same place and may vote or file their taxes together, they may be restricted in deducting travel expenses between these locations.

Example

A couple maintains a home in Baltimore, where the husband resides. The wife works in New York City during the week and travels to Baltimore each weekend. Even though Baltimore is the city she considers home, she cannot deduct her travel costs between Baltimore and New York City, nor her living expenses in New York City. Her tax home is New York City, not Baltimore, and she is not traveling on business when she returns to Baltimore each weekend.

Where to Claim the Benefit

If you are an employee whose job-related travel costs on temporary work assignments are covered by an employer's accountable plan, you do not have to do anything. Reimbursements for this travel are *not* included on your Form W-2. You do not have to deduct anything (your employer claims the deduction for your travel costs).

If you are an employee whose job-related travel costs on temporary work assignments are *not* covered by an accountable plan, you first figure your deductible travel costs on Form 2106 or 2106-EZ. Your deductible expenses are then entered on Schedule A of Form 1040.

If you are self-employed, you deduct your business travel costs on temporary work assignments on Schedule C or C-EZ.

You cannot claim a deduction for business travel expenses on temporary work assignments if you file Form 1040A or 1040EZ.

Conventions

Conventions and trade shows are a key way in which businesses can show off their wares, make new connections, and learn about industry developments. To find the best shows to market your products or services, visit www.tradegroup .com/resources/showdirectories.htm. Whether you are an exhibitor or a visitor, your attendance costs may be deductible.

Benefit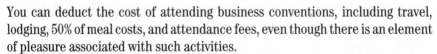

You can deduct the cost of attending business conventions, including travel, lodging, 50% of meal costs, and attendance fees, even though there is an element of pleasure associated with such activities.

There are restrictions, however, if you attend a convention held outside the North American area or on a cruise ship.

Conditions

You must be able to show that your attendance at the convention has some benefit to your trade or business. This can be shown by comparing the purpose of the convention as stated in its program or agenda with your official job duties or work.

The fact that you are appointed or elected as a delegate to the convention does not, by itself, establish a business benefit.

FOREIGN CONVENTIONS

If the convention is held outside the North American area, you must show that:

- The meeting is directly related to your trade or business.
- It is as reasonable to hold the meeting outside the North American area as in it. Reasonableness is based on the purpose of the meeting and activities taking place, the sponsoring group or organization, and the homes of active members. The North American area includes all of the locations detailed in Table 9.1.

TABLE 9.1 North American Area for Convention Deduction

American Samoa	Jarvis Island
Antigua and Barbados	Johnston Island
Aruba	Kingman Reef
Bahamas	Marshall Islands
Baker Island	Mexico
Barbados	Micronesia
Bermuda	Midway Islands
Canada	Netherlands Antilles
Costa Rica	Northern Mariana Islands
Curacao	Palau
Dominica	Palmyra
Dominican Republic	Panama
Grenada	Puerto Rico
Guam	Saint Lucia
Guyana	Trinidad and Tobago
Honduras	United States
Howland Island	U.S. Virgin Islands
Jamaica	Wake Island

CONVENTIONS ON CRUISE SHIPS

If you attend a business convention held on a cruise ship, your business deduction is limited to $2,000 per year (a limit in place since the Tax Reform Act of 1986 and not adjusted annually), regardless of the cost of the cruise or the number of convention cruises you take. And even this limited deduction can *only* be claimed if all 5 of these conditions are met:

1. The convention is directly related to your business.
2. The ship is a vessel registered in the United States.
3. All of the ports of call on the trip are in the United States or U.S. possessions.
4. You attach a signed statement to your return that includes the number of days for the cruise, the hours you spent each day devoted to scheduled business activities, and a copy of the program showing the scheduled business activities.
5. You also attach a signed statement by an officer of the organization or group sponsoring the meeting that shows the schedule of business activities each day and the number of hours you attended.

Planning Tip

Keep good records of your expenses at the convention, including a copy of the convention program with notations of the sessions you attended. If the convention has a sign-in book, be sure to sign in at every session.

If the convention is held on a cruise ship, follow the recordkeeping requirements discussed earlier.

Pitfall

If your spouse or other person accompanies you to the convention, you cannot deduct the expenses of your companion. This is so even if your companion is helpful to you.

However, as a practical matter, there may be no added cost for a second person in your room, so the only extras for your companion are meals and travel. And if you drive to the convention, even extra travel costs are eliminated.

Where to Claim the Deduction

If you are an employee whose job-related travel costs are covered by an employer's accountable plan, you do not have to do anything. Reimbursements for attendance at a business convention are *not* included on your Form W-2. You do not have to deduct anything (your employer claims the deduction for your travel costs).

If you are an employee whose job-related travel costs are *not* covered by an accountable plan, you first figure your deductible convention costs on Form 2106 or 2106-EZ. Your deductible expenses are then entered on Schedule A of Form 1040.

If you are self-employed, you deduct your business convention costs on Schedule C or C-EZ.

You cannot claim a deduction for business convention expenses if you file Form 1040A or 1040EZ.

Medical Travel

The days of doctors' house calls are all but over. To obtain medical assistance, you must go to the providers' sites—doctors' offices, hospitals, clinics, and other facilities. The tax law lets you treat your travel costs for medical purposes as a deductible medical expense.

Benefit ⊜

Medical insurance typically does not cover your expenses for getting to and from the doctor or pharmacy or other travel for other medical purposes. These costs are deductible as an itemized medical deduction. This means that the costs of medical travel are added to your other medical expenses, the total of which is deductible to the extent they exceed 10% of your adjusted gross income.

Conditions

To be treated as qualified medical expenses, the costs of travel must be related to obtaining a diagnosis, cure, mitigation, treatment, or prevention of disease or any treatment that affects a part or function of your body.

Deductible expenses include those paid not only for yourself, but also for a spouse and dependents. Who qualifies as a dependent is explained in Chapter 1.

EXAMPLES OF MEDICAL TRAVEL COSTS

- Ambulance hire
- Autoette (auto device for a handicapped person)
- Bus, cab, or train fare to see doctors, obtain treatment (including attendance at AA meetings, or to the gym if you are obese), or pick up prescriptions
- Car use to see doctors, obtain treatment (including attendance at AA meetings or to the gym if you are obese), or pick up prescriptions at 17¢ per mile for driving in 2017

- Medical conferences (travel costs and admission fees) on an illness or condition suffered by you, your spouse, or a dependent
- Lodging to receive outpatient care at a licensed hospital, clinic, or hospital-equivalent facility, up to $50 per night ($100 per night if you accompany a sick child)

Planning Tips

Keep good records of your expenditures for medical-related travel.

- For use of your car, note the date, purpose, and odometer reading at the start and end of each trip, as well as related parking and tolls
- For other travel costs, retain receipts of all expenses

Pitfall

You cannot deduct the costs of trips taken for general good health. For example, your car mileage to and from the gym is not deductible if you are there to improve your appearance or maintain general good health rather than to treat a condition such as obesity or high blood pressure.

Similarly, if you fly to Florida each winter to escape the cold of New Hampshire, you cannot deduct your travel costs, even though the warm climate may be beneficial to your health. You are not traveling for the purpose of obtaining treatment or for some other deductible medical purpose.

Where to Claim the Deduction

Medical travel costs, which are part of itemized medical expenses, are reported in the "Medical and Dental Expenses" section of Schedule A of Form 1040.

You cannot deduct medical expenses if you file Form 1040A or Form 1040EZ.

Charitable Travel

Volunteering for your favorite cause may cost you money; just getting to and from your volunteer activity can be an expense. The tax law lets you deduct your out-of-pocket travel costs incurred for charitable pursuits.

Benefit ⊜

If you use your car for charitable purposes, including attending meetings of organizations you serve, you can deduct either your actual car expenses for gas and oil or mileage at the rate of 14¢ per mile. Whichever method you select, you can also write off parking and tolls.

You can also deduct travel expenses, plus meals and lodging, for overnight trips away from home to serve as an official delegate to a convention of a church, charitable, veteran, or other similar organization.

Conditions

You qualify to deduct your car expenses to the extent that the use of your car is for a tax-exempt organization or governmental unit. To see whether the charity you work for is tax exempt, see Chapter 6.

You qualify for convention-related expenses that you are not reimbursed for if you serve as an official delegate on behalf of a religious, charitable, veteran, or other similar organization.

Planning Tip

Keep track of your mileage and out-of-pocket expenses on behalf of the charity. In a diary or logbook, note the odometer readings for every charity-related trip for which your car is used, as well as any related parking and tolls.

Pitfalls

You cannot deduct travel costs to work on a project for a nonprofit organization if there is a significant element of personal pleasure, recreation, or vacation involved.

You cannot deduct travel costs to attend a charity-related convention if you do not serve as an official delegate.

Where to Claim the Benefit

To claim a charitable deduction for your charity-related travel expenses, you must complete Schedule A of Form 1040. Enter your deduction for charity-related expenses in the "Gifts to Charity" section of Schedule A.

You cannot deduct donations if you file Form 1040A or Form 1040EZ.

Moving for Work

If you relocate your home because of a job or business and meet certain tests, you can deduct the cost of travel to your new location. If you use your car to move to your new home, you can deduct either your actual car expenses for gas and oil or a mileage rate of 17¢ per mile for driving in 2017. Whichever method you select, you can also write off parking and tolls.

For any of your travel costs to your new location to be deductible, you must meet the requirements for moving expenses, explained in Chapter 4.

Education-Related Travel

Unless you're taking classes online or via television from home or listening to teleconferences, you must travel to a classroom to learn. If the education is job-related, your travel costs may be deductible.

Benefit

Whether you drive across town to take college credits or fly across the country for a continuing education course, you can deduct your travel costs as a miscellaneous itemized deduction if the education is related to your job. For example, if you go to night school to take a computer course to keep you up-to-date for your job, which is working with computers, your travel from work to school and from school to home is deductible.

Education-related travel costs are added to your other miscellaneous itemized deductions, the total of which is deductible to the extent they exceed 2% of your adjusted gross income.

> **Example**
>
> In 2017, your adjusted gross income is $80,000. Your miscellaneous itemized deductions are $2,500. Since the first 2% of your adjusted gross income, or $1,600, is not deductible, you can write off $900 of such expenses.

Conditions

For educational travel to be treated as a deductible expense, the education you are traveling for must be job-related. This means that:

- You are employed (or self-employed). For example, you cannot deduct as job-related expenses the cost of an undergraduate education.
- You already meet the minimum job requirements for your position, based on employer standards and the laws and regulations of your state.
- The courses maintain or improve your current job skills.
- The courses do not lead to qualification for a new profession.

The rules on job-related education are explained more fully in Chapter 3.

EXAMPLES OF EDUCATIONAL TRAVEL COSTS

- Car expenses from work to school. You can deduct your actual costs or use the standard mileage rate for business travel (53.5¢ per mile in 2017), plus parking and tolls.

- Local transportation expenses (bus, subway, cab, train, or other fare) of going from your job to school.
- Car expenses or local transportation expenses (bus, subway, cab, train, or other fare) of going from school to home, *provided* you are regularly employed and going to school is a temporary endeavor (courses are expected to last no more than one year and do, in fact, end within this time).
- Travel costs away from home to attend a course (transportation to and from the course, lodging, and 50% of meals).

Example

You regularly work in New York City and every night for 6 weeks you take a refresher course. Since the course is temporary, you may deduct your travel expenses between work and school and school and home. It does not matter whether you go directly from work to school; your travel costs from home to school, in either or both directions, are deductible. The same is true if you take the refresher course on Saturday.

Planning Tip

If you are taking a course out of town and spend some time on personal activities, be prepared to prove that the primary purpose of the out-of-town travel was business-related education. This can be done by showing that you spend most of your time attending the course and only a relatively small amount of time on sightseeing or other personal activities.

Example

You travel from Boston, your place of employment, to Las Vegas for a 2-day continuing education program. If your total travel is 3 days, you can confidently show that the primary purpose of your trip is for the education so that your airfare to and from Boston is a deductible travel expense.

Example

Same facts except your trip to Las Vegas lasts 7 days. In this case, it may be difficult to show that the primary reason for the trip was job-related education since you spend 5 of the 7 days on personal activities. However, even if the airfare is not deductible, local transportation costs to and from the 2-day course are deductible.

Pitfalls

You cannot deduct travel that is educational in nature, even though it may be beneficial to your job. For example, a teacher may not deduct the cost of traveling to a foreign country to see the sights and absorb the culture. However, if the teacher takes courses abroad, then the travel costs become deductible even if the courses are not taken for credit. Decide whether it will save you money to pay for and take a course in order to deduct your travel costs.

If you are away from home for education purposes, you may not deduct travel costs for sightseeing, social visiting, or entertaining while taking the course.

You cannot deduct the cost of traveling to and attending investment seminars, despite how educational and beneficial they may be. The tax law specifically bans this deduction.

Where to Claim the Benefit

If you are an employee, then to claim a deduction for your education-related travel expenses, you must first complete Form 2106 or 2106-EZ to arrive at your unreimbursed employee business expenses. This total is then entered on the line provided for it on Schedule A of Form 1040.

If you are a self-employed individual, you enter your education-related travel on Schedule C or Schedule C-EZ.

You cannot deduct education-related travel if you file Form 1040A or Form 1040EZ.

National Guard and Military Reservist Travel

According to the 2017 Index of U.S. Military Strength, in the government's 2015 fiscal year, there were approximately 350,000 members of the National Guard and approximately 202,000 Military Reservists. If you're one of them, you likely have service-related costs and you may be able to deduct them.

Benefit

You can deduct your overnight travel costs as an adjustment to gross income rather than as an unreimbursed employee business expense subject to the 2% of AGI floor and the reduction of itemized deductions for high-income taxpayers.

Conditions

To claim the deduction, besides the obvious requirement of being a member of the National Guard or in the reserves, you must meet the following 3 conditions:

1. You must incur the costs to attend a meeting more than 100 miles away from home. You are considered to be away from home if you are away from

the permanent duty station long enough to require rest or sleep in order to complete your duties. For naval personnel of a drydocked submarine, your tax home is the area or vicinity of your principal place of employment or shore assignment (not the submarine itself).

2. The costs must relate to overnight transportation, meals, and lodging.

3. The amount of the deductible expenses cannot exceed the general federal per diem rate applicable to the locality to which you travel. You can find these per diem rates at www.gsa.gov (click on Per Diem Rates).

Planning Tips

Service-related travel expenses that cannot be deducted as an adjustment to gross income may be deductible as a miscellaneous itemized deduction (subject to the 2%-of-adjusted-gross-income floor).

Keep good records of your travel mileage and expenses to be able to substantiate the deduction you claim.

Pitfall

Only 50% of the cost of meals is deductible.

Where to Claim the Deduction

The deduction for travel expenses that meet these qualifications is claimed as an above-the-line deduction in the "Adjusted Gross Income" section of Form 1040.

You cannot claim this deduction if you file Form 1040A or 1040EZ.

Frequent Flier Miles

Whether you travel on business or for pleasure, you can build up frequent flier miles that can be cashed in for fares or upgrades. You can also earn frequent flier miles by charging goods and services to special credit cards that award mileage. Fortunately, there may be no tax cost to you for using frequent flier miles.

Benefit

You are not taxed on the value of frequent flier miles you earn on business travel and use for personal travel. For example, you earn enough points on your business travel throughout the year to receive free tickets for your summer vacation. You are not taxed on the frequent flier miles as they accrue, and you are not taxed when you use them for travel benefits—business or personal. The IRS, for the moment, has given up trying to tax this benefit because it is too difficult to assign a value to it. There is no dollar limit to the amount of this benefit that you can exclude from income.

Condition

To be excludable from income, frequent flier miles can be used only for in-kind benefits, which include free airline tickets or seat upgrades.

Planning Tips

Check on the expiration date of frequent flier miles you have earned so that you can use them up before it is too late.

Consider donating your frequent flier miles to charity. While you can't claim a tax deduction (there is no way to value the miles, and the donation is viewed as having been made to the user of the miles rather than to the organization), you'll benefit someone. For instance, Make-A-Wish Foundation needs over 2.8 billion miles annually to grant wishes to children with life-threatening medical conditions.

Pitfalls

If you convert frequent flier miles to cash, the cash value of the benefits must be reported as income in this case.

If you receive frequent flier miles as a bonus or gift, the miles *may* be taxable. For example, a few years ago Citibank ran a special promotion offering frequent flyer miles for opening deposit accounts and reported on a Form 1099 frequent flier miles at 2.5¢ per mile for those who opened new accounts.

Note: The IRS has said it may devise a way to tax frequent flyer miles, but to date no further information has been announced; see the Supplement.

Where to Claim the Exclusion

Since this employee fringe benefit is excluded from income, you do not have to report anything on your tax return. Frequent flier miles earned as an employee are not reported on your Form W-2.

Recordkeeping for Travel Expenses

The tax law requires you to keep records of your travel expenses as a condition for claiming a deduction. Your travel expense records must include the following information:

- *Amount.* The cost of each separate expense for travel, lodging, and meals. Incidental expenses can be totaled in any reasonable category (such as taxi fares). However, if you rely on a per diem rate for lodging, meals, and incidental expenses, you need not record these expenses nor retain receipts for them.

TABLE 9.2 Sample Weekly Travel Expense Record Keeper

Date: From: _____   To: _____

Expense	Sunday	Monday	Tuesday	Wednesday	Thursday	Friday	Saturday	Total
Airlines								
Excess baggage								
Bus								
Train								
Cab/limo								
Tips								
Other costs								
Hotel: Name City								
Breakfast								
Lunch								
Dinner								
Entertainment expenses								

- *Time.* Record the dates you leave and return for each trip and the number of days spent on business.
- *Place or destination.* Note the area of your travel (the name of the city, town, or other destination).
- *Business purpose.* Record the reason for the expense or the benefit to be gained, or expected to be gained, from the trip.

You can use the recordkeeper in Table 9.2 to record the amount of your travel expenses each week. You can also use a variety of apps for your smartphone or tablet to keep required records for deductible travel expenses.

In addition to your diary or logbook, you also need documentary proof of your expenses. This usually means retaining receipts, canceled checks, or other proof of what you paid for your travel expenses. However, you do not need receipts for expenses under $75 (except in the case of lodging, where proof is required regardless of the amount).

Entertainment

Alert

At the time this book was completed, Congress was considering important tax changes that could affect 2017 tax returns and planning for 2018. Check the online Supplement in February 2018 at www.jklasser.com or www.barbaraweltman.com to see what changes have been enacted and when they are effective.

Your personal entertainment costs—eating out, going to the movies or a ball game—are not deductible. But there's no law saying you can't combine business with pleasure—and make Uncle Sam foot the bill. It's common business practice to wine and dine customers, clients, and other business associates in the hopes of getting new business or keeping existing business. If you meet certain conditions, you can treat these expenses as deductible even though they may have provided some element of personal pleasure or recreation. But in view of the potential for abusing the write-off option, the IRS looks very closely at entertainment deductions. So be fully prepared to support any of your claims with the necessary proof to back up the positions you take on your tax return.

This chapter explains the types of entertainment costs you can deduct and the recordkeeping required to back up your write-offs. For more information, see IRS Publication 463, *Travel, Entertainment, Gifts, and Car Expenses*.

Meals and Entertainment

Wining and dining is a common business practice in just about every line of work. The government recognizes that this is standard operating procedure, but it doesn't want to underwrite the cost of a 3-martini lunch. So the cost of business meals and entertainment may be only partially deductible.

Benefit

In general, your meal costs are nondeductible personal expenses. But if your meal costs are business-related, they are deductible if certain conditions are met. It doesn't matter what time of the day you eat—breakfast, lunch, or dinner. Deductible costs include not only your meal expenses but also those of your guests. If you dine alone, your meal costs are deductible generally only when you are out of town on business.

You may be able to rely on standard meal allowances instead of keeping track of your actual meal costs (standard meal allowances and where to find these amounts are discussed later). Using a standard meal allowance simplifies your recordkeeping requirements.

Assuming you meet the conditions that transform your personal eating costs into a deductible business expense, you are then limited in most cases to writing off only 50% of your cost.

Conditions

For meals and entertainment when hosting business associates to be considered a deductible business expense, they must be an ordinary and necessary business expense (meaning a helpful and common practice in your trade or business), that is *either*:

- Directly related to the active conduct of your business ("directly related" test)
- Directly preceding or following a substantial and bona fide business discussion on a subject that is associated with the active conduct of your business ("associated with" test)

Business associates can include employees, agents, partners, your business accountant, your attorney, your insurance agent, your business banker, and suppliers—both established and prospective.

DIRECTLY RELATED TEST

The directly related test entails the conduct of business *at* the meal. There are 3 different ways in which you can meet the directly related test:

1. Show that the activity is generally related to your business. This means proving that you have more than a general expectation of getting future income or other business benefit (other than goodwill), whether or not such income or benefit ever materializes. Talk business during the meal, or at least have a reasonable intention of doing so.

2. Hold the meal in a clear business setting. Usually, if there are no distractions, just about any location can be considered a clear business setting because it is conducive to business discussions. Restaurants usually meet the bill, but nightclubs may not.

Example

You take a hospitality suite at a hotel where you display your business products. This is considered a clear business setting directly related to your business.

Example

You own a restaurant and give free meals to your supplier. This also is considered a clear business setting directly related to your business.

Example

You meet with several people, including some who are *not* business associates, at a cocktail lounge. This is *not* considered a clear business setting directly related to your business.

3. If your guest is an employee or your independent contractor, you can treat the meal as an expense made for the benefit of the guest as (1) compensation for service or (2) a prize or an award. In either event, the amount of the expense is deductible to you, but reported as income to the guest on Form W-2 as additional compensation to an employee or Form 1099-MISC

for an independent contractor (unless payments to the person are less than $600 for the year).

"ASSOCIATED WITH" TEST

Use this test when you are wining and dining in nonbusiness settings (such as nightclubs or dinner theaters) prospective clients, customers, or other business associates in the hope of getting new business or existing associates to engender goodwill that encourages continued business; the meal must come before or after you have conducted a genuine business discussion.

Example

You meet in your office to discuss the renewal of a contract with your supplier. Later that evening you take the supplier out to a nightclub. Since the dinner in this case follows a bona fide business discussion held earlier in the day in your office, you can treat the costs of your meal and the supplier's meal as a deductible business expense.

MEALS AWAY FROM HOME

You can't deduct your meal costs when you eat alone within the general area of your work. For example, if you eat lunch following a sales call on a customer across town, you cannot deduct the cost of the lunch. Or if you work overtime and grab a quick dinner before returning to the office for more work, you can't deduct your meal costs.

To deduct the costs of meals you eat alone, you must meet an overnight-sleep rule. You can only deduct meal costs incurred while away from home on a business trip that lasts longer than a regular workday (but not necessarily 24 hours) and requires you to take time off to sleep (not just to rest) before returning home. Taking a nap in your car on the side of the road does *not* meet the overnight-sleep test.

STANDARD MEAL ALLOWANCE

Instead of keeping track of your actual meal costs away from home, you can rely on government-set standard meal rates for your travel. You have several options for rates:

- *Maximum federal per diem rate*—an allowance for meals and incidental expenses (M&IE) for travel within the continental United States (CONUS). The rate you use depends on the location you are in. For the period October 1, 2016, through September 30, 2017, the rate for most locations is $51 per day. However, higher daily rates—$55, $59, $64, $69, and $74—apply in certain locations. For instance, the daily M&IE rate for Los Angeles and Manhattan is $74. For any changes in the rates for the period October 1, 2017, through September 30, 2018, see the Supplement.

- *High-low substantiation rate*—an allowance for meals and incidental expenses for CONUS travel. There are 2 rates: one for areas designated as "high-cost areas" and one for all other areas within CONUS. For the period starting October 1, 2016, the daily meal and incidental expenses rate for high-cost areas is $68; the daily rate for all other areas is $57. If the IRS increases the rates for high-low substantiation after September 30, 2017, they will be included in the Supplement.

- *Meal allowance for transportation industry workers*—an allowance for meals for employees and self-employed persons in the transportation industry. For the period October 1, 2016, through September 30, 2017, the standard daily meal allowance for travel within the continental United States is $63 per day, $68 for travel outside the continental United States. For any changes in the rates for the period from October 1, 2017, through September 30, 2018, see the Supplement.

For the fourth quarter of 2017, your employer may let you use the rates for October 1, 2016, through September 30, 2017, or the new rates that take effect on October 1, 2017. You can find rates for locations you travel to at www.gsa.gov (click on Per Diem Rates).

FIFTY PERCENT LIMITATION

Your deductible meal costs, whether entertaining others or dining alone out of town, are usually limited to 50%. This 50% limit applies whether you are an employee paying unreimbursed expenses or a self-employed individual in his or her own business. It also applies when you claim a standard meal allowance.

Example

Throughout the year you spend $480 on taking clients out to lunch and such costs are not reimbursed by your employer. You can deduct $240 (50% of $480) as an unreimbursed employee business expense.

Example

Throughout the year you spend $620 on meals you eat alone while out of town on business, which are not reimbursed by your employer. You can deduct $310 (50% of $620).

Because of the 50% limitation, it is necessary to allocate the cost of a hotel bill that includes your meals with your room charge—you separate the total cost between the expenses for the room itself and those for meals. Then apply the 50% limit to only the meal portion of the bill.

There are some important exceptions to the 50% limit. If you are an employee who is reimbursed for meal costs under an accountable plan, the 50% limit does not apply—tax-free reimbursement covers all of your meal costs.

For employees who work in the transportation industry and are subject to U.S. Department of Transportation (DOT) hours of service limitations, an increased percentage applies to meals consumed away from home. This limit for these workers is 80%.

If you are in business (these exceptions do not have application for employees), the 50% limit does not apply to:

1. Your employees' meal costs that you pay and treat as additional compensation.
2. Reimbursements to independent contractors for meal costs incurred on your behalf.
3. Company picnics and holiday parties open to all employees.
4. Meals included in advertising or promotional activities. For example, a real estate broker could deduct the cost of meals provided to potential investors attending his promotional seminar.
5. Meal costs for you and your staff if meals are sold to the public in the course of your business—for example, if you own a restaurant.
6. Food and beverages treated as *de minimis* fringe benefits to your employees. For example, if you provide doughnuts each morning for your staff, you can deduct their entire cost.

LAVISH AND EXTRAVAGANT

There is one more limitation that applies to meal and entertainment costs. They cannot be lavish or extravagant. There is no dollar amount used to make this determination; it depends on the facts and circumstances. If you use common sense and don't go overboard, the costs probably won't be considered lavish and extravagant.

Planning Tip

You may be able to deduct not only the costs for you and the business associate but for spouses as well. For example, if an out-of-town customer brings her spouse to dinner, the cost of meals for the customer, her spouse, and you and your spouse are deductible expenses.

Pitfall

You cannot convert nondeductible personal eating expenses by taking turns paying for meals with associates or business acquaintances. For example, you can't create an eating circle in which one person picks up the check in rotation in order to deduct costs for the group. If the directly related or associated with test is not satisfied, then no one within the group can pick up the check and write it off.

Where to Claim the Deduction

If you are an employee whose meal and entertainment costs are covered by an employer's accountable plan, you do not have to do anything. Reimbursements for these expenses are *not* included on your Form W-2. You are not allowed to deduct anything (your employer claims the deduction for your meals and entertainment costs).

If you are an employee whose meal and entertainment costs are *not* covered by an accountable plan, you first figure your deductible costs in Part II of Form 2106 or 2106-EZ. You enter your full expenses and the form then imposes the 50% limitation. Your deductible expenses are then entered on Schedule A of Form 1040.

If you are self-employed, you deduct your business meal and entertainment costs on Schedule C or C-EZ. You enter your full expenses and the schedule then imposes the 50% limitation.

You cannot claim a deduction for meal and entertainment expenses if you file Form 1040A or 1040EZ.

Company Holiday Parties and Picnics

Businesses commonly pay for certain activities to which employees have become accustomed—holiday parties, company picnics, and other annual events. How the costs of these activities are treated depends on which end you are on: Businesses may be able to deduct the costs, while employees who attend them usually aren't taxed on this benefit.

Benefit

If you are an employee, the value of company holiday parties, picnics, and other similar events you attend is treated as a tax-free fringe benefit. You are not taxed on this amount.

If you are a self-employed individual who pays for your company's holiday parties, picnics, or other similar events for your staff, you can deduct the cost of the event. The expense is fully deductible; even though meal costs are involved, they are *not* subject to the 50% limitation applied to most other business meal costs.

Conditions

To be a deductible entertainment expense for a self-employed individual, the company event must meet the entertainment expense requirements discussed earlier in this chapter.

Planning Tip

If your spouse or family attends the company event, you are *not* taxed on this benefit, either.

Pitfall

In most cases, you may not be able to deduct the costs you incur to enable you to attend a company event, such as the rental of a tuxedo.

Where to Claim the Deduction

If you are an employee who attends a company event, you are not taxed on the benefit you enjoy. Since the benefit is tax free, it is not reported on your Form W-2 and you do not have to report anything on your return.

If you are a self-employed individual, you deduct the cost of company-provided holiday parties, picnics, or other events as an entertainment expense on Schedule C of Form 1040. Make sure you do *not* apply the 50% limitation to these costs.

You cannot claim a deduction for these expenses if you file Form 1040A or Form 1040EZ.

Sporting and Theater Events

Business entertainment at sporting and theater events may be deductible. But because these are such clear recreational activities, strict conditions apply to make them deductible as business expenses. And then only a portion of the cost may be deductible.

Benefit

You can deduct the cost of tickets to sporting and theater events as long as you meet the general conditions for deducting entertainment expenses (discussed earlier in this chapter). Like other entertainment expenses, the cost of tickets is subject to a 50% limitation.

Special limits apply in the case of rental fees for skyboxes and private luxury boxes used for multiple events at sporting arenas or stadiums. In this case, your deduction usually is limited to the price of a nonluxury box seat ticket.

There is a special rule for tickets to events that benefit a charitable organization. In this case, your deduction is not limited to the face value of the ticket; you can deduct the full amount of what you pay for the event (which often exceeds the face or fair market value of the ticket) if you meet certain conditions. And the deduction is *not* limited to 50% of your costs.

Conditions

For the cost of tickets to sporting and theater events to be considered a deductible business expense, they must be an ordinary and necessary business expense (meaning helpful and common practice in your trade or business), which are either:

- Directly related to the active conduct of your business ("directly related" test)
- Directly preceding or following a substantial and bona fide business discussion on a subject that is associated with the active conduct of your business ("associated with" test)

Assuming you satisfy the directly related or associated with tests, then 50% of your costs are deductible as entertainment expenses.

These tests, including the 50% limitation, are explained in greater detail earlier in this chapter.

SKYBOXES AND PRIVATE LUXURY BOXES

How do you determine whether a skybox seat has been rented for more than one event? Count each game or performance as one event. For example, a skybox for a series of playoff games is treated as having been rented for each of these games. All skyboxes you rent in the same arena, plus any rentals by related persons (your close family members, related corporations, a partnership and its partners, a corporation and partnership with common ownership, or parties who have reciprocal arrangements to share boxes), are taken into account.

Example

You pay $2,000 to rent a 10-seat skybox at your local arena for 3 baseball games. The cost of a regular nonluxury box seat at each event is $20. You can deduct only $300 ([10 seats × $20] × 3 events = $600, which is then subject to the 50% limitation).

TICKETS TO SPORTS EVENTS BENEFITING CHARITY

You can deduct the full cost of what you pay for the events, even if the amount exceeds the actual ticket price, as long as you meet all 3 of these conditions:

1. The event's main purpose is to benefit a qualified charity. More details on qualified charities may be found in Chapter 6.
2. All of the net proceeds go to the charity.
3. The event uses volunteers to perform substantially all of the event's work.

Example

You pay $100 to enter your business in a golf tournament to benefit your local volunteer fire company at a local golf course where the greens fee is $30. All of the proceeds will be used to buy new firefighting equipment. The volunteer firefighters run the event. You can deduct the full $100, not merely the $70 in excess of the normal greens fee (and do not have to apply the 50% limitation), assuming your participation is a deductible entertainment expense.

"DIRECTLY RELATED" TEST

The directly related test entails the conduct of business *at* the entertainment event. There are 3 different ways in which you can meet the directly related test.

1. Show that the activity is generally related to your business. This means proving that you have more than a general expectation of getting future income or other business benefit (other than goodwill), whether or not such income or benefit ever materializes.
2. Talk business during the event, or at least have a reasonable intention of doing so.
3. Hold the event in a clear business setting. Usually, if there are no distractions, just about any location can be considered a clear business setting because it is conducive to business discussions. Sporting or theater events usually do not automatically fit the bill as a clear business setting because of the distractions.

"ASSOCIATED WITH" TEST

In the case of entertaining at sporting events or the theater, you are more likely to use the associated with test than the directly related test. This is because sports arenas and theaters aren't clear business settings. In this case, the event must come before or after you have conducted a genuine business discussion.

> **Example**
>
> You meet in your office to discuss the renewal of a contract with your supplier. Later that evening you take the supplier out to the theater. Since the entertainment in this case follows a bona fide business discussion held earlier in the day in your office, you can treat the costs of your ticket and the supplier's ticket as a deductible business expense.

Planning Tips

If you give business associates tickets to sporting or theater events *and* do not accompany them, you may have a choice on how to deduct expenses. You can treat them as entertainment costs (discussed earlier), which requires that you have bona fide business discussions preceding or following the event.

Alternatively, you can choose to treat the expense as a business gift, the cost of which is deductible up to $25 per gift per year. This deduction is *not* subject to the 50% limitation.

> **Example**
>
> Two out-of-town customers spend the afternoon at your office. You give them each theater tickets costing $40 apiece. You do not accompany them to the theater. You can deduct them as an entertainment expense, where your write-off is $40 ($40 × 2 × 50% limitation). Or you can deduct them as business gifts, where your write-off is $50 ($25 limitation on business gifts × 2). Since the gift option results in the larger deduction, you should select this option.

However, since the $25 gift deduction applies on a per-year basis, if you have already made deductible gifts to these customers this year, you can't use the second option and must treat the tickets as an entertainment expense.

You can even change your treatment of the cost at a later time by filing an amended return as long as it is not too late to still do so (generally, 3 years from the time you filed the return).

If you rent skyboxes and your deduction for tickets is limited (as explained earlier), you can also deduct food and beverages as a separate expense. Of course, the separate amount must be reasonable (you can't simply inflate the cost of the food and drinks as a way around the limit on skybox rentals).

Pitfall

As with other entertainment or gift expenses, you are required to keep good records to substantiate your deduction. The failure to do so can cost you the write-off you are otherwise entitled to claim.

Where to Claim the Deduction

If you are an employee whose entertainment costs are covered by an employer's accountable plan, you do not have to do anything. Reimbursements for this expense are *not* included on your Form W-2. You do not have to deduct anything (your employer claims the deduction for your entertainment costs).

If you are an employee whose entertainment costs are *not* covered by an accountable plan, you first figure your deductible costs in Part II of Form 2106 or 2106-EZ. You enter your full expenses and the form then imposes the 50% limitation. Your deductible expenses are then entered on Schedule A of Form 1040. If you are treating the cost of tickets as a business gift, do not apply the 50% limitation.

If you are self-employed, you deduct your business entertainment costs on Schedule C or C-EZ of Form 1040. You enter your full expenses and the schedule then imposes the 50% limit if applicable.

You cannot claim a deduction for entertainment expenses if you file Form 1040A or 1040EZ.

Home Entertainment

Entertainment of business clients, customers, and associates isn't limited to restaurants, clubs, and bars. You can easily conduct your entertaining at home. The cost of home entertainment is deductible within limits if certain conditions are met.

Benefit

If you entertain business clients, customers, or other business associates in your home, you may be able to deduct 50% of your costs. Your costs may include food, beverages, paper goods, dishware rentals, and even charges for a maid or bartender to assist you.

Conditions

The same conditions that apply to meals and entertainment costs in general (discussed earlier in this chapter) apply to home entertaining. You must meet the directly related or associated with test and apply the 50% limitation. Your expenses cannot be lavish or extravagant.

Planning Tips

This type of entertainment can raise eyebrows with the IRS. Dinners, which are conducive to business discussions, may be appropriate vehicles for business entertaining. It is probably a good idea to limit the guest list to no more than a dozen people. A larger crowd makes it more difficult to demonstrate that you conducted bona fide business discussions in your home.

Events such as pool parties may not easily satisfy the conditions for deductible entertainment costs and probably are not advisable.

Pitfall

You cannot claim a deduction for home entertainment for personal reasons. Parties for personal events, such as a child's birthday party, probably won't satisfy the conditions for deductibility. Even if business associates are invited, it may be difficult to prove that business discussions are carried on (court decisions on these types of events usually have not gone in favor of taxpayers).

Where to Claim the Deduction

If you are an employee whose entertainment costs are covered by an employer's accountable plan, you do not have to do anything. Reimbursements for this expense are *not* included on your Form W-2. You do not have to deduct anything (your employer claims the deduction for your entertainment costs).

If you are an employee whose entertainment costs are *not* covered by an accountable plan, you first figure your deductible entertainment costs in Part II of Form 2106 or 2106-EZ. Your deductible expenses are then entered on Schedule A of Form 1040.

If you are self-employed, you deduct your home entertainment costs for business on Schedule C or C-EZ.

You cannot claim a deduction for home entertainment expenses for business if you file Form 1040A or 1040EZ.

Entertainment Facilities and Club Dues

The "old boy" network is famed as a means of making connections helpful to business. This network, which isn't limited to men, is often found at country clubs, civic organizations, and other associations. The tax law heavily restricts your ability to deduct the costs of belonging to these groups, even though there is a strong business reason for doing so.

Benefit

You may *not* deduct the cost of buying or maintaining entertainment facilities, which include yachts, hunting lodges, fishing camps, swimming pools, tennis courts, hotel suites, company apartments, or homes in vacation areas. This ban applies even if the main reason for the facility is to entertain clients and customers. By law, the cost of entertainment facilities is not deductible.

You may not deduct the cost of membership in a golf, tennis, swim, or hunting club; an airline club; a hotel club; a business luncheon club; or any other club organized for pleasure, recreation, or social purposes. Again, this ban applies even if there is a strong business element involved.

However, there are 2 key exceptions to the bans on deducting the cost of entertainment facilities and club dues.

1. You can deduct expenses for food and drinks at the facility when your entertainment meets the conditions discussed earlier in this chapter.
2. You can deduct dues paid to civic or public service organizations, such as Kiwanis, Lions, and Rotary clubs; professional organizations such as medical or bar associations; and chambers of commerce, trade associations, business leagues, real estate boards, and boards of trade.

Conditions

Separate conditions apply, depending on which exception to the ban on entertainment facilities and club dues you are qualifying under.

FOOD AND DRINKS AT FACILITIES

To deduct the costs of food and drinks at entertainment facilities, you must meet the conditions discussed earlier for writing off entertainment costs.

CLUB DUES

You must be able to demonstrate that membership in any of the clubs listed earlier does not have a principal purpose of providing entertainment for members or their guests.

Planning Tips

If you maintain an entertainment facility, you can still write off any costs that would otherwise be deductible.

Example

You own a hunting lodge to which you bring clients and customers. You cannot deduct depreciation on the lodge, nor operating expenses such as utilities, security, and maintenance. But you can deduct real estate taxes and mortgage interest, which are deductible in any event.

If you are a self-employed individual who pays country club dues on behalf of employees, you can turn a nondeductible expense into a deductible one by treating the expense as additional compensation. You then deduct the expense as compensation. This option applies only if the employees use the club for business purposes (not if the employees use the club for personal purposes). You can make this election on an employee-by-employee basis. So, for example, if you are a shareholder-employee, there may not be any net benefit for making this election with respect to your compensation; you are merely shifting the tax from the corporation to you. But you can opt to treat the payment as compensation for your other employees, saving the corporation money.

Pitfall

If your employer pays for a membership on your behalf, your employer may opt to include this benefit in your income (so that it becomes a deduction for the employer). It is reported to you as additional compensation on your Form W-2 and is subject to income tax.

Where to Claim the Deduction

If you are an employee who pays for club dues that are not *barred* (e.g., dues to Rotary Club), you deduct your costs. You first enter these costs in Part I of Form 2106 or 2106-EZ. Your deductible expenses are then entered on Schedule A of Form 1040.

If you are self-employed, you deduct your allowable club dues on Schedule C or C-EZ.

You cannot claim a deduction for allowable club dues if you file Form 1040A or 1040EZ.

Recordkeeping for Meals and Entertainment Expenses

The tax law requires you to keep records of your meals and entertainment expenses as a condition for claiming a deduction, in addition to receipts and other proof of payment. Your meal and entertainment expense records must include the following information:

- *Amount.* Record the cost of each separate expense for meals and entertainment. Incidental expenses can be totaled in any reasonable category (such as taxi fares).
- *Time.* Record the dates of your meals and entertainment.
- *Place.* Note the location of the meals or entertainment. Also note the type of entertainment if it is not apparent.
- *Business purpose.* Record the reason for the expense or the benefit to be gained or expected to be gained from the meals or entertainment. For entertainment, note the nature of the business discussion or activity; whether the entertainment is directly before or after a business discussion; and the

TABLE 10.1 Sample Weekly Meal and Entertainment Expense Record Keeper—Details

Date: From: _____   To: _____

Date	Item	Place	Amount*	Business Purpose	Business Relationship

*You do not have to keep track of amounts for meals if you rely on a standard meal allowance.

date, place, nature, and duration of the business discussion. Identify the persons who took part in both the business discussion and the entertainment activity.

You can use Tables 10.1 and 10.2 to record the amounts of your meals and expenses each week. Enter the details of the expenses in Table 10.1. Then enter the totals in the appropriate spaces provided in Table 10.2.

As stated earlier, in addition to your diary or logbook, you also need documentary proof of your expenses. This usually means retaining receipts, canceled checks, or other proof of what you pay for your meals and entertainment expenses. However, you do not need receipts for any of these expenses under $75.

Gambling Losses

Legal gambling in casinos other venues, such as racetracks and online sites, and illegal gambling, such as office pools ($10.4 billion for March Madness 2017 according to the American Gambling Association), mean a lot of money is

TABLE 10.2 Sample Weekly Meal and Entertainment Expense Record Keeper—Summary

Date: From: _____   To: _____

Expense	Sunday	Monday	Tuesday	Wednesday	Thursday	Friday	Saturday	Total
Breakfast								
Lunch								
Dinner								
Entertainment expenses								

being wagered each year. Everyone knows that the odds always favor the house, whether it is a casino, race track, or state lottery. The chances of losing far outweigh those of winning. The tax law allows gambling losses to be deductible within limits under certain conditions.

Benefit

You can deduct gambling losses to the extent of your gambling winnings for the year. The losses do not have to result from the same gaming activities that produce the winnings.

If you are not a professional gambler, then gambling losses are claimed as miscellaneous itemized deductions, but they are *not* subject to the 2% of adjusted gross income floor that applies to most other miscellaneous itemized expenses.

If you are a professional gambler who devotes full time to this activity, you can treat your losses as a business expense. But even in this case gambling losses are limited to the extent of your winnings.

Example

During 2017, you spend $20 every week to play bingo ($1,040 for the year) and you do not win anything. But in December 2017, you win $500 on a state-sponsored scratch-off game. In 2017, you can deduct $500 of your bingo losses; the other $540 of your gambling losses is not deductible, and cannot be carried forward to offset winnings in a future year.

Conditions

You must report the gambling winnings that equal or exceed your claimed losses for the year. And you must have adequate records or receipts to prove your gambling expenses.

The Tax Court says that gambling winnings can include "comps" given to high rollers by a casino, such as a car, jewelry, and tickets to sporting events.

Planning Tips

Keep track of the amount you gamble throughout the year, since you don't know when in the year you will win. For example, retain all losing lottery tickets as proof of your gambling expenses so you can claim these losses when and to the extent you have winnings for the year. If you play the slots, whether you win or lose is calculated with reference to your wager for the day. If you wager $100 in slot tokens, for example, and at the end of the day redeem $60, you have a $40 loss even though you may have had a winning spin of $1,000 during the day.

For the slot machines, determine "losses" carefully. The IRS says your losses are determined as of the end of a calendar day or the casino's gaming day (at the casino's option). Compare what you start the day with against the amount you have at the end to determine your loss (or gain). For example, if you start with $100 and at the end of the day you have only $50, you have a $50 gambling loss even though you may have hit jackpots throughout the day of $200 or $2,000, or had losing spins of more than $50. The casino must report winnings of $1,200 or more on Form W-2G, with no reduction for the amount of the wager.

Pitfalls

Gambling winnings may be reported to you (and the IRS) on Form W-2G, *Certain Gambling Winnings*. The reporting threshold depends on the type of gambling (e.g., horse racing, slot machines, lotteries). If you claim losses in excess of amounts reported to the IRS, be prepared to show you had other winnings and that you reported these other winnings as income on your return.

Be sure to pay sufficient taxes on winnings to avoid estimated tax penalties. Winnings of $5,000 or more are subject to income tax withholding, but this withholding may not adequately cover your liability; you are entirely responsible for estimated taxes on smaller winnings.

Where to Claim the Deduction

If you are not a professional gambler, you claim a deduction for gambling losses in the space provided on Schedule A of Form 1040. The deduction for wagering losses is *not* subject to the reduction in itemized deductions for high-income taxpayers.

If you are a full-time professional gambler, you can treat your gambling losses as a business expense. The wages must be placed only for your own account. Gambling losses in this case are reported on Schedule C or Schedule C-EZ of Form 1040. You cannot claim a deduction for gambling losses if you file Form 1040A or 1040EZ.

Real Estate

Alert

At the time this book was completed, Congress was considering important tax changes that could affect 2017 tax returns and planning for 2018. Check the online Supplement in February 2018 at www.jklasser.com or www.barbaraweltman.com to see what changes have been enacted and when they are effective.

The housing market is recovering and the vast majority of Americans own real estate, with about 63.6% owning their own homes. (Tax write-offs for your main home are discussed in Chapter 4.) But owning a principal residence isn't the only way to invest in real estate. Many individuals also own second homes or invest in rental properties to generate income. These investments produce important tax breaks.

This chapter covers tax breaks related to real estate other than your principal residence. For more information, see IRS Publication 527, *Residential Rental Property (Including Rental of Vacation Homes)*; IRS Publication 587, *Business Use of Your Home (Including Use by Day-Care Providers)*; and IRS Publication 946, *How to Depreciate Property*.

Vacation Home

The rich have traditionally maintained more than one residence, summering in Newport, skiing in Aspen, escaping winters in Miami. But today, second homes aren't limited to the very rich; they are increasingly common among an ever-broadening populace. The tax law offers some tax breaks that help to make ownership of vacation homes more affordable.

Benefit

If you use your vacation home solely for your own personal enjoyment (you don't rent it out at any time during the year), you can deduct all of your real estate taxes and home mortgage interest (if the vacation home is designated as your second home under the home mortgage interest rules in Chapter 4). But, like your personal residence, you can't write off any of the costs of utilities, insurance, or upkeep.

If you rent out a home that you use for part of the year yourself, you may be entitled to certain tax benefits over and above those allowed for pure personal use of the home. The rules that apply to you depend on your rental period and the time that you use the home.

Conditions for Vacation Home with No Rentals

The conditions for deducting real estate taxes and home mortgage interest are explained in Chapter 4.

Conditions for Vacation Home with Rentals

The conditions you must meet and the benefits you are entitled to depend on how long you rent out the home and how long you use it for yourself during the year. There are 3 categories into which you can fall.

1. Rental of no more than 14 days during the year.
2. Rental of 15 days or more but personal use is for less than 14 days or 10% of the days of rental.

3. Personal use is more than 14 days or 10% of the total days the home was rented for a fair rental price.

TAX-FREE RENTAL INCOME

If you rent out your home for no more than 14 days during the year, you do not have to report the rental income. There's no dollar limit on this exclusion.

> **Example**
>
> In February 2017, because of your proximity to Super Bowl 50, you rented your home in Santa Clara, California, for 3 days. You receive a rental payment of $1,900 per day, for a total of $5,700. None of the $5,700 is taxable.

You cannot, however, deduct any expenses related to maintaining the home, depreciation, or any rent you pay. Of course, if you itemize your deductions, you can deduct your mortgage interest, if you designate the home as your second residence, and your real estate taxes (there is no limit on the number of homes for which you can deduct real estate taxes).

BUSINESS DEDUCTIONS

If you rent out your home for 15 days or more but you personally use the home for less than 14 days or 10% of the days of rental, your rental activities are viewed as a business.

> **Example**
>
> You rent out your home for 3 months and use it for only 1 week during the year. Since the rental period is more than 15 days (it is actually 92 days) and your personal use is less than 14 days or 10% of the days of rental (9 days), you fall within this rule for figuring your deductions from the rental activity.

As such, you must report all of the rental income, but you can deduct from rental income only the mortgage interest, real estate taxes, operating expenses, and depreciation prorated for rental use. If your prorated expenses, including depreciation on a home you own, exceed your rents for the year, you can use the loss to offset your income from other purposes (subject to the passive loss limitations discussed further on).

Personal use of your home includes any day the home is used by:

- You or any member of your family (unless a family member pays a fair rental price)
- Anyone else who pays less than a fair rental price

- Anyone under a reciprocal agreement who lets you use his or her home
- Any other person who owns a part of the home (unless it is rented to that person under a shared equity agreement)

You do not have to count your personal use during the year if your home is rented for at least 12 consecutive months.

Example

You move from your home in March 2017 and start renting it in April 2017. Assuming your rental lasts at least until through March 2018, you do not have to count your personal use in 2017.

However, your actual write-offs for the year may be limited by the passive activity loss rules discussed later.

LIMITED BUSINESS DEDUCTIONS

If your personal use is more than 14 days or 10% of the total days the home was rented for a fair rental price, you must report all of the rental income. Your deductions are limited to the amount of rents you receive. And the order in which you claim your deductions is carefully orchestrated:

1. Mortgage interest, real estate taxes, and casualty losses are fully deductible. You can claim them even if they exceed your rental income. But you must apply them first against your rental income to determine how much of your other deductions to claim.
2. Operating expenses, such as utilities and maintenance costs, are deductible only to the extent of your rental income after reduction for mortgage interest and so on.
3. Depreciation and other basis adjustments are deductible only to the extent that rental income has not yet been fully offset by the aforementioned deductions.

Example

You own a condo at the shore. You rent it out for June and July. You use it for August. Since your rental is 61 days and your personal use is 31 days, you must figure your deductions using this ordering rule. Assume you receive $6,000 for the 2 months of rental, and your deductions for the year are $2,000 for interest and $3,000 for taxes. In this case, you can deduct up to $1,000 of operating

(Continued)

(*Continued*)

expenses. Assuming you have at least $1,000 of operating expenses, then you cannot claim any depreciation. Your deductions, in effect, fully offset your rental income so you have no taxable income from your rental activity.

PASSIVE LOSS LIMITATIONS

If the rental of your vacation home is treated as a rental activity (your personal use is fewer than 15 days but the rental period is more than 2 weeks), you are subject to the passive loss rules. Generally, your deductions related to the rental of your home cannot exceed all of your passive activity income from the year (income from this rental activity plus any other passive activities). (The law calls them passive "losses" but really means deductions in excess of rental income.)

Example

The rental of a vacation home is your only passive activity. Rental income for the year is $6,000, while deductions are $8,000. You can deduct only $6,000 this year.

Passive activity losses in excess of passive activity income can be carried forward and used in a future year when there is passive activity income to offset it. There is no limit on the carryforward period.

There are 3 key exceptions to the ban on deducting passive losses in excess of passive activity income.

1. You can deduct all carryover losses from a passive activity in the year in which you dispose of your passive activity (e.g., sell your vacation home).
2. You can deduct up to $25,000 of passive activity losses in excess of passive activity income from a rental activity in which you actively participate (e.g., approve new tenants, decide on rental terms, and authorize capital expenditures and repairs). The $25,000 limit is phased out when your modified adjusted gross income exceeds $100,000 and is completely phased out when MAGI reaches $150,000. MAGI for this purpose means AGI without taxable Social Security benefits, the exclusion for interest from U.S. savings bonds used for higher education, the exclusion for employer-paid adoption expenses, and the deductions for IRA contributions and student loan interest. You cannot use the $25,000 allowance if you are married and file a separate return.

Example

You are single with MAGI of $135,000. You actively participate in the rental of your condo at a ski resort. Your rental loss in excess of passive activity income is limited to $7,500: $25,000 − 50% of ($135,000 − $100,000).

3. You are a "real estate professional" who meets certain tests in the tax law. In this case, your losses from rental realty are not subject to the passive activity loss rules. This is explained in greater detail later in this chapter under "Rentals."

Planning Tip

If you rent out your vacation home for more than 15 days and use it for less than 14 days or 10% of the days of rental, you are *not* subject to the passive activity loss limitations on your deductions if you are considered a "real estate professional." This means:

- More than 50% of your personal services during the year are performed in real estate trades or businesses in which you materially participate (e.g., work more than 500 hours for the year, which is 10 hours a week for 50 weeks, or your participation is substantially all of the participation for the activity during the year).

- You perform more than 750 hours of service in real estate trades or businesses in which you materially participate.

Pitfalls

Getting help with home renovations through an HGTV show may be taxable even if the show uses the home for fewer than 15 days. The value of the home improvements is not tax-free rental, but rather taxable income.

If you rent out your home for more than 15 days but use it for less than 14 days or 10% of the rental days, you cannot deduct the portion of home mortgage interest disallowed under the rental loss rules discussed earlier. In this case, since your home ceases to be treated as a personal residence, you cannot itemize any portion of the mortgage interest.

When you sell your vacation home, don't be surprised by the tax impact that can result. Your gain probably does not qualify for the home sale exclusion (see Chapter 4) because the vacation home is not your principal residence. As long as you own the home for more than one year, your gain is a long-term capital gain.

However, if you rented the home at any time and claimed depreciation on it, you must recapture the depreciation on the sale. This means that gain to the extent of your depreciation is taxed at 25% (assuming you are in a tax bracket at or above this rate).

Example

In 2017, you sell your vacation home for a profit of $100,000. You had bought the home in 2010 and claimed depreciation deductions for the rental of the home totaling $2,800. Of the $100,000 gain, $2,800 is taxed at 25%, while $97,200 is taxed at 15% (20% if you are in the 39.6% tax bracket).

If you realize a loss on the sale of your vacation home, your ability to claim the loss depends on whether or not the home was used for rental.

- If the home was used solely for personal purposes, no loss can be claimed on the sale.
- If the home was used some of the time for rental activities, you cannot claim a loss on the sale.
- If the home was converted solely to rental, you can then claim a capital loss on the sale. The loss is limited to the decline in value after the conversion.

Example

If the home was purchased for $150,000 and has declined in value to $125,000 when you decide to sell it, you can convert it to rental at this time and figure your deductible loss with reference to the $125,000 value. Assume you sell the home after a year on the market for $100,000. Your actual loss is $50,000 ($150,000 – $100,000), but your deductible loss is $25,000 ($125,000 – $100,000). Converting the home to rental means holding the property out for rental, even if you are unsuccessful in your efforts.

Where to Claim the Benefit

If you use your vacation home solely for personal purposes, you deduct your mortgage interest and real estate taxes on Schedule A of Form 1040 (as explained in Chapter 4).

If you rent out your vacation home, you report your rents and expenses in Part I of Schedule E of Form 1040 (unless rental income from your vacation home is tax free).

If you are subject to the passive activity loss limitations, you must complete Form 8582, *Passive Activity Loss Limitations*, to determine your deduction limit for the year.

If you have income from rental activities and you are not a real estate professional, this income is taken into account in determining the net investment income (NII) tax figured on Form 8960, *Net Investment Income Tax—Individuals, Estates, and Trusts*.

You cannot use Form 1040A or 1040EZ if you have rental real estate activities.

Home Office

The president of the United States works from home, but since he doesn't pay for the costs of the Oval Office, he can't claim any deduction for his home office. But if you work from your home, you may qualify for write-offs if certain conditions are met.

Benefit

If you use a part of your home for business, you may qualify to deduct costs related to the home office, including rent (if you lease your residence) or depreciation (if you own your home), maintenance and utilities, and other expenses. In effect, the personal expenses you are already paying become deductible business expenses, so the home office deduction is a write-off that doesn't require you to pay anything other than what you are already paying. Alternatively, you can opt to use an IRS-set standard amount for your home office deduction.

Generally, you figure your home office deduction by apportioning expenses to that space. The IRS generally wants you to make the apportionment based on square footage. For example, if your home is 2,500 square feet and you use 250 square feet of it for a home office, then generally 10% of your home's expenses are part of your home office deduction if you figure your deduction based on your actual expenses. If you use the IRS-set simplified method, you can take into account your square footage up to 300 square feet to figure your deduction.

If all your rooms are about the same size, you can opt to make your allocation based on the number of rooms. For example, if you have 8 rooms in your home and one is used for business, then one-eighth of your home's expenses are part of your home office deduction. If you use the IRS's simplified method, your deduction is $5 per square foot of up to 300 of square feet, for a maximum deduction of $1,500. If you base your deduction on your actual costs, the computation is more complex. There are 2 general categories of deductible expenses—those directly related to the home office and those indirectly related to the home office. The first category includes only costs for the office itself, and these costs are fully deductible; the second category includes costs related to the home in general, and these are deductible to the extent of your allocation.

> **Example**
>
> If you paint the office, it is a direct expense and is fully deductible. If you paint the outside of your home, it is an indirect expense and is deductible to the extent of your allocation. For example, if your allocation to the home office is 10%, then 10% of the outside paint job is part of your home office deduction.

If you own the home, you can claim depreciation on the portion of the house or other unit (not the land) used as a home office (see later in this chapter under Rentals). Usually, depreciation is figured using a 39-year recovery period on a straight line basis. However, if the office is within property qualifying as residential rental property (e.g., you use one room in your apartment within an 8-unit building you own), then depreciation is figured using a 27.5-year recovery period.

Conditions

To be eligible to treat costs related to a home office as a deductible business expense (regardless of how you figure the deduction), you must first show that the office is one of the following:

- Your principal place of business
- A place to meet or deal with patients, clients, or customers in the normal course of your business
- A separate structure (not attached to your residence) that is used in connection with your business

Then you must show that you use the home office regularly and exclusively for business. Assuming you meet this condition, you must have sufficient income from your home office activity. Finally, if you are an employee, you must satisfy an additional condition: Use of the home office must be for the convenience of your employer. This is explained later in this section.

PRINCIPAL PLACE OF BUSINESS

The home office must be the prime location for running your business. The business itself need not be your prime activity; you can claim a home office deduction for a sideline or moonlighting business. Usually, prime location means the place where you earn your money. For example, a freelance writer's prime location is her home office.

Your home office is treated as your prime location if it is used for substantial managerial or administrative activities and there is no other fixed location for these activities. For example, an electrician's prime location is the customers' homes where his fees are earned. But if he uses a home office to keep his books, schedule appointments, and order supplies, and he does not have another office, then the home office is treated as his prime location.

PLACE TO MEET OR DEAL WITH CUSTOMERS

You don't have to use your home office as your prime location. You merely have to use it on a regular basis to meet or deal with customers, clients, or patients. For example, an attorney with a downtown office who uses a home office several times each month to meet with clients qualifies as having a deductible home office. Merely using a telephone from a home office to talk with clients or customers is *not* considered meeting or dealing with them on a regular basis.

SEPARATE STRUCTURE

If you have a freestanding garage, barn, greenhouse, or studio that you use in connection with your business, it qualifies as a deductible home office. It does not have to be used as an office or qualify as a principal place of business or a place to meet or deal with customers. For example, a florist with a store in the city who uses a greenhouse on her property to grow orchids can treat the greenhouse as her home office.

EXCLUSIVE USE TEST

Whether you figure the deduction based on actual expenses or the IRS-set rate, you must show that you use the home office space regularly and exclusively for business. There is no minimum amount of time that the office must be used to show regular use. Regular use means more than just occasional use.

For purposes of showing exclusive use, you can't, for example, use the family den as an office by day and a family room by night. A piano teacher was able to show that her living room containing her baby grand piano was her home office; her family never used the room for personal reasons. However, incidental use, such as walking through the office to get to personal space because of necessity does not violate the exclusive use test.

You do not have to use an entire room as your office; a portion of a room can qualify. You don't even need to make a physical partition for the space. Just be sure it is used only for business. Furnish it appropriately for your business activity (e.g., a desk, and so on if you run a travel agency business from home).

There is a special rule if you run a day-care business from home (explained in IRS Publication 587, *Business Use of Your Home*).

GROSS INCOME LIMITATION

Your home office deduction cannot be more than your gross income from the home office activity whether you use the actual expense method or the IRS's simplified method. If you use your home office for a profitable business, this limitation should pose no problem. But if your business is merely a sideline generating modest income or a struggling business, you must check whether this limitation applies to you.

Gross income for purposes of the home office deduction means income from the business activity you run from home.

- If you are self-employed, this is your profit reported on Schedule C.
- If you are an employee, this is your salary earned from the home office.

If you find that gross income is less than your home office deduction, the deduction becomes limited. Under the actual expense method, your deduction for expenses that would otherwise be nondeductible (such as depreciation and utilities—category 1) cannot exceed gross income from the home office activity, reduced by the business portion of otherwise deductible expenses (such as home mortgage interest and real estate taxes—category 2), plus business expenses not attributable to business use of the home (such as salaries and supplies—category 3). In effect, this rather complex-sounding rule merely orders the categories of deductions you can claim.

Example

In 2017, you run a sideline business from home, showing a profit of $4,500 on Schedule C. You use the actual expense method and your deductions in the 3 categories of expenses are $1,200 for category 1, $1,400 for category 2, and $2,200 for category 3. Your category 1 deductions are limited to $900: $4,500 gross income − ($1,400 + $2,200).

If, after going through the computation, you have an unused home office deduction, you can carry it forward indefinitely. (There is no carryover if you use the IRS's simplified method.) The carryforward can be used in any future year in which there is gross income from the same home office activity to offset it. Using the carryforward is permissible even if you are no longer in the same home office.

Example

Same as the preceding example except that at the end of 2017 you relocate to a larger home. You continue to conduct your sideline business from your new home. In 2018, you can use the $300 home office deduction carryforward (assuming your sideline business has sufficient gross income).

CONVENIENCE OF THE EMPLOYER

If you are an employee who works from home, you have an additional condition to satisfy when claiming a home office deduction. As a telecommuter, you must be able to show that use of your home office is for the convenience of your employer (and not simply for your convenience or preference).

Be prepared to show a real need on your employer's part to have you work from home. This can be easily proven when there is no desk space for you at your employer's location. Just getting a letter from your employer stating your home office use is for the employer's convenience is not enough proof for the IRS; the letter must explain *why* it is for the employer's convenience (e.g., no space for you in the employer's location).

Planning Tips

If you were unable to claim the full home office deduction in a prior year due to income limitations, be sure to include any carryover of the home office deduction in your computations for the current year.

If you qualify for a home office, there are some ancillary benefits to consider. Travel to and from your home on business is deductible business travel. In effect, there is no such thing as nondeductible commuting when you have a home office.

Another ancillary benefit concerns depreciation on a computer used in your home office. A computer used in a regular business establishment is not treated as listed property for which you must prove that business use exceeds 50% in order to claim first-year expensing or accelerated depreciation. Since the computer is used in a home office, which is treated as a regular business establishment, you are presumed to use it more than 50% of the time on business. You do not have to maintain any logs showing the use of the computer.

Pitfalls

You cannot claim a home office deduction if you are an employee who leases the space to your corporation. The tax law specifically bars a home office deduction in this case. However, like any homeowner, you can continue to claim your regular deductions, such as mortgage interest, real estate taxes, and casualty and theft losses.

If you are an employee using a home office for the convenience of your employer, you cannot figure your deduction using the IRS's optional method if you receive advances, allowances, or reimbursements from your employer for the home office.

If you use the IRS's optional method and cannot claim a current deduction because of the gross income limitation, you *cannot* carry over the unused deduction to a future year. And, the year you use the optional method, you cannot claim any carryover of an unused home office deduction from a year in which the actual expense method was used.

When figuring the deduction using actual expenses, all expenses related to your home office are deductible. The cost of landscaping is not part of a home office deduction. Similarly the expenses of a telephone to a home office are not part of your home office deduction. You cannot deduct the basic service charge for the first line to your home. But the cost of a second phone line or even extra charges on the first line are separately deductible as a business expense that is not part of your home office deduction.

Claiming a home office deduction has often been called a red flag, a signal to the IRS to look closely at the deduction. However, if you are entitled to claim the deduction, then by all means do so; just be prepared to back up the position you take on your tax return.

If you own your home, then any depreciation claimed with respect to a home office after May 6, 1997, must be recaptured when your home is sold. Recapture means that this portion of your gain is taxed at a 25% rate (assuming you are in a tax bracket at or above this level). You must report your depreciation even if you qualify to exclude gain on the sale of your home; you cannot use the exclusion to offset depreciation recapture.

Where to Claim the Deduction

If you are an employee, you figure your home office deduction on a worksheet in IRS Publication 587 (you do *not* use the home office deduction form, Form 8829). The amount of your home office deduction is then entered on Form 2106 or 2106-EZ. Deductions from Form 2106 or 2106-EZ are then entered as miscellaneous itemized deductions on Schedule A of Form 1040.

If you are a self-employed individual, you figure your home office deduction using actual expenses on Form 8829, *Expenses for Business Use of Your Home*. The deduction using the IRS's simplified method is figured on a worksheet in the instructions to Schedule C.

In either event, you cannot claim a home office deduction if you file Form 1040A or 1040EZ.

Timeshares

Owning a timeshare entitles you to use your furnished unit in a resort location for a set period of time each year. In many cases, you can exchange yours for one in another resort or change your fixed time for another. According to the American Resort Development Association, there are more than 9.2 million vacation timeshares owned in the U.S. at more than 1,500 resorts in the U.S. (the most popular locations are California, Colorado, Florida, Hawaii, and South Carolina) and 5,000 worldwide. About 6.9% of all U.S. households own timeshares.

Owned for personal use. Timeshares owned for personal reasons are treated in the same way as vacation homes. Thus, the tax breaks available for such ownership include:

- Deducting mortgage interest as long as the debt is secured by the property.
- Deducting real estate taxes. The taxes are deductible whether you are billed directly (as is the case in California) or the tax is separately identified on the timeshare maintenance bills (as is the case in Florida).

As in the case of other realty owned for personal use, you cannot deduct homeowners insurance, maintenance fees, or special assessments. Gain cannot qualify for the home sale exclusion (see Chapter 4) because the timeshare can never be your principal residence. Thus, gain on the sale of your timeshare is taxed as capital gain; any loss is not deductible.

Owned for investment purposes. See rental property later in this chapter.

Rentals

Becoming a landlord by acquiring real estate and renting it out can be a sound financial activity. There is the possibility of making money both from rental income as well as property appreciation upon an eventual sale. The tax law helps to underwrite the cost of being a landlord, allowing for certain tax deductions. But there are limits on and special rules for write-offs associated with rental properties.

Benefit ⬆

If you rent out property, you can deduct your expenses against the rental income. Any loss resulting from having expenses in excess of rental income can effectively be used to offset your other income, such as salary or dividends.

However, losses from rental activities are subject to the passive loss rules that may restrict your deductions for the current year.

Conditions

If you own realty—a single-family home, a condo unit, a multifamily home in which you live and rent out a portion, an office building, a strip mall, or any other property—you can deduct expenses related to the property.

EXAMPLES OF DEDUCTIBLE RENTAL EXPENSES

- Advertising to find tenants
- Car expenses to and from the property
- Cleaning and maintenance

- Commissions to real estate brokers when finding tenants
- Depreciation
- Insurance
- Legal and professional fees (but not attorney's fees to buy the property)
- Management fees
- Mortgage interest on rental property
- Repairs
- Security system monitoring fees
- Supplies
- Taxes
- Utilities

PASSIVE LOSS LIMITATIONS

When you rent out property, you usually fall within the passive loss rules (exceptions to these rules are discussed later). Then, generally, your deductions cannot exceed all of your passive activity income from the year (income from this rental activity plus any other passive activities). (The law calls them passive "losses" but really means deductions in excess of rental income.)

Example

The rental of a single-family home in which you do not live during the year is your only passive activity. Rental income for the year is $6,000, while deductions are $8,000. You can deduct only $6,000 this year (unless you meet any of the 3 key exceptions in the list following).

Passive activity losses in excess of passive activity income can be carried forward and used in a future year when there is passive activity income to offset them. There is no limit on the carryforward period.

There are 3 key exceptions to the ban on deducting passive losses in excess of passive activity income.

1. You can deduct all carryover losses from a passive activity in the year in which you dispose of your interest in the realty in a taxable disposition (e.g., sell your vacation home).

2. You can deduct up to $25,000 of passive activity losses in excess of passive activity income from a rental activity in which you actively participate (e.g., approve new tenants, decide on rental terms, and authorize

capital expenditures and repairs). The $25,000 limit begins to phase out when your modified adjusted gross income exceeds $100,000 and is completely phased out when MAGI reaches $150,000. MAGI for this purpose means AGI without taxable Social Security benefits, the exclusion for interest from U.S. savings bonds used for higher education, the exclusion for employer-paid adoption expenses, deductions for IRA contributions, the deduction for contributions to Archer medical savings accounts, the domestic production activities deduction, the deduction for tuition and fees (if extended for 2017), and student loan interest. You cannot use the $25,000 allowance if you are married and file a separate return.

Example

You are single with MAGI of $135,000. You actively participate in the rental of your beachfront condo. Your rental loss in excess of passive activity income is limited to $7,500: $25,000 − 50% of ($135,000 − $100,000).

3. You are a real estate professional exempt from the passive loss rules. If you are in the real estate business and want to check whether you are treated as a real estate professional exempt from the passive loss rules, see the instructions to IRS Form 8582. Just know that if you have a full-time job in addition to your real estate activities, it's highly unlikely that you'll qualify as a real estate professional.

Planning Tips

Depreciation is a no-cost deduction (you don't spend any dollars to claim the write-off, other than buying the property). How do you figure this valuable write-off called depreciation? It is a deduction *only* for the building (you can't depreciate land), so you must allocate the cost of the property between the building and the land.

Example

You buy a single-family home for rental, paying $180,000. According to your county assessor's assessment for improvements (buildings), you allocate $155,000 to the house. This is your basis for depreciation.

If you convert personal property to rental property (for example, you move from your home and rent it out), your basis for depreciation purposes is your basis (as figured earlier) or the fair market value of the home at the time of conversion, whichever is less (exclusive of the land).

Example

You bought your home (exclusive of the land) for $200,000 in 2005. In 2017, you move from it and rent it out indefinitely. The value of the home in 2017 is $300,000. Your basis for depreciation is $200,000, which is the lower of basis or fair market value at the time of conversion.

The amount you claim for depreciation is based on the month in which you place the property into service as a rental and the type of realty involved:

- Residential rental property is depreciated over a period of 27.5 years using the straight-line method and a midmonth depreciation convention. Residential rental property is a building for which 80% or more of the gross rental income for the year is rental income from dwelling units. So, if you own an apartment building with stores at street level, you must see whether the property meets the 80% test.
- Nonresidential property is depreciated over a period of 39 years.

Depreciation is simply your basis in the home or building (but not the land) multiplied by the depreciation rate from the IRS table. Table 11.1 shows depreciation rates for residential property. Table 11.2 shows depreciation rates for nonresidential property.

If you sublease property—you are a tenant who leases the property to someone else—you cannot claim a depreciation deduction. Depreciation for the cost of the building can only be claimed by the owner of the property.

Leasehold improvements that you make can be deducted separately from depreciation on the building. Write-offs for leasehold improvements are explained later in this chapter.

Pitfall

Depreciation claimed on your rental realty is subject to a special capital gain rate for recaptured depreciation. This means that the gain you realize on the sale is taxed at 25% to the extent of depreciation deductions you have claimed. Gain in excess of this amount is taxed at no more than 20%, or 15% for most taxpayers (assuming you owned the property for more than one year).

TABLE 11.1 Depreciation Rates for Residential Rental Property

Year	Month											
	1	2	3	4	5	6	7	8	9	10	11	12
1	3.485%	3.182%	2.879%	2.576%	2.273%	1.970%	1.667%	1.364%	1.061%	0.758%	0.455%	0.152%
2–9	3.636	3.636	3.636	3.636	3.636	3.636	3.636	3.636	3.636	3.636	3.636	3.636
10	3.637	3.637	3.637	3.637	3.636	3.637	3.636	3.636	3.636	3.636	3.636	3.636

For years 11–28, see IRS Publication 946, *How to Depreciate Property*.

TABLE 11.2 Depreciation Rates for Nonresidential Rental Property (Placed in Service after May 13, 1993)

Year	Month											
	1	2	3	4	5	6	7	8	9	10	11	12
1	2.461%	2.247%	2.033%	1.819%	1.605%	1.391%	1.177%	0.963%	0.749%	0.535%	0.321%	0.107%
2–39	2.564	2.564	2.564	2.564	2.564	2.564	2.564	2.564	2.564	2.564	2.564	2.564

> **Example**
>
> On July 5, 2012, you bought an office building for $250,000 (exclusive of the land). You sell it on July 5, 2017, for $350,000. Depreciation deductions total $31,665. Your gain is $131,665 ($350,000 − $218,335). Of this gain, $31,665 is taxed at the 25% rate; $100,000 is taxed at 15% (assuming you are not in the 39.6% tax bracket). Your total tax is $22,916 ($7,916 + $15,000).

Where to Claim the Deduction

You report your rents and expenses in Part I of Schedule E of Form 1040. If you own a multifamily home in which you live, the portion of mortgage interest and real estate taxes is allocated between Schedule E (for the rental portion) and Schedule A of Form 1040 (for the personal portion of the home).

> **Example**
>
> You own a 3-family house and live in 1 unit. Two-thirds of your mortgage interest and property taxes and all of your rent-related expenses are reported on Schedule E; one-third of your mortgage interest and property taxes are reported on Schedule A.

If you own an interest in rental realty through a partnership or limited liability company that files a partnership return, you report your share of rental income or losses on Schedule E (you obtain the amount you must report from a Schedule K-1 that is given to you by the entity).

You must also complete Form 8582, *Passive Activity Loss Limitations*, to determine your deduction limit for the year under the passive activity rules.

You cannot use Form 1040A or 1040EZ if you have rental real estate activities.

Low-Income Housing Credit

The federal government wants to encourage investments in housing to accommodate low-income individuals. To make such investments attractive to investors, special tax credits have been made available. These credits effectively operate to replace the rental income investors do not receive because of the rent reductions or breaks provided to certain renters because of their income levels.

Benefit ✚

If you invest in low-income housing—to build it or substantially renovate existing structures—you may be eligible for a tax credit each year for a period of 10 years, generally starting with the year the building is placed in service. The amount of the credit depends on whether the building is new and whether any federal subsidies were used for construction or rehabilitation purposes.

The credit is based on 70% of the qualified basis of each new low-income housing building placed in service after 1986 or 30% of the qualified basis in the case of federally subsidized new or existing buildings. The credit itself is the present value of the 10 annual credit amounts determined as of the last day of the first year of the credit period. However, there is a minimum 9% for newly constructed nonfederally subsidized buildings.

Conditions

You can invest in low-income housing directly, by building the units or rehabilitating existing ones, or by putting money into a limited partnership that does the building or rehabilitating for you. Either way, to qualify for a credit, the building must be considered a low-income housing building.

LOW-INCOME HOUSING BUILDING

Low-income housing does not mean the property must be located in the slums or that the building itself is a tenement. Rather, the tax law requires only that the building offer a certain percentage of the rental units to tenants with income below fixed levels. For example, in the case of housing in suburban areas and smaller towns, the building is considered to be low-income housing if the tenants earn no more than 60% of the local median income. How do you know if your building qualifies? You must receive certification from an authorized housing credit agency. The agency allocates the credit to you on Form 8609, *Low-Income Housing Credit Allocation Certificate*.

The building must have been constructed after 1986; older buildings don't qualify.

Planning Tip

Generally, the first year of the credit is the year in which the building is placed in service for low-income housing. However, you can elect to start claiming the credit in the following year just by indicating your election on Form 8609. You may wish to do so if you cannot fully benefit from the credit in the year the building is placed in service (see "Pitfalls" that follow) or if you will have more income to offset in the following year.

Pitfall

If you dispose of your interest before the end of a set period, you are subject to recapture. This means that part of the benefit you received from claiming the credit is reported as an additional tax you owe in the year of recapture. The building must continue to meet certain requirements for a 15-year period. If not, then your recapture is figured on Form 8611, *Recapture of the Low-Income Housing Credit*.

Where to Claim the Credit

You figure your credit on Form 8586, *Low-Income Housing Credit*. The credit is part of the general business credit, which is figured on Form 3800, *General Business Credit*.

You may also need to figure whether the passive activity restrictions apply to your claiming the credit in the current year. You do this by completing Form 8582-CR, *Passive Activity Credit Limitations*.

The amount of the credit that can be claimed this year is then entered in the "Tax and Credits" section of Form 1040.

You cannot claim the credit if you file Form 1040A or 1040EZ.

Rehabilitation Credit

Fix it up or tear it down? The tax law provides key incentives for restoring certain older properties. These incentives are tax credits that may be claimed if certain conditions are met.

Benefit ⊕

If you spend money fixing up an old building, you may be eligible to claim a tax credit. The amount of the credit depends on the type of building you renovate:

- Certified historic structures—20% of your expenditures
- Buildings built before 1936—10% of your expenditures

There is no overall dollar limit on the credit. However, there are certain limitations that may restrict the amount you can claim in the current year.

Conditions

Only certain buildings are eligible for the credit. They include:

- Historic structures
- Pre-1936 buildings

Regardless of which type of building is involved, you must expend a certain amount on rehabilitation in order to claim a credit.

HISTORIC STRUCTURES

The 20% credit applies to both residential and nonresidential buildings (such as industrial and commercial buildings). The only criterion is that the building is a historic structure that has been recognized by a national or state registry (placed on the National Register of Historic Places or located in a registered historic district and certified by the Secretary of the Interior as being of historic significance to the district).

The National Park Service must certify that your planned rehabilitation of the building is in keeping with its historic status designation.

PRE-1936 BUILDINGS

The 10% credit applies only to nonresidential buildings; you cannot claim a credit for fixing up your home or other residential building. In making renovations, you must retain a certain portion of the original structure (this rule prevents you from basically tearing down the old building to put up a new one).

More specifically, at least 75% of the external walls must be intact, with at least 50% kept as external walls; and at least 75% of the existing internal structural framework must be kept in place. One federal court allowed the credit to be claimed for a building that was moved to a new location and then renovated where at least 75% of the walls were retained as external walls after the relocation.

MINIMUM REHABILITATION

You can't claim the credit simply for adding a doorbell or making other minor renovations. The credit is limited to expenses of at least a certain amount: $5,000 or your adjusted basis in the building, whichever is greater.

Example

You buy an old building for a cost of $50,000 (exclusive of the land). To claim the credit, you must spend at least $50,000 on renovations (since your basis of $50,000 is greater than $5,000).

The expenditures must be made within a 24-month period. This period is extended to 60 months if the rehabilitation is undertaken pursuant to a written architectural plan and specifications are completed before the rehabilitation begins.

Planning Tips

When shopping for real estate to purchase for investment or business, consider the impact that claiming the credit may have on your fix-up costs. Also explore any federal or state grants that may be available for restoring historic structures.

Check to see if there are state income tax credits or other incentives (such as real estate tax abatements) for rehabilitating certified historic structures or other old buildings. The rehabilitation credit can offset both regular tax and the alternative minimum tax.

Pitfalls

The tax credit for rehabilitating an old building falls under the passive loss rules. This means that the credit you are otherwise entitled to claim may be limited by passive activity restrictions. For more details, see the instructions to Form 8582-CR, *Passive Activity Credit Limitations*.

If you want to make a donation of a conservation easement, such as a façade easement (see Chapter 6), the amount of the contribution must be reduced by any rehabilitation credit claimed in the prior 5 years.

Where to Claim the Credit

You figure your credit on Form 3468, *Investment Credit*. The credit is part of the general business credit, which is figured on Form 3800, *General Business Credit*.

You may also need to figure whether the passive activity restrictions apply to your claiming the credit in the current year. You do this by completing Form 8582-CR, *Passive Activity Credit Limitations*.

The amount of the credit that can be claimed this year is then entered in the "Tax and Credits" section of Form 1040.

You cannot claim the credit if you file Form 1040A or 1040EZ.

Deduction for Energy-Efficient Commercial Buildings

The deduction for energy-efficient buildings expired at the end of 2016 but could be extended for 2017. If extended, the following information applies. It has been estimated that commercial buildings use one-quarter of all domestic energy consumption. To encourage owners and lessees of commercial property to make certain energy improvements, there was a special deduction that does not apply for 2017 unless Congress extends it.

Benefit

The cost of energy-efficient property can be deducted up to $1.80 per square foot. A reduced deduction of 60¢ per square foot can be claimed for a building that achieves only partial energy savings.

Conditions

To qualify for the full deduction, the addition of energy-efficient property must help a commercial building achieve a 50% energy savings as compared with similar property that meets benchmarks set by the Standard 90.1-2007 of the American Society of Heating, Refrigerating, and Air Conditioning Engineers and the Illuminating Engineering Society of North America. The savings is measured by the reduction in cost (not in the actual units consumed). Cost is determined on a fuel-neutral basis (e.g., without regard to whether the building is heated by gas, oil, or electricity) by reference to the Standard and not on the basis of the owner's actual costs.

The partial deduction (60¢ per square foot) is allowed for a building that fails the 50% energy-savings requirement but meets a lesser standard.

The deduction applies to improvements made to:

- The interior lighting system
- The heating, cooling, ventilation, and hot water systems
- The building envelop (exterior)

The building owner must obtain certification of a plan to reduce overall energy costs before installing the property. There are various ways to satisfy the certification requirement, including use of approved software to calculate energy consumption.

Planning Tip

Check for state tax incentives for making energy improvements. Many states provide deductions and/or tax credits for these improvements.

Pitfall

The basis of the property must be reduced by the amount of any deduction claimed. This will have the effect of reducing allowable depreciation for the property.

Where to Claim the Deduction

The deduction is a business expense reported by the building's owner or lessee on the proper tax return.

Leasehold, Restaurant, and Retail Improvements

If you make capital improvements to the interior of these commercial facilities, a deduction for your outlays is not tied to depreciation over 39 years for the cost of the building. Instead, you can deduct your outlays using first-year expensing, bonus depreciation, and special depreciation, which enables you to take significant write-offs in the first year.

Benefits

Capital improvements (not repairs) made to leasehold, restaurant, or retail property can be deducted up to $510,000 in 2017 using first-year expensing (Section 179 deduction). Bonus depreciation allows a 50% deduction for costs over this limit. Any costs not fully recovered through expensing and bonus depreciation can be depreciated over 15 years using straight-line depreciation (i.e., deducting the remaining costs ratably over this period).

Conditions

The deductions apply only to qualified property. Leasehold improvements are those done under the terms of a lease by the landlord (lessor), tenant (lessee), or a sublessee. Restaurant property means property more than 50% of which is devoted to the preparation of, and seating for on-premises consumption of, prepared meals. Retail property is property used for selling tangible personal property to the general public.

The rules for first-year expensing, bonus depreciation, and regular depreciation are covered in Chapter 15 under "Equipment Purchases."

Planning Tips

Make sure to distinguish between ordinary repairs and capital improvements. An improvement analysis applies to the building structure and each of the key building systems. The key building systems are the plumbing system, electrical system, HVAC system, elevator system, escalator system, fire protection and alarm system, gas distribution system, and the security system (although elevators and escalators don't qualify for these particular tax deductions).

There is a special safe harbor election for small taxpayers that allows improvements to be treated as ordinary repairs, which are currently deductible (i.e., not capitalized and deducted using expensing, bonus depreciation, and regular depreciation). This safe harbor applies if you are in business with average annual gross receipts less than $10 million and you own or lease property with an adjusted basis of $1 million or less. The safe harbor deduction can be claimed if the total amount paid for improvements does not exceed the lesser of 2% of the building's basis or $10,000.

Pitfalls

These deductions do not apply for enlarging the building, external improvements, internal structural framework changes, or elevators or escalators. These costs are recovered through regular depreciation.

Where to Claim the Deduction

Deductions for first-year expensing, bonus depreciation, and regular depreciation are reported on Form 4562. Total deductions from this form are then reported on the applicable business form (e.g., Schedule C for self-employed individuals, Schedule E for landlords). Anyone filing a business form must file Form 1040; Form 1040A or 1040EZ cannot be used.

Conservation Easements

You can benefit from your realty without disposing of it if you're willing to share. You can enjoy a current tax deduction if you donate a conservation easement to a charity, such as a local land trust. Find details in Chapter 6.

Special Breaks for Certain Disaster Victims

From time to time, when disaster strikes, special tax breaks have been created to encourage disaster victims to rebuild properties that have been destroyed. Special breaks had applied to victims in the Gulf Opportunity Zone and the Midwestern disaster area. These breaks have now expired, but future disasters may trigger new tax write-offs for disaster victims. Expect there to be legislation creating special breaks for victims of Hurricane Harvey. Developments on special breaks for certain disaster victims, if any, will be included in the Supplement to this book.

Borrowing and Interest

Alert

At the time this book was completed, Congress was considering important tax changes that could affect 2017 tax returns and planning for 2018. Check the online Supplement in February 2018 at www.jklasser.com or www.barbaraweltman.com to see what changes have been enacted and when they are effective.

With the prices of things rising, jobs tight, and investments performing weakly, it seems that every paycheck is stretched to the limit. We often choose or are forced to rely on credit to pay for the things we want or need. Whether you are a borrower or a lender, you may be eligible for tax breaks with respect to loan activities.

This chapter explains the tax rules related to borrowing money. For more information, see IRS Publication 550, *Investment Income and Expenses*, and IRS Publication 4681, *Canceled Debts, Foreclosures, Repossessions, and Abandonments*.

Home Mortgage Interest

If you are a homeowner repaying a mortgage, you can deduct the interest portion of your payments. There is no dollar limit on how much interest you can deduct. However, the law limits the amount of borrowing you can take into account in figuring your deductible interest on loans taken after October 14, 1987.

- For acquisition indebtedness to buy, build, or substantially renovate your home: $1 million

- For home equity debt, which is a loan other than acquisition indebtedness secured by your home (such as a home equity line of credit): $100,000

In effect, you can deduct all of the interest on up to a total amount of debt of $1,100,000 ($1 million acquisition indebtedness plus $100,000 home equity debt). These dollar limits are halved for married persons who file separate returns. The amount of the dollar limits for unmarried co-owners is not settled (courts are split).

Mortgage insurance premiums may also be treated as home mortgage interest. Home mortgage interest is deductible only as an itemized deduction; you cannot deduct the interest if you use the standard deduction.

For more details on deducting home mortgage interest, see Chapter 4.

Student Loan Interest

When you are repaying student loans, you may be able to deduct up to $2,500 of interest annually. The deduction is an adjustment to gross income, so you can claim it even if you do not itemize your other deductions and simply use the standard deduction.

The ability to deduct student loan interest depends on your modified adjusted gross income (MAGI). If your MAGI is too high, you cannot claim this benefit.

For more details on deducting student loan interest, see Chapter 3.

Borrowing from Retirement Plans

A 401(k) or other qualified retirement plan may allow you to borrow from your account. The loan proceeds from a qualified retirement plan are generally not taxable to you. No tax-free borrowing is allowed for IRAs and IRA-based plans, such as SEPs and SIMPLE-IRAs.

Benefit

Proceeds you receive when borrowing from your 401(k) or other qualified retirement plan are not taxable. The plan must allow for borrowing by participants; a plan is not *required* to offer this option. Assuming your plan does, then the maximum loan is limited to 50% of your vested account balance or $50,000, whichever is less.

Interest on the loan used for personal purposes, such as paying off credit card debt or college tuition, is generally not deductible (there's an exception for buying a home, explained later). Interest on the loan used for investment purposes is deductible under the investment interest rules (discussed later in this chapter), assuming you are not a "key" employee (a more-than-5%-owner, a more-than-1%-owner-employee earning more than $120,000, and a corporate officer with compensation over $175,000). Interest on the loan to buy a first or second residence is deductible if (1) you are not a key employee, (2) the account balance is not used to secure the loan, and (3) the residence is collateral for the loan.

Conditions

The loan can be taken for *any* reason; you don't even have to tell the plan administrator why you want to borrow money. However, the reason impacts the repayment term. If you use the loan to buy a principal residence for yourself, the repayment period can be any time frame that is reasonable (e.g., 15 years). If you borrow for any other purpose, you must repay the loan in substantially equal ("level") amounts that include interest and principal within 5 years. Repayment is made at least quarterly, and there may be a processing fee charged for the loan.

If you are married, your spouse must consent to the loan.

Planning Tip

The interest rate charged by the plan is usually very low compared with commercial loans. What's more, it is easy to arrange a plan loan. Just ask your plan administrator, complete a short form (you do not have to disclose any personal financial information), and the money is paid to you quickly (usually within days of your request).

Pitfalls

Because retirement plans are designed to build savings for your retirement, borrowing will limit your savings for the future. The money taken as a loan is no longer invested for growth. However, the interest you pay on the loan is repaid to your account. You are permitted to continue making contributions to the plan, but most people who borrow in this fashion use their wages for loan repayment and other purposes and effectively suspend making contributions until the loan is repaid, which means another missed opportunity for retirement savings.

If you fail to repay the loan, it is treated as a taxable distribution to you (immediately taxable and, depending on your age, subject to a 10% early distribution penalty). If you leave the company before repaying the loan, you usually will have to repay the loan immediately or have a taxable distribution. The amount that is taxable is reported to you on Form 1099-R, *Distributions From Pensions, Annuities, Retirement or Profit-Sharing Plans, IRAs, Insurance Contracts, etc.*

There is a distinction between loans that you take because you have a financial emergency and "hardship distributions." Hardship distributions, which may be allowed for certain severe financial hardships (e.g., facing foreclosure), are always fully taxable and, if you are under age 59$\frac{1}{2}$, subject to a 10% early distribution penalty.

Where to Report the Loan

The loan is not reported on your tax return because it is not taxable income.

Investment-Related Interest

You can deduct interest paid on loans used to buy or carry investments to the extent of your net investment income received (such as interest income). If your investment interest paid is more than your net investment income for the year, you can carry the excess interest forward indefinitely and use it in a future year. There is no overall dollar limit on this deduction.

You can deduct investment-related interest only if you itemize your deductions. You cannot claim a deduction if you use the standard deduction.

You cannot deduct interest on a loan used to buy tax-exempt securities, such as municipal bonds or muni-bond funds.

For more details on deducting investment-related interest, see Chapter 8.

Business Interest

Business in many cases runs on other people's money. Loans are used to start up a company, buy equipment, and pay operating expenses. Loans used for business come in all sizes—fixed loans for a set term, revolving lines of credit, or even basic credit card charges for purchases made. Fortunately, whatever type of business loan is involved, interest on the loan may be fully deductible.

Benefit 🛈

If you borrow money for business—by taking out a loan or charging a business purchase to a credit card on which you finance the payments—you can deduct the interest in full against your business income. There is no dollar limit on this deduction.

Condition

The source of the loan does not govern the treatment of the interest. Deductibility depends on what you use the proceeds for. If you use the proceeds for business—for example, to acquire a sole proprietorship—then interest is considered fully deductible business interest.

Interest on a loan used to buy shares in a corporation is viewed as investment interest, not business interest. Interest you pay on tax deficiencies related to your business (for example, a deficiency related to Schedule C of your sole proprietorship) is not deductible. This interest is treated as personal interest, not business interest.

Planning Tip

If you guarantee a loan made to your corporation, you can deduct interest on the loan as business interest, but only when and to the extent you are called upon to do so because the corporation cannot make the payment.

Pitfalls

You cannot deduct business interest that is otherwise required to be capitalized, such as construction period interest. In effect, you cannot deduct interest during the construction period. Construction period interest is added to the basis of the property.

If you borrow money from your corporation, the interest you pay back to the corporation is *not* automatically business interest just because of your relationship to the lender. Again, the treatment of interest depends on what you use the proceeds for. For example, if you borrow money from your corporation to take a vacation, the interest is nondeductible personal interest.

Where to Claim the Deduction

Self-employed individuals who pay business interest deduct these payments on Schedule C or C-EZ of Form 1040.

You cannot deduct business interest if you file Form 1040A or 1040EZ.

Accrued Interest on Bond Purchases

In the financial world, bonds are bought and sold in the secondary market: After an initial offering, they trade among investors at their current values. But when trades are made between interest payment dates, which is common, bond buyers pay for the interest that is actually received by the bond sellers; the interest is included in the cost of the bond. The tax law allows for a correction of this situation by allowing bond sellers a deduction.

Benefit

If you buy a bond between its interest payment dates, some interest may be included in the purchase price that doesn't belong to you. That interest is payable to the bond seller even though it is reported as payable to you. To correct this inequity, you can effectively deduct the accrued interest. This is not a tax deduction in the true sense of the word. Rather, you are allowed to make a subtraction that amounts to the same thing.

Condition

This subtraction applies only if you are a bond purchaser and there is accrued interest on the bond you buy. This occurs only when the purchase takes place between the bond's interest dates (typically twice a year).

Planning Tips

When purchasing a bond, you can ask your stockbroker about interest dates on the security. Knowing the interest dates will apprise you of whether there will be any accrued interest to deal with when you file your return.

If you *sell* a bond with accrued interest, you do not subtract it from interest income. Instead, you reduce the sales proceeds by the amount of accrued interest belonging to the purchaser (which reduces your gain or increases your loss). For example, if you sell a bond for which you paid $9,500 at $10,000 and have accrued interest of $180, you reduce the proceeds by this amount. As a result, your gain is $320 ([$10,000 proceeds − $180 accrued interest] − $9,500 basis).

Pitfall

Do *not* simply subtract from the interest reported to you on Form 1099-INT the accrued interest you paid when you purchased a bond. Netting the interest in this manner can trigger an examination of your return because your reporting does not match the information sent to the IRS on Form 1099-INT. Instead, follow the reporting instructions that follow.

Where to Claim the Benefit

Generally, you do not have to complete Part I of Schedule B of Form 1040 unless your interest income is over $1,500. However, you must do so, regardless of your total interest, if you want to deduct the accrued interest you paid on a bond purchase.

In Part I of Schedule B of Form 1040, report the full amount of interest shown on Form 1099-INT. Then, after entering any other interest you received, create a subtotal line reflecting the total of all entries. On the line immediately below the subtotal, write "Accrued interest" and enter the amount of accrued interest that you paid the seller. Subtract this amount from the subtotal and enter the result on line 2 of Part I of Schedule B.

You cannot effectively deduct accrued interest if you file Form 1040A or 1040EZ.

Below-Market Loans

In today's low-interest environment—*the federal funds rate at which banks borrow is still only 1% to 1.25% due to slight rate hikes in 2017*—it's hard to imagine that borrowers would bother to devise strategies for avoiding interest payments. But when rates were higher, it was common for business owners to borrow from their companies and for children to borrow from parents at little or no interest, realizing a considerable economic benefit. The tax law took note of this benefit, creating the below-market interest rate rules. Under these rules, phantom interest may be created for lenders and phantom interest deductions for borrowers. While the interest may be phantom, the income from this interest can be very real.

Benefit

If you lend money to or borrow from a relative, friend, or your business at no interest or at highly favorable low interest rates, there may be some tax issues to consider. Depending on who the parties are, the amount of the loan, and the interest rate charged, these results can ensue:

- *Gift loans up to $10,000.* Gift loans, compensation-related loans, and shareholder-corporation loans up to $10,000 have no consequences to the parties. No interest deduction can be claimed with respect to any interest that is not actually paid.
- *Gift loans in the range of $10,000 to $100,000.* No interest deduction can be claimed with respect to any interest that is not actually paid if the borrower's investment income is no more than $1,000.
- *All other loans.* In addition to interest actually paid, a deduction can be claimed for below-market interest (assuming that it is deductible interest). This is the interest that should have been charged, based on the government's applicable federal rate (AFR) for the term of the loan. The lender must report a like amount of income. However, the lender may be able to offset the income by deducting the forgiven interest in some way.

Example

You borrow $20,000 from your corporation interest free for 5 years. Assuming the AFR for this term is 1.5% at the time the loan originates, your annual interest deduction is $300 for each of the 5 years that the loan is outstanding (1.5% of $20,000). If the corporation treats the forgiven loan as compensation, you must report $300 as compensation. From the corporation's standpoint, it picks up $300 interest and deducts $600 compensation.

Keep in mind that even if you have imputed interest from a below-market loan, it may not necessarily be deductible. It depends on what you use the loan proceeds for. If you use the funds to buy stocks, for example, you can treat the imputed interest as investment interest (discussed earlier in this chapter). But if you use the funds to pay off your personal credit card debt or take a vacation, you cannot deduct the imputed interest; it is nondeductible personal interest.

Condition

Whether a loan falls within the below-market loan rules depends on the rate of interest, if any, fixed when the loan originates. Loans fall into 3 basic categories:

1. Short-term: 3 years or less.
2. Mid-term: over 3 but not over 9 years.
3. Long-term: over 9 years.

If the loan is payable on demand (there is no fixed term), then the interest rate used for a loan outstanding for the entire year is a blended rate announced by the IRS each July. For 2017, the blended rate is 1.09%.

Each month the IRS publishes AFRs. You can find an index of the AFRs monthly at https://apps.irs.gov/app/picklist/list/federalRates.html.

Planning Tip

When arranging loans between family or other related persons, keep the below-market loan rules in mind. With today's historically low interest rates, it is easy to keep loans from falling subject to the rules by charging the minimum AFR. But even if lower or no interest is charged so that income results, the arrangement may still be desirable.

Pitfall

If you are the lender of a below-market loan that does not meet the gift loan or other exemption rules, you have to report interest income even though you do not actually receive any payments.

Where to Claim the Benefit

If you are exempt from the below-market loan rules, do not report anything on your return. If you are a borrower subject to the below-market loan rules, you can deduct your interest payments if such interest is otherwise deductible. For instance, if the interest qualifies as investment interest, deduct it on Schedule A of Form 1040 (see Chapter 8 for more details about deducting investment interest).

Bad Debts

Lenders never loan money with the expectation they won't be repaid. They expect to collect interest during the term of the loan and recoup the amount of principal in the loan. But reality shows that some borrowers default. Taxwise, lenders may be able to write off these bad loans under certain conditions.

Benefit ⬆

If you loan money to someone who fails to repay you, you can claim a loss for the outstanding balance. The conditions for writing off the loss and the manner in which the loss is treated for tax purposes depend on the type of bad debt involved. There are 2 types:

1. Business bad debts, which are debts arising in the course of business. For example, your business is on the accrual method of accounting and fails to receive payment on an accounts receivable; this is a business bad debt. Loans made to protect your salary are treated as business bad debts. Business bad debts are fully deductible as ordinary losses against business income.

2. Nonbusiness bad debts, which are any other type of debt. For example, you loan money to your friend to buy a car and your friend fails to repay the loan; this is a nonbusiness bad debt. Nonbusiness bad debts also include loans that you make to protect your investments and uninsured bank deposits (explained in Chapter 8). Nonbusiness bad debts are deductible as short-term capital losses.

Condition

You must satisfy 4 conditions in order to deduct a bad debt loss:

1. It is a valid debt.
2. There was a debtor-creditor relationship.
3. The loan was made from your after-tax income or capital.
4. You must show that the debt has become worthless.

VALID DEBT

Your right to repayment must be enforceable and cannot depend on some future occurrence. For example, if the loan violates state usury laws, the debt cannot be deducted when it goes unpaid.

If you own a corporation and make loans to it, be sure that the arrangement is truly a loan and not merely an advance of capital. If the corporation is thinly capitalized (there is just too much debt compared with equity), the IRS may view a supposed loan to the corporation as an advance of capital.

DEBTOR-CREDITOR RELATIONSHIP

You must prove that there was a debtor-creditor relationship. In the context of a business loan, there is usually no issue.

But when you lend money to family or friends, there is the question of whether you are truly lending the money or really making a gift of it.

If you guarantee a loan made to someone else who defaults, you can claim a bad debt deduction when you make the payment *if* it is a business bad debt or a nonbusiness bad debt made to protect an investment. No deduction can be claimed for making good on your guarantee of a loan for personal reasons, such as a favor to a relative or friend.

LOAN FROM AFTER-TAX INCOME OR CAPITAL

If, like most individuals, you are on the cash basis of accounting, you cannot treat nonpayments of salary, rents, or fees owed to you as bad debts. Since you never reported the income (under the cash method you report as income only what you receive), you cannot claim a bad debt deduction for nonpayment.

Example

You are a consultant on the cash method of accounting. You complete a job for which you are owed $2,500. You never recover your fee because the client has gone out of business. You cannot deduct this amount as a bad debt because you never reported the consulting fee as income. While this may seem unfair because of the time and effort you put into the work, the tax law does not view you as having sustained a loss.

WORTHLESSNESS

You must show that the debt will never be repaid. If the debtor has gone out of business or filed for bankruptcy, this is a good indication that there is little hope of recovery. Show any steps you have taken to recover on the debt, such as suing for it in court or turning it over to a collection agency. You do not actually have to sue if this action would be futile because you would be unable to collect on a judgment.

In the case of nonbusiness bad debts, you must show that the debt is entirely worthless; a partially worthless bad debt cannot be claimed in this case.

To fix the year of worthlessness, show that the debt had some value on December 31 of the year prior to the year in which you believe the debt became worthless. Then show the identifiable event that leads you to conclude the debt is worthless.

You do not have to wait until the debt is due in order to claim a bad debt deduction if you know that it has already become worthless. You claim the deduction in the year it becomes worthless, not the year in which it is due.

Planning Tips

Whenever you make a loan, be sure to put all of the terms of the loan in writing. This will accomplish a couple of things: It will make the borrower aware of when and how much you expect to be repaid, and, in the case of default, you will have the proof that the arrangement was truly a loan and not a gift.

It's not always easy to tell when a debt has gone bad. You have 7 years in which to file an amended return for the year in which the bad debt became worthless in order to make a claim for a refund. The filing period generally runs 7 years from the due date of the return for the year of worthlessness.

Example

In June 2017, you discover that a loan you made to a friend became totally worthless in 2014. You have until April 15, 2012 (7 years from the original due date of the 2014 return, or April 15, 2015), to file an amended return for 2014 to report the nonbusiness bad debt.

Pitfalls

You cannot claim a bad debt deduction for unpaid child support. For example, if your former spouse owes you $10,000 in back child support, you cannot write this off as a bad debt. The reason: You do not have any basis in the debt so, for tax purposes, you do not have a loss (even though you surely have an economic loss).

Also, you cannot take a nonbusiness bad debt for any debt owed to you by a political party or committee.

If you deducted a bad debt in a prior year and to your amazement you receive repayment now, you must include the amount in income. But inclusion is required only to the extent that the deduction in a prior year reduced your tax in that year.

Where to Claim the Benefit

A business bad debt that you make in the course of your business is reported as a deductible item on Schedule C of Form 1040. But if you are a shareholder-employee with a loan to your corporation that has gone sour, determine whether it is a business bad debt or a nonbusiness bad debt. A business bad debt in this situation is only deductible as a miscellaneous itemized deduction subject to the 2% of AGI floor and the reduction of itemized deductions for high-income taxpayers.

A nonbusiness bad debt is reported as a short-term capital loss in Part I of Schedule D of Form 1040. In column (a), enter the name of the debtor and "Statement attached." On your own statement, which you attach to your return, include:

- A description of the debt, including the amount, and the date it became worthless.
- The name of the debtor and any business or family relationship between you.
- The efforts you made to collect the debt.
- Why you believe the debt is now worthless.

You cannot deduct your bad debts if you file Form 1040A or 1040EZ.

Loan Forgiveness

Usually, when a lender allows a borrower to pay less than the outstanding loan balance, the borrower has taxable income. However, in some special situations, loan forgiveness is not taxed.

Benefit

Certain debt forgiveness is tax free. This includes mortgage debt on certain primary residence foreclosures and workouts, student loan interest canceled in exchange for certain public service, and debt discharged while you are insolvent (when your liabilities exceed the fair market value of your assets) or through a bankruptcy proceeding. Forgiveness of student loan interest is explained in Chapter 3. Forgiveness of mortgage debt on a primary residence is explained in Chapter 4.

Condition

Student loan cancellation that is tax free requires public service to be performed under the direction of a governmental unit or tax-exempt organization.

Planning Tips

A price adjustment for an item purchased on credit is not taxable cancellation of debt.

Except in the limited circumstances where cancellation of debt is tax free, before accepting a lender's offer to reduce your loan balance (e.g., reduction of your home mortgage), consider the tax cost of the resulting income to you.

Pitfall

Taxable cancellation of debt is reported to you and the IRS on Form 1099-C, *Cancellation of Debt*.

Where to Claim the Benefit

If loan forgiveness is tax free, you do not have to report it on your return.

Debt Forgiveness

In some situations, lenders may be willing to accept less than the full amount owed in order to get your loan or other obligation off their books. Usually, income from the cancellation of debt (COD) is fully taxable. However, there are certain exceptions to this rule that allow you to exclude COD from your income. Thus, a bad economic situation may have a good tax result.

Benefit

COD income is tax free if you can qualify under any category described next.

Conditions

To be nontaxable, the cancellation of debt must fall within a specific category:

- You are bankrupt.
- You are insolvent at the time the debt is canceled. Insolvency means that your debts exceed the fair market value of your assets immediately before the discharge.
- The debt is on your main home and you meet certain requirements. Cancellation of mortgage debt is explained in Chapter 4 and is not discussed further in this chapter. *This exclusion ended in 2016 but Congress may extend it for 2017.*
- The debt is qualified farm indebtedness.
- The debt is qualified real property business indebtedness.

- The debt is a student loan made by a qualified lender. Cancellation of these student loans is explained in Chapter 3 and is not discussed further in this chapter.

Planning Tip

If you're excluding COD income because you are insolvent, be sure to retain good records of your assets and liabilities at the time of the debt forgiveness. This will be helpful in case the IRS questions your return.

Pitfalls

If you exclude COD income, you must reduce certain tax attributes (described next) by the amount of the excluded COD income (but not below zero). There is a set order to the reduction of tax attributes, depending upon the reason for the cancellation of debt. When excluding COD income, you must usually reduce tax attributes so that you effectively increase your income in other ways (e.g., losing deductions or reporting greater gain on the sale or property). The order of reduction is as follows unless a special election (beyond the scope of this book) is made:

- Net operating losses (including carryovers)
- General business credit carryover
- Minimum tax credit
- Net capital losses (including carryovers)
- Basis of property
- Passive activity losses and credits (including carryovers)
- Foreign tax credit

If the cancellation of debt is because of bankruptcy or insolvency and is not because of qualified principal residence indebtedness, the basis of personal-use property (e.g., a home, home furnishings, a car) is made if there is no tax attributes to be reduced.

When you pay less than the full amount of the money owed on a loan or other obligation (e.g., credit card debt), this adversely affects your credit rating (FICO score). However, the sooner you settle up, the sooner you can begin to rebuild a good credit rating.

Where to Claim the Benefit

Forgiven debt is reported to you by the lender on Form 1099-C, *Cancellation of Debt*. If you are excluding cancellation of debt income, you must complete Form 982, *Reduction of Tax Attributes Due to Discharge of Indebtedness*. There is no income to report on your return; just attach the completed Form 982 to the return.

Insurance and Catastrophes

Alert

At the time this book was completed, Congress was considering important tax changes that could affect 2017 tax returns and planning for 2018. Check the online Supplement in February 2018 at www.jklasser.com or www.barbaraweltman.com to see what changes have been enacted and when they are effective.

No one likes to think about bad things happening, but happen they do, as seen in severe winter storms in Oklahoma and Oregon, spring floods in Arkansas and Missouri, flooding, landslides, and mudslides in West Virginia, and of course, Hurricanes Harvey and Irma. Natural disasters, accidents, illnesses, and now terrorist activities, such as the Pulse nightclub incident in Orlando, Florida, and war all present serious personal and financial threats that can become reality. When faced with such catastrophes, insurance may carry you just so far, with economic losses outstripping your insurance recoveries. But you may be able to mitigate your financial losses with certain tax write-offs.

This chapter explains the tax rules related to insurance and catastrophes. Mortgage insurance is covered in Chapter 4. Losses to your bank deposits are discussed in Chapter 8. For more information, see IRS Publication 547, *Casualties, Disasters, and Thefts (Business and Nonbusiness)*; IRS Publication 584, *Casualty, Disaster, and Theft Loss Workbook (Personal-Use Property)*; and IRS Publication 2194, *Disaster Resource Guide for Individuals and Businesses*.

Casualty and Theft Losses

Things happen beyond man's control, such as hurricanes and wildfires, that damage or destroy property. If there is insurance, it may only partially cover the loss. The tax law allows a deduction for losses resulting from a casualty event or theft. But strict rules apply to limit the amount of the write-off.

Benefit ⊜

If you suffer property damage due to a casualty or theft, any insurance proceeds you recover are tax free. If your loss is not fully covered by insurance, you may be able to deduct your loss as an itemized deduction. There is no overall dollar limit on the amount you can deduct. Your itemized deduction is *not* subject to the overall reduction in itemized deductions for high-income taxpayers (explained in the Introduction).

The amount of your loss, however, is limited to the decrease in the value of property from the casualty or its adjusted basis (usually your cost), whichever amount is smaller. *Rule of thumb:* For property that appreciates in value, your loss is usually based on your adjusted basis; for property that declines in value, your loss is usually based on the decrease in value. Any casualty or theft loss must be reduced by insurance or similar recoveries.

Example

Your car is damaged in an accident and you do not have collision coverage. Before the accident, your car was worth $8,000. After the accident it was worth only $2,000. Your adjusted basis for the car (what you paid for it) was $19,000. Your casualty loss is the decrease in value of $6,000 ($8,000 – $2,000), which is less than the car's adjusted basis of $19,000.

> **Example**
>
> You bought a painting several years ago for $2,500 that was valued at $25,000 before it was stolen (you did not have any insurance). Your loss is limited to your adjusted basis of $2,500, which is lower than the loss in value of $25,000.

Conditions

To deduct a loss relating to your personal property, such as your home or car, you must meet all 4 of these conditions:

1. The loss must result from a casualty event or theft.
2. You must have proof of the casualty loss or theft.
3. You must reduce your loss by any insurance or other reimbursements.
4. The amount of your loss must exceed certain limits if the loss is exclusive to personal items (there are no such limits for business losses).

CASUALTY EVENT

A casualty is a sudden, unexpected, or unusual event, such as an earthquake, explosion, fire, flood, hurricane, storm, or tornado. Generally, deciding whether an event qualifies as a casualty is not too difficult. But when damage or loss results from something that is progressive in nature, you can't claim a deduction because it is not a casualty.

> **Example**
>
> If the pipes in your house burst because of freezing and the water damages your carpeting, you have suffered a casualty loss. But if the pipes leak because of corrosion over time, the resulting water damage to your carpeting is not due to a casualty and you can't deduct the loss.

THEFT EVENT

For tax purposes, a theft includes any unlawful taking of your money or property. Thefts include burglary, embezzlement, larceny, and robbery.

If you lose money through extortion, kidnapping, threats, or blackmail, these are considered thefts for tax purposes if you meet both of the following conditions:

1. The taking was illegal under local law.
2. It was done with criminal intent.

PROOF OF YOUR CASUALTY LOSS OR THEFT

You must show all 4 of these conditions for a casualty loss:

1. The type of casualty, such as hurricane damage to your home.
2. The date of the casualty.
3. The connection between the casualty and your loss (that is, that your loss is the direct result of the casualty event).
4. That you are the owner of the property. If you lease property, you cannot claim a casualty loss; this right belongs only to the owner unless you are contractually obligated to return the property in the same condition (in effect, you bear the risk of loss).

For a theft, you must show all 3 of these conditions:

1. When you discovered that your property was missing.
2. That your property was stolen through a robbery, embezzlement, or otherwise.
3. That you are the owner of the property.

INSURANCE REIMBURSEMENTS

If you carry property insurance coverage, you may have little or no loss for tax purposes. You cannot create a tax loss by not submitting an insurance claim to which you are entitled. If you do not submit a claim for a covered loss, you cannot claim a casualty loss deduction, even for the portion of the loss not covered by insurance.

Example

You have insured an item for $10,000 for which you paid $12,000; it is now worth $15,000. If the item is destroyed in a casualty and you do not submit an insurance claim because you do not want the premiums increased on your other property or for any other reason, you cannot deduct any loss. You cannot even deduct the $2,000 that you would have been entitled to had you made the claim and received the full coverage.

What if you have made a claim but have not received any reimbursement from the insurance company by the end of the year? File your return using an estimate of what you expect for reimbursement.

If you receive more in a later year than you had estimated, report the additional insurance recovery as "Other income" on your return for that later year (do not file an amended return for the year of the casualty event) to the extent you received a tax benefit from the deduction you should not have claimed. (Whether you realized any tax benefit is a difficult determination for which you may need to consult a tax expert.)

Example

In 2017, you suffer a casualty and figure your loss deduction based on the assumption you will receive $10,000 from the insurance company. In 2018, you receive a check from the insurance company for $12,000. On your 2018 return, report $2,000 as "Other income."

If you later receive *less* than you had estimated, you need to file an amended return to increase your loss deduction.

$100 LIMIT

You must reduce each loss from a personal casualty or theft event by $100 (business and investment losses, including losses from Ponzi schemes as explained in Chapter 8, are not subject to this limitation). The dollar reduction applies per event (not per item lost or damaged in the event). Thus, you figure your loss separately for each item but then apply only one $100 reduction per event.

Example

On June 1, 2017, you are robbed of $1,000 cash plus jewelry you just purchased for $8,000 (assume your loss is not covered by insurance). Your loss for tax purposes is $8,900 ($1,000 + $8,000 − $100).

If you are unfortunate enough to suffer 2 such losses in the same year, you must reduce your loss for each event by $100 (effectively, your total losses are reduced by $200).

10% OF AGI LIMIT

You can deduct personal casualty and theft losses only to the extent that the total of all such losses for the year exceeds 10% of your adjusted gross income (business losses, including losses from Ponzi schemes, as explained in Chapter 8, are not subject to this limitation).

Example

You determine that the unreimbursed damage to your home from a tornado is $8,400 (after reducing your loss by the $100 limit). If your adjusted gross income for the year is $75,000, you can deduct $900 ($8,400 − 10% of $75,000). If your adjusted gross income is $84,000 or more, you cannot claim any casualty loss deduction.

Losses that cannot be claimed because of the 10% limit are lost forever; you cannot carry forward the unused amount.

Planning Tips

How do you determine the decrease in value? There are a few alternatives:

- Obtain an appraisal. Use a qualified appraiser to determine the value of the property before and after the casualty (the tax treatment of appraisal fees is discussed later in this chapter).

- Use the cost of repairs or restoration as the measure of loss. You can rely on this cost if the repairs are necessary to bring the property back to its precasualty condition, the amount spent is not excessive, and the value of the property after the repairs is not more than it was before the casualty.

- If the loss involves your car, you can use various online valuation services to determine the value of your car, including Kelley Blue Book (www.kbb.com) and NADA Appraisal Guides (www.nadaguides.com).

If you are married and one spouse suffers a casualty loss (for example, an expensive uninsured piece of jewelry is stolen), it may be advisable to file separate returns. This is so where the spouse with the lower AGI suffers the loss. The lower AGI may entitle the spouse to a deduction that would otherwise be blocked because of the couple's combined AGI. Of course, other factors must be taken into account when filing separate returns, such as eligibility to claim other tax benefits that require filing a joint return.

Review your insurance coverage carefully to understand what it does and does not cover. You may be able to expand the coverage under your existing policy; or you may need to obtain other coverage (for example, flood insurance if you are located within a flood zone). In some cases, you may not be able to obtain coverage because it is just not sold or the premiums are prohibitive. For example, even though federal legislation has provided underwriting guarantees to carriers for claims due to terrorist attacks, many major carriers are simply not covering such events.

When you are in a vehicular accident, be sure to take photos and obtain a police report. Then, if you have losses not covered by insurance, you'll be able to prove that you experienced a casualty.

Pitfalls

Not all losses related to a casualty are deductible. You cannot deduct your personal living expenses in temporary housing when a casualty event forces you out of your home. You cannot deduct cleanup costs from the casualty.

Your deduction is limited to your economic loss from the casualty or theft. You cannot recoup anything related to sentimental value.

> **Example**
>
> Your wedding album is ruined during a fire in your home. The pictures cost a few hundred dollars, which is the limit of your tax loss, even though their value to you may have been priceless.

Poor home construction because of shoddy work does not constitute a theft loss by the contractor in the absence of showing that the contractor committed fraud.

Where to Claim the Deduction

You must file Form 4684, *Casualties and Thefts*, to report the loss and figure the amount of the deduction. The deduction is then entered on Schedule A of Form 1040. The deduction is not subject to the reduction in itemized deductions for high-income taxpayers.

You cannot claim a deduction for casualty or theft losses if you file Form 1040A or 1040EZ.

Disaster Losses

Disaster losses are losses to property within areas designed as eligible for federal disaster relief as a result of a disaster. From a tax perspective, disaster losses are a type of casualty loss, but special breaks apply.

Benefit ⊜

If you suffer property damage or loss because of a disaster—a storm, tornado, wildfire, earthquake, or other event in an area eligible for assistance from the federal government—you can claim a disaster loss. A disaster loss is a type of casualty loss with this difference: You can deduct it in either the year of the loss or the prior year. Having the option of claiming the deduction for the prior year may give you an immediate infusion of cash (a tax refund) to use to rebuild from the disaster.

Like ordinary casualty losses, there is no dollar limit on the amount you can claim as a disaster loss. And your reduction for a disaster loss is not subject to the overall reduction of itemized deductions for high-income taxpayers (explained in the introduction).

Whether or not you qualify for a disaster loss deduction, you may be able to exclude from income certain disaster relief payments you receive as a result of a disaster (discussed later in this chapter).

Conditions

In addition to meeting *all* of the conditions for claiming a casualty loss deduction (discussed earlier in this chapter), there are 2 additional conditions:

1. The loss must occur within a federally declared disaster area.
2. You must act within set time limits if you want to claim the loss on the return for the prior year.

DISASTER AREAS

The loss must result in an area designated by the president as qualifying for federal disaster relief. Generally, you will know that the designation has been given and probably already have had contact with the Federal Emergency Management Agency (FEMA). If you are unsure, you can check on designations at www.fema.gov. The IRS also publishes an annual list of federal disaster areas (for example, in 2016, there were more than 3 dozen designated disasters nationwide for storms, flooding, earthquakes, mudslides, tornados, and fires); find 2017 disaster areas listed at www.irs.gov/uac/Tax-Relief-in-Disaster-Situations or from FEMA at https://www.fema.gov/disasters/grid/year/2017.

TIME LIMITS

You can claim the loss on the return for the year of the disaster, which gives you plenty of time to amass the information needed to establish your loss when completing your return.

But if you want to claim the loss on a return for the prior year, you must act no later than 6 months after the original due date of the return for the year of the disaster. This 6-month period applies whether or not you obtain a filing extension for your return.

Example

On February 1, 2017, you experience a natural disaster in an area declared eligible for federal disaster assistance through FEMA. The due date for the 2017 return is April 17, 2018. You have an additional 6 months from April 15 to make the election to deduct the disaster loss on a 2016 return; this extends the election period through October 15, 2018.

You have 90 days after the due date for making the election to change your mind and revoke your choice by returning to the IRS any refund or credit you received. If you revoke your choice before receiving a refund, you must return the refund within 30 days after receiving it in order for the revocation to be effective.

Planning Tips

Which year should you claim the loss—the year of the disaster or the prior year? Generally, choose the year in which you have a lower adjusted gross income threshold for figuring your loss.

Example

In 2017, you have a $22,800 disaster loss (after the $100 reduction). Your adjusted gross income (AGI) for 2017 is $86,000. Your AGI for 2016 was $75,000. If you take the deduction on your 2017 return, your AGI threshold is $8,600, so only $14,200 of your loss is deductible. If you take the deduction on your 2016 return, your AGI threshold is $7,500, allowing you to deduct $15,300. In this situation, claiming the disaster loss deduction on the prior year's return provides a greater tax benefit.

If your home and its contents are damaged or destroyed in a disaster, figure the loss separately for the home and for the furnishings.

If you are living in a federal disaster area, you may be entitled to certain tax breaks, even if you don't qualify to claim a disaster loss (you might be fully compensated by insurance or might not have had any loss). For example, you may be eligible for a one-year postponement of tax deadlines, including the due date for filing returns and making IRA contributions. The IRS may also abate the interest and penalties on underpayment of income tax for the length of any postponement of tax deadlines.

Pitfall

Just because you suffer property damage during a disaster does not automatically mean you have a tax loss. You can even have a tax *gain* as a result of a disaster (for example, where insurance or other recoveries exceed your basis in the property). You need to work through the numbers to determine whether and to what extent you have a tax loss.

Where to Claim the Deduction

You must file Form 4684, *Casualties and Thefts*, to report the disaster loss and figure the amount of the deduction. The deduction is then entered on Schedule A of Form 1040.

You cannot claim a deduction for disaster losses if you file Form 1040A or 1040EZ.

If you are claiming a disaster loss for the prior year for which you have not yet filed a return (for example, in January 2018 you have a casualty loss that you report on your 2016 return to be filed by April 17, 2018), write at the top of the return "DISASTER LOSS." If you are claiming a disaster loss for the prior year for which you have already filed a return, you must file an amended return, Form 1040X. At the top of the return write "DISASTER LOSS."

Disaster Relief Payments

When disaster strikes, the federal government may provide needed assistance. The Federal Emergency Management Agency (FEMA) steps in to provide grants and other assistance to affected individuals and businesses. (For more information about disaster assistance, check www.fema.gov.) To avoid adding insult to injury, certain government assistance can be received tax free.

Benefit

You are not taxed on disaster relief payments you receive from federal agencies or charitable organizations to cover personal expenses. There is no dollar limit on the amount you can exclude from income. Your exclusion does not depend on your income or need.

Conditions

Only "qualified disaster relief payments" are excludable. These include payments, regardless of the source, for the following reasonable and necessary expenses:

- Personal, family, living, or funeral expenses incurred as a result of a presidentially declared disaster.

- Expenses incurred for the repair or rehabilitation of a personal residence due to a presidentially declared disaster (whether you own the home or rent it as a tenant).
- Expenses incurred for the repair or replacement of the contents of a personal residence due to a presidentially declared disaster.

Grants under the Disaster Relief and Emergency Assistance Act are excludable from income, but you cannot deduct a disaster loss to the extent you are reimbursed for it by the grants. Cancellation of all or part of a federal disaster loan is also considered reimbursement for a loss (it reduces your casualty loss deduction).

Disaster relief mitigation payments are also excludable from income. These are payments made under the Robert T. Stafford Disaster Relief and Emergency Assistance Act or the National Flood Insurance Act for hazard mitigation of your property.

Planning Tip

If you are the victim of a disaster, be sure to check with your local authorities as well as with FEMA to see whether there are any grants or relief payments you may be entitled to.

Pitfall

Disaster relief payments for business-related expenses, lost wages, or unemployment compensation may not be excluded from income and are fully taxable.

Where to Claim the Benefit

Since qualified disaster relief payments are not taxable, you do not have to report them on your return.

Damages

In 2015 (the most recent year for statistics), there were more than 50,000 civil lawsuits filed in federal courts and many, many more filed in state courts in the United States to redress wrongs, such as medical malpractice claims and breach of contract. The tax law allows only certain types of damages to receive favorable tax treatment.

Benefit

If you receive compensatory damages for personal *physical* injury or illness, you can exclude your recovery. For example, if you recover damages for a medical malpractice incident that affected your body, the damages are tax free. There is no dollar limit on the amount you can exclude from income.

There is a special exclusion for persons who were persecuted by the Nazis. They can exclude *all* amounts received as restitution payments for their ordeal. The exclusion applies to:

- Heirs or estates of such persons who suffered on the basis of their race, religion, physical or mental disability, or sexual orientation.
- Restitution payments for assets that were lost or stolen before or during World War II.
- Life insurance issued by European insurance companies immediately before and during the war.
- Interest earned on escrow accounts and funds established in settlement of Holocaust victim claims.

There is a special exclusion for restitution for victims of human trafficking. Even though the restitution payments are not limited to physical injury, the payments are fully excludable.

There is also a special exclusion for compensation paid to the wrongfully incarcerated even though the payments do not relate to physical injury. This exclusion became law in December 2015, but applies to previous awards under a transition rule that expired in 2016.

Damages arising out of the purchase of property are treated as a recovery for injury or damage to a capital asset. As such, damages are tax free to the extent of your basis in the property.

Example

You buy land for $100,000. After the sale you learn it is contaminated and sue the seller, who settles with you for $25,000. You are not taxed on these damages. They serve to reduce your basis in the land to $75,000.

If you receive damages for any other reason, including punitive damages for physical injury or any type of damages for personal injury that is not physical, the damages are fully taxable. Nonphysical personal injuries for which damages are taxable include injury to reputation, discrimination, and back pay.

Conditions

To claim the exclusion for damages, the award must relate to some physical injury or sickness. Damages for emotional distress are excludable only if they are attributable to a physical injury or sickness and compensate you for related medical expenses.

"Soft injuries," such as headaches, weight loss, and insomnia, arising from a work-related case (e.g., discrimination, sexual harassment) are viewed as emotional distress and not as physical injuries for which damages are tax free. However, any awards for these soft injuries are excludable to the extent they compensate for medical costs.

The damages must be compensatory, meaning that they aim to make you whole from your loss (covering medical expenses, etc.). Punitive damages are not tax free, even if they relate to physical injuries.

The damages award can be a negotiated settlement or an award fixed by a court.

Planning Tip

If an action involved both physical and nonphysical injury aspects, be sure that the complaint allocates the degree of injury to each part.

Example

Suppose you are injured in a car accident in a state that does not have a no-fault law. You sue for $75,000 for personal injuries and $25,000 for damage to your car. You settle with the other party for $40,000. Of this amount, three-quarters, or $30,000, relates to personal injuries and is tax free; $10,000 relates to property damage and is taxable.

Pitfalls

If you receive interest on an award for physical damages, you are taxed on the interest even though the award itself is tax free.

If you obtain a recovery under a contingent fee agreement with your attorney, you must include the *entire* award in income if such awards are taxable (e.g., defamation actions). How you treat the attorney's fees depends on the nature of the action (see Chapter 16).

Where to Claim the Benefit

Since damages for personal physical injury are excludable from your income, you do not have to report them on your return.

If you receive damages for personal injuries that are not physical (for example, for libel), they are taxable and must be reported as "Other income" on Form 1040. You cannot file Form 1040A or 1040EZ if you have taxable damages.

Disability Coverage

The statistics about disability from the Social Security Administration and the Census Bureau are startling. More than one in 4 of 20-year-olds today will become disabled before they reach the normal retirement age for collecting Social Security retirement benefits. About 19% (nearly one in 5) of the U.S. population is classified as disabled according to the U.S. Census Bureau; one in 10 are classified as severely disabled. To protect against this possibility, it is advisable to carry disability insurance. The tax law does not treat disability coverage in the same way as medical insurance; special rules apply that *may* allow a deduction for premiums.

Benefit ⊗

Disability benefits you receive under a policy on which you paid the premiums are tax free. There is no dollar limit on the amount of disability benefits you can exclude from income. If your employer paid the premiums on a policy that you are now collecting on, the benefits are taxable to you. If you and your employer shared the cost of premiums, you must allocate the benefits accordingly; you can exclude only the portion that relates to *your* payments.

Disability coverage under Social Security is treated for tax purposes in the same way as Social Security retirement benefits—they may be wholly excludable or included in income in the amount of 50% or 85% of benefits, depending on your filing status and income. Generally, the payment of disability benefits under Social Security ends once you attain your full retirement age (for example, 66 years old for someone born in 1943 through 1954; the age increases gradually until it reaches 67 for those born after 1959). At that time you start receiving Social Security retirement benefits.

Condition

Tax-free treatment applies to benefits paid under a policy for which you paid the premiums with after-tax dollars. Tax-free treatment also applies to these types of disability payments:

- Disability pensions from the Department of Veterans Affairs
- Pensions for combat-related injuries or injuries from a terrorist attack
- Disability pensions for anyone who has injuries resulting from terrorist attacks after September 10, 2001

Planning Tips

If your employer gives you the choice between accepting employer-paid disability coverage or paying for such coverage yourself, you may prefer to pay for it so that benefits will be tax free if you become disabled. While your employer's payment of disability insurance premiums may be tax free to you, the price for this benefit is taxability of any disability payments you later receive.

If you are totally and permanently disabled and receive little or no Social Security benefits, you may be eligible for a tax credit called the credit for the elderly and disabled.

Pitfall

If you retire on disability and receive a lump-sum payment for accrued annual leave, you cannot exclude this payment; it is fully taxable as additional compensation.

Where to Claim the Benefit

If you are entitled to exclude disability payments you receive, you do not have to report them on your return. In this event, it does not matter whether you file Form 1040, 1040A, or 1040EZ.

Taxable disability pension payments shown on Form 1099-R are reported on your return as compensation if you have not reached the minimum retirement age set by your employer (use the same line you would for reporting salary, wages, etc.). Once you have attained the minimum retirement age, the disability pension payments are reported on lines 16a and 16b of Form 1040.

To determine the portion of Social Security disability payments that are excludable from income, complete the worksheet for Social Security benefits in the instructions to Form 1040. Ignore the words "Retirement Benefits" on this worksheet and enter your disability benefits in substitution. You must file Form 1040 or 1040A to report the taxable portion, if any, of your disability payments from Social Security (report Social Security disability payments on the line in the "Income" section of Form 1040 or 1040A used for Social Security benefits). You cannot file Form 1040EZ to report Social Security disability payments; there is no line on Form 1040EZ for reporting this income.

Accelerated Death Benefits

A life insurance policy may provide more than just death benefits. In some cases, it can be used to provide funds during the insured's lifetime. The tax law treats the proceeds during life, called accelerated death benefits, the same as post-death payments (that is, tax free), if certain conditions are met.

Benefit

Accelerated death benefits are an insurance company's payment of some or all of the death benefits under a life insurance policy on account of terminal or chronic illness of the insured. Viatical settlements involve the selling of a cash-value life insurance policy to a company in the business of buying such policies. Accelerated death benefits and viatical settlement proceeds received by a terminally ill individual are tax free.

Such payments to a person who is chronically ill can be excluded in full to the extent used to pay long-term care costs; per diem payments in excess of care costs are excludable only up to a set dollar limit per day ($360 in 2017).

Conditions

Tax-free treatment of accelerated death benefits and viatical settlement proceeds apply for someone who is terminally ill. This means you have a condition or illness that is expected to result in death within 24 months of certification by a physician. The exclusion applies without regard to the use of the benefits or proceeds.

To qualify for favorable treatment as a chronically ill individual, you must be certified by a licensed health-care practitioner that, within the preceding 12 months, you are unable to perform for a period of at least 90 days 2 or more of the following activities:

- Eating
- Toileting
- Bathing
- Dressing
- Continence
- Transferring (such as getting in and out of bed)

A person also qualifies as chronically ill if certified as requiring substantial supervision for one's own health and safety because of cognitive impairment (for example, the person has Alzheimer's disease).

For a chronically ill individual, excludable amounts must be used to pay long-term care expenses. These are necessary diagnostic, preventive, therapeutic, curing, treating, mitigation, and rehabilitative services, as well as personal care services. The services must be provided under a plan of care prescribed by a licensed health-care practitioner (which includes a doctor, registered nurse, or licensed social worker).

Planning Tip

When shopping for life insurance, inquire about accelerated death benefit options under the policy. You want to have as many options as possible, even if you never need to use them.

Pitfall

Generally, it is not advisable for someone who is terminally or chronically ill to use life insurance proceeds to cover lifetime care expenses. The purpose for which the policy was originally purchased, such as the care of surviving family members or the payment of funeral expenses and estate taxes, is frustrated by such use. Thus, using a life insurance policy for lifetime needs is usually a last resort for paying care expenses.

Where to Claim the Benefit

If accelerated death benefits or viatical settlement proceeds are excludable, they are not reported on the return.

Legal Fees

In most cases, there is no requirement that a lawyer be used to bring a lawsuit or conduct other types of business. But it is usually advisable to use an expert to protect your rights. Of course, this assistance may not come cheaply. Whether you can deduct legal fees depends on the type of activities involved.

Legal fees are discussed in Chapter 16.

Appraisal Fees

When property is damaged or destroyed, how do you know the true extent of the economic loss? Typically, you must rely on experts who can assess your unique situation. Experts, called appraisers, generally charge for their services. Fortunately, the tax law allows you to deduct appraisal fees if certain conditions are met.

Benefit

If you pay fees to an appraiser in order to determine the amount of a casualty, disaster, or theft loss, you may deduct the appraisal fees as a miscellaneous itemized deduction. You do *not* include appraisal fees as part of the loss.

The deduction is part of miscellaneous itemized expenses, which are deductible only to the extent the total exceeds 2% of your adjusted gross income and is subject to the reduction in itemized deductions for high-income taxpayers. There is no dollar limit on the deduction for appraisal fees.

Conditions

There are no specific conditions to meet in order to deduct your appraisal fees. Simply retain proof of this cost (keep it with copies of your tax return).

Planning Tip

Find the right appraiser for the item for which you are claiming a loss. For example, if your home is damaged by a storm, use a qualified real estate appraiser to assist in determining your loss.

In general, to find a qualified appraiser, see:

- American Society of Appraisers (www.appraisers.org)
- Appraisal Institute (www.appraisalinstitute.org)
- International Society of Appraisers (www.isa-appraisers.org)

Pitfall

If your miscellaneous itemized deductions do not exceed 2% of your adjusted gross income, you do not receive any benefit from the write-off of appraisal fees. In effect, the deduction is lost forever.

Where to Claim the Deduction

You claim the deduction for appraisal fees as a miscellaneous itemized deduction on Schedule A of Form 1040.

You cannot claim the deduction if you file Form 1040A or 1040EZ.

Corrosive Drywall Damage

Several years ago, homeowners in 23 states reported damage from certain drywall (called Chinese drywall because it was manufactured in China), including blackening or corrosion of electrical wiring and copper components in household appliances, as well as sulfur gas odors. Damage from the corrosive drywall to residences and appliances may be deductible. Hopefully, by now most affected homeowners have discovered the problem and remedied it. Those who have not can claim an itemized deduction (for details see IRS Revenue Procedure 2010-36).

Identity Theft

Identity theft is all too common in the United States today. According to the Javelin 2016 Identity Fraud Survey, there were an estimated 13.1 million individuals who had their personal identities stolen, with total fraud amounting to $15 billion. If you become a victim, you can experience damage to your FICO score, delays in tax refunds, and various financial losses.

Financial losses as a result of identity theft may be tax deductible because it usually constitutes a theft under state law (see the rules for deducting theft losses earlier in this chapter). However, the time and effort you expend to fix problems caused by identity theft (e.g., contacting credit bureaus; talking with creditors) are not tax deductible. Neither is the cost of identity theft insurance or similar coverage to protect your personal identity.

However, identity theft protection services that you receive (as a consumer or an employee) as a result of a company's data breach is not taxable. Such services include credit reporting and monitoring services, identity theft insurance, identity restoration services, and other similar services.

Identity Theft and Tax Relief

The IRS has been working to combat the growing number of identity theft cases where taxpayer information is used to obtain tax refunds, often preventing the legitimate person from receiving his or her refund on a timely basis. The IRS has a landing page for information and assistance on identity theft at www.irs.gov/Individuals/Identity-Protection. Here you'll find a link to the Taxpayer Guide to Identity Theft.

If you think you may be a victim of identity theft, you can protect yourself with respect to your tax return by filing Form 14039, *Identity Theft Affidavit*, with the IRS. This will help to ensure that you receive any tax refund you're entitled to. You must obtain an IP PIN if you receive a notice from the IRS (CP01A) giving you a new IP PIN or because you should have had one because your return was rejected without it. You may choose to get one if you received an invitation from the IRS to opt in or your return last year was filed in the District of Columbia, Florida, or Georgia (areas rampant with identity theft in which the IRS has a pilot program to combat it). Find details at www.irs.gov/getanippin.

Hurricanes Harvey and Irma Relief

In late August 2017, as a result of Hurricane Harvey, unprecedented flooding occurred in Houston and many other parts of Texas as well as Louisiana. It was estimated that as many as 40,000 homes and up to a half a million vehicles were destroyed. An estimated 70% of homes had no flood insurance. Similarly, catastrophe struck Florida and Georgia as a result of Hurricane Irma in September 2017. It is expected that Congress will create special tax rules for relief related to this property damage. Check the Supplement for details.

Your Job

Alert

At the time this book was completed, Congress was considering important tax changes that could affect 2017 tax returns and planning for 2018. Check the online Supplement in February 2018 at www.jklasser.com or www.barbaraweltman.com to see what changes have been enacted and when they are effective.

Your job not only is what occupies the majority of your time during the greater part of each week and, hopefully, provides satisfaction; it also gives you a paycheck and perhaps other benefits. While your earnings are taxable in most cases, some of the fringe benefits may be tax free.

In order to earn that paycheck, you may have to expend your own dollars on various things. Fortunately, you may be able to deduct your out-of-pocket job-related costs.

This chapter explains the write-offs and other breaks you can claim with respect to your job. Job-related moving expenses are discussed in Chapter 4. Employment-related travel and entertainment expenses are explained in Chapter 9.

For more information, see IRS Publication 3, *Armed Forces' Tax Guide*; IRS Publication 535, *Business Expenses*; and IRS Publication 587, *Business Use of Your Home*.

Job-Hunting Expenses

In today's tight job market, it may take considerable time and effort to land a new position. The costs incurred in this endeavor may be deductible if certain conditions are met.

Benefit

The cost of searching for a new job in your same line of work is deductible as a miscellaneous itemized deduction. There is no dollar limit on the amount of this deduction. You can claim the deduction whether or not a new job is found.

Miscellaneous itemized deductions can be claimed only to the extent they exceed 2% of your adjusted gross income (the 2% of AGI floor). They are also subject to the reduction in itemized deductions for high-income taxpayers.

If your employer or former employer pays for certain job placement costs, you are not taxed on this benefit. For example, if you are laid off and your employer provides outplacement services (including office space and resume preparation), this benefit is tax free.

Condition

The only condition for claiming this deduction is that your search relate to the same line of work you are currently or most recently in. For example, if you are an out-of-work programmer seeking a job as a programmer, this is considered to be in the same line of work. But if you are looking for a job in teaching, something you did 10 years ago, this is a new line of work.

If you are just out of college seeking your first full-time job in your field, you cannot deduct job-hunting expenses. If you are seeking work in a new line of business, you cannot deduct job-hunting expenses. If you are out of work for a long time, the IRS may question whether your job-hunting expenses are deductible.

Example

You leave your job when your first child is born, returning to the workforce when she enters kindergarten. Your job-hunting expenses in this case would probably *not* be deductible because of the 5-year period since your last job, even if you are searching for employment in the same line of work that you left.

EXAMPLES OF JOB-HUNTING EXPENSES

- Employment agency fees
- Postage and supplies
- Resumes
- Telephone costs
- Travel costs (for example, an out-of-town trip to interview for a job)

Planning Tip

Keep track of your job-hunting costs to support the amount of the deduction you claim.

Pitfalls

You cannot deduct job-hunting expenses for your first job. This is so even if you do find employment. The reason: Since you are not yet an employee, job-hunting expenses cannot be work-related as yet.

You cannot deduct job-hunting expenses that relate to a new line of work. For example, you are a teacher who attends law school in the evening. You cannot deduct job-hunting expenses to find a job as an attorney.

If you pay an employment agency fee to obtain a job and deduct this amount in the year of payment only to be reimbursed by your new employer in the following year, you must report the reimbursement as income to the extent that the deduction provided you with a tax benefit. Do not file an amended return for the year in which you claimed the deduction to back the deduction up.

Where to Claim the Deduction

If this is your only unreimbursed employee business expense, the deduction for job-hunting expenses is included with miscellaneous itemized deductions and entered directly on Schedule A of Form 1040. If you have other employee business expenses, you must complete Form 2106, *Employee Business Expenses*, or Form 2106-EZ, *Unreimbursed Employee Business Expenses*, to report your employee business expenses; the total amount is then entered on Schedule A of Form 1040.

You cannot deduct job-hunting expenses if you file Form 1040A or 1040EZ.

Dues to Unions and Professional Associations

According to the Bureau of Labor Statistics, there were about 14.4 million union members nationwide in the public and private sectors by the end of 2016. In addition, millions of professionals belong to trade or professional associations. The cost of this membership is generally deductible.

Benefit

Dues you pay to unions or professional associations are deductible. The dues are treated as a miscellaneous itemized deduction. Miscellaneous itemized expenses are deductible only to the extent they exceed 2% of adjusted gross income (the 2% of AGI floor) and are subject to the reduction of itemized deductions for high-income taxpayers.

There is no dollar limit on the amount of dues you can deduct each year.

Condition

Dues that you pay to a union or a professional association are deductible if they are ordinary and necessary business expenses (helpful to your job).

EXAMPLES OF DEDUCTIBLE PAYMENTS TO UNIONS

- Dues
- Initiation fees
- Mandatory payments for unemployment benefits (required as a condition for remaining in the union)
- Monthly service charges to nonunion members

EXAMPLES OF DEDUCTIBLE PAYMENTS TO PROFESSIONAL ASSOCIATIONS

- Chamber of commerce if it is conducted to advance the business interests of its membership
- Community booster club dues conducted to attract tourists and settlers to your locality
- Professional societies if you are a salaried accountant, attorney, doctor, teacher, or other professional

- Stock exchange if you are a securities dealer
- Trade association dues if the association is conducted to further the business interests of its membership

Planning Tip

Check to see what benefits you may be entitled to because of membership in a union or trade or professional association. The savings you can realize on member benefits may well exceed the cost of dues.

Pitfall

Just because funds are collected by your union or payments relate to your union does not automatically mean they are deductible. You may not deduct the following types of payments:

- Assessments for a construction fund to build union recreation facilities
- Campaign costs for running for union office
- Mandatory contributions to a union pension fund applied toward the purchase of an annuity (you are treated as having purchased the annuity and cannot deduct your cost)
- Voluntary payments to a union unemployment benefit or strike fund

Where to Claim the Deduction

If this is your only unreimbursed employee business expense, the deduction for dues to unions and professional associations is included with miscellaneous itemized deductions and entered directly on Schedule A of Form 1040. If you have other employee business expenses, you must complete Form 2106, *Employee Business Expenses*, or Form 2106-EZ, *Unreimbursed Employee Business Expenses*, to report your employee business expenses; the total amount is then entered on Schedule A of Form 1040.

You cannot deduct dues to unions or professional associations if you file Form 1040A or 1040EZ.

Work Clothes and Uniforms

Everyone wants to look his or her best on the job. But only certain types of workers can deduct the cost of work clothes, provided certain conditions are met.

Benefit

The costs of work clothes and uniforms are deductible. They are treated as a miscellaneous itemized deduction. Miscellaneous itemized expenses are deductible only to the extent they exceed 2% of adjusted gross income (the 2% of AGI floor) and are subject to the reduction of itemized deductions for high-income taxpayers.

There is no dollar limit on the amount you can deduct for work clothes and uniforms.

If your employer provides you with a clothing allowance, you can exclude this amount from your income as long as you are required to substantiate your purchases to your employer (for example, provide your employer with receipts showing how you spent the allowance). If you spend more than the substantiated amounts, you can treat the excess costs as a deductible expense, provided you satisfy the following conditions.

Conditions

There are 2 conditions for deducting the cost of work clothes and uniforms; you must satisfy both conditions:

1. You are required to use such wear to keep your job. Generally, these include items necessary to keep you safe and enable you to perform your job, such as protective clothing, steel-tip shoes, eye goggles, and protective gloves.

2. The clothing is not suitable for ordinary street wear. The fact that your job requires you to wear expensive clothing is not a justification for deducting your costs; if the items can be worn off the job, even if you would not have bought them but for the job, the costs are not deductible. Similarly, those involved in many types of sports cannot deduct warm-up clothing and similar clothing that is suitable for wear off the job.

EXAMPLES OF PROFESSIONALS HAVING DEDUCTIBLE WORK CLOTHES AND UNIFORMS

- Airline pilot
- Bakery salesperson (uniform with company label)
- Baseball player
- Bus driver
- Cement finisher (gloves, overshoes, and rubber boots)
- Civilian faculty member of a military school
- Commercial fisherman (protective clothing such as oilskins, gloves, and rubber boots)
- Dairy worker (rubber boots, white shirts, trousers, and cap for inside use)
- Dance instructor (jazz shoes)
- Doctor (scrubs)
- Electrical worker (coveralls and protective gear)

- Entertainer (theatrical clothing used solely for performances)
- Factory foreman (white coat with company name and "foreman" designation)
- Factory worker (safety shoes)
- Firefighter
- Hospital attendant (clothes used only on the job with patients having contagious diseases)
- Jockey
- Letter carrier
- Meat cutter (special white shoes)
- Musician (formal wear)
- Paint machine operator (high-top shoes and long leather gloves)
- Plumber (special shoes and gloves)
- Police officer
- Railroad conductor
- Reservists (uniform costs in excess of military allowances for clothing prohibited from wearing off duty)
- Roughneck for oil drilling company (protective clothing)

Planning Tips

In addition to a deduction for clothes and uniforms, you can also write off costs of cleaning, laundering, and alterations for such items.

If your employer provides you with uniforms, safety goggles, or other similar items, you are not taxed on this benefit.

EXAMPLES OF DEDUCTIBLE CLEANING EXPENSES

- Clothing in need of daily laundering
- Clothing viewed as a hazard if not freshly pressed (baggy clothing could become caught in machinery)
- Meat cutters required to wear clean work clothes
- Shoeshines for military-like shoes worn by pilots only with uniforms

If your employer provides you with uniforms, safety goggles, or other similar items, you are not taxed on this benefit.

Pitfall

The fact that your union or your position requires you to wear certain items does *not* make their costs deductible. For example, painters in the painters' union may be required to wear white bib overalls, but this does not make the cost of the overalls deductible. The Tax Court did not allow a bartender required by his employer to wear an all-black ensemble (black shirt, black tie, and black pants) to deduct the cost of clothing because the ensemble was not a uniform; it was suitable for ordinary street wear.

Where to Claim the Deduction

If this is your only unreimbursed employee business expense, the deduction for work clothes and uniforms is included with miscellaneous itemized deductions and entered directly on Schedule A of Form 1040. If you have other employee business expenses, you must complete Form 2106, *Employee Business Expenses*, or Form 2106-EZ, *Unreimbursed Employee Business Expenses*, to report your employee business expenses; the total amount is then entered on Schedule A of Form 1040.

You cannot deduct expenses for work clothes and uniforms if you file Form 1040A or 1040EZ.

Subscriptions to Professional Journals, Newsletters, and Podcasts

It has been estimated that information in the world now doubles every 13 months. How can you keep up with developments affecting your job or profession? Journals, newsletters, magazines, online subscription sites, podcasts, and other mobile information resources help to provide needed information for your work, the cost of which may be deductible.

Benefit

The cost of subscriptions to professional journals and newsletters are deductible. This applies to print as well as online versions. The cost is treated as a miscellaneous itemized deduction. Miscellaneous itemized expenses are deductible only to the extent they exceed 2% of adjusted gross income (the 2% of AGI floor) and are subject to the reduction of itemized deductions for high-income taxpayers.

There is no dollar limit on the amount you can deduct for subscriptions to professional journals and newsletters.

Conditions

The subscriptions must be an ordinary and necessary expense of your job or profession. For example, an accountant who subscribes to tax newsletters can treat the cost as a deductible job expense.

Planning Tip

You may be able to save on subscription costs by opting for online or fax versions of newspapers and newsletters instead of receiving them by mail.

Pitfall

If you pay for multiyear subscriptions, under a so-called 12-month rule you cannot deduct subscription costs that cover a period of more than 12 months or the 12-month period that ends on or before the last day of the income year following the year in which the payment was incurred.

Example

In July 2017, you take out a 1-year subscription to a trade journal. Because the period does not exceed 12 months, you can deduct the entire payment in the year you make it. But if you take out a 3-year subscription, you can deduct only 6 months for the 3-year subscription in 2017, 12 months in 2018, 12 months in 2019, and 6 months in 2020.

Where to Claim the Deduction

If this is your only unreimbursed employee business expense, the deduction for professional journals and newsletters is included with miscellaneous itemized deductions and entered directly on Schedule A of Form 1040. If you have other employee business expenses, you must complete Form 2106, *Employee Business Expenses*, or Form 2106-EZ, *Unreimbursed Employee Business Expenses*, to report your employee business expenses; the total amount is then entered on Schedule A of Form 1040.

You cannot deduct expenses for professional journals and newsletters if you file Form 1040A or 1040-EZ.

Work Tools and Equipment

Tools of the trade don't always come with the job. Sometimes it's up to you to provide them. When you do, the tax law lets you write off their cost under certain conditions.

Benefit

The cost of work tools is deductible. The cost is treated as a miscellaneous itemized deduction. Miscellaneous itemized expenses are deductible only to the extent they exceed 2% of adjusted gross income (the 2% of AGI floor) and are subject to the reduction of itemized deductions for high-income taxpayers.

There is no dollar limit on the amount you can deduct for work tools. The question you must decide is *when* to claim the write-offs: the year of the purchase or over a set number of years based on the recovery period of the tools. The answer depends on the useful life of the tools. If a tool has a useful life of no more than one year, you can simply deduct its cost in full in the year of purchase. But if it has a longer useful life, you must depreciate its cost or elect first-year expensing.

Conditions

You must show that the tools or equipment are an ordinary and necessary expense of your job. This means that you need the tools or equipment to do your job properly and your employer does not provide such items. Merely obtaining a letter from your employer stating that the item is required does not, by itself, prove your necessity; include the *reason* why it is required (e.g., safety).

Example

You are a salesperson and purchase a tablet to make sales presentations at customer locations. You cannot make sales presentations without the tablet and your employer does not provide you with a tablet. In this instance, the tablet may be deductible. But if the tablet is merely helpful (e.g., you keep notes for yourself), a deduction is not allowed, even though it is used on the job.

EXAMPLES OF DEDUCTIBLE WORK TOOLS AND EQUIPMENT

Camera, watch, and gun of a federal investigator

Cellular phones

Computers, laptops, and tablets

iPods used to download work-related podcasts

Smartphones

Tools of your trade (e.g., for plumbing or electrical work, painting and plastering, or woodworking)

Planning Tip

Ask whether your employer can supply you with the necessary tools for your job, eliminating your need to make the purchase, since the 2% of AGI floor may bar you from claiming any deduction if you make the purchase.

Pitfall

If you use the tools or equipment for personal purpose in addition to job-related use, only the portion of the cost related to the job is deductible. For example, if you use a computer for work (and show it is required for you to do your job) but also use it on your off time, allocate the cost of the computer between job and personal use.

Where to Claim the Deduction

If this is your only unreimbursed employee business expense and the work tools have a useful life of no more than one year, the deduction for work tools is included with miscellaneous itemized deductions and entered directly on Schedule A of Form 1040. If you have other employee business expenses, you must complete Form 2106, *Employee Business Expenses*, or Form 2106-EZ, *Unreimbursed Employee Business Expenses*, to report your employee business expenses; the total amount is then entered on Schedule A of Form 1040. If tools have a useful life of more than one year, you must file Form 4562, *Amortization and Depreciation*, to figure depreciation on the tools. Depreciation is explained in greater detail in IRS Publication 946, *How to Depreciate Property*.

You cannot deduct expenses for work tools and equipment if you file Form 1040A or 1040-EZ.

Miscellaneous Job-Related Expenses

Not every expense related to a job fits neatly into a set category. But just because you can't find a specific rule for the expense doesn't mean you can't claim a deduction for it. Various types of miscellaneous job-related expenses can be deductible if certain conditions are met.

Benefit 🖹

Just about any type of expense related to your job that can be viewed as ordinary and necessary may be deductible. These miscellaneous job-related expenses are treated as a miscellaneous itemized deduction. Miscellaneous itemized expenses are deductible only to the extent they exceed 2% of adjusted gross income (the 2% of AGI floor) and are subject to the reduction of itemized deductions for high-income taxpayers.

There is no dollar limit on the amount you can deduct for miscellaneous job-related expenses.

Conditions

The expense must be an ordinary and necessary expense of your job. This generally means that the item must be appropriate and helpful to your particular job or position.

No deduction can be claimed if the expense is really a company expense that you voluntarily make.

EXAMPLES OF DEDUCTIBLE MISCELLANEOUS EXPENSES

- Breast implants of an exotic dancer that made her the abnormal size of 56N.
- Laboratory breakage by a research scientist.
- Office decorations. In one case, an office manager purchased his own furniture when the company moved to new quarters and the Tax Court allowed him to depreciate the cost of the furniture, which was appropriate and helpful to his image as a successful manager.
- Politician's expenses in excess of a government allowance for such costs as employee salaries, office rent, and supplies. The expense is allowable whether the position is full time or part time.
- Private airplane operating costs of a salesman whose territory, covering 6 states, was not near commercial airports (even though expenses were large in relation to his compensation).
- Repayment of layoff benefits upon being rehired (essentially, payments required as a condition of reemployment).
- Stockbroker's repayment to his firm for a client's loss that the firm made good due to his trading errors.

Planning Tip

If you claim a deduction that is out of the ordinary, be prepared to support your deduction not only with proof of the cost but also with the reason on why the cost should be deductible.

Pitfall

Not all seemingly ordinary and necessary job-related costs are deductible. Even though the expense may have some relation to the job, it may be primarily a nondeductible personal expense. Here is a roundup of cases in which taxpayers lost their claimed deductions:

- Campaign costs of running for union presidency.
- Currency loss on converting a U.S. paycheck into foreign currency of a government employee stationed abroad.
- Donations to political parties in order to secure a job.
- Gifts to superiors.
- Haircuts by a pilot required to keep his hair short and neat at all times. The same results apply to service personnel and to secretaries' coiffures.
- Health club membership, even if the job requires physical fitness (for example, a police officer could not deduct membership fees).
- Insurance premiums withheld from pay to cover disability insurance.

- Makeup for a television newsman.
- Pension fund assessments.

Where to Claim the Deduction

If this is your only unreimbursed employee business expense, the deduction for miscellaneous job-related expenses is included with miscellaneous itemized deductions and entered directly on Schedule A of Form 1040. If you have other employee business expenses, you must complete Form 2106, *Employee Business Expenses*, or Form 2106-EZ, *Unreimbursed Employee Business Expenses*, to report your employee business expenses; the total amount is then entered on Schedule A of Form 1040.

You cannot deduct miscellaneous job-related expenses if you file Form 1040A or 1040EZ.

Educator Expenses

There are about 3.6 million teachers in grades K–12, according to the National Center for Education Statistics. Most teachers spend money from their own pockets to pay for classroom expenses. The tax law lets them deduct their costs, up to a limit, regardless of whether they itemize deductions.

Benefit ⬲

If you are an educator, you can deduct up to $250 of what you spend out-of-pocket for classroom expenses and professional development courses related to curriculum as an adjustment to gross income; you do not have to itemize deductions to claim this benefit. The $250 limit can be adjusted annually for inflation, but because of low inflation, there is no increase in the limit for 2017.

Conditions

You must be an educator in grades K–12. This includes not only teachers, but also principals, guidance counselors, and aides. The Tax Court allowed a high school coach to deduct his costs for sports over IRS objections that only classroom expenses counted; the track was his classroom.

You must work at least 900 hours a school year in a school that provides elementary or secondary education.

You must pay qualified expenses. This includes supplies, books, computer equipment, and other materials used in the classroom (including health and physical education courses). As mentioned earlier, it also includes professional development expenses, which are courses related to the curriculum that the educator teaches.

Planning Tip

If out-of-pocket classroom costs exceed the $250 limit, the excess can still be deducted as an unreimbursed business expense if you itemize your deductions.

Pitfall

If you homeschool your child, you cannot claim this deduction.

Where to Claim the Deduction

Enter the amount of your out-of-pocket expenses up to $250 in the "Adjusted Gross Income" section of Form 1040.

You cannot claim the deduction if you file Form 1040A or 1040EZ.

Home Office Deduction

Global Workplace Analytics reports that 3.7 million employees (2.8% of the workforce) now work at least half the time from home. The numbers are even greater when considering employees who work at least one day a week from home. This number should grow substantially as governments and private employers are increasingly offering or mandating telework as one solution to high gas prices. Those who work from home may be eligible to deduct some of their housing costs as a job expense as long as they meet certain conditions.

Benefit

If you telecommute or use a portion of your home as an office for your job, you may be entitled to deduct expenses related to that portion of your home, including rent (if you are a tenant) or depreciation (if you are a homeowner), utilities, insurance, and maintenance.

The home office deduction is treated as a miscellaneous itemized deduction. Miscellaneous itemized expenses are deductible only to the extent they exceed 2% of adjusted gross income (the 2% of AGI floor) and are subject to the reduction of itemized deductions for high-income taxpayers.

There is no dollar limit on the amount you can write off as a home office deduction if you are using the actual expense method. If, instead, you rely on an IRS-set rate (the simplified method), you can deduct $5 per square foot up to 300 square feet of space. You cannot use the simplified method if you receive an advance, allowance, or reimbursement from your employer for your home office.

For a further discussion of the home office deduction, see Chapter 15.

Conditions

Employees have a unique requirement to be eligible for a home office deduction: The home office must be used for the convenience of your employer.

Convenience of the employer does not mean that your employer just supports your preference to work from home. Rather, it usually means that your employer *needs* you to work from home (for example, there is no office space at the company's location). Simply obtaining a letter from your employer stating that your home office use is for the convenience of the employer is generally not sufficient to prove your employer's convenience; the letter must explain the reason why use of a home office is for the employer's convenience (e.g., space considerations).

Planning Tip

Discuss your work arrangement thoroughly with your employer so you'll know whether you satisfy the condition for eligibility. If you do, then ask your employer for a letter stating that working from home is for the employer's convenience and add the employer's reason why (for example, there is no desk space for you at the company office).

Pitfall

You cannot claim *any* home office deduction if you lease the space to your employer. Mortgage interest, real estate taxes, and casualty losses otherwise deductible by any homeowner continue to be deductible even if you rent space to your employer; only utilities, insurance, maintenance, and other office-related costs are not deductible. You must, of course, report as income any rent you receive from your employer.

Where to Claim the Benefit

You figure your home office deduction on a worksheet contained in IRS Publication 587, *Business Use of Your Home* (you do *not* use Form 8829 for this purpose; only self-employed individuals filing Schedule C complete that form).

If this is your only unreimbursed employee business expense, the deduction for home office expenses is included with miscellaneous itemized deductions and entered directly on Schedule A of Form 1040. If you have other employee business expenses, you must complete Form 2106, *Employee Business Expenses*, or Form 2106-EZ, *Unreimbursed Employee Business Expenses*, to report your employee business expenses; the total amount is then entered on Schedule A of Form 1040.

You cannot claim a home office deduction if you file Form 1040A or 1040EZ.

Prizes and Awards

Recognition for a job well done is always appreciated. When it is accompanied by a monetary item, it may be valued even more. Taxwise, a prize or award may be tax free under very limited circumstances.

Benefit ⊗

If you receive certain prizes or awards *other than cash*, you can exclude the amount you receive from income. These include awards of tangible personal property, such as the proverbial gold watch, given as awards for length of service or safety achievements, and your employer is permitted to deduct the cost of those awards. However, other prizes and awards are fully taxable.

Conditions

Generally, your ability to exclude employment-related prizes and awards depends on your employer's ability to deduct the payments. But you don't have to be the company's comptroller to determine this; the company will report to you the tax treatment of the award on your Form W-2.

Just to give you some idea of the extent of what you can exclude, your employer's deduction depends on whether the award is part of a qualified award plan. If yes, then up to $1,600 may be given to the same employee during the year. If the award is not part of a qualified award plan, then the annual limit per employee is $400.

Planning Tip

If you receive a valuable prize or award that is *not* tax free, your employer will automatically withhold income taxes on the payment (at the flat rate of 25%). If this withholding is not enough to cover your estimated tax requirements, ask your employer to withhold an additional amount.

Pitfall

If you win a sales or other contest on the job and receive a prize, such as a vacation, you can decline the award to avoid taxation on the benefit. If you accept the prize, you are generally taxed on the value of the benefit.

Where to Claim the Benefit

Prizes and awards that are tax free need not be reported on your tax return.

Performing Artists

Actors, singers, dancers, comedians, and other performing artists can deduct the same job expenses as any other worker. But the tax law provides a special rule on *how* to claim deductions.

Benefit 🔼

If you are a performing artist with income below a set amount, you can deduct your employment-related expenses as an adjustment to gross income rather than as a miscellaneous itemized deduction. This means that your employment-related expenses become fully deductible; they are not subject to the 2% of AGI floor (discussed earlier in this chapter).

Conditions

You must meet all of the following 3 conditions to treat your job-related expenses as an adjustment to gross income rather than as an itemized deduction:

1. You have 2 or more employers in the performing arts during the year with at least $200 of earnings from at least 2 of them.

2. Your expenses from acting or other services are more than 10% of your gross income from such work. For example, you spend $8,000 during the year on voice lessons and earn $22,000 doing voice-overs and other jobs in the performing arts. Since $8,000 is more than 10% of $22,000, you meet this condition.

3. Your adjusted gross income from all sources (not just performing arts) is no more than $16,000.

SPECIAL RULE FOR MARRIED INDIVIDUALS

You must file a joint return if you are married, unless you live apart from your spouse for the entire year.

If both you and your spouse work in the performing arts, you figure the two-employer requirement and the 10% requirement separately for each of you. Compare your personal employment-related expenses to the money you earn from performing arts jobs.

For purposes of your adjusted gross income, the $16,000 applies to your *combined* AGI.

Planning Tip

As with any other type of expense, it is vital to keep good records of your job-related outlays. Retain receipts for lessons you take. Use a diary or other record keeper to note travel expenses and other items.

Pitfall

Even $1 of adjusted gross income over the $16,000 limit means your expenses can be deducted only as a miscellaneous itemized deduction subject to the 2%

of AGI floor. If you anticipate AGI of about this amount, weigh carefully the after-tax cost of accepting work that puts you over the limit.

Example

You earn $15,000 from your work in acting, have expenses of $7,000, and meet the other conditions for treating your expenses as an adjustment to gross income. This means your AGI after the deduction becomes $8,000. But if you have $1,000 more of AGI, your expenses are deductible in excess of $320, so your write-off is limited to $6,680. The $1,000 of additional income nets you only $680 ($1,000 – $320 lost deduction).

Where to Claim the Benefit

You figure your deductible work-related expenses on Form 2106 (or Form 2106-EZ, if eligible). Your total amount is then entered on the line for this item in the "Adjusted Gross Income" section of Form 1040.

State or Local Government Officials Paid on a Fee Basis

Not every bureaucrat is a regular employee on the government's payroll. Some government employees are paid under a contract arrangement. Those who are can write off their related employee expenses in a special way.

Benefit

If you are an employee of a state or local government and are paid in whole or in part on a fee basis, you can deduct the business expenses related to these services as an adjustment to gross income rather than as a miscellaneous itemized deduction.

Conditions

The only conditions for treating your business expenses as an adjustment to gross income are:

- You are an employee of a state or local government.
- You are paid in whole or in part on a fee basis.

Planning Tip

If you are a state or local government employee, ask to arrange partial compensation on a fee basis (for example, related to a specific government project) to create an above-the-line deduction for your job expenses.

Pitfall

There is no downside to treating these business expenses as an adjustment to gross income.

Where to Claim the Deduction

You figure your deductible work-related expenses on Form 2106 (or Form 2106-EZ, if eligible). Your total amount is then entered on the line for adding up your adjustments to gross income in the "Adjusted Gross Income" section of Form 1040; there is no specially labeled line for this deduction. On the dotted line alongside the total adjustments to gross income write "FBO" to indicate that the deduction is for a fee-basis official.

Repayment of Supplemental Unemployment Benefits

While unemployed, you may receive benefits in addition to regular state unemployment benefits. These "supplemental" benefits may have to be repaid once you obtain employment. If so, you may be able to write them off, either as a deduction or as a tax credit, if certain conditions are met.

Benefit

If you are required to repay supplemental unemployment benefits in order to qualify for trade readjustment allowances, you can claim a deduction for the repayment as an adjustment to gross income, even if you do not itemize your other deductions.

In some cases, you may even be eligible for a tax credit (instead of a deduction) for your repayments.

Example

In 2016, you received supplemental unemployment benefits and your tax bill was $3,800. In 2017, you repay $5,000. You recompute your 2016 tax, eliminating the $5,000 from income. Without this income, you would have paid $2,774. Therefore, your credit is $1,026 ($3,800 – $2,774).

Conditions

To claim the deduction, you must be required to repay supplemental unemployment benefits that you included in income in a prior year. The deduction is designed to wipe the slate clean; you already paid tax on the benefits when you received them and now you are entitled to a deduction to reduce your income, effectively backing out the benefits.

To claim a credit, your repayment must exceed $3,000. Then figure your credit by recomputing the tax you would have paid had you not received the repaid amount in the initial year, and compare the tax with what you actually paid.

Planning Tip

If you repaid supplemental unemployment benefits in the same year in which they were received, you do not have to do anything; the benefits were never reported as income, so there is no offsetting deduction necessary.

Pitfall

You cannot choose to file an amended return for the year in which the supplemental unemployment benefits were originally paid to subtract your later repayment. Your only choice in handling the repayment is to deduct it or, if eligible, claim a tax credit in the year of repayment.

Where to Claim the Benefit

If you are claiming the deduction, enter the amount of your repayment in the "Adjusted Gross Income" section of Form 1040; there is no specially labeled line for this deduction. On the dotted line alongside the total adjustments to gross income write "subpay TRA" to indicate that the deduction is for repayment of unemployment benefits due to trade readjustment allowances.

If you opt to treat repayments exceeding $3,000 as a tax credit, enter the credit as another payment in the "Payments" section of Form 1040. Write in "IRC 1341" to indicate the type of credit you are claiming.

Jury Duty Pay Turned Over to Your Employer

Jury duty is a civic duty that is hard to avoid. If you are called to serve, you are paid a nominal amount that is taxable income. But if you also receive your regular wages from your employer and must hand over your jury duty pay, you can claim a deduction for the income you don't get to keep.

Benefit

If you receive your regular pay while serving on jury duty and turn over your jury duty pay to your employer, you can claim a deduction for this action as an adjustment to gross income, even if you do not itemize your other deductions. This deduction is intended to offset your having to include the jury duty pay in income. There are no dollar limits on this deduction.

Condition

You must be required by your employer to turn over jury duty pay as a condition of receiving your regular compensation.

Planning Tip

Ask your employer whether you can keep your jury duty pay and simply receive your ordinary compensation in excess of this amount so that you reduce your FICA taxes (and your employer saves a like amount in FICA taxes).

Example

Your regular daily pay in 2017 is $150. Assume you serve on a jury for 5 days and receive $40 per day. If your employer pays you only $110 and allows you to retain the $40, you save $15.30 in taxes ($40 × 5 days × 7.65% rate for Social Security and Medicare taxes).

Pitfall

Don't overlook this deduction for jury duty pay, especially if you receive it early in the year. It's easy to forget about it since payments of less than $600 are not reported to you on an information return from the government.

Where to Claim the Deduction

If you are claiming a deduction for jury duty pay turned over to your employer, enter the amount in the "Adjusted Gross Income" section of Form 1040; there is no specially labeled line for this deduction. On the dotted line alongside the total adjustments to gross income, write "jury pay" to indicate that the deduction is for the amount of jury duty pay that you turned over to your employer.

Impairment-Related Expenses

Having a disability may necessitate certain additional expenses in order to work. The tax law recognizes this added cost and allows these work-related expenses to be deductible under a special rule.

Benefit

If you suffer from a physical or mental impairment and you must incur special expenses to enable you to work, you can deduct these impairment-related expenses as an itemized deduction. This deduction is *not* subject to the 2% of AGI floor discussed earlier with respect to certain other employment-related expenses but is subject to the reduction of itemized deductions for high-income taxpayers.

There is no dollar limit on this deduction. The deduction may be claimed without regard to the amount of your income.

Conditions

To be eligible for the deduction, you must meet both of the following conditions:

1. You have a physical or mental disability that results in a functional limitation of employment that substantially limits one or more major life activities.
2. You must pay the expenses in order to work. For example, if you require an attendant at work so you can perform your job, your cost for these services is a qualified expense.

EXAMPLES OF IMPAIRMENTS

Any one of these impairments entitles you to deduct job-related expenses without regard to the 2% of AGI limit:

- Blindness
- Deafness
- Impairment limiting your ability to perform manual tasks
- Inability to speak or walk

Planning Tip

You may be able to avoid paying some or all of your work-related expenses due to your impairment (no cost to you is better than a deductible one). Under the Americans with Disabilities Act (ADA), your employer must provide reasonable accommodations to enable you to perform your job duties. This may include special equipment or assistance. For more information about benefits to which you may be entitled by the ADA, visit www.usdoj.gov/crt/ada/adahom1.htm.

Pitfall

You cannot claim a double deduction for the same expense, so if you treat some impairment-related costs as a job expense, you cannot also deduct them as a medical expense. For example, Braille books for your work are an impairment-related job expense and also qualify as a deductible medical expense, but if you treat them as a job expense, you cannot also deduct them as a medical expense.

Where to Claim the Deduction

You must complete Form 2106, *Employee Business Expenses*, or Form 2106-EZ, *Unreimbursed Employee Business Expenses*, to report your impairment-related expenses along with other unreimbursed employee business expenses. The total amount is then entered as a miscellaneous itemized deduction not subject to the 2% of AGI floor on Schedule A of Form 1040.

You cannot deduct impairment-related expenses if you file Form 1040A or 1040EZ.

Military Benefits

Serving your country in the military won't make you rich, but it may entitle you to a variety of benefits and other assistance. The tax law looks favorably on those in the service by allowing tax-free treatment for a long list of benefits.

Benefit

If you are a member of the armed forces, including the National Guard and the reserves, you may be entitled to certain benefits because of your job status.

EXAMPLES OF TAX-FREE BENEFITS

- Adjustments in pay to compensate for losses resulting from inflated foreign currency
- Benefits under the Servicemembers' Group Life Insurance
- Combat pay
- Death allowance for burial services, gratuity payments to survivors up to $5,000, and travel of dependents to burial sites
- Death benefit payable to family members of those killed in combat
- Defense counseling payments
- Disability pay
- Dislocation allowance (intended to partially reimburse expenses such as lease forfeitures, temporary living costs in hotels, and other expenses incurred in relocating a household)
- Dividends on GI insurance
- Education, training, or subsistence allowances paid under any law administered by the Veterans Administration (VA) (deductible education costs must be reduced by the VA allowance)
- Family allowances for education expenses of dependents, emergencies, evacuation to a place of safety, and separation

- Housing allowances (Basic Allowance for Housing, Variable Housing Allowance, temporary lodging expense allowance, and a moving-in allowance intended to defray costs such as rental agent fees, home security improvements, and supplemental heating equipment associated with occupying leased space outside the United States)
- Interest on dividends left on deposit with the VA
- Living allowances (Basic Allowance for Subsistence)
- Medical or hospital treatment
- Payments to former prisoners of war
- ROTC educational and subsistence allowances
- State and local payments of bonuses to active or former military personnel or their dependents by reason of such personnel's service in a combat zone
- Survivor and retirement protection plan premium payments
- Travel allowances for annual round-trip for dependent students, leave between consecutive overseas tours, reassignment in a dependent-restricted area, and transportation for you or your dependents during ship overhaul or inactivation
- Uniform allowances

Condition

There are no specific conditions for claiming these benefits; you are entitled to them if you are a member of the armed forces.

Planning Tips

If you receive a Basic Allowance for Housing (BAH), you can still deduct your mortgage interest and real estate taxes on your home, even though you pay these expenses with your BAH.

Military personnel can treat tax-free combat pay as earned income for purposes of making contributions to a traditional or Roth IRA.

Military personnel can also treat tax-free combat pay as earned income for purposes of the earned income credit (see Chapter 1).

For purposes of the home sale exclusion for gain on the sale of a principal residence, military personnel have a 10-year period (in place of a 5-year period) in which to have owned and used the home as their main home (see Chapter 4).

Pitfall

Nearly half the states tax military retirement pay, so check with your state for details.

Where to Claim the Benefit

Benefits that are excludable need not be reported on your return.

Contributions to State Benefit Programs

You may deduct mandated employee contributions to state unemployment, disability, and family leave programs as an itemized deduction. This deduction is explained in Chapter 16 under State and Local Income Taxes.

Fringe Benefits

Wages, or salary, are only one aspect of remuneration for working. Your job may entitle you to a wide range of benefits, called perquisites ("perks") or fringe benefits. Many of these benefits are fully or partially tax free.

Benefit ⊗

If your employer pays for certain benefits, you may be able to exclude from your income some or all of these items. In many cases, however, tax-free treatment does not apply if you are an employee of an S corporation in which you own more than 2% of the stock.

There are various limitations and conditions for different fringe benefits, many of which are discussed in other chapters in this book (see Table 14.1).

You may be unaware of certain fringe benefits because you do not have to sign up for them as you would for, say, health coverage or a retirement plan, and they are not reported on your annual Form W-2. These fringe benefits include:

De minimis (minimal) fringe benefits. These are items so modest that accounting for them would be an administrative burden on your employer. For example:

- Birthday cakes
- Doughnuts, coffee, and soda
- Flowers or fruit for special occasions
- Occasional personal long-distance calls
- Occasional lunch or dinner money
- Photocopying
- Postage on personal items once in a while
- Tickets bought by the company for sporting or entertainment events
- Use of employer's car if not more than once a month

Caution: Some companies have a policy against personal phone calls or other personal use of company property (e.g., photocopying) and such use can be considered a theft, so ask about your employer's policy on this matter.

TABLE 14.1 Fringe Benefits in 2017

Type of Benefit	Dollar Limit on Exclusion	Other Limitations	For More Details, See Chapter
Accident and health plans	None (except for long-term care benefits)		2
Achievement awards	Up to $1,600 ($400 for nonqualified awards)		
Adoption assistance	$13,570	Income limitations	1
Athletic facilities	None		
Bicycle commuting	$20/month		
De minimis (minimal) benefits			
Dependent care assistance	$5,000		1
Educational assistance	$5,250		3
Employee discounts			
Employee stock options			
Free parking	$255/month		
Group term life insurance	$50,000		
Lodging on business premises			
Meals on business premises for convenience of employer			
Meals—*de minimis*			
Moving expense reimbursements		50-mile distance test and 39-week employment test	4
No-additional-cost services			
Transit passes	$255/month		
Working condition benefits			

Employee discounts. Typically, these are limited to 25% to 30% of the cost of goods such as store merchandise (usually 20% of the cost of services such as dry cleaning).

No-additional-cost services. These are items for which your employer does not incur any additional cost when you use them. For example:

- Flights for airline employees and their families on a standby basis
- Hotel rooms for hotel workers when there is a vacancy

Working condition fringe benefits. These include expenses that would be deductible as an unreimbursed employee business expense on your return if you, rather than your employer, had paid for them. For example:

- Clothing and uniforms to wear on the job
- Dues to professional or trade associations
- Subscriptions to work-related publications
- Travel, entertainment, and meals
- Work-related continuing education courses

Transportation fringe benefit. This includes free parking, transit passes, and vanpooling of $255 per month in 2017. It also includes bicycle commuting up to $20 per month. You can receive all transportation benefits, other than bicycle commuting, each month. The bicycle commuting benefit—for the purchase, maintenance, and storage of a bicycle used to get to and from work—cannot be claimed in any month in which another transportation fringe benefit is used.

Conditions

Different fringe benefits have different conditions and limitations. Table 14.1 contains a survey of various fringe benefits that are excludable, including any other limitations that may apply, and references, where appropriate, to the chapter in which you will find an additional explanation.

Planning Tips

Congress may increase the types of tax-free benefits that employers can provide to workers, so check with your employer for benefits for which you may be eligible.

If a fringe benefit is tax free, it may also be exempt from Social Security and Medicare (FICA) taxes. Table 14.2 shows which benefits are exempt from Social Security and Medicare taxes.

TABLE 14.2 Benefits Exempt from Social Security and Medicare (FICA) Taxes

Benefit	FICA Taxes
Accident and health benefits	Exempt (except for S corporation shareholders owning more than 2% of the stock)
Achievement awards	Exempt up to $1,600 ($400 for nonqualified awards)
Adoption assistance	Not exempt
Athletic facilities	Exempt
De minimis benefits	Exempt
Dependent care assistance	Exempt up to $5,000

Pitfalls

Employees in an S corporation who own more than 2% of the stock cannot exclude the following types of fringe benefits from income:

- Accident and health benefits.
- Achievement awards.
- Adoption assistance.
- Lodging on the business premises.
- Meals furnished for the employer's convenience.
- Moving expenses.
- Transportation benefits (free parking and transit passes). However, transit passes up to $21 per month can be excluded if the value of the passes is not more than this amount (if more, then all of the benefit is taxable; you cannot exclude the $21 per month).

Certain benefits payable to highly compensated employees (generally executives and other highly paid workers, even those who are not S corporation shareholders) are not excludable. These benefits include:

- Self-insured medical reimbursement plans
- Dependent care assistance if the program favors these employees
- Employee discounts
- No-additional-cost services

Where to Claim the Benefit

Tax-free fringe benefits need not be reported on your return. Many fringe benefits are listed on your Form W-2, with any necessary reporting requirements included in the instructions to the form.

Income Earned Abroad

Working abroad does not relieve citizens of their obligation to file U.S. tax returns and pay taxes here. But to make things easier for those working overseas, the tax law lets a limited amount of income be received tax free each year as long as certain conditions are met.

Benefit ⊗

If you live and work abroad, you are not taxed on up to $102,100 of foreign earned income. If you are married and both you and your spouse have foreign income, you may each be eligible for an exclusion. If your foreign earned income is more than $102,100, you are taxable only on amounts in excess of $102,100.

This exclusion is not automatic; you must elect it.

Conditions

To qualify for the foreign earned income exclusion, you must meet 3 conditions:

1. Your tax home is in a foreign country.
2. You meet either a foreign residence test (you live abroad for an uninterrupted period that includes one full year) or a physical presence test (you live abroad for 330 days during a 12-month period).
3. You do not work for the U.S. government or a government agency.

You can apply the exclusion only to foreign earned income, not to other types of foreign income.

FOREIGN EARNED INCOME

You must have income from the performance of personal services. This includes:

- Allowances from your employer for housing or other expenses
- Bonuses
- Business profits tied to the performance of services
- Commissions
- Professional fees
- Rents and royalties tied to the performance of services
- Salaries
- Value of an employer-provided car or housing
- Wages

The earned income must be received no later than the year after the year in which you performed the services.

If you qualify under the foreign residence or physical presence test for only part of the year, you can prorate the exclusion. Proration is made on a daily basis.

Example

On January 1, 2016, you move to England and reside there until you move back to the United States on July 1, 2017. Since you have satisfied the foreign residence test (you lived abroad for an uninterrupted one-year period) and you lived abroad in 2017 for 181 days, you can exclude 181/365 of $102,100, or $50,492.

If you receive payment this year for foreign earned income earned last year, you can exclude this amount this year to the extent that you did not use up your exclusion in the prior year.

Example

In 2016, you earned $75,000 but were paid only $65,000, which you excluded. In 2017, you earn $120,000 and receive the $10,000 for 2016 services. In 2017, you can exclude a total of $112,100 ($10,000 for 2016 pay because you did not use up your 2016 exclusion of $101,300, plus $102,100 exclusion for 2017). You are taxable on $17,900 of your 2017 earnings.

Not all foreign income is eligible for the exclusion. Nonqualified payments include:

- Alimony
- Annuity income
- Capital gains
- Dividends
- Gambling winnings
- Interest income
- Pensions
- U.S. government pay (if you work for the government and are stationed abroad, your pay is not tax free)
- Value of tax-free meals or lodging

If you work in Antarctica, you cannot exclude your income (Antarctica is not considered a foreign country by the IRS).

Planning Tips

What happens if you haven't met the foreign residence or physical presence test by the time your return is due? You cannot claim the exclusion before you have met either test, but you have a choice: You can ask for a filing extension if you expect to meet either test within the extension period.

Example

Your return for 2017 is due June 15, 2018, but you request a filing extension to October 15, 2018, because you expect to satisfy the 330-day test in July 2017, so that you can claim the exclusion on your 2017 return.

Alternatively, you can file your return to report the foreign earned income and then file an amended return to claim the exclusion once you satisfy either test.

Example

Same as the preceding facts except that you won't satisfy the 330-day test until after October 15, 2018. You file your 2017 return and pay tax on the foreign income. Once the test is met, you file an amended return to receive a refund.

Once you make the election to exclude foreign earned income, it remains in effect for subsequent years unless you revoke it. You revoke the election by attaching a statement to your return indicating revocation.

Weigh carefully whether you want to revoke the election to claim the foreign earned income exclusion. Following a revocation, you may not use the exclusion for 5 years unless the IRS grants you permission to do so. The IRS may grant permission under these circumstances:

- You return to the United States for a period of time.
- You move to a different foreign country that has different tax rates.
- You change employers.
- There is a change in the tax law of the foreign country in which you reside.

If you are eligible to exclude foreign earned income, you may also qualify to exclude housing. The basic limit on housing expenses in areas that are not designated as high-cost areas in 2017 is $30,630 ($83.92 per day). The maximum exclusion for areas where the basic limit applies is $14,294 (the basic housing expense minus the basic housing amount, which is $16,336 [16% of the foreign earned income exclusion of $102,100]).

Pitfalls

If you elect to exclude your foreign earned income, you may not deduct any expenses related to such income.

You cannot base a contribution to an IRA or a Roth IRA on excludable foreign earned income.

You cannot claim the foreign tax credit or a deduction for foreign taxes related to excludable foreign earned income. In fact, if you had claimed the foreign earned income exclusion in the past and claim a foreign tax credit this year, you have effectively revoked your election to claim the exclusion. You cannot claim the exclusion for at least 5 years unless the IRS grants you permission to claim the exclusion.

Under a "stacking rule," excluded foreign income is taken into account in figuring the tax rate you pay on income that is taxable.

You cannot claim the foreign earned income exclusion for work in Antarctica, in international waters, or in international airspace.

You cannot claim the foreign earned income exclusion with respect to earnings from any country subject to U.S. government travel restrictions. Countries subject to travel restrictions may be found at www.state.gov/travel. Restrictions for Cuba were lifted, so those who meet the foreign residence or physical presence test there may be eligible for the foreign earned income exclusion.

Where to Claim the Benefit

To elect the foreign earned income exclusion, file Form 2555, *Foreign Earned Income*, which you attach to Form 1040. You can use a simplified Form 2555-EZ, *Foreign Earned Income Exclusion*, if your foreign wages are no more than $101,300, you do not have any foreign self-employment income, and you do not claim the foreign housing exclusion or deductions for foreign housing, moving, or business expenses.

You cannot claim the foreign earned income exclusion if you file Form 1040A or 1040EZ.

Your Business

Alert

At the time this book was completed, Congress was considering important tax changes that could affect 2017 tax returns and planning for 2018. Check the online Supplement in February 2018 at www.jklasser.com or www.barbaraweltman.com to see what changes have been enacted and when they are effective.

The United States is an entrepreneurial country—it is the American dream to own your own business, and millions already do. It has been estimated that there are now more than 29.6 million small businesses, 80% of which have no employees. Most expenses related to running a business are deductible, but timing issues and limitations may come into play. The tax rules for your business apply whether you operate a full-time or a sideline business. This chapter deals primarily with business deductions for a sole proprietor, independent contractor, or freelancer who files Schedule C (or, for farming, Schedule F). Of course, many rules discussed in this chapter apply to partnerships, limited liability companies, and corporations.

This chapter explains the tax rules for various business-related deductions and other tax breaks. These rules apply whether your business is full time or part time (e.g., you do freelance work in the "gig" economy). The rules for claiming a home office deduction are in Chapter 11. Retirement plans for self-employed individuals are discussed in Chapter 5.

For more information, see IRS Publication 15, *Circular E, Employer's Tax Guide*; IRS Publication 225, *Farmer's Tax Guide*; IRS Publication 334, *Tax Guide for Small Business*; IRS Publication 535, *Business Expenses*; IRS Publication 536, *Net Operating Losses*; IRS Publication 587, *Business Use of Your Home*; and IRS Publication 946, *How to Depreciate Property*. Also see *J.K. Lasser's Small Business Taxes 2018* by Barbara Weltman.

Start-Up Costs

The term "start-up" has a very specific meaning for tax purposes. When you think of the start-up phase of a business, you typically think about the first few years of operation when the business gets going. But for tax purposes, start-up means that period of time just *before* you actually focus on the business you then begin. It is the period in which you are looking for a business to go into.

Benefit ⬆

When you decide to start a business, you may incur certain costs. Usually, these costs are viewed as capital expenditures that are not currently deductible. But you can deduct up to $5,000 of start-up costs in the year the business begins. If start-up costs exceed $5,000, the balance can be amortized (deducted ratably) over 180 months.

If start-up costs exceed $50,000, the $5,000 deduction limit is reduced dollar for dollar by the excess over $50,000. If start-up costs exceed $55,000, no immediate deduction is allowed; such costs can be amortized over 180 months.

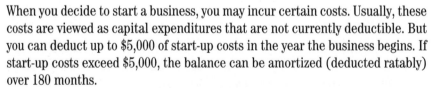

Example

You've been looking into a business to start and have incurred expenses for research, travel, and other related costs of $5,900. You begin business in

2017. You can deduct $5,000, plus 1/180 of $900, or $5 for a total of $5,005 in 2017. In 2018 and for the next 13 years, you'll deduct 1/180 of $900, or $5 each year. If your start-up costs had been $54,000, you could have deducted $1,000 ($5,000 − [$54,000 − $50,000]), plus 1/180 of $53,000 in the first year. If your costs had been $55,000 or more, then all of the costs would be deducted ratably over 15 years (1/180 each year).

Conditions

Start-up expenses include ordinary and necessary business costs related to deciding *whether* to go into business and which business to buy or start. This is referred to as the "whether and which" test.

EXAMPLES OF START-UP COSTS

- A survey of potential markets
- Advertisements for the opening of the business
- An analysis of available facilities, labor, and supplies
- Salaries and fees for consultants and executives
- Travel and other expenses incurred to get prospective distributors, suppliers, and customers

Expenses incurred after the start-up phase that relate to starting the business cannot be amortized; they must be capitalized (added to the cost of the business).

Example

You find a business you want to purchase and ask your accountant to review the company's books. Then you ask your attorney to draw up a contract of sale. Since you have already identified a particular business, you are beyond the start-up phase for tax purposes and accountant's and attorney's fees cannot be currently deducted or amortized as part of start-up expenses; they are simply part of the basis (cost) of your business, along with the purchase price of the company.

Planning Tips

Remember to keep track of your annual deductible amount so you don't overlook the write-off opportunity in the coming years if you do not write them off in full in your first year of business.

If you sell your business before the end of the amortization period (assuming your start-up costs were not initially fully deducted), you can deduct any unamortized amount in the final year of business.

The $5,000 deduction limit and 180-month amortization period applies to certain other expenses you may incur in forming a business: incorporation costs and partnership organizational costs. Like start-up costs, make sure that the items fit within the write-off category and then apply the $5,000 deduction limit and 180-month amortization rule.

Pitfall

Start-up costs are limited to expenses incurred *before* you begin operations. Once you have passed the start-up phase, which means you've identified the business or type of business you'll start, you can no longer include expenses in your pot of start-up expenses.

Where to Claim the Benefit

Report the amortizable amount of your start-up costs on Schedule C (or Schedule F) as "Other expenses." If you have more than one expense, you must list each of them in the space provided for this on Schedule C (or Schedule F).

You cannot claim a deduction for start-up expenses if you file Form 1040A or 1040EZ.

Equipment Purchases

It usually takes more than just your brains and hard work to make a business run. You need equipment, from technology-based items (e.g., computers, tablets, and smartphones), to furniture (e.g., desks, file cabinets, and chairs), to industry-specific items (e.g., carpentry tools and heavy machinery). For tax purposes, all of these items are viewed as "equipment" for which special tax treatment may be claimed. Today, the tax law encourages investments in equipment as a means of spurring the economy by allowing an immediate deduction for purchase costs if certain conditions are met.

Benefit ⬆

You can deduct amounts you pay for equipment used in your business as an ordinary business expense. However, tax law dictates when and how much of your cost you can deduct. Four sets of rules come into play:

1. *First-year expensing.* Up to a set dollar limit can be deducted in the year the equipment is placed in service. Higher dollar limits apply for equipment placed in service in certain distressed areas; a lower dollar

limit applies for vehicles weighing more than 6,000 pounds. The limit for 2017 is $510,000.

2. *Bonus depreciation.* Fifty percent of the cost of equipment is allowed to be deducted if purchased and placed in service in 2017. There is no dollar limit on bonus depreciation, but it applies only to new property.

3. *Depreciation.* A percentage of the equipment's basis is deducted over a set term (a recovery period fixed for various types of assets). There is no dollar limit on depreciation.

4. *De minimis safe harbor rule.* If you don't capitalize the cost of an item (i.e., you don't add it to your balance sheet), you can immediately deduct up to $2,500 per item or invoice if you make such an election on your tax return.

Conditions

Equipment purchases are not limited to machinery; the term "equipment" includes just about any type of property other than most real estate.

EXAMPLES OF EQUIPMENT

- Answering machine
- Bookshelves
- Cars (see Chapter 7)
- Computers
- Copiers
- Desk accessories
- Desk chairs
- Desks
- Farming equipment (see later in this chapter)
- Fax machines
- File cabinets
- Floor models and displays
- Leasehold, restaurant, and retail improvements
- Machinery
- Musical instruments for musicians
- Printers
- Signs
- Smartphones
- Software purchased off the shelf

- Tablets
- Telephones
- Tools of your trade
- Trucks (see Chapter 7)
- Vacuum cleaner

Slightly different rules apply to the different write-off methods. For example, a particular item may qualify for the Section 179 deduction but not for bonus depreciation.

The rules on depreciation are quite complex, and a complete discussion is well beyond the scope of this chapter. Here you will gain an overview of the rules that apply. To learn more, see IRS Publication 946, *How to Depreciate Property* or *J.K Lasser's Small Business Taxes 2018*.

Conditions for First-Year Expensing

There are 3 basic conditions for claiming first-year expensing:

1. You must elect it.
2. Your total equipment purchases for the year cannot exceed a set dollar amount.
3. Your taxable income must at least equal your expense deduction.

ELECTION

You must elect to claim first-year expensing (also referred to as a Section 179 deduction because of the section in the Internal Revenue Code governing the deduction).

EQUIPMENT PURCHASES

To qualify for the election, your total equipment purchases for the year cannot exceed a set dollar amount. For 2017, you can claim the expensing deduction only if your total purchases are no more than $2,030,000. The dollar limit phases out on a dollar-for-dollar basis for total purchases over $2,030,000. *Note:* Higher dollar limits applied in certain designated areas not covered in this book.

CERTAIN IMPROVEMENTS TO COMMERCIAL SPACE

Qualified leasehold, restaurant, and retail improvements to the internal space of a commercial building can also qualify for first-year expensing up to $510,000 in 2017. Write-offs for these properties are explained in Chapter 11.

TAXABLE INCOME

Your first-year expensing deduction cannot be more than the taxable income from the active conduct of a business. Taxable income for this purpose means your net income (or loss) from all businesses you actively conduct. If you are married and file a joint return, your spouse's net income (or loss) is added to yours. Taxable income also includes Section 1231 gains and losses (from the sale of certain business property) and salary or wages from being an employee. Taxable income must be reduced by the deduction for one-half of self-employment tax and net operating loss carrybacks and carryforwards.

Example

You own a sole proprietorship that shows a $5,000 profit for the year, and your deduction for the employer portion of self-employment tax is $353. Your spouse works as an employee with a salary of $50,000. Your taxable income for purposes of figuring your first-year expensing deduction is $54,647 ($5,000 − $353 + $50,000).

Conditions for Bonus Depreciation

The only 2 conditions are that the property be new (not preowned) and it must qualify for this special deduction. Qualified property includes:

- Tangible property depreciated under the modified accelerated cost recovery system (MACRS) with a recovery period of 20 years or less
- Off-the-shelf computer software
- Qualified leasehold improvement property, qualified restaurant property, and retail improvement property

Conditions for Depreciation

Depreciation is a method for recovering your investment in property over a period of time fixed by law, called a recovery period. You apply a set percentage (based on the property's recovery period) to the property's basis (generally, its cost) to arrive at your annual deduction. These percentages may be found in IRS Publication 946.

Example

In 2017, you place in service a used copier machine (5-year property) for which you do not claim any first-year expensing because you are not profitable. Assume the cost of the machine is $8,000 and does not qualify for bonus depreciation. Your depreciation percentage for the year that 5-year property is placed in service is 20%, so your depreciation deduction is $1,600 ($8,000 × 20%).

Different types of property are classified by their recovery periods:

- 3-year property, such as taxis, tractors, racehorses over 2 years old when placed in service, and breeding hogs
- 5-year property, such as cars, trucks, copiers, assets used in construction, and breeding and dairy cattle
- 7-year property, such as office fixtures and furniture, fax machines, assets used in printing, assets used in recreation (e.g., billiard tables), and breeding horses and workhorses

There are also 10-year, 15-year, and 20-year types of property as well as realty (27.5 years for residential realty and 39 years for nonresidential realty such as office buildings, strip malls, and factories). Leasehold, restaurant, and retail improvements have a 15-year recovery period.

CONVENTIONS

Special depreciation rules, called conventions, come into play to determine your write-offs for the year.

- For property other than realty, a mid-year convention makes a hypothetical assumption that the property has been placed in service in the middle of the year. As a result of the mid-year convention, 5-year property is depreciated over 6 years.
- For property other than realty, a mid-quarter convention applies. If you place in service more than 40% of all your equipment purchases for the year in the final quarter of the year, a special rule dictates the amount of depreciation you can claim for each item placed in service during the year. This special rule is called a mid-quarter convention and generally operates to limit write-offs (although in some cases it may enable you to take greater deductions than under regular depreciation rules).
- For realty, a mid-month convention assumes that the property has been placed in service in the middle of the month it is actually placed in service. The mid-month convention is built into the depreciation rate tables applied to realty.

Conditions for De Minimis *Safe Harbor Rule*

You must be consistent in your treatment of the items, which means that if you use the de minimis rule to treat items as materials and supplies, you can't treatment them as an asset on your balance sheet. You must attach your own statement that you are electing to use this safe harbor rule. The statement must make reference to Reg. Sec. 1.263(a)-1(f).

Planning Tips

The amount of your write-offs does not depend on whether you pay cash for the equipment or finance your purchase. If, for example, you finance your purchase, you may wind up deducting more in the first year than you pay out of pocket.

Example

In December 2017, you buy a machine for $25,000, financing it over 5 years at 8% interest. In 2017, you can claim a first-year expensing deduction of $25,000, even though you have not yet paid a penny.

Decide whether to make the first-year expensing election and/or forgo bonus depreciation. Generally, if your current income is modest but you expect it to increase in coming years, it may be preferable to forgo the deduction now in favor of using it against future income that would otherwise be taxed at higher rates.

Bonus depreciation can be used to create or increase a net operating loss (NOL). Thus, even if you do not have sufficient current taxable income to use bonus depreciation, the write-off can be taken into account in figuring an NOL.

Pitfalls

Special rules apply to so-called listed property, which includes cars and computers and peripherals not used at a regular business establishment. You cannot use first-year expensing or accelerated depreciation *unless* business use of a listed property item is more than 50% of total use.

Example

You buy a computer that is used 75% for business and 25% for personal purposes. Since business use exceeds 50%, you can use first-year expensing or accelerated depreciation for the portion of the computer (75% of its purchase price) used for business.

If you sell or cease using property for which first-year expensing has been claimed, you *may* be subject to recapture. This means you're required to report a portion of the previous write-off as income in the year of the disposition of the property. Discuss this rather complicated matter with a tax adviser.

Where to Claim the Deduction

You figure your deduction for equipment purchases on Form 4562, *Depreciation and Amortization.* You enter the amount of your deduction on the line provided for this write-off on Schedule C (or Schedule F).

If you are claiming depreciation this year on an item placed in service in a prior year and you do not have any new items to report, you do not have to file Form 4562. Simply attach your own schedule to the return showing the amount of depreciation you are claiming this year.

You cannot claim a deduction for equipment purchases if you file Form 1040A or 1040EZ.

Payment for Services

You may not be able to do it alone and may therefore need to hire employees to work for your business. The costs of wages, salaries, bonuses, and other payments are deductible if certain conditions are met.

Benefit

Amounts you pay to individuals who provide services to you are deductible as ordinary expenses against your business income. Such payments fall into 2 general categories:

1. Wages and compensation to employees.
2. Fees and payments to independent contractors.

There are no dollar limits on the amount you can deduct for payments for services.

In addition to a deduction for wages and compensation to employees, you may be eligible to claim a tax credit for a portion of these payments.

Conditions

There are several conditions for determining how much to deduct for payments to workers:

- It must be determined whether the worker is an employee or independent contractor.
- Amounts paid must be reasonable.
- Payment must relate to work actually performed.
- Payments must be made in a timely fashion.
- Employer credit for wage differential payments to activated reservists.

WORKER CLASSIFICATION

First, you must determine whether workers are your employees or independent contractors. The key reason for making the distinction is the obligation to pay employment taxes—Social Security and Medicare (FICA) taxes, federal unemployment insurance (FUTA), and state unemployment and other payroll taxes. If you are the employer, you are responsible for the employer's share of taxes as well as withholding income taxes and the employee's share of FICA. If your worker is an independent contractor, then he or she is responsible for employment taxes.

Generally, worker classification as an employee or independent contractor is based on control. If you control when, where, and how work is to be performed, the person is your employee regardless of what label you may attach. If the person is in his or her own business and provides services to you, the person is usually treated as an independent contractor. Worker classification is a perennial "hot" IRS audit issue, so work with a knowledgeable tax adviser to get it right.

REASONABLE PAYMENTS

Compensation paid to your employees must be "reasonable." There's no set dollar amount. Reasonable depends on many factors, including job responsibilities, education level, and location of the business. Payments to yourself as a sole proprietor are not treated as deductible compensation because you are not an employee.

Payments paid to independent contractors must also be reasonable.

PERFORMANCE OF WORK

You can deduct only payments for work actually performed. Generally, this poses no problem for your rank-and-file employees. But if you put family members on the payroll, the IRS may look closely at the relation between their wages and work performed. Keep track of the hours they worked and the tasks they performed as proof that they earned the compensation you paid.

TIMELINESS OF PAYMENT

You can deduct only payments you actually make (if you are on the cash method of accounting for your business). If you are on the accrual method (which is unusual for self-employed individuals and most small businesses), payments to rank-and-file employees must be made no later than $2^{1}/_{2}$ months after the close of the year (e.g., by March 15, 2018, for compensation earned in 2017). (Different rules apply to payments to shareholders in C and S corporations.)

Planning Tips

Compensation paid to certain employees may entitle you to claim a tax credit (more details may be found later in this chapter). These include:

- Work opportunity credit
- Empowerment zone credit for workers within designated areas (if this break is extended for 2017)
- Indian employment credit for workers on Indian reservations (if this break is extended for 2017)

- Social Security tax credit on certain tips for workers in restaurant and tavern businesses
- Employer wage differential payment credit

Certain small employers engaged in research and development can opt to use up to $250,000 of a research credit as an offset to the employer share of Social Security taxes rather than offsetting income taxes. See the instructions to Form 8974, *Qualified Small Business Payroll Tax Credit for Increasing Research Activities*.

Pitfall

If your workers are employees, you are responsible for employment taxes. This requires you to withhold federal and, if applicable, state income taxes from their wages, as well as the employee share of FICA tax. You must also pay the employer share of FICA as well as FUTA and state employment taxes. If you fail to pay over these taxes in a timely fashion, you may be personally liable for them.

Where to Claim the Deduction

You report the deduction for compensation to employees on the line designated as "Wages" on Schedule C of Form 1040. Wages are reduced by employment tax credits you claim (listed earlier in "Planning Tip"). You report payments to independent contractors on the line marked "Commissions and fees" of this schedule.

For farming-related activities, the deduction for wages to employees is reported on the line marked "Labor hired" on Schedule F of Form 1040. Wages are reduced by employment tax credits you claim. You report payments to independent contractors on the line marked "Customer hire" of this schedule.

Employment tax credits to which you may be entitled are figured on the following forms:

- Work opportunity credit: Form 5884
- Empowerment zone credit: Form 8844*
- Indian employment credit: Form 8845*
- Social Security tax credit on certain tips: Form 8846
- Credit for employer wage differential payments: Form 8932

*If these credits are extended for 2017.

Supplies

To paraphrase Benjamin Franklin, for want of a paper clip, your business may be lost. Despite predictions of a paperless society, most businesses use reams of paper and other supplies every year. The tax law allows a full write-off for the cost of ordinary supplies as long as certain conditions are met.

Benefit ①

Office supplies (including paper, pens, tape, and toner replacements) and cleaning supplies (such as detergent, paper towels, and sponges) are deductible against your business income. There is no dollar limit on this deduction.

Supplies that are part of your inventory are *not* currently deductible; they are part of the cost of goods sold.

Conditions

For supplies to be currently deductible, they must be ordinary and necessary business expenses. They cannot be items with a useful life of more than one year. If they have a longer useful life, they are treated as equipment (discussed later in this chapter).

EXAMPLES OF DEDUCTIBLE SUPPLIES

- Binders and presentation material
- Boards and easels
- Business cards
- Cleaning supplies
- DVDs and thumbdrives
- Filing and storage material
- Ink cartridges and toners
- Labels, envelopes, and shipping material
- Paper clips, tape, and staples
- Paper, pads, and notes
- Pens, pencils, and markers
- Replacement parts (which are not part of inventory)
- Rubber stamps
- Small wares of restaurants and taverns (e.g., glassware, paper or plastic cups, dishes, pots and pans, and bar supplies)
- Stationery
- Trash bags

Planning Tips

From a nontax standpoint, it may not make economic sense to load up on supplies even though you can deduct them. You are incurring costs now that could be paid later.

While the cost of supplies is generally deductible, it is a good business practice to economize on purchases. Look for discounts and special business incentives from such office supplies companies as:

- Office Depot (www.officedepot.com) (Office Max is part of Office Depot)
- Staples (www.staples.com)
- The Ultimate Green Store (www.theultimategreenstore.com/s-3-office.aspx)

Pitfalls

Supplies that are part of your inventory are *not* separately deducted. Instead, they are included as part of your cost of goods sold.

Watch the timing of ordering supplies. A current deduction is allowed for supplies used within the year. A deduction for supplies *not* used within the current year but kept on hand may still be claimed as long as doing so does not distort income, no records are maintained to indicate when supplies are actually used, and no inventory is taken of the amount of supplies on hand at the beginning and end of the year.

Where to Claim the Benefit

Report supplies used in your business on the line provided for this item on Schedule C (or Schedule F) of Form 1040. You do not have to complete any additional form or schedule for this purpose.

You cannot deduct business supplies if you file Form 1040A or Form 1040EZ.

Gifts

Gifts generally are given because of personal feelings without any expectations or strings attached. But business gifts are usually motivated by gratitude for some business activity or hope for future business activity. In recognition of this fact, the tax law allows a deduction for business gifts, but only in very limited amounts.

Benefit

You may wish to bestow some gratuitous benefit on employees, customers, dealers, distributors, or other business relations. You can qualify for a deduction for business gifts, but the amount you can deduct is limited. Generally, you cannot deduct more than $25 per gift for any person each year (the same dollar limit in place since 1962). The dollar limit applies even if you attempt to make an indirect gift (for example, you give the gift to a company that is intended for the eventual personal use of a particular person).

Conditions

To claim a deduction for business gifts, you must meet both of the following conditions:

1. Dollar limit
2. Substantiation

DOLLAR LIMIT

The deductible amount of the gift cannot exceed $25 per person per year. The dollar limit does not include incidental costs, such as wrapping, insuring, or shipping the gift.

> **Example**
>
> You give a new vendor a gift that cost you $60. You paid $10 more to insure and ship it. You can deduct $35 ($25 of the $60, plus incidental expenses of $10).

In determining your $25 annual limit, you do not have to count any gifts of nominal value ($4 or less) with your company name imprinted on them that you distribute to a number of clients or customers (e.g., calendars at Christmastime).

SUBSTANTIATION REQUIREMENTS

You must show the cost of the gift, a description of the gift, the date it was given, and to whom. You must also state the reason for the gift (such as the business to be gained from making it). This information should be recorded on an expense log or business diary.

In addition, you must have evidentiary proof of the expense, such as a canceled check or receipt for the item.

Planning Tips

Gifts to your employees are *not* subject to this $25 limit because payments to them are usually treated as compensation (discussed earlier in this chapter). As long as regular compensation plus any purported gifts are reasonable, the total is deductible as compensation.

Certain items can be treated as gifts, such as an entertainment expense, which is *not* subject to the $25 limit. You have the option of using this treatment if you give tickets to the theater or a sports event and do *not* attend the event yourself. In making the choice, keep in mind that the entertainment deduction is subject to a 50% limit (without regard to a dollar amount).

> **Example**
>
> You buy your best customer tickets to a local golf tournament for $80. Assuming you do not attend, you are better off treating the ticket as an entertainment expense so you can deduct $40 (50% of $80), rather than as a business gift, which would be deductible at only $25.

If you treat the ticket as a business gift, you have 3 years in which to change your mind and file an amended return to report the ticket as an entertainment expense.

If you give food or a beverage intended to be consumed by your customer or other businessperson, you *must* treat the item as a gift (you do not have the choice to treat it as an entertainment expense).

Pitfall

You must substantiate your business gifts in order to support your deduction. If you fail to meet full substantiation requirements, your deduction is lost. For example, merely retaining a receipt for the gift is not sufficient; you need to note all the information listed earlier as full substantiation for the gift.

Where to Claim the Deduction

You report the gifts as "Other expenses" on Schedule C (or Schedule F) of Form 1040. If you have more than one such expense (for example, in addition to business gifts, you are deducting environmental cleanup costs), you must list each type of expense in the space provided (or on your own attachment if more space is required).

You cannot deduct any business gifts if you file Form 1040A or 1040EZ.

Hobby Losses

When does a hobby become a business? The tax law says this happens when you are profitable. In effect, if you lose money, you bear the cost entirely, but if you make money, the government shares in your good fortune. You can deduct losses from activities that might be viewed as hobbies only under certain conditions.

Benefit

If you do not have a profit motive for running an activity—especially one involving some element of personal recreation or pleasure, such as coin collecting or dog breeding—then your expenses are deductible only to the extent of your income from the activity. The hobby loss rule acts as a limitation on your deductions—dictating how much you can deduct and where to claim the deduction for your business expenses.

Hobby losses are treated as miscellaneous itemized deductions, which are deductible only to the extent they exceed 2% of adjusted gross income and are subject to the reduction of itemized deductions for high-income taxpayers.

Conditions

You want to avoid application of the hobby loss rule so that your business expenses in excess of business income are deductible. If your business is unprofitable year after year, the IRS may question whether you are in it for a profit or are merely trying to deduct the costs of a hobby.

To avoid the hobby loss rule, you must be able to demonstrate that you are in the activity to make a profit. Of course, this is a subjective determination based on your reasonable expectations and beliefs. But certain objective criteria are used to show you really mean business. No single factor is determinative; the more you can muster, the better off you will be:

- You run the activity in a businesslike manner (e.g., have a business plan, keep good records separate from your personal activities, and have a business bank account, telephone, stationery, and other indications of a business).
- You put in substantial time and effort.
- You depend on income from the activity for your livelihood (if you have other sources of income, this tends to show the activity is merely a hobby).
- You consult with advisers to make the business profitable.
- You have profits in some years (the bounty in your good years can support a profit motive).
- You expect to see a profit from the appreciation of assets used in the activity.

Planning Tips

You can opt to rely on a presumption that you are in the activity for a profit—opting for this presumption delays any IRS inquiry about your activity. You are presumed to be in an activity for profit if you make a profit for at least 3 of the first 5 years you are in business (2 out of 7 years if the activity is breeding, training, showing, or racing horses).

To use the presumption, you must file Form 5213, *Election to Postpone Determination as to Whether the Presumption Applies That an Activity Is Engaged In for Profit*. The form can be filed with the first return for your activity; it must be filed within 3 years of the due date of the return for the first year of the activity.

Of course, the downside to making this election to postpone inquiry into your activity is that you are extending the statute of limitations under which the IRS may question your deductions. Generally, the IRS has only 3 years, but filing Form 5213 means it has 5 years—and you can expect to have your returns examined at the end of the 5-year period.

If you make the election but fail the presumption, you are not precluded from arguing you really had a profit motive, even though you had losses in many years. One of the key ways to show a profit motive is to have a written business plan spelling out how you expect to make the activity profitable and when you anticipate that this will occur.

Pitfall

The hobby loss rule applies to individuals, including partners and members of limited liability companies; it does not apply to C corporations. In the case of pass-through entities, the determination of a profit motive is made at the entity level (for example, you might be in a partnership to make a profit but it is up to the partnership to prove it has a profit motive).

Where to Claim the Benefit

If you are subject to the hobby loss rule, you report your income from the activity as other income in the "Income" section of Form 1040 and expenses from the activity as miscellaneous itemized deductions on Schedule A of Form 1040.

You cannot claim any hobby loss deduction if you file Form 1040A or 1040EZ.

Self-Employment Tax Deduction

Self-employed individuals pay both the employer and employee share of Social Security and Medicare taxes. But self-employed persons are treated as their own employers to the extent they are permitted to deduct the employer share of these taxes.

Benefit ⬆

If you pay self-employment tax on your net earnings from self-employment, you can deduct one-half of the tax as an adjustment to gross income, even if you do not itemize your other deductions.

Conditions

Self-employment tax is the employer and employee share of Social Security and Medicare taxes figured on your net earnings from self-employment. As long as you show a profit in your self-employment activities of at least $400, you owe self-employment tax and can deduct the portion representing the employer share. The same is so if you opt to pay self-employment tax even if you had a loss or a small amount of income.

Planning Tips

To figure your deduction, simply look at Schedule SE, *Self-Employment Tax*, the form used to figure your self-employment tax. The last line of the short or long form of Schedule SE allows you to figure your deduction. You deduct the employer portion of 7.65% (6.2% of Social Security taxes on earnings up to $127,200 in 2017, plus 1.45% of Medicare taxes on all net earnings from self-employment in 2017).

Pitfall

The deduction for one-half of your self-employment tax is *not* a business expense, but a personal one. It does not reduce your profits on which you pay income and self-employment taxes.

Where to Claim the Benefit

You report the deduction on the line provided in the "Adjusted Gross Income" section of Form 1040. No separate form or schedule is required for this purpose.

Home Office Deduction

The number of home-based businesses is put between 18 million and 38 million; exact figures are not available. Whatever the number, the cost of operating an office from home may be deductible as long as certain conditions are met. The term "home office" isn't limited to clerical space; it can include a workshop, greenhouse, artist studio, or any other area of a home used for business. The rules for claiming a home office deduction are explained in Chapter 11.

Farming-Related Breaks

According to the U.S. Department of Agriculture, there were more than 2.17 million farms in the United States in 2012 (the next farm census is in December 2017 with data to be collected in 2018). Farming is considered a type of business and is therefore entitled to deductions available to any other business. But the tax law provides special breaks just for farms.

Benefit

If you operate a farm or farming activity, many of your costs are deductible against your farming income. In addition to any business expense you could claim in a nonfarming business, you may be entitled to special write-offs. Generally, there are no dollar limits on your farming-related deductions.

Some benefits payable to farmers may be tax free, and some expenses paid by farmers may qualify for a tax credit.

Conditions

Like other business expenses, farming-related deductions must be ordinary and necessary expenses.

EXAMPLES OF FARMING-RELATED DEDUCTIONS

- Chemicals
- Conservation expenses for soil and water
- Custom hire (machine work)
- Enhanced deduction for donations of conservation easements (100% of the contribution base, which is essentially adjusted gross income)
- Feed purchased (there are limits on how much you can deduct for feed to be consumed beyond this year)
- Fertilizers and lime
- Freight and trucking
- Gasoline, oil, and other fuel
- Ginning
- Hired labor (reduced by any employment-related tax credits discussed earlier in this chapter)
- Insect sprays and dusts
- Seeds and plants purchased
- Storage and warehousing
- Tying materials and containers
- Veterinary and breeding fees and medicine

Planning Tips

Some payments to farmers may be tax free. These include:

- Cost-sharing payments under The Conservation Reserve Program (CRP)
- Soil and water conservation assistance payments under a special federal program, which may run as high as $50,000
- Agricultural management assistance program payments

In addition to deductions for farming expenses, you may be eligible for certain tax credits related to farming. These include:

- Credit for federal excise tax paid on kerosene used in your home for heating, lighting, and cooking
- Credit for federal excise tax paid on gasoline, special motor fuels, and compressed natural gas used on a farm for farming purposes
- Credit for federal excise tax on fuels used in running stationary machines, for cleaning purposes, or in other off-highway vehicles

You can claim the credits on your return or claim a refund of the excise taxes you already paid. The credits and your options on claiming them are explained in more detail in IRS Publication 225, *Farmer's Tax Guide*.

Pitfalls

Not all farming-related expenses are deductible. You may not deduct your personal living expenses, such as taxes, insurance, and repairs to your home.

The IRS began conducting a one-year audit program of 2015 returns that began on April 1, 2017, to verify if deductions claimed on Schedule F were allowable.

Where to Claim the Deduction

Report the deduction on the line provided for it on Schedule F of Form 1040. If there is no specific line for the type of deduction you are claiming, list it in the space provided for other expenses (attach your own explanation or description of the expense if not self-explanatory).

You cannot deduct farming-related expenses if you file Form 1040A or Form 1040EZ.

Domestic Production Activities Deduction

If your business makes something in the United States, whether it's by manufacturing, agriculture, mining extraction, construction, filming, software development, or certain other approved activities, you can claim a deduction that effectively reduces the tax rate you pay on your business profits. The best part of the deduction: You don't have to spend any separate money to get it (you are entitled to it because of your activities).

Benefit

You may deduct 9% of the net income from qualified domestic production activities. The deduction for individuals is claimed as a subtraction after you have figured the other deductions in the adjusted gross income section of your return.

Conditions

There are several conditions to claiming this deduction:

- You must derive income from a qualified activity.
- The deduction must meet a W-2 limit.
- The deduction must meet an adjusted gross income.

QUALIFIED DOMESTIC ACTIVITY

You must derive the net income from a qualified activity, which includes:

- Selling, leasing, or licensing items manufactured, produced, grown, or extracted in the United States in whole or significant part (see safe harbor following).
- Selling, leasing, or licensing films produced in the United States.
- Construction in the United States including both erection and substantial renovation of residential and commercial buildings (but not cosmetic activities, such as painting).
- Engineering and architectural services relating to a construction project performed in the United States.
- Software developed in the United States, regardless of whether it is purchased off the shelf or downloaded from the Internet. The term *software* includes video games. But, with some de minimis exceptions, the term does not include fees for online use of software, fees for customer support, and fees for playing computer games online.

Under a safe harbor, you are treated as conducting activities in the United States if labor and overhead costs incurred in the United States for the manufacture, production, growth, and extraction of the property are at least 20% of the total cost of goods sold of the property.

Net income is figured by reducing gross receipts from qualified domestic activities by expenses allocated to these receipts. Under a de minimis rule, if less than 5% of total gross receipts is derived from nonqualified domestic production activities, you do not have to make any allocation; all gross receipts are treated as attributable to qualified domestic production activities.

If there is a service element in the activity, allocate gross receipts between the qualified activity and the services. However, no allocation is required if the gross receipts relate to a qualified warranty and other gross receipts from these services are 5% or less of the gross receipts from the property.

W-2 LIMIT

The deduction cannot exceed 50% of your business's W-2 wages paid in the calendar year that are allocable to domestic production activities. W-2 wages include both taxable compensation and elective deferrals (e.g., employee contributions to 401(k) plans).

ADJUSTED GROSS INCOME LIMIT

The deduction cannot exceed your adjusted gross income.

Planning Tips

In order to increase your W-2 limitation, consider hiring employees rather than using independent contractors. Weigh the added cost of employment taxes against the tax savings derived from the higher production activities deduction because of additional W-2 wages.

If you are an owner of a pass-through entity (partnership, limited liability company, or S corporation), your share of the business's qualified production activities income and W-2 wages are reported on your Schedule K-1.

Pitfalls

You cannot claim the deduction if you lease or license property to a related party.

You cannot claim the deduction for the sale of food or beverages prepared at a retail establishment. However, if a business both manufactures food and sells it at a restaurant or take-out store, income and expenses can be allocated so that those related to manufacture and wholesale distribution qualify for the deduction. Thus, in the so-called Starbucks situation, roasting and packaging coffee beans could qualify, but selling the beans or brewed coffee at their stores would not.

Where to Claim the Deduction

The production activities deduction is figured on Form 8903, *Domestic Production Activities Deduction*, and is reported in the "Adjusted Gross Income" section of Form 1040. First report all of the other deductions in this section; then enter your production activities deduction (subject to the adjusted gross income limitation).

You cannot claim the deduction if you file Form 1040EZ or Form 1040A.

Other Business Deductions

Not every expense fits neatly into a business deduction category. The tax law provides a catchall deduction rule, referred to as the ordinary and necessary expense rule, under which an expense can be written off as long as certain conditions are met.

Benefit 🔼

A variety of miscellaneous expenses you incur in your business are currently deductible against business income.

Condition

The only condition for deductibility of miscellaneous expenses is that they are ordinary and necessary for your business. "Ordinary" means that they are usual. "Necessary" means they are helpful and appropriate.

EXAMPLES OF OTHER BUSINESS DEDUCTIONS

- Advertising costs—promotional costs as well as goodwill advertising to keep your name in the public eye.
- Asbestos removal.
- Banking fees.
- Depletion for certain oil, gas, and mineral as well as timber properties.
- Dues to professional and trade associations.
- Environmental cleanup costs—expenses to restore property to its precontamination condition.
- Insurance (for self-employed health insurance, see Chapter 2).
- Intangibles (e.g., goodwill and covenant not to compete) that are acquired (must be amortized over 15 years).
- Interest on borrowing (for example, financing of equipment purchases).
- Leasing costs for equipment.
- Licenses and regulatory fees paid annually to state or local governments.
- Merchant authorization fees for credit card payments.
- Moving equipment and machinery.
- Rent for office and other business-related space.
- Repairs to keep property in working order (if repairs add to the value or usefulness of the property, the cost must be capitalized in most cases).
- Repayments of income reported in prior years. *Note:* If the amount of repayment is more than $3,000, you may be able to take a tax credit in lieu of a deduction to obtain a greater benefit from the write-off.
- Shipping and postage.
- Storage and warehousing.

- Subscriptions (see Chapter 14).
- Telephone. If you operate your business from a home office, the basic service charge of the first landline to your home is not deductible. But this ban does not apply to additional charges, such as business long-distance calls and the cost of a second business line. The monthly cost of cell phone use is deductible.
- Utilities. Gas, electric, water, and other charges are deductible. If you claim a home office deduction, the treatment of these charges is discussed earlier in this chapter.

Planning Tip

As with all business expenses, keep good records, including receipts, canceled checks, and bills of sale.

Pitfall

Not all expenses you incur in your business are deductible. The tax law specifically prevents you from writing off certain expenses, even though they may be ordinary and necessary to your business.

EXAMPLES OF NONDEDUCTIBLE EXPENSES

- Bribes and kickbacks—even if customary or common business practice, if they are in violation of the law. For example, an insurance broker who pays a "referral fee" to car dealers who refer customers to him cannot deduct the fee because the car dealers are not licensed to sell insurance.
- Club dues for clubs organized for pleasure, recreation, or any other social purpose. Exceptions to this rule are discussed in Chapter 10.
- Demolition expenses to raze a building. These costs are added to the basis of the land on which the building was demolished.
- Fines and penalties.
- Interest on a business-related tax deficiency.
- Lobbying expenses to influence legislation. *Exception:* Up to $2,000 of in-house costs for influencing legislation and communicating directly with a covered executive branch official can be deducted.

Where to Claim the Deduction

Deductible miscellaneous business expenses are reported on Schedule C (or Schedule F) either on the line provided for the type of expense (e.g., "Advertising" on Schedule C) or as "Other expenses." If you have more than one such expense, you must list each type of expense in the space provided (or on your own attachment, if more space is required).

Business Credits

Not every business expense is treated as a deductible item. Some expenses qualify as tax credits that can be used to reduce tax liability on a dollar-for-dollar basis.

Benefit ⊕

Other expenses you incur in your business may entitle you to a tax credit, which reduces your taxes dollar for dollar. In Table 15.1 you will see a listing of tax credits, the forms you use to figure them, and where the credits are discussed in this book.

Conditions

Each credit has its own conditions. However, many of the credits are part of the general business credit, which acts as an overall limitation on these credits. The limit for the general business credit is your regular tax liability (after credits other than those that are part of the general business credit), plus any alternative minimum tax liability, minus whichever of the following is larger:

- Tentative AMT from Form 6251
- 25% of your regular tax liability (after other credits) over $25,000

Planning Tip

Credits in excess of the general business credit limitation can be carried back one year and forward for up to 20 years until they are used up. Be sure to keep track of carryfowards so you do not fail to claim credits to which you may be entitled.

Pitfall

A special limitation applies to tax credits related to passive activities. See Chapter 11 for more details.

Where to Claim the Credits

Figure the credits on the forms specified for each one. Then, if required, complete Form 3800, *General Business Credit*, to figure the overall limitation on certain credits.

The credits are entered in the "Tax and Credits" section of Form 1040. You cannot claim these business credits if you file Form 1040A or 1040EZ.

TABLE 15.1 Tax Credits

Tax Credit	IRS Form	For More Information, See Chapter
Alcohol fuels credit	6478	15
Alternative fuel vehicle refueling credit*	8911	
Alternative motor vehicle credit	8910	
Biodiesel and renewable diesel fuel credit*	8864	
Credit for contributions to certain community development corporations	8847	
Credit for employer-paid FICA on certain tips received by employees of food and beverage establishments	8846	15
Credit for wages paid in an empowerment zone*	8844	15
Disabled access credit	8826	
Distilled spirits credit	8906	
Employer-provided child care facilities and services	8882	
Employer credit for wage differential payments to activated military reservists		
Energy efficient home credit*	8908	
Indian employment credit*	8845	15
Investment credit (including rehabilitation property credit)	3468	11
Low-income housing credit	8586	11
Low sulfur diesel fuel production credit	8896	
New markets credit	8874	
Nonconventional source fuel credit	8907	
Orphan drug credit	8820	
Plug-in electric vehicle credit	8834	
Railroad track maintenance credit*	8900	
Renewable electricity production credit	8835	
Research credit	6765	
Small employer health credit	8941	
Small employer pension plan start-up costs credit	8881	
Work opportunity credit	5884	15

*These credits expired at the end of 2016 but could be extended for 2017 (see the Supplement for details).

Net Operating Losses

Not every business can be profitable year in and year out. What happens if your business suffers a loss from its operations that effectively wipes out more than your tax liability for the year? You may then have what is called a net operating loss. You may be able to use this loss to reduce taxes in prior and/or future years.

Benefit ⬆

If your business expenses for the year outweigh your income, your loss may give rise to a net operating loss (NOL) that can be used to offset income in other tax years. Such loss can be carried back to offset income in prior years (producing an immediate tax refund); unused amounts can be carried forward to offset future income. There are limits on the carryback and carryforward years.

The net operating loss deduction is not an additional loss deduction. Rather, it is the result of having deductions exceed your business income and applying this excess against income in other years.

Conditions

You must determine whether having a loss in your business for the year results in a net operating loss. You have an NOL if your adjusted gross income is a negative figure. But adjusted gross income for purposes of an NOL does not include certain deductions you are otherwise allowed to take. When figuring your NOL, increase your adjusted gross income by all of the following that apply to you:

- IRA deduction
- Alimony deduction
- Net capital losses (capital losses in excess of capital gains)
- Self-employed person's contribution to a qualified retirement plan

While this computation may sound complicated, you need only follow the line-by-line instructions to Form 1045, *Application for Tentative Refund*, to see how you adjust your income and determine your net operating loss.

CARRYBACK AND CARRYFORWARD PERIODS

The years to which you carry the loss backward and forward depend on the year in which the NOL arises.

- General rule: 2 years back; 20 years forward
- Special rule for small businesses (average annual gross receipts of $5 million or less during the 3 prior years) that have losses resulting from a federally declared disaster: 3 years back; 20 years forward

- Farmers and rangers: 5 years back; 20 years forward
- Product liability losses: 10 years back; 20 years forward

Planning Tips

You can obtain a quick refund from an NOL carryback, money you can put into your business or use for any other purpose. To obtain a quick refund file Form 1045, *Application for Tentative Refund*, with the IRS. Usually you'll receive your refund within 90 days of filing the form.

Alternatively, you can obtain a refund by filing an amended return, Form 1040X.

You can elect to forgo the carryback and simply carry the NOL forward until it is used up. This election makes sense if you expect to be in a higher tax bracket in coming years than you were in prior years. Keep in mind, however, that tax rates are declining over the next several years.

Another reason to forgo the carryback is to avoid drawing attention to a prior year in which you may have taken a questionable tax position.

If you make the election to forgo the NOL carryback, it applies for alternative minimum tax purposes as well.

Be sure to keep track of NOLs arising in different years, especially since they may be subject to different carryback and carryforward periods.

Pitfalls

An NOL carryback does *not* allow you to refigure your self-employment tax and obtain a refund of that tax.

Net operating losses that are not used up within the carryforward period of 20 years are lost forever.

Where to Claim the Deduction

There is no special form required to be used in figuring a net operating loss. As a practical matter, you can figure your NOL on Schedule A of Form 1045.

A net operating loss is reported as a negative income item; it is not a direct offset to your business income. For example, if your net operating loss carryforward is $4,400, enter –4,400 on the "Other income" line in the "Income" section of Form 1040.

Miscellaneous Items

Alert

At the time this book was completed, Congress was considering important tax changes that could affect 2017 tax returns and planning for 2018. Check the online Supplement in February 2018 at www.jklasser.com or www.barbaraweltman.com to see what changes have been enacted and when they are effective.

There are some tax benefits that simply defy classification so they cannot be included in any other chapter. You may be entitled to claim them nonetheless.

This chapter explains a variety of miscellaneous tax breaks you may be entitled to claim. The standard deduction amount that can be claimed instead of itemizing personal deductions is explained in the Introduction to this book. For more information see IRS Publication 525, *Taxable and Nontaxable Income*, and IRS Publication 529, *Miscellaneous Deductions*.

State and Local Income Taxes

Individuals in all but 7 states (Alaska, Florida, Nevada, South Dakota, Texas, Washington, and Wyoming) and the District of Columbia may be subject to income taxes (those in New Hampshire and Tennessee have an income tax on interest income and dividends only). There may also be income taxes on the local level. These taxes are deductible for federal income tax purposes if you itemize deductions.

Benefit

If you pay state and local income tax, through withholding or estimated tax payments, you can deduct the total amount as an itemized deduction. There is no dollar limit to this deduction.

Conditions

There are no conditions for claiming this deduction. Whatever amount you pay is deductible, provided you itemize your deductions and do not opt to deduct state and local sales taxes.

State income tax withholding reported on Form W-2 is deductible. Withholding includes not only state and local income taxes, but also mandatory contributions you make to state unemployment, disability, or family leave programs. States with one or more of these programs include Alaska, California, New Jersey, New York, Pennsylvania, Rhode Island, Washington, and West Virginia.

As mentioned earlier, you may not deduct your state and local income tax if you opt to deduct state and local sales taxes, explained next.

Planning Tips

You may increase your deduction for state income tax for 2017 by prepaying the fourth installment of estimated tax. Generally, the fourth installment for 2017 is due on January 16, 2018. This fourth installment would normally be deductible for federal income tax purposes in 2018. However, you can pay it before the end of the year to increase the deduction for 2017.

If you deduct state and local income taxes as an itemized deduction, do not forget to add to your 2017 payments any 2016 state and local estimated taxes that were paid in January 2017.

Pitfalls

If you do not deduct state and local sales taxes (you do not itemize, or if itemizing, you opt to deduct state and local sales taxes), you lose any tax benefit from contributions you make to state unemployment, disability, or family leave programs. Such amounts are withheld from your pay nonetheless.

Do not prepay state income tax if you are subject to the alternative minimum tax (AMT). State income tax is not deductible for AMT purposes, so prepaying effectively wastes the deduction.

Recognize that the deduction for state and local income taxes is subject to a phaseout for high-income taxpayers (see the Introduction).

Where to Claim the Deduction

The deduction is claimed on Schedule A of Form 1040. There is no special form or worksheet needed to figure your deduction.

You cannot claim this deduction if you file Form 1040A or 1040EZ.

State and Local Sales Taxes

There are about 10,000 state and local sales tax jurisdictions throughout the United States. The amount of tax you pay depends on how much you buy each year and the state (or states) in which you live. The deduction for state and local sales taxes can be claimed only if you itemize deductions and you do not deduct state and local income taxes.

Benefits

You can deduct state and local sales taxes paid during the year as an itemized deduction. You can claim your actual payments based on receipts for purchases or rely on an IRS table in the instructions to Schedule A of Form 1040. There is no dollar limit to this deduction (although the deduction is subject to a phaseout for high-income taxpayers, as explained in the Introduction).

Conditions

There are no conditions for claiming this deduction. Whatever amount you pay (or the figure for your state of residence, income level, and number of exemptions claimed on your return) can be deducted. "Income" for purposes of the IRS tables is based on total available income, which is taxable income increased by nontaxable items such as tax-exempt interest; veterans' benefits; nontaxable combat pay; workers' compensation; nontaxable part of Social Security and Railroad Retirement benefits; nontaxable part of IRA, pension, or annuity distributions (but no rollovers); and public assistance payments.

As mentioned, you may not deduct state and local sales taxes if you opt to deduct state and local income taxes.

Planning Tips

You can increase the deduction from the IRS tables by state and local general sales taxes paid on the following items *only*:

- Car
- Motorcycle
- Motor home
- Recreational vehicle
- Sport utility vehicle
- Truck
- Van
- Off-road vehicle
- Leased motor vehicle

You can also add in sales taxes paid on an aircraft, a boat, a mobile home, a prefabricated home, or home building materials as long as the tax rate is the same as the general sales tax rate.

If you live in more than one state, you must allocate the deduction found in the IRS tables for the number of days you lived in that state. For example, if you lived in Arizona for 6 months and New Jersey for the other 6 months, your total deduction for state and local sales taxes is one-half of your amount from the table for Arizona and one-half of your amount from the table for New Jersey.

Just because you live in a state in which you pay income taxes, do not assume that that deduction will be larger than the one for state sales tax. You may have a higher sales tax deduction if you fall into any of the following situations:

- A retiree whose income is primarily from Social Security benefits, certain types of annuities and pensions, and interest on Treasury securities.
- A self-employed individual who had a bad year.
- A family with a large number of exemptions.
- A person who was laid off from a job.
- A disabled worker who receives nontaxable state disability and workers' compensation payments.

Pitfall

State and local sales taxes that are itemized are not deductible for alternative minimum tax (AMT) purposes, so claiming the deduction in this manner can trigger or increase your AMT liability.

Where to Claim the Deduction

The deduction is claimed on Schedule A of Form 1040. Be sure to check the appropriate box on the schedule to indicate that you are claiming a deduction for general sales taxes.

Certain Federal Taxes

Most federal taxes you pay, such as income taxes, are not deductible. But there are some deductible federal taxes:

- Employer equivalent portion of self-employment tax (see Chapter 15)
- Estate tax paid on income in respect of a decedent (see Chapter 16)

Tax Refunds

The IRS reported in July 2017 that it had thus far issued more than 106 million refunds out of the 142 million returns for 2016 processed thus far, with the average refund exceeding $2,700. Certain refunds such as refunds of federal income taxes, are fully tax free; state tax refunds may be taxable or tax free in the year in which you receive them, depending on the situation. You don't have to amend any prior year's return if some or all of your refund is taxable.

Benefit ✪

The receipt of a tax refund may be taxable, or partially or fully tax free. Federal tax refunds are *always* tax free (because you are not allowed to deduct your federal income taxes). State and local tax refunds may be partially or fully taxable or tax free, depending on whether you itemized your deductions in the year in which the taxes were paid and certain other factors.

Conditions

If you receive a refund of state (and/or local) income tax for the year in which you claimed the standard deduction, none of the refund amount is taxable to you. For example, suppose you claimed the standard deduction on your 2016 federal income tax return. In 2017, you receive a check for $946 from your state representing a refund of state income tax that you overpaid for 2016. You do not have to report this refund on your 2017 federal income tax return.

If you itemized deductions on your 2016 federal income tax return and receive a refund of 2016 state income taxes in 2017, figure whether none, some, or all of the refund is taxable to you in 2017, based on the tax benefit rule (the benefit that the tax deduction afforded you). If you receive a refund of state income tax, the portion that is taxable and the portion that is tax free depends on the amount

WORKSHEET 16.1 State and Local Income Tax Refund

1. Enter the income tax refund from Form(s) 1099-G (or similar statement), but not more than the amount of your state and local income taxes shown on your 2016 Schedule A, line 5a.　　1. _____

2. Enter your total allowable itemized deductions from your 2016 Schedule A, line 30.　　2. _____

3. Enter the amount shown below for the filing status claimed on your 2016 Form 1040.
   - Single or married filing separately—$6,300
   - Married filing jointly or qualifying widow(er)— $12,600
   - Head of household $9,300　　3. _____

4. Did you fill in line 39a on your 2016 Form 1040?
   ☐ No. Enter -0-.
   ☐ Yes, Multiply the number in the box on line 39a of your 2016 Form 1040 by $1,250 ($1,550 if your 2016 filing status was single or head of household).　　4. _____

5. Add lines 3 and 4.　　5. _____

6. Is the amount on line 5 less than the amount on line 2?
   ☐ No. None of your refund is taxable.
   ☐ Yes. Subtract line 5 from line 2.　　6. _____

7. Taxable part of your refund is the smaller of line 1 or line 6.　　7. _____

of your total itemized deductions as well as what you could have deducted for state and local sales tax instead of deducting state and local income tax.

The taxable recovery cannot be more than the difference between your standard deduction for the year in which the state income taxes were itemized and your total itemized deductions for the year.

To figure the taxable part of any refund, use Worksheet 16.1.

You cannot use this worksheet, and your computations become more complex, if your refund is more than the excess of the deduction you claimed for state and local taxes over what you could have deducted for state and local sales taxes. Generally, the full amount of the refund is taxable if it is less than the excess of the deduction claimed for state income tax in the prior year over what could have been deducted for sales tax, but you'll need to complete a separate worksheet found in IRS Publication 525.

Planning Tip

Many taxpayers look forward to receiving their federal income tax refunds, but this is poor tax planning. If you are entitled to a refund, then you've made an interest-free loan to the government. A better way is to adjust wage withholding and/or estimated tax payments so you more closely approximate your actual tax bill for the year. Given today's low interest rates, it is probably better to err on the side of underpaying (so you'll owe the government money and some interest), rather than overpaying.

Pitfalls

Whether you actually receive a refund check of state income taxes or apply it to your next year's state income tax bill, you'll have to determine whether none, some, or all of it is taxable, as explained earlier.

If you are owed a federal tax refund or rebate check, the government can apply it to any outstanding federal tax liability, delinquent child support payments, outstanding student loan payments, or certain other payments. The government will inform you by letter of how it applied your refund or rebate amount.

Where to Claim the Benefit

You do not have to report your federal tax refund and/or rebate check on your federal income tax return. Refunds of state income taxes are reported to you on Form 1099-G, *Certain Government Payments*. If the state income tax refund is tax free, you do not have to report it on your return.

If any portion of a state income tax refund is taxable, it is reported on line 10 of Form 1040. Where appropriate, be sure to enter your refund as a *negative* number on Form 6251 so you reduce the income reported for purposes of the alternative minimum tax (AMT).

Tax Preparation Costs

The cost of tax return preparation and filing can be a few dollars for mailing a return by certified mail, a little more for buying tax preparation software or an online option, or hundreds of dollars in professional fees. Fortunately, whatever you spend may be deductible.

Benefit

Whatever way you prepare your personal federal and, if applicable, state income tax returns each year, you can deduct your expenses as a miscellaneous itemized deduction. This deduction can be claimed only to the extent that the total exceeds 2% of your adjusted gross income and is subject to the reduction of itemized deductions for high-income taxpayers.

The cost of tax preparation for returns for your business or rental activities is deductible as a business expense against your business or rental income.

There is no dollar limit on what you can deduct for tax preparation costs.

Conditions

There are no set conditions for writing off the cost of preparing and filing your tax returns; whatever you pay is a deductible expense.

EXAMPLES OF TAX PREPARATION COSTS

- Books on taxes and tax preparation (including the cost of this book)
- Online (electronic) filing fees
- Tax preparation software (such as TurboTax)
- Tax preparer fees (such as H&R Block charges and accountants' fees)

Planning Tip

To minimize your tax preparation costs, see if you qualify for free online preparation and filing through a commercial software company. FreeFile is open to Schedule C filers who meet certain requirements. Owners in partnerships and S corporations may be eligible to use FreeFile to report business income on their personal returns. FreeFile cannot be used to prepare Forms 1065, 1120, or 1120S. You can learn about eligibility requirements for FreeFile at the IRS website (www.irs.gov and click on *freefile*).

Pitfall

Be sure to claim tax preparation costs in the right year.

Example

In April 2017, you pay an accountant to prepare and file your 2016 returns. Your deduction for these tax preparation costs is claimed on your 2017 return.

Where to Claim the Deduction

You report your tax preparation costs for personal returns as a miscellaneous itemized deduction on Schedule A of Form 1040.

You report tax preparation costs related to your business or investment properties on the appropriate form: Schedule C, Schedule E, or Schedule F of Form 1040.

You cannot claim any deduction for tax preparation costs if you file Form 1040A or 1040EZ.

Tax Audits

The law does not require professional representation during the course of a tax audit; taxpayers can represent themselves. But it is common practice to use knowledgeable tax professionals during an audit, especially if the dollars at stake justify the cost of their professional fees. Fortunately, whatever you spend on these fees may be deductible. Alternatively, you may be able to get the government to pay for them if certain conditions are met.

Benefit ⊜

Fees to pay to your accountant or attorney to assist or represent you in a tax audit are deductible as a miscellaneous itemized deduction, which is subject to the 2% of adjusted gross income floor. There is no dollar limit on how much you can deduct for your audit costs. You can also deduct transportation costs to and from the audit or other audit-related travel at the rate of 53.5¢ per mile in 2017, as well as other out-of-pocket audit costs (e.g., photocopying).

If you contest an IRS audit and substantially prevail, you may be able to recover attorney's fees and costs if the IRS's position was not substantially justified. Generally, your recovery of attorney's fees is limited to a set dollar amount ($200 per hour in 2017).

Conditions

The conditions for deducting your audit costs are the same as those discussed earlier in this chapter with regard to tax preparation costs.

The following conditions relate to recovering your costs from the government. In order to recover your out-of-pocket costs for contesting an IRS audit through the administrative level as well as in the courts, you must meet all 5 of these conditions:

1. You exhaust administrative remedies.
2. You substantially prevail against the IRS.
3. The IRS position is not substantially justified.
4. Your request for reimbursement is reasonable.
5. You meet net worth requirements.

EXHAUST ADMINISTRATIVE REMEDIES

This means you must proceed through the IRS appeals process and cooperate at every level. You cannot unreasonably delay the proceedings.

SUBSTANTIALLY PREVAIL AGAINST THE IRS

This means you must win on the key issue or issues or the amount of tax involved. Once you satisfy this requirement, you are entitled to a recovery unless the IRS can show that it was substantially justified in pursuing the case.

THE IRS POSITION NOT SUBSTANTIALLY JUSTIFIED

The IRS position is substantially justified if it is reasonable. The IRS is presumed *not* to be reasonable if it fails to follow Treasury regulations and IRS rulings, procedures, notices, announcements, and private letter rulings. Of course, this is only a presumption that the IRS is free to rebut. In deciding whether the IRS position is substantially justified, a court may consider whether the same IRS position has already been rejected in a federal appellate court.

REASONABLE REIMBURSEMENT

You can recover only reasonable administrative costs of proceeding within the IRS and reasonable litigation costs, such as expert witnesses, court costs, and attorney's fees, in a court action. Attorney's fees are generally limited to a fixed rate per hour ($200 in 2017). However, a higher rate may be granted in special circumstances, such as the limited availability of local tax expertise.

NET WORTH REQUIREMENTS

Even if you meet all of the previous 4 conditions, you cannot recover anything related to your personal taxes unless your net worth is no more than $2 million. Net worth is based on your acquisition costs for assets, and not on the fair market value of the assets. If you file a joint return, jointly petition the Tax Court, and jointly incurs costs, the $2 million net worth limitation is for both you and your spouse. If you file a joint return but separately petition the Tax Court and have separate costs, the limitation is for each of you. The net worth limit is measured at the time the action begins.

If the recovery relates to your business as a sole proprietorship, you cannot have a net worth over $5 million or more than 500 employees.

Planning Tip

To make a claim for reimbursement of reasonable administrative costs, you must make an application for the amount to the IRS before the 91st day after the date on which the IRS mailed you its final decision. If the IRS denies your claim for payment, you must then petition the Tax Court within 90 days from the date the IRS mailed you its denial.

Pitfall

You may not recover any attorney's fees if you represent yourself (pro se).

Where to Claim the Deduction for Audit Costs

You report your audit costs related to your personal taxes as a miscellaneous itemized deduction on Schedule A of Form 1040.

You report audit costs related to your business or investment properties on the appropriate form: Schedule C, Schedule E, or Schedule F of Form 1040.

You cannot claim any deduction for audit costs if you file Form 1040A or 1040EZ.

If you successfully recover attorney's fees and other costs from the government, you do not have to report this income. It is tax free to you.

Legal Fees

William Shakespeare said, "Let's kill all the lawyers." But when a person today wants to right a perceived wrong, he or she usually turns to a lawyer for assistance. The cost of this help, which can be very steep, can be deducted only in certain circumstances.

Benefit

Legal fees you pay for actions that include discrimination are deducted as an adjustment to gross income. Legal fees for certain other personal matters are deductible as miscellaneous itemized deductions, which are subject to the 2% of adjusted gross income floor and the reduction in itemized deductions for high-income taxpayers.

Legal fees related to your business that meet deductibility conditions are ordinary and necessary business expenses that offset business income.

Condition

To be deductible, legal fees must relate to your business, the production of income (which includes, for example, the receipt of taxable alimony or a taxable award), or income taxes.

EXAMPLES OF DEDUCTIBLE FEES

Fees related to these matters can be deducted:

- Action to keep your job, win a promotion, or fight discrimination or sexual harassment.
- Estate planning advice.
- Personal injury actions other than for physical illness or injury, (e.g., defamation suits).
- Marital actions in which you seek alimony.
- Social Security benefits contest (assuming your benefits are partially taxable, then that portion of legal fees is deductible).
- Tax actions, including return preparation and audits. Legal fees related to tax advice are also deductible.

To deduct legal fees as an adjustment to gross income, the claim must be for unlawful discrimination (such as age discrimination on the job), claims against the federal government under Subchapter III of Chapter 27, Title 31, of the U.S. Code, and a private cause of action under the Medicare Secondary Payer statute.

Planning Tip

When engaging an attorney for representation, be sure you fully understand the fee arrangement. For example, even in a contingency fee arrangement (in which you owe no money if you do not recover anything), you may owe the attorney money to cover expenses, such as photocopying and postage, in addition to any portion of the award.

Pitfall

Not all legal fees are deductible. Some nondeductible legal fees may be capitalized (added to the basis of property), so that they will, in effect, be recovered when the asset is disposed of.

Example

You buy investment property for $100,000 and pay $5,000 in legal fees. You cannot deduct the fees, but you can add them to the basis of the property. Assume that a few years from now you sell the property for $150,000. Your gain is $45,000 ($150,000 − [$100,000 + $50,000]). In effect, you have reduced your gain for tax purposes by the $5,000 in legal fees you added to the property's basis.

EXAMPLES OF NONDEDUCTIBLE FEES

Fees related to these matters cannot be currently deducted:

- Acquisition of an asset, including a home or a business (the fees are added to the basis of the asset)
- Obtaining child support
- Defending title to property
- Marital actions in which you are required to pay alimony or make a property settlement (or actions in which you receive a property settlement), other than amounts related to tax advice
- Name change
- Personal injury actions involving physical injury or illness
- Will preparation, other than amounts related to tax advice, provided it is separately billed

You cannot deduct legal fees which are part of miscellaneous itemized deductions for alternative minimum tax (AMT) purposes. This means that if you have claimed a large write-off for regular tax purposes, the deduction of legal fees might trigger or increase your AMT liability.

Where to Claim the Benefit

You report deductible legal fees paid for personal matters other than discrimination claims as a miscellaneous itemized deduction on Schedule A of Form 1040.

You report legal fees related to discrimination claims up to the amount of the award in the "Adjusted Gross Income" section of Form 1040. Write "UDC" on line 36 to indicate that you are deducting legal fees for an unlawful discrimination claim. You report legal fees paid in connection with an award from the IRS for information provided to help the IRS detect tax law violations ("whistleblower award") up to the amount of the award in the "Adjusted Gross Income" section of Form 1040. Write "WBF" on line 36 to indicate that you are deducting legal fees for an unlawful discrimination claim.

You report deductible legal fees related to your business or investment properties on the appropriate form: Schedule C, Schedule E, or Schedule F of Form 1040.

You cannot claim any deduction for legal fees if you file Form 1040A or 1040EZ.

Gifts You Receive

Whether your birthday gift is a tie, a set of golf clubs, or a check for $25,000, you usually can treat the gift as tax free for income tax purposes. The gift doesn't have to relate to a special occasion, such as Mother's Day or an anniversary, and it doesn't have to come from a relative. All you need is for the transfer to be a true gift and not something else (such as disguised compensation).

Benefit ⊗

Gifts you receive from just about anyone are tax free. Gifts can be in cash or property. There is no dollar limit on the amount of gifts you can exclude from income each year.

Important: Your income tax treatment is separate and distinct from the gift tax rules imposed on the gift's giver (the donor). Thus, the fact that a donor can make gifts free from gift tax only up to a set dollar amount per person per year ($14,000 in 2017) does not affect your receipt of the gift. Even if the donor exceeds this limit, your receipt is still entirely tax free for income tax purposes.

Condition

To be treated as a tax-free gift, the transfer must be made with donative intent (a substantive view toward making a gift) and the recipient cannot pay any consideration for receiving it. In most cases, it is entirely clear that a transfer of property is intended as a gift. There are 2 key situations, however, in which the transfer may not be entirely clear and tax-free treatment is not assured:

1. When money is really intended as a loan rather than a gift (see Chapter 12 for rules on distinguishing between a gift and a loan, especially when the parties are related).
2. When money or property is given to employees (see "Pitfalls").

Planning Tip

When you receive a gift of property, be sure to obtain from the donor the following information needed to determine your gain or loss when you later dispose of the property:

- *The donor's basis.* If the basis of the property at the time of the gift was at least equal to its value at that time, then your basis becomes the donor's basis. If the gift's value was less than its basis at the time of the gift (the property had declined in value), then your basis for purposes of determining gain is the donor's basis, but your basis for determining loss is the value of the gift at the time it was made to you. It is possible under the right circumstances that because of these special basis rules, you may realize neither a gain nor a loss when you sell the gift.
- *The donor's holding period.* You can add to the time you own the property all of the donor's holding period. For example, assume the donor purchased stock on July 1, 2013, and gives you the shares on May 1, 2017. If you sell those shares on May 15, 2017, your gain or loss is *long-term* gain or loss because the shares are considered to have been held for more than one year (the holding period begins with the donor's holding period).

A donor who is required to file a gift tax return must provide you with the following information within 30 days after the gift tax return's due date (generally April 15 of the year after the year of the gift):

- The name, address, and telephone number of the person required to file the tax return.
- The information specified in the gift tax return (a description of the gift and its value at the time of the gift).

Pitfalls

Money or items received from your employer that are labeled as gifts may, in fact, be nothing more than additional compensation. Small items, such as a holiday turkey or ham, are tax-free gifts to you. But gifts of *any* cash or cash equivalents (such as gift certificates) and more expensive items (such as golf clubs) are considered taxable compensation, not tax-free gifts.

Income earned on a gift is taxable (unless such income is also tax-free income).

Example

You receive a gift of $10,000. The receipt of the gift is tax free to you. You use the money to buy a Treasury bill: Interest on the investment is taxable to you. If you use the money to buy a municipal bond, however, the interest on the investment is tax free (because municipal bond interest is tax free).

There is no income tax deduction for *making* a gift. While some gifts may be free from gift tax, there is no break for income tax purposes when you make a gift.

Where to Claim the Benefit

Since gifts are tax free, you do not have to report them on your return.

Inheritances

Whether you inherit your uncle's gold watch or your mother's entire million-dollar estate, you are not taxed on this inheritance. There are no limits to the amount you can inherit tax free.

While the receipt of an inheritance is always tax free, some inheritances may produce taxable income later on. For example, if you inherit a $100,000 traditional IRA, you are not immediately taxed on the inheritance; there's no tax as long as the funds remain in the IRA. However, as you start to withdraw funds from the IRA, you are taxed on this amount. Fortunately, you are entitled to claim a tax deduction for any federal estate tax attributable to this taxable income, called income in respect of a decedent (IRD), which is explained later in this chapter.

Benefit

Inheritances you receive are tax free. There is no dollar limit on the amount of an inheritance you can exclude from income.

In addition to tax-free treatment for an inheritance, you may also be entitled to a tax deduction from the estate. This occurs when an estate is not settled immediately but operates, receiving income and incurring deductions for income tax purposes. The estate becomes a taxpayer until the affairs of the estate are settled. If the estate's income tax total deductions in its last year are more than its gross income for that year, then beneficiaries who succeed to the estate's property can claim a deduction. This is a one-time deduction that can be claimed only in the year in which, or with which, the estate terminates, whether the year of termination is a normal tax year or a short tax year. The executor of the estate should supply any necessary information to enable you to claim a deduction. The deduction can be claimed only as a miscellaneous itemized deduction subject to the 2% of AGI floor and is subject to the reduction of itemized deductions for high-income taxpayers.

Condition

There are no conditions on the tax-free receipt of an inheritance other than the fact you receive the inheritance on account of the death of a person. Inheritances include amounts paid to you under a will, or by the state's rules of intestacy (if the person died without a will), jointly owned property you receive in full when your co-owner dies, and other amounts you receive as a named beneficiary (for example, a person's pension benefits left to you as the designated beneficiary).

Planning Tips

When you inherit property, your basis usually becomes the value of the property for estate tax purposes (generally, the property's value on the date of death). This is called a "stepped-up basis." Also, you automatically have a long-term holding period, regardless of how long the decedent owned the property before death or how long you hold it after you inherit it.

Example

On December 20, 2016, you inherit 100 shares of X Company from a decedent who purchased them on November 15, 2010, at $10,000. On the date you inherit them, they are worth $12,000. Two weeks later in 2017, you sell them for $13,000. You have a long-term capital gain of $1,000 ($13,000 − $12,000).

However, for inheritances from certain decedents dying in 2010, there was a modified carryover basis rule (very few estates opted to use this rule). If the estate elected to use the zero estate tax rule, then the basis to an heir is the same as the basis that the decedent had in the property. However, the stepped-up basis rule continues to apply to the first $1.3 million of an estate, with an additional $3 million passing to a surviving spouse, this amount is allocated by the executor to property passing from the decedent.

Pitfalls

If you inherited property from a person whose estate tax return was required to be filed after July 31, 2015, and received Schedule A of Form 8971 from the estate, you must use the basis specified on this schedule. This is the same amount that the estate used on the decedent's estate tax return. If you use a basis for inherited property that is inconsistent with the amount reported on this schedule, you may be subject to a 20% accuracy-related penalty.

If you anticipate an inheritance and sell your right to receive it, the proceeds you receive are taxable as ordinary income. This is so even though you would have received tax-free income had you waited for the inheritance itself.

If you are named as the executor, administrator, or personal representative of an estate, payment of fiduciary fees to you are *not* tax-free inheritances (even if you are also an heir to the estate).

Income earned on an inheritance is taxable (unless the income is also tax-free income—see the earlier example under "Gifts"). Income includes amounts on assets that previously have gone untaxed, such as traditional IRAs and annuities.

Example

You are named as the beneficiary of your father's IRA. When he dies, there is $100,000 in the IRA. Your inheritance of this IRA is tax free. However, since your father never paid income tax on the funds, you must do so under the required minimum distribution (RMD) rules for IRAs (explained in IRS Publication 590-B, *Distributions from Individual Retirement Arrangements*). You are taxable when and to the extent you take withdrawals from the IRA.

Where to Claim the Benefit

Since inheritances are tax free, you do not have to report them on your return.

If you are entitled to deduct the estate's deduction from its final year, report the deduction as a miscellaneous itemized deduction subject to the 2% of AGI floor on Schedule A of Form 1040.

You cannot claim this deduction if you file Form 1040A or 1040EZ.

Life Insurance Proceeds

The beneficiary of a life insurance policy generally can receive the proceeds free from income tax. There is no requirement that the beneficiary be related to the insured (the person on whose life the insurance is based), and there is no limit on the amount of proceeds that can be received tax free.

Benefit

Life insurance proceeds you receive on account of the death of the insured are tax free to you. There is no dollar limit on the amount you can receive tax free.

Condition

To be tax free, life insurance proceeds must be payable on the death of the insured. The insured may be the same person as the owner of the policy or may be someone else.

Planning Tip

Life insurance proceeds can be used during the insured's life on a tax-free basis under certain conditions. The treatment of accelerated death benefits is explained in Chapter 2.

Pitfalls

If you leave insurance proceeds with the insurance company, interest you receive is taxable. (Only surviving spouses of someone who died before October 23, 1986, can exclude the first $1,000 of interest each year.)

If you paid any consideration for the life insurance policy, then you are taxable on the proceeds. You are treated as having paid consideration if you become the policy owner and there is an outstanding loan on the policy.

Example

A mother has a $100,000 life insurance policy against which she has borrowed $10,000. She gives the policy to her daughter (receipt of the policy is a tax-free gift to the daughter). Shortly thereafter, the mother dies and the daughter collects $90,000 ($100,000 face value of the policy minus the outstanding loan of $10,000). The daughter is taxed on the $90,000.

Where to Claim the Benefit

Since life insurance proceeds received on account of the death of the insured are tax free, you do not have to report them on your return.

Estate Tax Deduction on Income in Respect of a Decedent

If you inherit something on which you must pay income taxes because the person who left you the inheritance never did, then you may be eligible for a special deduction related to federal estate taxes paid on certain types of assets left to you. To claim this special deduction, certain conditions must be met.

Benefit ≡

If you inherit a traditional IRA, annuity, or other income in respect of a decedent (IRD) and must report income from this inheritance, you may be eligible for an itemized deduction for the portion of federal estate tax related to this property. This itemized deduction is *not* subject to the 2% of adjusted gross income floor. There is no dollar limit on this deduction.

Conditions

To claim this deduction, the IRA, annuity, or other income in respect of a decedent (any income that the decedent earned before death but was not taxable to him or her at that time) must have been part of an estate that was subject to federal estate taxes. State estate or inheritance taxes are not deductible.

Examples of IRD:

- Accounts payable to self-employed business owners on the cash basis
- Benefits from 401(k) and other qualified retirement plans
- Damage awards from lawsuits
- Deferred compensation
- Health Savings Accounts
- Interest on U.S. savings bonds that has been deferred
- Royalties
- Survivor annuities
- Traditional IRAs

Assuming there has been federal estate tax paid on income in respect of a decedent, then figure the portion of the estate tax deductible in the current year. If, for example, you withdraw all of the IRA funds, then all of the estate tax related to this asset is deductible this year.

Example

You inherit a $120,000 IRA from your brother and your sister inherited an $80,000 IRA from him, so the total IRD from his estate is $200,000. The tax on your brother's estate is $94,600. The estate determines that without including the IRA and other income in respect of a decedent, the estate tax would have been $48,400. The estate tax that qualifies for a deduction is $46,200 ($94,600 − $48,400). This year you empty the inherited IRA, and thus include $120,000 in your gross income. You can take an itemized deduction of $27,720 for your share of the estate tax, figured as follows:

$$\frac{\text{Value included in your income}}{\text{Total value of IRD}} \times \text{Estate tax qualifying deduction}$$

$$\frac{\$120,000}{\$200,000} \times \$46,200 = \$27,720$$

The calculation on the portion of estate tax can become complex when only part of the IRA is withdrawn within the year. A full explanation of how to figure this deduction may be found in IRS Publication 559, *Survivors, Executors, and Administrators*.

Planning Tips

This deduction is often overlooked. If you inherited an IRA and have not been claiming the deduction every year in which you report a distribution from the account, consider filing amended returns for all open tax years. You generally have 3 years from the due date of the return to file an amended return. This means you may be able to file for the prior 3 years and obtain tax refunds for each year.

When you receive an inheritance of IRD, be sure to ask the executor for information about estate taxes so you can figure your deduction. Find out about the amount of federal estate tax, the total estate, and what portion of it is the IRD you inherited.

Pitfall

There is no downside to claiming this deduction where allowable.

Where to Claim the Deduction

Generally, you report this deduction as a miscellaneous itemized deduction on Schedule A of Form 1040. It is *not* subject to the 2% floor but it is subject to the reduction of itemized deductions for high-income taxpayers. However, when the income in respect of a decedent is long-term capital gain (such as an installment payment on a sale made before the decedent's death), the deduction is not claimed separately but rather treated as an expense of sale. This means you still get the benefit of the deduction, but in the form of a reduction of the gain you report.

You cannot claim this deduction if you file Form 1040A or 1040EZ.

Rebates and Discounts

Retailers may offer various rebates or discounts to induce you to buy their products. You may receive an immediate price reduction or, if you submit paperwork, you can get a check in the mail. These rebates and discounts are not taxable to you.

Benefit ⊗

The receipt of a check representing a rebate for purchasing an item is not income. For instance, if you buy a car, you may be able to apply a $1,000 manufacturer's rebate to the purchase price of the car, saving you $1,000 on the spot. Or, if you purchase a computer within a certain time, you may be able to send in a copy of your receipt and proof of purchase to receive a check payable to you (you often have to wait 6 to 12 weeks for this check).

Either way, the IRS says this rebate arrangement doesn't produce any taxable income for you. Instead, it's as if the rebate simply reduced the price of the item you purchased.

Planning Tips

While mail-in rebates have declined (and only 40% of these are redeemed correctly), the number of rebates offered through smartphones continues to increase. Check for rebates when you purchase goods.

If your credit card has a rebate program under which you have the option of receiving cash or donating your accrued benefit to charity, the IRS says you are *not* taxed on the benefit, whichever option you choose. What is more, if you itemize and apply your benefit to a charity, you can claim a charitable contribution deduction as long as you meet substantiation requirements (i.e., obtain a written acknowledgment for a donation of $250 or more).

Pitfall

There is no downside to submitting rebate claims, other than the brief time it takes you to do this.

Where to Claim the Benefit

You do not have to report any rebates or discounts that qualify as tax free to you.

Government Benefits

Individuals may receive payments from the federal and/or state government for a variety of reasons. In many cases, these benefits may be received entirely tax free.

Benefit

Most government payments can be received tax free; they are excludable without regard to their amount or your income.

If you must repay Social Security benefits in excess of annual benefits received, you may deduct the excess amounts as a miscellaneous itemized deduction to the extent total itemized deductions exceed 2% of adjusted gross income and the reduction in itemized deductions for high-income taxpayers.

Condition

As a practical matter, many types of government benefits are payable to individuals whose incomes are below the level at which a tax return must be filed and taxes are owed. Most government benefits or payments are tax free. Any taxable amounts are usually reported to you on an information return:

- Form RRA-1099, Payment by the Railroad Retirement Board
- Form SSA-1099, Social Security Benefit Statement
- Form 1099G, Certain Government Payments (for unemployment benefits, RTAA payments, agricultural payments, and taxable grants)

EXAMPLES OF TAX-FREE GOVERNMENT BENEFITS

- Black lung benefit payments.
- Crime victim payments from a state fund for this purpose.
- Disaster relief and disaster mitigation grants (see Chapter 13).
- Energy conservation subsidies paid by public utilities.
- Federal Employees' Compensation Act (FECA) payments for personal injury or sickness (including death benefits to beneficiaries).
- Federal income tax refunds.
- Foster care provider payments (see Chapter 1).
- Foster Grandparents Program payments for supportive services or reimbursement for out-of-pocket expenses.

- Grants for homes designed for wheelchair living of disabled veterans.
- Grants for motor vehicles for veterans who have lost their sight or the use of their limbs.
- HFA Hardest Hit Fund payments to distressed homeowners.
- Historic preservation grants under the National Historic Preservation Act.
- Holocaust victims restitution (see Chapter 13).
- Interest on insurance dividends left on deposit with the Department of Veterans Affairs.
- Military benefits (see Chapter 14).
- Mortgage assistance payments under Section 235 of the National Housing Act (the homeowner cannot deduct interest paid by this assistance).
- Nutrition Program for the Elderly food benefits.
- Peace Corps payments for housing, food, utilities, and clothing.
- SCORE payments for supportive services or reimbursement for out-of-pocket expenses.
- Senior program payments for supportive services or reimbursement for out-of-pocket expenses.
- Social Security lump-sum death benefit of $255 payable to a surviving spouse.
- State income tax refunds if you did not itemize deductions in the year to which the payments relate.
- Supplemental Security Income (SSI) and Supplemental Security Disability Income (SSDI).
- Survivor benefits of deceased public safety officers (police and law enforcement officers, firefighters, chaplains, and rescue squad and ambulance crew members).
- Volunteer tax counseling for the elderly (TCE) reimbursements for transportation, meals, and other expenses.
- Volunteers in Service to America (VISTA) volunteers, living expense allowances.
- Welfare benefits.
- Winter energy cost reduction payments to qualified individuals.
- Workers' compensation benefits.
- Work-training program payments from state welfare agencies (as long as the payments, exclusive of extra allowances for transportation or other costs, do not exceed public welfare benefits otherwise receivable).
- Wrongful incarceration payments payable to those who were wrongfully incarcerated.

TABLE 16.1 Income Threshold for the Excludable Portion of Social Security Benefits

	100% Excludable	50% Excludable	15% Excludable
Married filing jointly	Up to $32,000	Over $32,000 but not over $44,000	Over $44,000
Married filing separately	—	—	Automatically applies
Other taxpayers	Up to $25,000	Over $25,000 but not over $34,000	Over $34,000

Planning Tips

Social Security benefits may be fully or partially tax free, depending on your filing status, the amount of Social Security benefits, and other income, including tax-exempt interest. (The same rules apply to equivalent Railroad Retirement benefits.) Table 16.1 shows the portion of benefits excludable from income. The income threshold includes total income plus tax-exempt interest and one-half of Social Security benefits.

Example

In 2017, you are single with income from wages and taxable interest of $18,000. You also receive $12,000 in Social Security benefits and $1,000 of tax-exempt interest, with no adjustments to gross income. Since total income ($18,000 + 50% of $12,000 + $1,000) does not exceed $25,000, none of your benefits are included in income; they are tax free.

This explanation of the taxation of Social Security benefits is a brief overview that does not include many nuances to be taken into account. For more complete information about excluding Social Security benefits, see IRS Publication 915, *Social Security and Equivalent Railroad Retirement Benefits*.

If Form SSA-1099 shows a negative number (the benefits you are required to repay for any reason exceed your annual benefits), you may deduct the negative number as a miscellaneous itemized deduction to the extent total miscellaneous deductions exceed 2% of adjusted gross income. If the negative number exceeds $3,000, you may qualify to figure tax for the year in a special way (see "Repayment of Supplemental Unemployment Benefits" in Chapter 14).

Pitfalls

Disability payments from Social Security are taxed in the same way as Social Security retirement benefits.

Just because a payment comes from the government does not automatically mean it is tax free. Some government payments are taxable.

EXAMPLES OF TAXABLE GOVERNMENT BENEFITS

- Alaska Permanent Fund dividend income
- Election precinct officials' payments
- Jury duty pay
- Peace Corps payments for leave allowances, readjustment allowances, and termination payments
- State lottery winnings

Where to Claim the Benefit

Those government benefits that are tax free do not have to be reported on your return.

Olympic Medals

American Olympians and Paralympians are not taxed on their winnings after 2015. This impacts winners in the 2016 Summer Olympics, as well as those in the Winter Olympics in 2018 and future Olympics. The exclusion applies to the cash payments ($25,000 for gold, $15,000 for silver, and $5,000 for bronze) as well as the value of the medals (estimated at $600 for gold and $300 for silver; the bronze have little value).

However, athletes with adjusted gross income exceeding $1 million ($500,000 for married persons filing separately) cannot exclude their winnings.

Alternative Minimum Tax

The alternative minimum tax (AMT) is a parallel tax system that exists to ensure all taxpayers pay at least some tax, even if they can reduce their regular tax through legitimate deductions. You pay AMT to the extent it exceeds your regular tax. According to the Tax Policy Center, while only 20,000 filers paid AMT in 1970, today about 4.4 million pay AMT. Throughout this book, you have seen many examples of items that receive different tax treatment for regular tax and AMT purposes.

Benefit ⬤

You can claim an AMT exemption that may eliminate or at least minimize your AMT liability. The 2017 exemption amounts are $84,500 for married filing jointly,

$54,300 for single taxpayers and heads of households, and $42,250 for married persons filing separately.

Conditions

There are no conditions for claiming this exemption. Simply apply the correct one for your filing status.

Planning Tips

Even if the exemption amount does not eliminate AMT liability, you can use various personal tax credits to reduce this liability. All nonrefundable personal credits could offset AMT liability.

Pitfall

The AMT exemption is subject to a phaseout for those with alternative minimum taxable income (AMTI) over a set amount. The exemption is reduced by $1 for every $4 over the phaseout threshold. Table 16.2 shows the phaseouts for 2017.

Example

A married couple filing jointly in 2017 have AMTI of $199,700. Because their AMTI is $40,000 over the threshold amount for their filing status, their exemption is $74,800 ($84,500 − [$199,700 − $160,900] × .25]).

Where to Claim the Exemption

The exemption is claimed on Form 6251, *Alternative Minimum Tax— Individuals*, which is attached to Form 1040. If any AMT is owed, it is entered in the Tax and Credits section of Form 1040. If you are required to complete this form, you cannot file Form 1040A or 1040EZ.

TABLE 16.2 2017 Phaseout Thresholds for the AMT Exemption

Filing status	AMTI
Single and head of household	$120,700
Married filing jointly and surviving spouse	160,900
Married filing separately	80,450

Items Adjusted Annually for Inflation

Law changes are one important way in which write-off amounts and restrictions on them change each year. But another, less obvious way is adjustments to certain amounts and limits reflecting cost-of-living changes. Not all items subject to adjustment actually change each year, but the list of the items subject to change continues to grow.

To help you plan your taxes for the future, it's helpful to know that certain limits affecting exclusions, deductions, and credits are raised in step with increases in the cost of living (although some items may be adjusted downward if the times demand it). The following exclusions, deductions, and credits are subject to annual adjustments for inflation:

401(k) 403(b), and 457 plan elective deferrals

accelerated death benefits daily dollar amount that can be paid tax free from a life insurance policy on account of chronic illness

adoption assistance programs the maximum dollar amount and AGI phaseout range

adoption credit the maximum dollar amount and the AGI phaseout range

affordable health coverage provided by an employer and which prevents eligibility for the premium tax credit

alternative minimum tax (AMT) exemption amount

alternative minimum taxable income for the 26% rate

Archer medical savings accounts the definition of a high-deductible plan (i.e., the range for an annual deductible) and the limit on out-of-pocket costs

attorney's fee recovery from the government

benefits limit for defined benefit plans the dollar limit on benefits under these plans for which contributions are figured on an actuarial basis

child tax credit the value used in determining the refundable credit

compensation on which qualified retirement plan deductions are based the amount of compensation or self-employment income taken into account in figuring deductions for plan contributions

contribution limit for profit-sharing and other defined contribution plans the dollar limit on deductible contributions to these plans

contribution limit for SEPs the dollar limit on deductible contributions to these plans

dollar limit for depreciation and first-year expensing on luxury cars the maximum deduction for depreciation or first-year expensing for cars and light trucks weighing no more than 6,000 pounds

earned income credit the earned income amount, the maximum amount of the credit, and the AGI phaseout range

educator deduction out-of-pocket costs for grades K–12

first-year expensing limit dollar limit on amount of equipment that can be expensed as well as the taxable income limit

flexible spending accounts for medical costs the employee salary reduction contribution limit

foreign earned income exclusion the dollar amount that can be received tax free for performing services abroad

Health Savings Accounts annual deductibles and contributions limits to HSAs for high-deductible health plans

insubstantial benefits from charities dollar limit on what constitutes insubstantial benefits (ignored when figuring charitable contribution deductions)

interest exclusion on savings bonds AGI phaseout range

interest on student loans AGI phaseout range

IRAs MAGI limit for active participants to make deductible IRA contributions

Lifetime learning credit MAGI phaseout range

long-term care premiums dollar limit on annual contributions treated as deductible medical expenses

low-income housing credit amounts used to calculate the state housing credit ceiling

parking dollar limit on employer-provided tax-free parking

payments received under long-term care policies or accelerated death benefits daily dollar limit excludable without regard to long-term care expenses or terminal illness

personal exemption dollar amount

phaseout of itemized deductions for high-income taxpayers

phaseout of personal exemptions for high-income taxpayers

premium tax credit income eligibility threshold

retirement savers credit MAGI limit on eligibility to claim a credit for making certain elective deferrals and IRA contributions

Roth IRAs MAGI limit on eligibility to contribute to this retirement savings plan

shared responsibility payment for failing to have minimum essential coverage and not qualifying for exemption

Social Security wage base for FICA and self-employment tax limit on income taken into account in figuring the Social Security portion of FICA and self-employment tax

standard deduction dollar amount

standard mileage rate for business travel the cents-per-mile rate may be increased or decreased

standard mileage rate for medical or moving the cents-per-mile rate may be increased or decreased

transportation fringe benefits dollar limit on excludable free parking, monthly transit passes, and van pooling

Not all of the dollar amounts covered in this book are indexed annually for inflation. There are certain dollar amounts set by law or the IRS that are not adjusted for inflation. In doing tax planning for future years, you can rely on these fixed amounts (unless Congress decides to change them).

Achievement awards. An exclusion for receiving these awards is limited to $1,600 for qualified awards and $400 for nonqualified awards.

Alimony payments. If alimony payments decline by more than $15,000 in the second or third year, some of the previously claimed deductions are recaptured.

Bank deposit losses. If the bank fails and deposits are not covered by FDIC insurance, you can opt to treat up to $20,000 ($10,000 if married filing separately) of losses as a miscellaneous itemized deduction.

Business gifts. These are deductible only up to $25 per recipient each year.

Business travel substantiation. No receipts are needed for travel costs under $75 (except for lodging).

Capital losses. Up to $3,000 ($1,500 if married filing separately) of capital losses in excess of capital gains for the year can be used to offset ordinary income.

Casualty losses. There is a $100 reduction in the amount of each casualty loss; it applies per event (not per item lost).

Charitable contribution substantiation rules. The dollar thresholds for certain types of substantiation are fixed by law. Donations of $250 or more require a written acknowledgment from the charity. Donations of cars or other vehicles valued over $500 require a special acknowledgment. Appraisals are needed for donations of property valued over $5,000. Additional appraisal rules apply to donations of art valued at $20,000 or more.

Child tax credit. The maximum credit is $1,000 per eligible child.

Coverdell Education Savings Accounts (ESAs). The maximum annual contribution is capped at $2,000 per year for an eligible beneficiary, and the MAGI limit for making a full contribution is up to $95,000 for singles and $120,000 for joint filers.

Cruise ship travel for business. The deduction is limited to $2,000.

Dependent care assistance. Employer assistance is tax free up to $5,000 annually. If your employer offers a dependent care flexible spending account, you can contribute up to $5,000 annually from your compensation; the amount contributed is not taxed to you.

Dependent care credit. The maximum amount of eligible expenses taken into account in figuring the credit is $3,000 for one child and $6,000 for two or more children.

Flexible spending account carryover. If the plan allows for unused contributions to be carried forward, the cap is $500.

Foreign tax credit simplified reporting. This is restricted to a foreign tax credit of no more than $300 ($600 on a joint return).

Gift loans. The below-market loan rules do not apply to gift loans up to $10,000 per recipient.

Health savings account additional contribution limit. Those who are age 55 and older by year-end can add $1,000 to their applicable contribution limit for the year.

Home sale exclusion. Up to $250,000 of gain ($500,000 on a joint return) on the sale of a principal residence can be excluded if certain conditions are met.

IRA catchup contributions. The additional annual contribution by those age 50 or older is $1,000.

IRA early distribution penalty exception for first-time homebuyers. There is a $10,000 cap on penalty-free IRA distributions.

Loans from qualified retirement plans. The maximum loan is 50% of your vested account balance or $50,000, whichever is less.

Lodging for medical treatment. Lodging to receive outpatient care is deductible up to $50 per night ($100 per night if you are accompanying a sick child).

Mortgage insurance. Assuming the deduction is extended to 2017, the deduction for mortgage insurance is limited for those with adjusted gross income (AGI) below set limits. The full deduction applies for AGI up to $100,000 ($50,000 for married persons filing separately).

Mortgage interest. For purposes of deducting interest, the cap on the amount of qualified acquisition is fixed at $1 million and the cap on home equity debt is $100,000.

Performing artists. The conditions for such individuals to deduct their job expenses from gross income rather than as an itemized deduction are fixed. Adjusted gross income from all sources (not just performing) cannot exceed $16,000.

Qualified charitable distributions. If you are age 70½ or older, you can transfer up to $100,000 directly from your IRA to a public charity tax free.

Rental losses. You can deduct up to $25,000 of rental losses each year if you actively participate in the rental activity and your adjusted gross income is no more than $100,000. Married couples must file jointly to use this deduction.

Recovering attorney's fees and administrative costs from the government. There is a net worth cap on individuals seeking a recovery. The cap is $2 million.

Reporting payments to independent contractors. Only payments of $600 or more to an independent contractor must be reported to the IRS.

Section 1244 losses. You can treat losses on certain small business stock as ordinary (rather than capital) losses up to $50,000 ($100,000 on a joint return).

Standard mileage rate for charitable driving. The rate is 14¢ per mile.

Student exchange program. If you host an exchange student in your home under an agreement with a charitable organization, you can deduct $50 per month as a charitable contribution.

Student loan interest. The maximum annual deduction is $2,500.

Tuition and fees deduction. The modified adjusted gross income limited on eligibility for this above-the-line deduction remains constant.

Checklist of Tax-Free Items

When items are not included in income, and in some cases not even reported on the return, there are considerable tax savings. Here is a list of tax-free items for 2017 tax returns.

- 529 plan withdrawals to pay qualified higher education costs
- ABLE account withdrawals to cover qualified expenses for a disabled beneficiary
- Accelerated death benefits under a life insurance policy
- Adoption costs paid by employer up to $13,540
- Awards to certain employees (usually up to $1,600)
- Bequests
- Black lung benefit payments

- Capital gains and capital gain distributions for those in the 10% or 15% tax bracket
- Charitable transfers of IRA distributions up to $100,000 by those age 70½ and older
- Child support payments
- Coverdell education savings account withdrawals to pay education costs
- Crime victim payments from a state fund for this purpose
- Damages received for personal physical injury
- Damages received for wrongful incarceration
- Debt discharged during insolvency or bankruptcy
- Dependent care expenses paid by employer up to $5,000
- Disability payments under a policy in which you paid the premiums
- Disaster relief payments and disaster mitigation grants
- Discounts on purchases you make
- Dividends for those in the 10% or 15% tax bracket if the dividends are "qualified"
- Education courses paid by employer (fully excluded if job-related; up to $5,250 if not job-related)
- Federal Employees' Compensation Act (FECA) payments for personal injury or sickness (including death benefits to beneficiaries)
- Federal income tax refunds
- Flexible spending arrangement contributions from salary for health care or dependent care
- Foreign earned income up to $102,100
- Foster care payments
- Foster Grandparents Program payments for supportive services or reimbursement for out-of-pocket expenses
- Frequent flyer miles you earn
- Fringe benefits from employers ("perks") if they are de minimis, an employee discount, working condition fringe benefits, or transportation fringe benefits
- Gifts
- Grants for homes designed for wheelchair living of disabled veterans
- Grants for motor vehicles for veterans who have lost their sight or the use of their limbs
- Health insurance tax credit for coverage months (the portion of premiums paid by the federal government)

- Health reimbursement arrangement (employer plan)—all reimbursements
- Health savings account distributions to pay for medical costs
- Historic preservation grants under the National Historic Preservation Act
- Home sale gain up to $250,000, or $500,000 on a joint return
- Inheritances
- Interest on insurance dividends left on deposit with the Department of Veterans Affairs
- IRA rollovers
- Life insurance proceeds
- Long-term care benefits under a policy to pay for the care of someone chronically ill ($360 per day limit if benefits are paid under a per diem contract)
- Meals and lodging furnished on the employer's premises for the employer's convenience (accepting onsite lodging must also be a condition of employment)
- Military benefits, including combat pay and death benefits
- Minister's housing allowance
- Mortgage assistance payments under Section 235 of the National Housing Act
- Mortgage debt cancellation on a principal residence up to $2 million, or $1 million for married filing separately
- Mortgage loan proceeds (including proceeds on refinancing)
- Moving expenses paid or reimbursed by employer
- Municipal bond interest
- Nutrition Program for the Elderly food benefits
- Payment for wrongful incarceration
- Peace Corps payments for housing, food, utilities, and clothing
- Prizes to certain employees (usually up to $1,600)
- Public safety officers' survivor benefits
- Rebates on purchases you make
- Restitution payments for Nazi victims and victims of human trafficking
- Retirement planning advice paid for by an employer
- Roth IRA distributions (all contributions, plus earnings in the account at least 5 years that are withdrawn after age 59$\frac{1}{2}$, or on account of disability, death, or first-time homebuying)

- Savings bond interest if used to pay qualified higher education costs of certain taxpayers
- Scholarships, fellowships, and grants covering tuition, fees, books, supplies, and equipment for a degree program
- SCORE payments for supportive services or reimbursement for out-of-pocket expenses
- Senior Companion program payments for supportive services or reimbursement for out-of-pocket expenses
- Senior Corps program payments for supportive services or reimbursement for out-of-pocket expenses
- Small business stock gain up to 50% (75% of the gain for stock acquired after February 17, 2009, and before September 28, 2010; 100% for stock acquired after September 27, 2010)
- Social Security benefits if your income is below a threshold amount
- Student loan debt cancellation by a qualified lender for those who work in certain professions
- Supplement Security Income (SSI) and Supplement Security Disability Income (SSDI)
- Transportation fringe benefits up to $255 per month
- Tuition reduction for employees of educational institutions
- Vacation home rental income if the rental is no more than 14 days during the year

Checklist of Nondeductible Items

Alert

At the time this book was completed, Congress was considering important tax changes that could affect 2017 tax returns and planning for 2018. Check the online Supplement in February 2018 at www.jklasser.com or www.barbaraweltman.com to see what changes have been enacted and when they are effective.

Unfortunately, not everything you spend your money on gives rise to a tax deduction. Most of your personal expenses, such as food, clothing, and recreation, are nondeductible items. The tax law also specifically bans certain write-offs. Of course, in some cases, while a deduction may be banned as a general rule, there may be circumstances under which it becomes deductible (so check throughout the book for exceptions to the general rule).

The IRS has identified a number of scams (the IRS calls them the "Dirty Dozen") in which sharp promoters incorrectly advise taxpayers to claim certain types of write-offs. Here are some types of situations that the IRS has over the years cautioned taxpayers against:

- *Pervasive telephone scams.* Callers pretend to be from the IRS in order to steal money or identities. If you know you don't owe money (i.e., you never received a bill from the IRS), don't respond. *Instead, call the Treasury Inspector General for Tax Administration at 800-366-4484 to report the call.*

- *Phishing.* Scammers purporting to be from the IRS send e-mails seeking to obtain personal information used for identity theft. *The IRS never contacts taxpayers by e-mail without prior notice of the communication; the IRS already has taxpayers' personal information.*

- *Identity theft.* This has topped the list of scams in the past several years, despite considerable IRS efforts to thwart it where taxes are concerned. Thieves are looking for ways to use a legitimate taxpayer's identity and personal information to file a tax return and claim a fraudulent refund. *Avoid problems with obtaining your legitimate refund by safeguarding your tax information; contact the IRS Identity Protection Specialized Unit.*

- *Preparer return fraud.* Dishonest preparers, often promising refunds too good to be true, can leave taxpayers owing taxes and penalties for underpayments. Or they may have client refunds directed to themselves, leaving clients with difficulty obtaining what they are owed. *Taxpayers remain liable for taxes owed on their returns.*

- *Hiding income offshore.* The IRS is working with some offshore banks to learn the identity of depositors who fail to report their offshore income on their U.S. returns. *The IRS continues to develop investigation procedures to catch nonreporters.*

- *Filing false documents to hide income.* This usually involves inflating earned income to maximize the earned income tax credit to which a taxpayer is not eligible (or at least not in the amount claimed). *Taxpayers can be subject to penalties, interest, and even criminal prosecution.*

- *Excessive claims for fuel tax credits.* Scammers induce taxpayers to claim credits that are meant for fuel used in off-highway vehicles (e.g., farm equipment). *Taxpayers who agree to submit these claims may be liable to penalties of $5,000 for frivolous arguments as well as criminal prosecution.*

- *Trust deductions for personal expenses.* Promoters tell taxpayers to transfer their assets to trusts and have the trusts deduct the cost of food, clothing and other personal expenses. *Personal expenses, other than those explained throughout the book, are not deductible.*

- *"Abuse of charitable deductions."* These abuses include attempts by donors to maintain control over donated assets or income from donated property. They also include schemes involving the donation of noncash assets, including easements on property, closely held corporate stock, real property, and overvaluations of property donations. *No deductions are allowed for illusory donations, and there are penalties for significant overvaluations.*

- *"No gain realized" deduction.* Like the claim of right doctrine, promoters tell taxpayers to claim a miscellaneous itemized deduction on Schedule A equal to their adjusted gross income. *There is no such deduction.*

- *Zero returns.* Promoters instruct taxpayers to enter all zeros on the return (rather than reporting their actual income items). *Income must be reported unless there is a specific tax rule for exemption or exclusion.*

- *Slavery reparations.* Promoters suggest that African-Americans can claim a deduction or credit for reparations. *There are no such reparations and no such allowable deduction or credit.*

- *Home-based businesses.* While there is a deduction allowed for legitimate home-based businesses, promoters tell taxpayers to fictitiously create a business run from home so that a deduction will be allowed. *Fake businesses do not support real deductions.*

- *Shared earned income credits.* Promoters tell taxpayers that they can "share" dependents in order for multiple taxpayers to claim the earned income credit with respect to the same dependents. *Only eligible taxpayers can claim the earned income credit and only one credit is allowed for each dependent.*

Nondeductible Items

Here is a listing of other items you may *not* deduct:

Additional Medicare taxes on earned income and net investment income for high-income taxpayers

Attorney's fees on buying a home

Bank fees, such as monthly checking fees on a personal account

Bar examination fees

Blood donations

Bribes

Burial fees

Car expenses for personal use of the car

Child support payments

Club dues for recreational, social, and athletic clubs

Commuting expenses

Compensation to housekeepers and other domestic employees

Cosmetic surgery

Country club membership

Credit card interest incurred for personal expenditures

Debts belonging to another person that you pay

Demolition costs

Disability insurance premiums

Education costs for your child's primary and secondary school

Elective deferrals to 401(k) and similar plans

Estimated tax penalties

Expenses of earning tax-exempt income

Federal income tax

Fifty percent of meal and entertainment costs for business

Fines

Funeral expenses

Gambling losses in excess of winnings

Gift tax

Gifts you make to family and friends

Health spa expenses

Hobby losses in excess of hobby income

Interest on loans to buy or carry tax-exempt securities

Investment seminars

IRA contributions by participants with AGI over set limits

Job-hunting costs for a first job

Kickbacks

Life insurance premiums

Lobbying expenses (other than in-house expenses up to $2,000)

Losses from the sale of your home, furniture, car, and other personal items

Losses in excess of at-risk limits

Losses on sales to related parties

Lost or misplaced cash or property

Lunches with coworkers

Organ donations (e.g., a kidney)

Over-the-counter medications

Partially worthless securities

Passive activity losses in excess of passive activity income

Penalties

Personal disability insurance premiums

Personal interest (such as credit card interest)

Personal living expenses (such as food, clothing, rent, and utilities)

Pet food

Points paid to refinance a home mortgage

Political contributions

Professional accreditation fees

Property settlements when dissolving a marriage

Reimbursed expenses you receive under an accountable plan

Repairs to your home or personal car

Repayment of loans

Rollover contributions

Roth IRA contributions

Sales tax if you deduct state and local income taxes

Social Security and Medicare (FICA) taxes

Spousal travel costs

State inheritance taxes

Stockholder meetings, expenses of attending

Tax penalties

Telephone line (basic service charges of first residential line to home)

Title insurance

Toiletries

Travel as a form of education

Vacations

Veterinary fees

Voluntary alimony payments

Voluntary unemployment benefit fund contributions

Wash sale losses

Index